D1569199

BIRMINGHAM BYZANTINE AND OTTOMAN MONOGRAPHS

About the series:

Birmingham Byzantine and Ottoman Monographs is a new series of studies devoted to all aspects of the history, culture and archaeology of the Byzantine and Ottoman worlds of the East Mediterranean region from the fifth to the twentieth century. It aims to provide a forum for the publication of work carried out by scholars while at the Centre for Byzantine, Ottoman and Modern Greek Studies at the University of Birmingham, or who are connected with the Centre and its research programmes.

About the volume:

This volume combines a catalogue of the early churches of Cilicia and Isauria (southern Asia Minor) with an analysis of their significance for the general development of ecclesiastical architecture during the fourth to sixth centuries. Although not wealthy, the region has a dense concentration of surviving churches from the late fifth century, and particularly from the reign of the Isaurian emperor Zeno (474-91). In the absence of late fifth century monuments in Constantinople, these churches in Cilicia and Isauria serve as indicators for building patterns which were developing in the critical decades before the great 'Domed Basilicas' were built in Constantinople in the first half of the sixth century. Cilician and Isaurian basilicas include transepts, ambulatories and various subsidiary chambers and passages, and it is argued that such modifications to the basic basilical plan helped in the evolution of the basilica towards the more centralized forms of the sixth century. The volume includes discussion of major monuments such as Alahan and Meryemlık.

About the author:

Stephen Hill has conducted extensive fieldwork on the early Byzantine monuments of Turkey. Most recently he has directed survey work on the Byzantine fortifications of Amastris on the Black Sea, and he is currently directing a rescue excavation of an early Byzantine site at Çiftlik, near Sinop. Stephen Hill has recently served as Honorary Secretary of the British Institute of Archaeology at Ankara, and after many years in the Department of Classics and Ancient History is now Associate Director of Open Studies at the University of Warwick. He is an Associate Fellow of the Centre for Byzantine, Ottoman and Modern Greek Studies at the University of Birmingham.

Frontispiece: The interior of the East Church at Alahan in 1826
(De Laborde, 1838).

THE EARLY
BYZANTINE CHURCHES OF
CILICIA AND ISAURIA

BIRMINGHAM BYZANTINE AND OTTOMAN MONOGRAPHS

Volume 1

General Editors

Anthony Bryer
John Haldon

Centre for Byzantine, Ottoman and Modern Greek Studies
University of Birmingham

THE EARLY
BYZANTINE CHURCHES OF
CILICIA AND ISAURIA

Stephen Hill

VARIORUM
1996

Published by   VARIORUM
                    Ashgate Publishing Limited
                    Gower House, Croft Road,
                    Aldershot, Hampshire GU11 3HR

                    Ashgate Publishing Limited
                    Old Post Road
                    Brookfield, Vermont 05036
                    USA

ISBN 0 86078 607 2

British Library Cataloguing-in-Publication Data
Hill, Stephen
    The early Byzantine churches of Cilicia and Isauria
    1. Basilicas - Cilicia - History 2. Basilicas - Byzantine Empire - History
    I. Title
    726.5'09495

Printed in Great Britain by Galliard (Printers) Ltd, Great Yarmouth

Birmingham Byzantine and Ottoman Monographs
Volume 1

CONTENTS

LIST OF FIGURES

LIST OF PLATES

1. Alahan, general view from west (Gough).
2. Alahan, Cave Church, view from west (Gough).
3. Alahan, West Church, view from east before excavation (Gough).
4. Alahan, West Church, view from east showing primary church (Gough).
5. Alahan, West Church, view from east showing secondary church (Gough).
6. Alahan, East Church from north (Gough).
7. Alahan, East Church from southeast (Gough).
8. Alahan, East Church from west (Gough).
9. Alahan, East Church, interior looking west (Hill).
10. Alahan, East Church, interior looking east (Hill).
11. Alahan, East Church, interior of tower looking east (Gough).
12. Alahan, East Church, east side of tower (Gough).
13. Alahan, Baptistery, interior from northeast (Hill).
14. Alahan, Baptistery, exterior from southwest (Gough).
15. Alahan, East Church, north end of narthex (Gough).
16. Alahan, East Church, capital with eagles (Gough).
17. Ayaş, Temple-Church, apse (Gough).
18. Anavarza, Rock-Cut Church from southwest (1905, Bell C193).
19. Batısandal from west (Hill).
20. Batısandal, sockets at mouth of apse (Hill).
21. Batısandal, east façade (Hill).
22. Bodrum, North Church, exterior of apse (ca 1925).
23. Bodrum, South Church, exterior of apse (ca 1925).
24. Canbazlı, Basilica from west (Hill).
25. Canbazlı, Basilica from south (Hill).
26. Canbazlı, Basilica, south colonnade (ca 1925).
27. Canbazlı, Basilica, gallery (ca 1925).
28. Cennet Cehennem, Temple-Church, apse from south (Hill).
29. Cennet Cehennem, Temple-Church, apse from west (Hill).
30. Cennet Cehennem, Temple-Church, inner face of north wall (Hill).
31. Cennet Cehennem, Chapel of St Mary from south (Hill).

32. Cennet Cehennem, Chapel of St Mary, domical vault in southern side-chamber (Hill).
33. Corycus, Church A, 'Cathedral', apse from west (Hill).
34. Corycus, Church G, Transept Church extra muros, south façade (1905, Bell D4a-b).
35. Corycus, Church G, Transept Church extra muros, east façade (Hill).
36. Corycus, Church G, Transept Church extra muros, interior looking east (Hill).
37. Corycus, Church G, Transept Church extra muros, base of south pier of triumphal arch (Hill).
38. Corycus, Church H, Tomb Church extra muros, south façade from southeast (ca 1925).
39. Corycus, Church H, Tomb Church extra muros, inner face of south wall (ca 1925).
40. Corycus, Church H, Tomb Church extra muros, interior looking east (ca 1925).
41. Corycus, Church H, Tomb Church extra muros, interior looking northwest (Hill).
42. Corycus, Church H, Tomb Church extra muros, atrium and narthex from southeast (Hill).
43. Corycus, Church H, Tomb Church extra muros, pier capital at northeast corner of nucleus (Hill).
44. Corycus, Church H, Tomb Church extra muros from northeast (1905, Bell D16)
45. Corycus, Church B, apse from west (Hill).
46. Corycus, Church I, 'Große Armenische Kirche extra muros' from west (Hill).
47. Corycus, Church I, 'Große Armenische Kirche extra muros' from south (Hill).
48. Corycus, Church I, 'Große Armenische Kirche extra muros' from east (Hill).
49. Corycus, Church J, Monastic Church, general view from southwest (Hill).
50. Corycus, Church J, Monastic Church, west façade of court (1905, Bell D28).
51. Corycus, Church J, Monastic Church from southeast (Hill).
52. Corycus, Church K, Northwest Church inside Land Castle from southeast (Hill).
53. East of Corycus, Funerary Chapel from west (Hill).
54. East of Corycus, Funerary Chapel, apse and hypogaeum from south (Hill).
55. North of Corycus (Demirciören), interior looking northwest (Hill).
56. North of Corycus (Demirciören), east end from southwest (Hill).
57. North of Corycus (Demirciören), east façade (Hill).
58. North of Corycus (Demirciören), southeastern chambers from west (Hill).
59. North of Corycus (Demirciören), capital (Hill).
60. Çatıkören from south (Gough).
61. Çatıkören, interior looking west (Gough).
62. Dağ Pazarı, Basilica, narthex from south (Ballance).

This book is dedicated to the memory of
Michael and Mary Gough.

'Every valley shall be exalted, and every mountain
and hill be laid low: and the crooked shall be
made straight and the rough places plain.'
Isaiah 40.4

PREFACE

This study of the early Byzantine churches of Cilicia and Isauria began life as a thesis which was not originally meant to be an architectural study of early Byzantine churches. I first visited Cilicia in 1973, at Martin Harrison's suggestion, with the intention of resolving the identification of some unpublished photographs in the Gertrude Bell Archive at the University of Newcastle upon Tyne. Following this work, I embarked on a study of settlement patterns in late Roman Cilicia. What has emerged is the product of circumstances: any account of ancient settlement needs its fixed chronological points, which may be historical, archaeological, or architectural. In my case it seemed useful to attempt an analysis of the most prominent monuments of the Cilician and Isaurian Cilicia, and the result was that churches became the exclusive focus of the thesis (Hili 1984). Since then the works of Hild and Hellenkemper, especially their *Tabula Imperii Byzantini* volume for Cilicia (Hild and Hellenkemper 1990), have provided the necessary study of the available historical literature with an invaluable gazeteer of the known sites of the region in Byzantine era. This volume now offers a study of the churches of the early Byzantine period in Cilicia and Isauria. In reality this is a study of basilicas since the region is remarkable for the fact that its early churches are all basilicas. Cilicia and Isauria ignored other available plans, and do not have the circular, cruciform, square and polygonal forms which are common enough in the neighbouring provinces of Anatolia and Syria. Whilst Cilicia was ecclesiastically distinct from the rest of Asia Minor, it fell within the see of Antioch, and the differences between Cilician and Syrian churches demonstrate how there can be considerable local variation within the same diocese. As for the chronological range, later churches in Cilicia and Isauria tend to be simple, single-chambered buildings, often very small, so there is a convenient cut-off in the seventh century when the tradition of basilica building seems to have stopped in the context of Persian and Arab incursions.

Cilicia seems to have been relatively ignored both by ancient writers and modern excavators. There are, of course, exceptions to these generalizations. Basil of Seleucia's accounts of the life and miracles of St Thecla make very lively reading, and give us some idea of conditions in late Roman Cilicia, and there have been some excavations, notably those of Michael Gough at Alahan and Dağ Pazarı and James Russell at Anemurium. The list of epigraphists, too, who have worked in Cilicia, is long and distinguished. Our knowledge of the province owes much to the publications of Heberdey and Wilhelm, Keil and Wilhelm, and, more recently, Gough, Bean and Mitford, Dagron and Feissel and Hild and Hellenkemper. Cilicia had its share of travellers and explorers in the nineteenth century. Although they did not normally concern themselves with the churches, their accounts, written while transhumance was still a normal way of life, are always lively, and often valuable. The full list would be long and hardly germane here, but one could not write about Cilicia without acknowledging the works of Beaufort, de Laborde, Langlois, and Davis. The late nineteenth century saw a surge of interest in Cilicia, which produced the first 'scientific' publications relating to the province. Thus in quick succession the region was explored by Bent, the formidable trio of Ramsay, Hogarth and Headlam, whom a later traveller, Sykes, was to hear referred to as 'the men with hats on', and Heberdey and Wilhelm. Headlam's publication, *Ecclesiastical Sites in Isauria*, appeared in 1892 and was the first to take serious account of the early Byzantine monuments of the region. A short-lived rush of enthusiasm for the subject was inspired by the publication of Strzygowski's stirring volume *Kleinasien, ein Neuland der Kunstgeschichte* in 1903. Strzygowski never visited Cilicia, but, on the basis of Headlam's account of Alahan, he began the whole controversy about 'Domed Basilicas'. His book inspired Gertrude Bell to extend her travels in Syria to include a trip through Cilicia in Spring 1905. In 1907 Herzfeld and Guyer, following Strzygowski's injunction 'Meriamlik muss ausgegraben werden', worked at Meryemlık and Corycus, whilst Keil and Wilhelm explored the district between the Göksu and the Lamas, and found further copious evidence for the richness of the Christian remains of the region.

This spurt of activity was interrupted by the First World War, and the publications of the work of Herzfeld and Guyer, and Keil and Wilhelm did not appear until 1930 and 1931 respectively. From 1907 until 1949 there seems to have been no interest in the early Byzantine monuments of Cilicia, and faced by the literary silence concerning the province, most scholars have tended to assume that it was, at best, a quiet backwater or, at worst, to have agreed with Cicero that it was the back of beyond, infested by pirates and brigands.

Cilicia, especially Rough Cilicia, is, however, still rich in standing monuments which often stand three stories high in extensive settlements whose populations dwindled in the wake of Arab incursions and have never recovered. Some Cilician churches have attracted attention, especially the 'Domed Basilicas', which are found at better known sites such as Meryemlık, Corycus and Alahan, but understanding of these has been bedevilled by preconceived ideas, especially the assumption that since Cilicia was a backwater its churches were, in the last analysis, derivative and conservative. This study attempts to redress this balance by showing that the churches of Cilicia and Isauria are innovative and had significant influence beyond their immediate locality.

Gough's work in the area began immediately after the Second World War and, although he began by studying Cilicia's Classical inscriptions and monuments, he soon became fascinated by the richness of its early Byzantine antiquities, and his researches did much to restore some respectability to the region. I must mention here, too, Mary Gough, who accompanied her husband in his travels, and whose book *The Plain and the Rough Places* captures the feeling of Cilicia far more successfully than any 'academic' work on the subject, and gives the reader an intimate understanding of the practical problems which beset fieldworkers in Cilicia. As well as excavating at Alahan and Dağ Pazarı, Gough travelled regularly and widely through the district and published long articles on Anavarza and Ayaş as well as a mass of shorter notes on other sites. Gough's major contribution has been to establish a sound basis for the dating of Alahan, which can be confidently assigned to the late fifth century. He died, tragically early, in 1974, before his work at Alahan was finished, and in the midst of plans to return to Dağ Pazarı. His wife produced a report on Alahan (Mary Gough 1985) before her death in 1992.

Gough and Guyer are the only scholars to have conducted lengthy researches on the Cilician churches, but the region has seen some spectacular flying visits. The first of these was made by Gertrude Bell in 1905. She brought the churches at sites like Anavarza, Kanlıdivane, and Corycus to the attention of architectural historians, and there is still much useful material in her descriptions and conclusions, and her photographs record several buildings which have disappeared. Bell evidently believed that the Cilician churches were both important and architecturally independent, but her views were ignored until George Forsyth rushed through Cilicia in 1954, visiting the major coastal sites as well as Alahan and Dağ Pazarı. His two subsequent articles were major landmarks in the study of early Byzantine architecture for he was the first to see some system in the peculiarities of Cilician church planning, and made the first attempt to place it in its wider context. The first of his subsequent articles was evidently modelled on Gertrude Bell's account, and attempted to disentangle some of the confused conclusions of Guyer. Forsyth's articles were major landmarks, since he was the first person to apply careful architectural reasoning to the study of the structure of the Cilician churches. Otto Feld passed through Cilicia in the early 1960's, and like Forsyth and Bell, published a series of useful findings in short articles. Cyril Mango's short article on the 'Isaurian Builders' (Mango 1966) was a seminal contribution, because it marked the beginning of the thinking which was to move our perception of Cilician and Isaurian churches forward from the belief that they were provincialised and insignificant to seeing them as a vital part of the dynamic processes in early Byzantine architecture in the late fifth century.

Recent years have seen further great advances in our knowledge of Cilician churches. Semavi Eyice has conducted extensive fieldwork in Rough Cilicia in the region around Silifke which has considerably increased our knowledge of the impressive monuments of that part of the region. Most importantly Hild and Hellenkemper have conducted systematic fieldwork in the region which has resulted in the recording of various hitherto unknown, or poorly understood, monuments (Hild and Hellenkemper 1986) and the production of a comprehensive gazeteer of the region (Hild and Hellenkemper 1990). Now there are new young scholars working on the early Byzantine monuments of the region, and we must look forward to seeing the results of fieldwork and study conducted by Richard Bayliss and Gabrielle Mietke.

The Christian basilicas are preserved in such numbers, and display such a variety of forms that they stand up to comparison with the churches of much more famous centres such as Thessalonica or Ravenna. In the absence of a systematic study it has been impossible to establish an adequate chronology for the churches, and they have tended to be categorized as provincial copies of hypothetical metropolitan models originating in Antioch or Constantinople. I started this study with the same preconceived notion that Cilicia could not have been architecturally independent, and I was drawn, almost reluctantly, to attempt a survey of the churches in the hope that such conventional and derivative buildings could be dated by reference to other provinces. I was confronted immediately by two problems. If the Cilician basilicas were so derivative, where were their archetypes? If the generally accepted view of their dating was correct, what circumstances in Cilician history could account for such a profusion of monuments attributed to the sixth century? The burden of the argument which follows is that the Cilician churches were much more important than has formerly been realized.

It follows from what has been said that there exists no architectural survey of the early Byzantine churches of Cilicia as such, and I have, therefore, been obliged to attempt to create one. Much of this volume is therefore cast in the form of a catalogue. But the catalogue is not a simple recital of factual data, for each building poses problems of interpretation which have had to be discussed separately. The catalogue is rigidly alphabetical since it would have been very unfortunate to dismember such sites as Alahan and Meryemlık, and to attempt a typological classification by individual monument would have involved prejudging the conclusions. There has been a structural problem which has been difficult to resolve. The catalogue contains conclusions which are drawn on in the opening chapters which themselves contain the definitions. In the end it seemed most effective to put the catalogue after the discussion.

Certain practical problems have affected the work. The area is large, and I have not had a permit to survey all the late Roman monuments of Cilicia. The plans which are attached to this thesis are, in the main, revisions of those in existing publications incorporating observations in the field and information in the archives of Gertrude Bell and Michael Gough. Plans of sites which I have discovered (e.g. Yanıkhan and Öküzlü) are not properly measured drawings, for to undertake such would have been illegal, though hopefully they will serve to give an impression of the dimensions and layout of the buildings concerned. Anyone who has worked in Turkey will also understand that fieldwork does not follow the logical plans one may have formed for it.   Thus I discovered Yanıkhan quite by chance after four days wandering through the Lamas hinterland in the course of which I failed to reach Tapureli, but did manage to visit Canbazlı.   The possibility of such chance discoveries underlines the point that a work like this could never be complete since much remains to be discovered, especially in the more unpopulated regions of the Taurus foothills.

I should like to acknowledge the assistance of various institutions.   I have received grants to help fund my travels from the Seven Pillars of Wisdom Fund, The Gerard Averay Wainwright Fund of the University of Oxford, the Committee for Fieldwork and Excavation of the University of Newcastle upon Tyne and the Research and Innovations Fund of the University of Warwick. The British Institute of Archaeology at Ankara regularly provided welcome lodging and the use of its invaluable library and Landrovers.   My thanks are due to the University of Newcastle upon Tyne for permission to reproduce photographs taken by Gertrude Bell in 1905.

To attempt to list individuals who have helped is doubtless invidious, but I must mention a few.   Firstly I must acknowledge the help of my wife, Fiona, who often accompanied me on my travels, and who, with the rest of my family, has had to suffer the composition of this opus.   Jim Crow was a stimulating companion in 1979, not least because from his comments on the urban fortifications of Cilicia, I was able to derive support for my own view that the ecclesiastical remains of the sixth century were infrequent and unambitious.   It was Jim, too, who disturbed the dog at Öküzlü!

I must thank my supervisor, the late Martin Harrison and his wife Elizabeth for their encouragement and support.   I owe an enormous debt to Leo Gough who granted me complete access to his parents' papers without which this book would have been very much poorer.   I am also indebted to Michael Ballance for his thoughts on geographical identifications and for allowing me to reproduce his photographs of Dağ Pazarı.   I must thank the late Richard Krautheimer for sending me a copy of Guyer's annotations on Gertrude Bell's articles, and Andrew Keck who gave me C. R. Morey's annotated copy of Rott's *Kleinasiatische Denkmäler.*   My former colleague, Charles Morgan, proved to be a fund of useful information. Gabrielle Mietke and Richard Bayliss shared their ides on Akören and Kadirli respectively.   Practical assistance in production of the text has been freely given by William Baker, Richard Bayliss, Gina Couthard, Sandy Fury, Fiona Hill, Penny McParlin, Lynn Ritchie, Daniel Smith, Diana Wardle and Kenneth Wardle.   Finally it would not have been possible to produce this volume without the heroic efforts of Richard Bayliss who produced all the drawings for the figures, and in doing so came up with innumerable bright ideas and taxing criticisms: I am deeply indebted to him for his efforts.

My biggest debt is to the late Michael and Mary Gough.   One of my greatest regrets is that I never actually met Michael Gough.   The news of his death came only days after a cheerful letter from him asking for photographs of Fiona and myself which were to be attached to the application for a permit to work at Dağ Pazarı, for we were to have joined him there in the summer of 1974. Through correspondence he was gracious enough to take a sincere and stimulating interest in my early enthusiasm for his subject. After Michael's death Mary was extraordinarily generous in passing on all sorts of information from Michael's papers and from her own experience of working in Cilicia and Isauria. Both Michael and Mary took a generous and unstinting interest in my efforts and those of any young scholars interested in the area which they loved. This book, which has benefited immensely from the help and encouragement of both Michael and Mary Gough, is therefore humbly dedicated to their memory.

DISCUSSION AND CATALOGUE

1

INTRODUCTION

This volume is concerned with the early Byzantine churches of an area which a Roman of the high empire would have understood to be Cilicia. In round terms this was the eastern half of the southern coastlands of Asia Minor. That is to say that I have defined Cilicia as the region which was separated from Pamphylia by the Melas river, from Syria by the Amanus mountains, and the northern boundary of which was formed by the Taurus peaks. The early Byzantine churches within this region form a coherent group which can be distinguished on grounds of plan and building methods from those of surrounding areas. The northern boundary, as it is shown on figure 63 follows the assumption that, where there is no other indication, the watersheds on the Taurus should be regarded as dividing Cilicia from Anatolia. The region thus defined conforms to the provincial boundaries suggested by Mitford (see the maps in Mitford 1982). The boundaries of eastern Cilicia are reasonably certain since there is a clear distinction between Cilicia and the provinces of Cappadocia, Commagene and Syria. It is much more difficult to define any lines which divides western Cilicia from Lycaonia, since these cut through the area which is, in the broadest sense of the term, Isauria.

In Classical antiquity Cilicia was always thought of as consisting of two distinct regions. The richer, more populous, eastern area included the Cilician Plain, and was known as Cilicia Pedias. The western part of Cilicia was known, appropriately enough since it is a mountainous district with little coastal plain, if any, between the Taurus foothills and the Mediterranean, as Cilicia Tracheia, Rough Cilicia. The Cilician Plain included the great cities of Tarsus and Anazarbus, and is now dominated by Adana, which is the fourth largest urban centre in modern Turkey. Today, as in antiquity, the population of the Plain greatly outnumbers that of Rough Cilicia, with the result that there are far fewer standing monuments in eastern Cilicia than western Cilicia, where large tracts of land are still the preserve of the occasional band of transhumant Yürüks. A distribution map of known ancient monuments in Cilicia would, by showing far more sites in Rough Cilicia, be a good inverse indicator of the extent of modern exploitation of different parts of the region, and would give some impression of the terrain, since monuments tend to survive in direct proportion to their inaccessibility. But such a distribution map would, like this volume, show fewer sites in the Plain, and would ignore Tarsus, which as the birthplace of St Paul, and the first capital of the Roman province, is likely to have had the grandest Cilician churches of all. There is inherent in this observation a critical problem. Cilicia was under the ecclesiastical jurisdiction of Antioch, but the surviving remains, most of which are in Rough Cilicia, display a stubborn independence. Those churches which survive in eastern Cilicia tend to display closer affinities with Syrian models.

It is necessary here to explain a problem of terminology, for I have used the terms Isauria and Cilicia more or less interchangeably. The ecclesiastical see of Isauria was based on Seleucia, and in the late Roman period the term was essentially coincident with what was also called Cilicia Tracheia. This was, at least on paper, distinct from the region which Sir William Ramsay used to call 'Isaurika' or in Mango's terminology 'old Isauria' (Mango 1966, 363-4), which includes the great stronghold of Isaura itself at Zengibar Kalesi. It might be thought odd that that a book which is concerned with the churches of a province called at one time Isauria has not included discussion of the monuments in the mountainous area around Zengibar Kalesi, but the ancient administrative nicety that this region was part of Lycaonia is reflected in the Anatolian architectural vocabulary of its churches. Thus the cross churches and barrel-vaulted hall-churches of 'old Isauria' are types which were common on the plateau. This is not to say that they do not require re-examination, for they have not been surveyed since the Prague Expedition in 1902 (Swoboda et al. 1935), but they should have to form the subject of a separate study. The ancients were prepared to live with such anomalies in terminology: thus Egeria reported that the Church of St Thecla, which was in Isauria, since it was situated at Meryemlık, just outside Silifke, the metropolis of Isauria, was protected by a great wall from the raids of the Isaurian mountaineers. The Count of Isauria might have derived his title either from the name of the territory he governed, or, in the manner of the Count of the Saxon Shore, from the peoples who were likely to attack his command. There is no escape from this inconvenient nomenclature, although it is necessary to understand that an 'Isaurian builder' is more likely to have originated from Corycus than Isaura.

Isaurian mountaineers were, of course, racially akin to the Cilicians. There was a veneer of Classical urbanization in the coastlands of Rough Cilicia, but the Hellenistic urban communities were not, as has sometimes been suggested, entirely distinct from the Cilician pirates who flourished in Mediterranean waters until they were subdued by Pompey's famous campaign of 67 BC. The old pirate who was mentioned in Vergil's fourth *Georgic* was a man of Corycus, and Pompey's long term solution to the problem of Cilician piracy seems to have been to restore the economic basis of cities like Coracesium and Soli, the latter of which was renamed Pompeiopolis in his honour. Piracy and brigandage were, in other words, a natural means to maintain a balanced economy for a community which, owing to limited locally available land resources, could only practise subsidence, pastoral agriculture. Even the urban foundations along the coastline of Rough Cilicia, where there was some hope of arable farming, cannot have produced an agricultural surplus, and their presence must have made the lot of the inhabitants of the interior much harder. There was also a tension in Cilicia between the pastoral nomads of the hinterland and the more settled city dwellers. Hopwood has explored the epigraphical evidence for this (Hopwood 1983), and has suggested that the phenomenon of brigandage can be explained as an aspect of the need for farmers in marginal lands to diversify their work. The same is true of piracy, which is outside the law, mercenary soldiering which is just within it, but hardly respectable, and working as a contract labourer.

All these activities were taken up by Cilicians, and in the late Roman period the word Isaurian suggested one of two things - mercenary or builder. The former concerns the present thesis only indirectly, but the latter is particularly relevant. The phenomenon of the 'Isaurian builders' was first discussed by Mango (1966) and has been developed by Gough (1972) and the present writer (Hill 1975, 1977). It may be compared to the movement of Irish 'navvies'. Conditions at home were, for reasons of geography, rather less than stable in terms both of economy and security. The mountainous limestone country of Rough Cilicia has relatively small pockets of thin soil which are regularly washed away by the spring floodwaters which result from the melting of the snow on the Taurus highlands. Even this water drains quickly since the limestone is deeply fissured, and there are numerous underground water-courses which cannot easily be tapped. In most places outcrops of the finely-grained limestone are readily available for the cutting, washed clean by the ephemeral, but powerful, rains, and often broken into convenient blocks by the action of winter frosts. Quarrying is often hardly necessary, although frequently enough, to save on transportation, Cilician buildings, modern and ancient alike, stand on the sites of the quarries from which their materials were extracted. The North Church at Yanıkhan is a good example of this process. Cilicia was also rich in timber. It was for this reason that Antony gave the region to Cleopatra, and the masts of the Egyptian fleet at Actium were in all likelihood made from Isaurian cedar. The Isaurian juniper does not achieve anything like the height of the stands of cedar, but it is one the toughest woods available for use as a building material.

Rough Cilicia is rich in goats, for pastoral nomadism has not yet died out, but it is on the decline, since, as was the case in the Roman empire, nomads do not fit conveniently into 'civilized' societies, which require people to be counted and taxed. But there are still three commodities which are available in surplus, building stone, timber, and manpower. As Gough wrote:

'Isaurian geography goes far to explain a native skill in stone-working. Most of the province is mountainous, and the few little pockets of fertile land that do exist are correspondingly valuable and to be defended at all costs. In the language of the guide-book, 'hardy independence' is characteristic of mountaineering folk, and in antiquity independence was best guaranteed by fortifications and strong-points.' (Gough 1972, 199)

The extract just given comes from Gough's article entitled 'The Emperor Zeno and some Cilician Churches', in which he argued that some of the churches which have come to be known as the 'Domed Basilicas' should be assigned to the reign of Zeno on grounds of architectural similarity. This argument represented a response to a proposal tentatively advanced by Mango in his article on 'Isaurian Builders' that the famous churches of Cilicia might belong to the late fifth century (Mango 1966, 364). I shall return to this issue but first would like to make a point which, curiously, neither Mango nor Gough seems to have made.

We have seen that geographical conditions in Rough Cilicia precluded the possibility of settled arable farming on any scale, and encouraged transhumant pastoralism, since the goatherds and shepherds had to move their flocks between winter and summer grazing grounds. Transhumance seems to have been practised on a grand scale. It is possible that Ura and Uzuncaburç were, respectively, the winter and summer settlements of the same city. Gough even suggested that the sudden transition to illiteracy half way through the dedicatory inscription in the mosaic floor of the church at Karlık was the result of the departure of the archdeacon to summer quarters (Gough 1974, 417). Russell sees the city of Anemurium ending with a whimper rather than a bang.

'In the end, discouraged by the uncertainty and disruption of their lives, the remaining families in the once flourishing city of Anemurium abandoned their homes and sought security in the mountain pastures. There would be no returning. A tiny trickle of coins excavated at the site indicates limited activity into the early eighth century after Christ, but for all practical purposes the city's life had already come to an end around AD 660. There are no signs of violent destruction or a last-ditch stand - the citizens simply gave up city life and headed for the hills.' (Russell 1980, 40)

The point I am making is that the Isaurian environment fostered not only pastoralism and stone-working skills, but also encouraged a migratory pattern of life. The main non-pastoral agricultural product of Rough Cilicia was olive oil. Neither the pasture of goats, nor the production of olive oil is labour intensive except at certain critical times of year, to wit the seasons of lambing and the olive harvest, and the times when it was necessary to move flocks from between pastures. Because local conditions did not encourage a variety of agricultural practices, there would have been long periods, even in the summer months, when there was not sufficient work to keep all the menfolk of a community in gainful employment, and it would have been entirely natural, in a society which was in any case used to transhumance, to emigrate in order to find seasonal building work. Mango made a start on tracing the movements of the Isaurian builders by collecting literary references to their activities in Constantinople and Syria in the sixth century (Mango 1966). It would be possible to trace their influence by analysis of archaeological remains from Egypt to Italy but that is not the purpose here.

The extent to which the inhabitants of Rough Cilicia were involved in the building trade can be gauged by a glance at the cemeteries. Keil and Wilhelm recorded numerous stone-workers amongst the citizens of Seleucia and Corycus. Of ten inscriptions which gave the profession of the deceased at Uzuncaburç, five were concerned with the building trade, and these included an architect and a marble-mason. The fine churches of Rough Cilicia, which are evidently the home productions of a people who possessed specialized architectural and building skills, are likely to contain their architectural experiments. But it is something of a problem to explain how a people who seem to have been driven into regular temporary exile in order to balance the uncertain local economy could have afforded such extravagant enterprises.

This is surely the place to develop the point made by Mango and Gough that the late fifth century was a period of prosperity for Cilicia, thanks to the ascendancy and subsequent accession to the purple of the Isaurian Tarasis, son of Codisas, better known as the emperor Zeno, who reigned from 474 to 491. His power base was the Isaurian military faction which was so prominent under his predecessor Leo. It would have been entirely natural for him to extend financial support to his home province, and there could have been no better method of fostering his own popularity and employing large numbers of his countrymen than to inaugurate building schemes in Cilicia and throughout the empire. It would also have been entirely natural for him to have filled his court with his own countrymen. Among their numbers there would doubtless have been master-builders who would have had secure financial backing for their more imaginative schemes. The effect, I believe, was to turn Cilicia for a time into a sort of architectural hothouse, where designs of new styles of churches suitable for the capital were forced into fruition. It is, I believe, pointless to talk of hypothetical Constantinopolitan architectural archetypes which may have influenced church design in Cilicia: while the Isaurians were in the political ascendant they also appear to have been dominant architecturally. For a while the architecture of the capital and one of the provinces were thrown into fertile identity. The remarkable wealth of churches with advanced plans in Cilicia should be seen, as it were, as the apprentice-pieces and experiments of architects and builders who were profiting from sudden imperial favour.

This argument depends on the assumption that the more remarkable Cilician churches, especially those with transepts, and the 'Domed Basilicas' were all built within the space of a few decades. I will argue that this is not merely likely for historical reasons, but also the conclusion which can be drawn from the architectural and archaeological evidence, and that all the factors which would have been required to foster such developments are inherent in the plans of Cilician churches from the fourth century.

The accession of the hostile and parsimonious Anastasius in 491 would have brought a sudden cessation of imperial funding, and the immediate end of the local building bonanza. The dire effects of this would have been accentuated by the civil wars which afflicted the province from 492 to 498. As a result there would have been a serious problem of unemployment in the building industry. Anastasius would have had no shortage of conscript labour for his extraordinary frontier foundation at Dara (Anastasiopolis), and it is small wonder that Mango was able to find references to bands of Isaurian labourers who apparently turned up uninvited at Syrian building sites in the hope of casual employment. To misapply Mango's concluding sentence in his article on Isaurian builders:

'The same consideration would also account for the reference to Isaurians without qualification: an Antiochene author of the 6th century might naturally have assumed that all Isaurians were construction workers.' (Mango 1966, 365)

The sites which are critical for the development of these arguments are Alahan, Dağ Pazarı, Meryemlık, Corycus, Kanlıdivane, Öküzlü and Yanıkhan.. Their distribution and associations are suggestive. We know that Zeno took an interest in the sanctuary of St Thecla since Evagrius (III. 8) tells us that he donated a μέγιστον τέμενος there in commemoration of a victory over a rival. It is possible that Zeno may have felt he had a personal association with Thecla, who was, in effect, the patron saint of Rough Cilicia, and whose sanctuary was a pilgrimage centre of international repute. Alahan was another pilgrimage centre which had strong associations with two local monks called Tarasis, who were Zeno's namesakes before he changed his name, and one of whom was evidently at least a local saint since a silver reliquary bearing his name was found at Çirga. Corycus and Kanlıdivane are but a short distance along the coast from Meryemlık. In other words, the critical 'Domed Basilicas' and Transept Basilicas form a coherent group in architectural and geographical terms, and I will argue they fall close together in chronological terms, and may reasonably be supposed to have benefited from imperial support.

It follows from this, although again this is in a sense beyond the scope of the present work, that the major churches of Cilicia occupy a critical position in the general history of the development of early Byzantine architecture. Even if only some of them may be seen as the products of the late fifth century, as a group they are the prototypes of the great churches of the sixth century, amongst which are such famous buildings as Santa Sophia. The significance of this is that it can finally be stated that the so-called 'Domed Basilicas' did not burst upon a surprised world in full-fledged form in Constantinople in the early sixth century, but were in fact the product of a process of gradual evolution within a province where architecture and building were a local pre-occupation, and which held, for a period in the late fifth century, a share of the imperial limelight. It was from such a chance combination of factors that the major development in architectural thinking, which is represented by the great sixth century churches of Constantinople, could proceed.

As far as it can be reconstructed, the history of Cilicia after Zeno is somewhat depressing. The province never seems really to have recovered from the civil wars under Anastasius. The subsequent urban decline has been demonstrated by excavations at Anemurium and Dağ Pazarı where the public buildings fell into general disrepair during the sixth and seventh centuries and, in the case of Anemurium, were taken over for industrial use, and by squatters (Russell 1976b, 16).

Few churches in Cilicia and Isauria can be assigned to the sixth century with confidence. One is the Rock-Cut Church at Anavarza which was built in 516. Even this is somewhat puzzling, since, according to Procopius (*Secret History* 18, 10), Anazarbus was rebuilt after earthquakes during the reigns of Justin and Justinian. Few of the surviving monuments at Anavarza, including its fine circuit of walls, can be so late, and the Church of the Apostles, which was in all probability the cathedral, gives every sign of having been flattened by an earthquake, and never repaired.

Procopius (*Buildings* 5, 9) also informs us that Justinian restored a monastery at Apadnas in Isauria. Headlam (1892, 18) hesitantly proposed that this should be identified with Alahan, but since Gough showed so conclusively that Alahan was built in the fifth century, and was never finished, the idea was for a while forgotten. Hild and Hellenkemper (1990, 193-4), for whatever reason, have returned to the proposal and I am inclined to accept the identification, since the name Ἀπάδνας is not far removed from the ἀπαντητηρία which Tarasis is recorded as having founded. The word is sufficiently obscure to have confused Procopius, and the extensive patches in the floor of the East Church might then well be the surviving evidence of a Justinianic restoration of the church after its dome had fallen. If so, the Justinianic restoration, with a simpler wooden roof, was a poor substitute for the ambitious fifth century structure. Some indication of the sad state of affairs in the sixth century can also be derived from the observation that two of the churches at Dağ Pazarı were destroyed by fires in the sixth century and were not repaired.

Definitely identified churches of the seventh century are in still shorter supply. The 'Cathedral' at Corycus has a dedicatory inscription which has been argued to give a foundation in the year 629/30. It was a fine building, but constructed entirely from spolia which appear to have originated from the ruins of two nearby basilicas of fifth century date, one of which, at least, was a church of greater architectural distinction. The replacement 'Cathedral' was presumably the best that could be created in the immediate aftermath of the Persian occupation of the city.

The Necropolis Church at Anemurium was repaired in the seventh century by the erection of a small chapel against the original apse. The rest of the basilica was left unroofed and used for burials. Such reductions of the early Byzantine basilicas provide graphic evidence of the extent to which the population must have declined by the seventh century. Single chambered chapels, similar to that at Anemurium, were erected within Church 1 at Kanlıdivane and the West Church at Alahan. Further excavation would probably reveal that they were the normal form of church existing in Cilicia in the last years before the Arab conquest, and these single-chambered chapels are very like the medieval chapels which were still being built during the period of the Armenian kingdom of Cilicia. There may, therefore, be reason to suppose that there was some continuity of settlement in Cilicia even after the region had, in effect, become no man's land between Islam and Christianity. If there was continuity, it was on a sadly reduced scale, and I would certainly agree with Russell that the majority of the population simply took to the hills.

It is even possible that Cilician Christians did not merely take to the hills in the seventh century, but actually crossed them into Anatolia. Church 32 at Binbirkilise is unique amongst the surviving basilicas of Lycaonia since it had galleries, eastern side-chambers, and a simple transept (Ramsay and Bell 1909, 209-21; figures 164, 172-80). Bell believed that the church was a late addition to a previously existing monastery. The combination of so many unparalleled Cilician elements in one building allows room for speculation that a band of immigrant Cilicians were clinging tenaciously to a familiar church plan even after they had crossed into another province. The same reasoning may explain the very battered ruins of a basilica at Tomarza, on Erciyes Dağı south of Kayseri, which is without parallel in southern Cappadocia, for it had a tripartite east end; the outer face of the main apse was rounded not polygonal; and, in a region which was distinguished by squatly planned basilicas, conformed to longitudinal Cilician proportions.

2

CHARACTERISTICS OF CILICIAN
AND ISAURIAN CHURCH PLANNING

BUILDING METHODS AND MATERIALS

Local limestone is almost invariably the chosen building material. The limestone is a bright orangey red when freshly cut, and weathers to a dull grey. It is normally sufficiently fine in texture to allow delicate carving, and is generally available throughout the province, although it would have had to be transported short distances to the alluvial parts of the Plain, and to the deltoid area around Silifke. In western Rough Cilicia limestone was mixed with a coarse micaceous slate, and at Erzin the local black basalt was used.

The stone was dressed in various ways. Polygonal masonry, which often includes blocks in excess of a cubic metre, is fairly common in Hellenistic and Roman buildings, but relatively unusual in churches. This cannot have been because it was falling out of use, since it was always a common technique used in domestic structures, but it may well have been thought unnecessary, since the exterior faces of most of the churches which were not constructed from large ashlars seem to have been covered with stucco. It was presumably more impressive to construct large buildings from regular blocks of stones if the technology and finance were available to cut them. Cheaper constructions in coursed or uncoursed small stone were rendered to give the impression of ashlar construction. Polygonal masonry was, however, often used in foundations (e.g. Üç Tepe, South Church; Yanıkhan, North Church), and was employed above ground level in the churches at Tapureli. Large, regular ashlars were, however, normally used for foundations, quoins, apses and vaults, and the limestone was strong enough to be cut into monolithic jambs and lintels. Occasional buildings were constructed throughout from friction-bonded ashlars (e.g. the churches at Alahan), but in most buildings walls which were not subject to great stress consisted of a rubble and mortar core faced on both sides by coursed small, wedge-shaped stones which have square outer faces. These less substantial walls are usually about 50 centimetres thick.

Bricks were hardly employed in the churches, although commonly used in contemporary cisterns and bath houses. Thus at Meryemlık, although the churches were built from ashlars, there are numerous brick vaulted cisterns, including one immediately to the east of the main apse of the Basilica of St Thecla, under its eastern passage. The same building shows how bricks were occasionally used for repairs since there are patches of brickwork in the outer face of the apse. The bricks in the secondary arcades of the North Church at Bodrum are likely to have been brought from an earlier building. Brick was also employed for the secondary apse of one of the churches at Erzin.

Cilician mortar was of particularly high quality, since the volcanic soils in the vicinity of the Amanus were similar to the pozzolana which was exploited so effectively in Roman architecture in Italy. Cilician mortar is often so strong that the cores of walls are preserved when the faces have been eroded away. Simple limestone mortar was used as stucco to render the surfaces of the walls: this has often fallen away to reveal the trowel marks in the stronger mortar which was used in the walls. The cheaper walls were constructed by building the faces in lifts of 1 to 1.5 metres and then pouring in the wet rubble and mortar mixture. Wooden scaffolding poles ran through the thickness of the walls, and were lopped off when construction was finished. The poles were usually left in place in the wall, and it is common to see arrays of holes piercing the outer walls of the basilicas (good examples of this are the west façade of Church 1 at Kanlıdivane, and the north wall of the church north of Corycus). The scaffolding was presumably left in position until the roof was finished; thus, in cases where the putlog holes have been filled with mortar, it is normal to find fragments of broken tile in the filling (e.g. the church east of Corycus).

Most buildings employ a mixture of small stone and ashlar work, and butt joints can often be seen where the construction technique changes. It must be emphasised that such butt joints do not constitute evidence for remodelling in the absence of other indications. In the North Church at Yanıkhan theapse, and the west walls of the side-chambers at ground level are constructed from fine ashlars, and the rest of the church is in small stone work. Accordingly, there are two butt joints in the north and south faces of the church, where the ashlars at the ends of the west walls of the side-chambers meet the small stones of the rest of the walls, with the latter at points riding over the former. It would appear that here the apse must have been erected before the rest of the church was constructed, and it would be reasonable to assume that different gangs of builders were involved, with the more skilled group being responsible for the apse and its semi-dome and less skilled, perhaps very local, workmen completing the building project.

The east façade of the Transept Church at Corycus presents a great variety of building techniques, and has a selection of butt joints, but it is clear from the vaults of the apses that it is all of one period, and the changes in building technique are related to the stresses imposed on the different parts of the walls. Thus the wall of the eastern passage, and faces above the vaults are in small stone work, whilst the foundation plinth, and the lower walls of the apses are constructed from heavy ashlars. The walls of the subsidiary apses were constructed from especially large ashlars, and are, remarkably, thicker than the walls of the main apse, presumably in order to support a second pair of subsidiary apses at first floor level. This tendency to use superior materials and techniques for critical parts of the structure, especially apses, explains why so often an apse has remained standing when the rest of the basilica has fallen.

Little is known about the decoration of these churches, since none is intact, and so few have been excavated. Marble is occasionally found. This is sometimes the red Isaurian marble from which was carved the altar table of the Funerary Basilica at Dağ Pazarı, and probably the window columns of the temple-church at Silifke. Most commonly fragments of white marble are found. The most common use of marble was for revetting the inner faces of the walls of the apse (as in the Basilica of St Thecla at Meryemlık), or of other important chambers (notably the domical eastern chamber in the South Church at Yanıkhan, and the fifth century interior of the Cave Church at Meryemlık). Marble was also used for columns, capitals, and other pieces of decorative sculpture, and where it appears is probably an indicator of rich, or even imperial, patronage. Thus all the details of the 'Cupola Church' at Meryemlık, even the massive font, are carved from Proconnesian marble, and it is likely that the same was true in the fifth century Cathedral (Church C?) at Corycus, pieces of which can be seen re-used in the seventh century 'Cathedral' (Church A). The columns in the portico of the Basilica of St Thecla at Meryemlık were pieces of red porphyry, but this precious stone is not to be found elsewhere in Cilicia, and may be another indicator of the imperial support for the building campaign at Meryemlık.

When marble was not available, or could not be afforded, plaster surfaces could be painted to mimic marble veneer (e.g. West Church at Alahan). This said, the fine local limestone was the normal material for architectural sculpture. Its quality can be gauged, for instance, at Alahan where it was used to very impressive effect throughout the complex.

All churches had plastered walls, and traces of simple wall paintings have been found in some excavated buildings, although it is likely that the traces of paintings of saints which can still be seen in some of the churches were originally applied in the medieval period. In the Funerary Church at Dağ Pazarı, the architectural members, columns and voussoirs, were covered with painted plaster.

Glass paste tesserae have been found in the churches at Meryemlık, the West Church at Alahan, the 'Domed Ambulatory Church' at Dağ Pazarı, and the South Church at Yanıkhan. In the last mentioned, and also the Cave Church and 'Cupola Church' at Meryemlık, these included gold glass tesserae, and it seems likely that these would have come from mosaics which covered domical or vaulted surfaces. It is impossible to tell from such loose finds whether the wall mosaics included figures, although Gough did suggest this possibility for the West Church at Alahan.

Floor surfaces vary from the native rock (Mazılık; North Church at Yanıkhan), through limestone flags, which are easily the most common surviving flooring material, to opus sectile and tesellated mosaic pavements. Opus sectile floors have been found in the aisles of the Basilica at Dağ Pazarı, whilst the floor of its nave was covered with flags. Similarly, the aisles of the 'Domed Ambulatory Church' at Dağ Pazarı were covered with geometric mosaics, whilst the nucleus appears to have had plain flagstones. Occasionally the bema was given exceptional treatment (as in the Funerary Church at Dağ Pazarı), but this seems to have been more the exception than the rule. In general, the more public areas of the churches appear to have had the most elaborate floors. Thus the narthex of the Basilica at Dağ Pazarı had a particularly handsome mosaic which may represent the birds of Thecla's sanctuary, and the west end of the mosaic pavement of the nave of the basilica at Karlık was much more impressive than the east end. I have already mentioned that the floors of the aisles of two of the churches at Dağ Pazarı were more lavishly covered than those of the nave: in the same way, the most impressive floor mosaics in the Basilica at Misis were those in the north aisle.

In all cases main roofs consisted of timber and tiles. In most cases such roofs covered longitudinal basilicas, but the vaults and domes of the 'Domed Basilicas' were also protected with tiles. The provision of side-chambers and eastern passages simplified the task of roofing the basilicas, since the main apse could either be included under a continuation of the roofing system of the nave (e.g. Canbazlı, Basilica), or covered by a simple lean-to across the width of the west end of the church (e.g. Kanlıdivane, Church 4). Cornices can still be seen at Kadirli, the Basilica at Canbazlı and on the northeast corner of the Transept Church at Corycus. In the latter building the cornice is supported by consoles which hold it well beyond the building line of the north wall. Rainwater from the roof would thus have been projected well beyond the building. In the Tomb Church at Corycus, there is evidence to suggest that the rainwater from the roof was collected. There are still fragments of lead pipe set in the east end of the south wall which presumably led storm water into the cistern underneath the apse.

COURTYARDS AND ATRIA

Courtyards of one sort or another are common, but by no means invariable. Occasionally, (Anemurium, Necropolis Church; Canbazlı, Basilica; Cennet Cehennem, Temple-Church; Dağ Pazarı, 'Domed Ambulatory Church'; Meryemlık, Basilica of St Thecla; Uzuncaburç, Temple-Church) the church was surrounded by a temenos which was inherited from an earlier building, usually a pagan temple. In spite of Evagrius' statement that Zeno donated a temenos to Meryemlık, there is no example of such an enclosure which can be assigned unequivocally to the early Byzantine period. This is not to say that they did not exist, but none have been recognized, though sometimes, as at Emirzeli and

Karakilise, what appear to be sections of early Byzantine compound walls survive. Some churches did have large irregular courtyards to north or south of the building (notably Corycus, Monastic Church; Emirzeli, Church 1; Ura, Monastery; Uzuncaburç, Church of Stephanos; and the Temple-Church at Ayaş could perhaps be added). These courtyards are often associated with monastic churches, and are probably identical in function with the large, irregular courtyards on the west side of such monastic churches as Mahras and Church B at Tapureli. There was a similar enclosure between the major churches of the monastery at Alahan, where it was defined by the north wall of the colonnaded walkway.

There is also a group of churches with regularly planned courtyards on the western side. Three of these (Kanlıdivane, Church 4; Tapureli, Churches A and C) seem to have been without a peristyle, but there were full colonnaded atria in some important churches (Corycus, Transept Church and Tomb Church; Meryemlık 'Cupola Church' and North Church; Yanıkhan, South Church). The sample is too small to enable us to define a typical Cilician atrium. Three had simple peristyles, but there were square chambers at the western corners of the atria of the Transept Church at Corycus and the 'Cupola Church' at Meryemlık. Guyer thought that the latter, at least, had two storeys, and it may be that the rooms at the western angles contained staircases. In no case did the peristyle continue round all four sides of the atrium. This would have been unnecessary, since very few Cilician basilicas lacked a narthex, and the normal triple-arched portal of the Cilician narthex provided a colonnade on the east side of the atrium. In at least two churches (Corycus, Tomb Church; Meryemlık, 'Cupola Church') there were arched openings between the narthex and the north and south sides of the peristyle. In both cases, there seems to have been a particular reason for this: in the Tomb Church there was a basin in an apse at the south end of the narthex, and in the 'Cupola Church' there was an apsidal structure, perhaps a bath, against the south aisle of the church.

In most cases, the atrium could be entered only from the west. The atrium of the Tomb Church at Corycus also has entrances on its north and south sides. Unusually, there is no western entrance to the atrium of the South Church at Yanıkhan, although it could be approached from either north or south, and was preceded on the south side by a monumental doorway and a long flight of steps. No fountain has been discovered in a Cilician atrium, but there were well-heads for cisterns in the atria of the Tomb Church at Corycus and the South Church at Yanıkhan. The bath house immediately to the west of the 'Cupola Church' at Meryemlık was probably built at the same time as the church.

Mention must also be made of three remarkable fore-courts. Two 'Domed Basilicas', the 'Domed Ambulatory Church' at Dağ Pazarı and the 'Cupola Church' at Meryemlık had semi-circular western courtyards: in the latter building the hemicycle actually preceded the atrium proper, and possibly had a propylaeum on its east side. The fore-court of the North Church at Öküzlü is five-sided, being the greater part of a somewhat irregular octagon. These unusual fore-courts recollect contemporary palatial architecture, and are a striking feature of the ambitious basilicas to which they are attached.

THE NARTHEX
The narthex was a normal feature of Cilician basilicas. One was present in almost all basilicas in Rough Cilicia where the west end can be examined, and where no particular local circumstances rendered the building of a narthex impossible. Some of the churches in the Plain (Akdam; Akören I, Church 2; Anazarbus, Church of the Apostles and Southwest Church; Mazılık) can be shown to have had no narthex. The nartheces of the basilicas at Bodrum and Kadirli were evidently secondary additions. This is one respect in which there was a consistent difference between the churches of Pedias and Tracheia. Syrian basilicas were not necessarily provided with nartheces, and it is likely that at first the churches in the Plain followed Syrian custom in this respect, whereas a narthex was included in the earliest Rough Cilician basilicas as a matter of course. The addition of nartheces to some of the basilicas in the Plain and the fact that they conformed to the Rough Cilician pattern suggests that, in architectural terms, Pedias came to follow Tracheia. It is likely, of course, that the Isaurian builders would have become involved in the construction of the churches in the Plain.

The great majority of nartheces took the form which is still preserved as the west façade of Church 1 at Kanlıdivane, that is a two-storeyed hall with a triple-arched portal at ground level, and a large arched window at gallery level. The form can be attested in the fourth century, since the first Basilica of St Thecla at Meryemlık and both basilicas at Yanıkhan had this type of narthex, and it was still included in the apparently seventh century 'Cathedral' at Corycus. When the Temple at Uzuncaburç, was converted into a Christian basilica, the three central columns of the west façade were left unblocked in order to create the central triple entrance. In all known examples the arches of the narthex portal were supported by columns: this was true even in the North Church at Üç Tepe, where the nave arcades were supported by piers. The columns were invariably surmounted by decorated capitals, even if these were lacking inside the church: this suggests that considerable importance was attached to the narthex portal as the centrepiece of the main façade of the church.

The little we know about nartheces in the Plain suggests that they followed the Rough Cilician type. Thus a fine example of the triple-arched portal can be seen in Langlois' illustration of the Church at Manaz. There was, however, a tripartite narthex of Anatolian type in the Rock-Cut Church at Anavarza.

In the Tomb Church at Corycus, the narthex portal had five arches rather than three. This is evidently a more impressive variant of the normal type, which was probably also present in the Basilica of St Thecla and the 'Cupola Church' at Meryemlık, and also in the Basilica at Canbazlı. The most remarkable narthex in Cilicia is that provided for Church 1 at Akören I: this narthex in effect goes round three sides of the building with five-arched portals on each side.

Variant types of entrance portal are infrequent, and can often be explained by local circumstances. The narthex of the West Church at Alahan, which had one entrance, was built around the apse of the Cave Church, and that of the East Church was joined to the end of the colonnaded walkway, and was accordingly long enough only for a double archway of a type which is very reminiscent of the double arched entrances of the churches of Lycaonia. This Anatolian connection may be significant since some of the churches of Dağ Pazarı and Balabolu have only one doorway: it may be that these northern Isaurian churches were particularly exposed to architectural influences from the other side of the Taurus. The narthex of Church 3 at Kanlıdivane has no west doorway, but its west wall was inherited from an earlier building. Both churches at Susanoğlu were cut deeply into the rock at the west end, and may have had entrances in the west wall at gallery level, although at ground level the nartheces are somewhat formless, that of the Town Church having no entrance in any of its outer walls. There was no narthex at the west end of the basilicas at Mazılık and Şaha, although the latter did have a tower-like structure which protected the single door in the west wall of the nave. In both cases, however, there were corridors against the south sides of the church and it seems likely that they included the main entrances to the church. At Mazılık, the south corridor included the entrance to the caves beneath the basilica. At Şaha the south corridor was two storeys high, and a pair of columns which lie in front of it suggest that it may have had the form of a normal western narthex. In Church 2 at Akören I the main entrance was on the south side of the building.

The exact form of the narthex of the basilica at Dağ Pazarı is obscure, because it was remodelled in antiquity, and the foundations of its north end support a modern stable: what is certain is that it was added to the building. The secondary nature of the narthex confirms my theory that the church was a conversion of a secular basilica, since it would otherwise be the only regular Isaurian basilica to have been constructed without a narthex, where one was actually possible. The Cemetery Church at Uzuncaburç, was built around a pre-existing tomb cut into a cliff at the west end of the building, and, therefore, had no narthex, but the arrangements in the Temple-Church at Uzuncaburç were also unusual in that it was provided with a staircase chamber at the north end of the narthex.

Doorways at the north and south ends of the narthex were commonly provided in churches where there was a passage along the north or south side of the building (e.g. Akören II, Church 1; İmamli; Kanlıdivane, Church 2), or where the side-chambers were used as a baptistery. Thus there is a wide arch at the south end of the narthex of the church north of Corycus, where the southern side-chambers appear to have been used as a baptismal suite which had its own narthex-like entrance hall.

There was an upper floor in every narthex which survives to a height sufficient to give information concerning this point. The upper floor of the narthex was necessary to provide communication between the galleries over the aisles. Staircases were often provided in the north end of the narthex (e.g. Corycus, Transept Church; Kanlıdivane, Church 4; Uzuncaburç, Temple-Church), or else were attached to it. Thus there was a wooden staircase against the outside of the narthex in the North Church at Yanıkhan, and a wooden staircase in the northwest corner of the north aisle in the church north of Corycus rose to the upper floor of the narthex.

Churches were often enough built on the site of the quarries from which their materials were extracted, and, as a result, were sometimes set deeply into bedrock. This fact could be exploited to provide direct access to the church at gallery level. The doorway into the north end of the gallery of the narthex of the East Church at Alahan can still be seen: its threshold is slightly raised, presumably in order to prevent rainwater running into the building. It is likely that there was direct access to the upper floor of the narthex in both churches at Susanoğlu. Where the east wall of the narthex survives to any height central windows are preserved which would have given an excellent view of the nave. The windows in the East Church at Alahan, and the Basilica at Manaz had triple arches. There was probably a similar window in Church 4 at Kanlıdivane, but it stood inside the jambs of a much taller window which rose into the gable end of the west wall of the nave. At Manaz, too, there was a window in the apex of the west gable. It follows that the large window in the gallery of the narthex was essentially used for viewing the interior of the church, and windows had to be provided above the roof of the narthex in order to admit the light of the afternoon sun into the nave.

Water was often available in the narthex. Stoups in arched niches have been found in the east sides of the nartheces of three basilicas (Balabolu, Necropolis Church; Susanoğlu, Cemetery Church; Yanıkhan, North Church), and there are similarly positioned niches which might have held basins in the East Church at Alahan and the Town Church at Susanoğlu. There was a well-head against the west wall of the fifth century Basilica of St Thecla at Meryemlık, and there was possibly a bath at the south end of the narthex of its fourth century predecessor. It is also possible that there was a bath off the south end of the narthex of the 'Cupola Church' at Meryemlık. The south end of the narthex of the Tomb Church at Corycus is apsidal, and appears to have contained a large marble basin which was presumably filled from the cistern whose well-head was just outside the entrance to the narthex. The well-head of the cistern of the South Church at Yanıkhan is in the same position, but there the narthex is too poorly preserved to show whether provision for ablution was provided. There was a cistern under the narthex at Halil Limanı.

The association of water with the narthex was sometimes baptismal: thus in the Basilica at Dağ Pazarı, and probably also at Şaha, there was a baptistery at the north end of the narthex, and it is possible that the chamber at the south end of the narthex of the Basilica at Canbazlı was used for baptisms, since it was built over a cistern. The Cave Church at Alahan, to which was attached the narthex of the West Church, also appears to have been used for baptisms.

Bench seating was sometimes provided inside the narthex as in the North Church at Yanıkhan, or against its west wall, as in the 'Domed Ambulatory Church' at Dağ Pazarı.

Between the narthex and the church proper there were three doorways, the central of which was often wider and taller than the others, and more elaborately decorated (e.g. both churches at Yanıkhan). These were the real outer doors of the church, since the west side of the narthex was normally an open colonnade. Only in the 'Cupola Church' at Meryemlık is there definite evidence for doorways between the columns of the west portal. The solidity of the doorways between the narthex and the church proper was indicated by the iron studs, door plates, and key which were found with the carbonized fragments of the door between the narthex and the south aisle in the Basilica at Dağ Pazarı. In the Funerary Basilica at Dağ Pazarı the doorway between the narthex and the north aisle was at some point filled with masonry and plastered over. Since there was only one doorway in the centre of the west wall, a substantial room would have been created at the north end of the narthex. The Anatolian influence on this basilica, which had no side-chambers at the east end, can thus be seen to have been particularly strong. Only in the basilica at Hasanalıler would there appear to have been no doorways between the narthex and the aisles.

The provision of an exo-narthex is not normal in Cilicia. There are only two possible cases of such a feature. What appears to be an exo-narthex in Church C at Tapureli may be nothing more than the narthex proper in a church where the gallery ran across the west end of the nave (the same system is probably attested at Şaha, which did not have a proper western narthex). The exo-narthex in the Monastic Church at Corycus is rather more convincing, but there it is impossible, without excavation, to disentangle the medieval alterations from the original early Byzantine building.

NAVE AND AISLES

Almost all the Cilician churches, apart from the smallest chapels (e.g. Canbazlı, small church; east of Corycus; Takkadın; and perhaps the little Temple-Church at Ayaş) were divided longitudinally into nave and aisles. In some of the 'Domed Basilicas', particularly the Tomb Church at Corycus, this division is rendered less apparent by the presence of a transverse element across the west end of the church: such anomalies will be considered later. The division was in most cases effected by arcades supported on rows of columns. There were probably trabeated colonnades in three early churches (the Basilica at Dağ

Pazarı and both churches at Yanıkhan). Some churches had arcades supported by rectangular piers (İmamli; Hasanalıler; both churches at Üç Tepe). There were also secondary piers in the North Church at Bodrum, and the columns of the great Basilica of St Thecla were encased or replaced by substantial square piers, probably after the collapse of the fifth century roof and galleries. Although piers are clearly late features of the latter two basilicas, it would be rash to suppose that they have any significance in general terms for dating. They are more likely to be another indicator of the links with the early Christian architecture of Anatolia.

It is likely that all Cilician churches, whether parish or monastic, had galleries. The most convincing case for the absence of galleries can be made for the Basilica at Dağ Pazarı. There, at least, excavation did not uncover two orders of columns and capitals, but there are also good reasons to suppose that the church was a conversion of an earlier secular basilica. I do not accept Guyer's argument that there were no galleries in the fifth century Basilica of St Thecla: if this had been the case, then the columns of the arcade must have been 9.8 metres high, although they were only 58 centimetres in diameter. In most cases the galleries had an upper order of stone columns and capitals which was smaller and simpler than the lower order. In the Basilica at Canbazlı and the East Church at Alahan there are slots in the lower parts of the gallery columns which must have received wooden screens, and it is likely that wooden parapets were normally provided between the columns at gallery level. The gallery in the North Church at Yanıkhan was evidently constructed entirely from wood, and it is probable that there were similar wooden galleries also in the church north of Corycus and at Mazılık.

Lighting at ground level is never lavish, and is often provided by openings which are little more than arrow-slits (Canbazlı, Basilica; Tapureli, Church C). Even arrow slits are often entirely lacking in the north wall. The latter observation suggests that the early Byzantine architects were fully conscious of the problem of winds coming off the Taurus in the winter months, but considerations of security or privacy are also likely to have been important, since there are usually windows in the apse where there was sufficient height for the windows, which in any case often had to be above the synthronum, to be set at a high level. Churches of more generous proportions would have had higher aisles, and in these buildings high windows may be found at ground level (e.g. Corycus, Transept Church and Tomb Church). There seems to have been much more lavish provision of fenestration at gallery level, and it is likely that most Cilician basilicas would also have had clerestory lighting, although this can be certainly attested in only two churches (Alahan, West Church; Öküzlü, North Church). The North Church at Öküzlü demonstrates how transverse roofing structures were possible in churches with transepts and that clerestory lighting could be inserted above the transept as well as above the nave.

Doorways in the south walls of the church are very common and some of the larger basilicas had northern entrances as well. Sometimes, especially in the Plain which presumably followed Syrian practice in this respect, the south entrance was more important than the west entrance (Mazılık; Şaha). Such doorways might be thought to detract from the axiality of the basilical plan, but it is clear that in many Cilician basilicas the central apse was not the only focus, since considerable importance was attached to the area behind it, where ambulatory passages were provided, and to the side-chambers which were regularly used as baptisteries. In order to facilitate communication with the various important points at the east end of the church, passages, or colonnaded walkways were often provided along either the north or the south side of the church. Sometimes the north passage had the appearance of an extra aisle, separated from the body of the church by an open arcade (this was the arrangement of the north passages at İmamli, the Necropolis Church and Church III 10 C at Anemurium, and perhaps the basilica at Misis and the Monastic Church at Corycus). South passages, on the other hand, tended to be open colonnades (Meryemlık, Basilica of St Thecla; Tapureli, Church B; Yanıkhan, South Church; and perhaps Şaha, if the southern hall there was not in fact the narthex). Most commonly, the passage was a simple corridor along the north side (Kanlıdivane, Church 2; Susanoğlu, Cemetery Church) or the south side of the church (Ura, and perhaps Mazılık, if the passage there was not a southern narthex). Even the single naved chapel at Kümkuyu had a simple north corridor. The 'Große Armenische Kirche' at Corycus was provided with passages along both north and south sides.

THE MAIN APSE
Churches were usually oriented and had the main apse at the east end of the nave. Only converted buildings had very eccentric alignments (Ayaş,Temple-Church; Dağ Pazarı, Basilica). Apses were variously semi-circular and horse-shoed in plan, and were sometimes stilted. The semi-domes, too, were either hemi-spherical or horse-shoed. Their masonry was usually superior to that of the rest of the church, either consisting of dressed ashlars, or having larger square stones to face the rubble and mortar fill.

There was no standard form for the exterior of the main apse. In most cases the outer face of the apse was rounded, whether or not it projected from the east wall of the church, or was included within it in what was in effect a continuation of the east walls of the side-chambers. In the latter event, the side-chambers often had irregular plans when no attempt was made to disguise the curved outer face of the apse. In the Plain, the apse was usually contained by the side-chambers, but projected slightly to allow the positioning of three windows in its curve (Anazarbus, Southwest Church; Bodrum, both churches; Kadirli, Ala Cami; Karlık): the same arrangement can be seen in three churches in Rough Cilicia (Dağ Pazarı, 'Domed Ambulatory Church'; Ura, Town Church;

Uzuncaburç, Church near the Theatre), and is not a feature which can be attested in Syrian basilicas. Two large apses (Meryemlık, Basilica of St Thecla; Yemişkum, Church 1) had external buttresses.

Although the outer face of the apse was occasionally straightened, in order to tidy the appearance of the side-chambers or the eastern passage (hence the slanting walls in the Temple-Church at Uzuncaburç, and the basilica at Çatıkören), the only apse with a polygonal external appearance was that of the seventh century 'Cathedral' at Corycus, which was built in a period when there seems to have been some degree of architectural interchange between Cilicia and Anatolia. In the better built churches the side-chambers were made rectangular, and the apse was therefore encased in very thick walls (e.g. Canbazlı, Basilica; Alahan, East Church).

The apse usually had one or more arched windows. These tend to range in number from one to three, although there were pairs of double windows in the Temple-Church at Silifke, and the Basilica of St Thecla at Meryemlık. Presence or absence of windows seems to have been completely unrelated to the provision of an eastern passage. Thus in the South Church at Yanıkhan, the apse window may have had some purpose in lighting the eastern passage, but cannot have provided any light for the nave. It may also be regarded as normal for there to be a simple sima moulding at the level of the springing of the semi-dome, but this is not a universal rule. This moulding often marked the point of transition from small stones to better cut larger blocks. Since churches without the sima include the South Church at Yanıkhan, the Town Church at Ura, which is probably a converted temple, and Church 3 at Kanlıdivane, which was apparently converted from a domestic structure, it may be that the absence of this moulding should be seen as an early feature.

A row of sockets is visible at a high level inside the apses of several churches (e.g. Alahan, East Church; north of Corycus; Kanlıdivane, Church 2; Şaha). I suggest that these may have held supports for lamps. In most cases the sockets are at such a level that they might have held brackets, but the sockets in the East Church at Alahan are set into the semi-dome, and might have held hooks for hanging lamps. Artificial lighting would have been particularly necessary in churches where the apse had no window, or where there was an eastern passage.

The presence of a synthronum is very common. These varied in form considerably from a simple bench round the inner face of the apse (Cennet Cehennem, Temple-Church) to a multi-tiered form with a raised central cathedra (Alahan, West Church). Most surviving examples are stone, but joist-holes which must have supported a wooden synthronum are visible in the apse of Church 2 at Kanlıdivane. Synthrona have been discovered in most basilicas where the apse has been excavated, and they may be regarded as a normal Cilician feature. In both major churches at Alahan, the secondary extensions of the synthronum blocked the doorways between the choir and the side-chambers.

A cathedra at the centre of the synthronum should also be regarded as a normal feature.

SIDE-CHAMBERS

Side-chambers are a common feature, but there is no reason to suppose that churches without side-chambers are earlier than those with tripartite east ends. Although no positively dated fourth century church in Cilicia had simple side-chambers, their presence in the Temple-Church at Uzuncaburç, in the Basilica at Dağ Pazarı, and even in the single-naved Chapel of St Mary at Cennet Cehennem leaves no room to doubt that they were included in the plans of the earliest Cilician churches. The occasional churches which can definitely be shown to have been without either side-chambers or an eastern passage appear to have been monastic (Tapureli, Church B; Ura, Monastery; Uzuncaburç, Church of Stephanos). To these may be added the Funerary Basilica at Dağ Pazarı: I have already suggested that this church may have been particularly open to Anatolian influences since the doorway between the north aisle and the narthex was blocked in order to create a chamber at the north end of the narthex. This chamber closely resembles those at the ends of the narthex in Lycaonian basilicas which, with the single important exception of Church 32 at Binbirkilise, always lack eastern side-chambers. The absence of chambers beside the apse in the Funerary Basilica at Dağ Pazarı may thus also be a reflection of Anatolian practice, or may have resulted from the simple fact that the apse is cut deeply into the hillside.

The tripartite plan has a strong Syrian flavour and its appearance in fourth century Cilician churches probably reflects the metropolitan influence of Antioch. But the term 'side-chamber' can often be applied only loosely in Cilicia, since in churches with an eastern passage the spaces normally occupied by the side-chambers were little more than corridors linking the aisles with the passage behind the apse. This is the point which Krautheimer was making when he wrote:

> 'In a number of churches in and near Kanlıdivane (Kanytelideis), these flanking side-rooms become somewhat formless spaces extending on either side and behind the apse in a provincialised version very characteristic of Cilicia.' (Krautheimer 1986, 111)

It is clear from the churches at Susanoğlu and Yanıkhan that the eastern passage was already being included in Cilician basilicas in the fourth century, but it is convenient to consider first those side-chambers which could be considered conventional. It seems likely but by no means certain that Cilician churches followed Syrian practice in having the prothesis in the south side-chamber, and the diaconicon in the north side-chamber. There is a certain amount of evidence to suggest that the north side-chambers were more secure than those on the south sides of churches. There are often larger and more numerous windows in the south side-chamber, and in one church where this difference in fenestration is evident, the Basilica at Canbazlı, there is a cupboard recess in the south side-chamber which is not matched in the north side-chamber. But it is most common to find cupboard recesses in both side-chambers (e.g. Alahan, East Church; Öküzlü, North Church). In Church 3 at Kanlıdivane, the south side-chamber has a tiny arrow-slit at a high level, and is considerably smaller than the north side-chamber which has a double window.

The uncertainty of the evidence concerning the function of the side-chambers probably reflects Cilician practice, since it is likely that the usage of the side-chambers was not as predictable as it may have been in Syria. Even in churches without eastern passages the side-chambers were sometimes open to the ends of the aisles through arches (e.g. Kanlıdivane, Church 1; Tapureli, Church B), and thereby lost much of their independent character. Often enough, too, the side-chambers housed the baptistery. This was commonly placed in the south side-chamber (as in Corycus, Tomb Church; Meryemlık, 'Cupola Church'; and probably the church north of Corycus): in the Necropolis Church at Anemurium the north side-chamber was used in this way. There is no reason in any of these cases to suppose that the use of the side-chamber for baptismal purposes involved the conversion of the prothesis, for in all cases except the Necropolis Church at Anemurium the baptistery consisted of a pair of parallel chambers which appear to have been part of the original plan of the church. A more meaningful conclusion would be that the standard Cilician baptistery consisted of two parallel rectangular chambers, which might well occupy what would normally be the position of a side-chamber. It is possible that further excavation would establish that the practice of placing the baptistery on one or other side of the apse was more common than can currently be attested.

These observations do tend to suggest that in Cilicia the side-chambers were not necessarily used for the purposes for which they were included in the Syrian basilica. During the fifth century, as Cilician church plans became more and more complex, the side-chambers increasingly lost their identity as independent units. The blocking of the access from the chancel to the side-chambers of both churches at Alahan would also seem to suggest that the side-chambers were losing their importance. In the churches where the side-chambers retain their significance by the late fifth century, there is often a specific reason. Thus in the 'Cupola Church' at Meryemlık the south side-chambers were positioned beyond the eastern passage, which hugged the outer face of the apse, in order to preserve the unity of the side-chamber which was used as a baptistery. Similarly in the Basilica of St Thecla at Meryemlık, and the Transept Church at Corycus, the north side-chambers, which in both cases were apsidal, appear to have been expensively decorated with marble cladding and glass mosaics in a manner which suggests that they may have been independent chapels. Subsidiary apses are a feature of the side-chambers of several important fifth century churches (as well as the two just mentioned, the Corycus, Tomb Church; the church north of Corycus; Öküzlü, North Church: the secondary side-chamber of the sixth century Rock-Cut Church at Anazarbus was also apsidal). It could be argued from this that even in churches where side-chambers were provided as late as the late fifth century, there was usually a specific reason which did not necessarily reflect the usual functions of pastophories.

This lack of interest in the usual functions of the side-chambers was probably inherent in Cilician liturgical practice from an early date, and related to the provision of eastern passages. But even in churches which were not equipped with an ambulatory the side-chambers were sometimes open to the east ends of the aisles through wide arches (e.g. Kanlıdivane, Church 1; Tapureli, Church C), and cannot, accordingly, have been seen as independent terminal units. In their provision of side-chambers which do not always appear to have been used for their Syrian purposes, the Cilician churches can be seen to stand in an intermediate position between Syria and Anatolia, and even, it might be argued, to be looking towards Constantinople where the early basilicas had openings at the east ends of the aisles, although these did not lead to enclosed spaces.

The three churches with ambulatory apses (Akören II, Church 2; Anavarza, Church of the Apostles; Ovacik) represent a distinctive plan present in both Plain and Rough Cilicia in which the traditional positioning of side-chambers is impossible since the ambulatory round the columnar exedra, which occupied the position of the apse at the end of the nave, involved having the spaces on either side of the exedra fully open for circumambulation.

Although I have suggested that by the late fifth century the side-chambers were losing their original significance, it can, nevertheless, be demonstrated that in certain circumstances they were actually gaining in size. There is a group of basilicas in which the side-chambers project westwards from the mouth of the apse, and thus define a rectangular sanctuary bay. I believe that this development had little to do with the significance of the side-chambers, but was rather connected with increasing elaboration of sanctuary arrangements in the fifth century. The list of churches with these extended side chambers is extensive (Batısandal; Canbazlı, Basilica; Kanlıdivane, Church 1; Kızılaliler; Tapureli, Churches A and C; Takkadın; Yeniyurt Kale; and, most significantly, the West Church at Alahan). As a group these churches may be attributed to the fifth century, and they stand as important links in the chain of architectural development which leads to the appearance of various forms of transept in the basilicas of Cilicia by the late fifth century. The extension, and more precise definition, of the sanctuary in these fifth century churches could be seen as a response to the declining importance of the side-chambers. Once this was effected, it was a relatively simple matter to place an arch between the west walls of the side-chambers, thus defining the sanctuary still more positively by the inclusion of a triumphal arch on its west side. This is precisely what was accomplished in the West Church at Alahan, since the engaged columns at the corners of the side-chambers must have supported such a triumphal arch across the east end of the nave. This simple development must surely have been mirrored in other Cilician churches which have yet to be discovered, or in which the evidence awaits excavation. The inclusion of a triumphal arch to the west of the mouth of the apse allowed two major developments in Cilician basilicas, since it defined a transverse unit at the east end of the nave, which could be converted into a transept by the simple expedient of opening up the side-chambers, and also had the effect of creating a bay immediately in front of the apse, which could potentially be surmounted by a tower. The bay in front of the apse of the West Church at Alahan could have supported some form of elaborated roof: even if it did not, the church was considerably more significant in architectural terms than has hitherto been suggested.

SANCTUARIES
Churches with no eastern passage, and where the side-chambers were not occupied by a baptistery or for some other function not normally associated with the pastophories, could presumably have followed Syrian liturgical practice exactly. But such basilicas are in a very small minority, and, even if the side-chambers were originally meant to be used as the prothesis and the diaconicon, Cilician usage seems to have moved away from this. The functions of the diaconicon could perhaps have been carried out in the upper floor of the side-chambers, but such a shift would hardly have been convenient for the preparations for the Eucharist, which would normally have been carried out in the prothesis. It is quite clear, in fact, that in the Cilician basilicas the sanctuaries regularly occupied a large area of the eastern part of the nave, and were separated off not by low parapets, as was the case in Syria and Anatolia, but by high chancel screens which were could be over 2 metres high. Parts of such screens have survived in many Cilician churches: their height may be gauged from the indications in the 'Cathedral' and Transept Church at Corycus, the West Church at Alahan, and, most completely, from the chancel-screen of the Funerary Church at Dağ Pazarı (plate 74). In these churches the chancel screens were formed from a combination of elaborately carved stonework with wooden screens and curtains. Some less pretentious churches had a simple stone wall (Takkadın; and probably also the church at Çukurkeşlik). In all cases there was a doorway at the centre of the chancel screen. The Dağ Pazarı screen was high enough to allow the suspension of a sanctuary lamp from the arch of the doorway.

There are occasional signs that a wooden screen was erected across the mouth of the apse at the same level as the gallery floors. In Church 3 at Kanlıdivane, which has simple side-chambers this was presumably the chancel-screen. In both the case of the church at Batısandal, which had extended side-chambers, and the 'Große Armenische Kirche' at Corycus, which had a transept, the chancel-screen would usually have been set further to the west, and the purpose of these extra wooden screens is uncertain.

The high Cilician chancel-screen must have resembled very closely the high iconostasis which is such a feature of later Greek churches. They would have functioned in the same way to hide the altar and the apse, and it is reasonable to assume that, since the side-chambers in Cilician basilicas so often appear to have been public parts of the church, the offices which would otherwise have been carried out in the prothesis must have been accomplished in the extended and elaborately screened area in front of the apse.

The altar stood in a central position either on the chord of the apse or on a raised bema immediately to the west. It would thus have been visible from the nave when the door or curtain at the centre of the chancel screen was opened. Where some evidence has been preserved (Alahan, West Church and Baptistery; Corycus, 'Cathedral'; Dağ Pazarı, Funerary Church) the altar consisted of a square or oblong marble slab supported by four (or three in the perverse instance of the Baptistery at Alahan) wooden legs which were set into sockets in a stone base. The altar bases sometimes contained sealed compartments which contained reliquaries (Dağ Pazarı, Funerary Church; Çırga).

So few churches have been excavated that it is impossible to generalize about other aspects of sanctuary planning and church furniture. In the Funerary Basilica at Dağ Pazarı, the ambo, which consisted of a circular stone base which supported a wooden parapet, projected from the chancel-screen into the north half of the nave. It was approached from the chancel by a short raised path, which could just about be classified as a solea. Herzfeld and Guyer found the remains of similar ambones in the 'Cupola Church' and the North Church at Meryemlık. The former was lying on the west side of the central nucleus, beside a rectangular slab which appeared to have been its base. Since it is evident that the central bay in the 'Domed Basilicas' was included within the sanctuary, the position of the ambo at Meryemlık conforms to the position at Dağ Pazarı, and this may have been the normal practice.

This last point raises the issue, to which I shall return, that it is likely that the large Cilician sanctuaries, with their high chancel-screens, were a major factor which led to dramatic architectural developments. I have already noted that in a group of fifth century churches the side-chambers project westwards from the mouth of the apse, enclosing the north and south sides of the sanctuary. When, as was the case in the West Church at Alahan, a triumphal arch was included between the west walls of the extended side-chambers, the sanctuary became a unit at the centre of the church which was clearly defined by the architecture.

EASTERN PASSAGES

The regular provision of a passage behind the apse is easily the most remarkable characteristic of Cilician church planning. The feature was present in the earliest Cilician basilicas, and was, I believe, a major factor which influenced subsequent architectural developments. These ambulatory passages have puzzled scholars since Gertrude Bell, who wrote 'I have searched in vain for any exact parallel to the arrangement of apses illustrated by the church at Sheher' (Şaha) 'and by many others in the Kanytelideis district' (Bell 1906b, 390). She concluded that they were probably 'a kind of retro-choir containing a separate chapel' (Bell 1906b, 395). This has the merit of simplicity, but is somewhat vague. Bell was unaware of any passages without subsidiary apses and attributed more significance to the apses than the passages to which they were attached. Guyer took this idea a stage further, and considered this Cilician peculiarity so unlikely that he was inclined to assign all churches with multiple apses to the Armenian period (Herzfeld and Guyer 1930, 12). It was as a result of this groundless reasoning that the 'Große Armenische Kirche' acquired its monstrous title. With surpassing illogicality, Guyer was nevertheless able to accept that the passages of the Basilica of St Thecla at Meryemlık and the Tomb Church at Corycus, which did not have subsidiary apses, although their side-chambers did, were early Byzantine features. Forsyth's initial mistrust of these passages is evident from the special pleading by which he argues that the passage of Church 4 at Kanlıdivane 'is clearly a later addition', although he admits that every aspect of its construction has 'exactly the same character' as the rest of the church (Forsyth 1961, 132). More recently, as has been noted, Krautheimer has categorized the eastern apartments of Cilician basilicas as 'somewhat formless spaces' (Krautheimer 1986, 111), although he evidently accepts their antiquity. This statement was a simple reiteration of what was said in the first edition of his book *Early Christian and Byzantine Architecture*, which appeared in 1965. Forsyth, however, searching for parallels for the plan of the Church of St Catherine at Mount Sinai, had meanwhile made tentative steps in the direction of discovering the purpose of the Cilician passages, although he did not himself understand them: 'no reason is apparent for these Cilician chapels to enclose a small court behind the apse' (Forsyth 1968, 18). It seems that, like Guyer, Forsyth was prepared to accept the antiquity of passages which were set between the side-chambers and entered from them through doorways, but ignored passages where the side-chambers were non-existent, or at most had had their walls reduced to residual arches.

The eastern passages, in their various forms, demand attention if only because the list of churches in which one was present is so formidable (Akören II, Church 2; Anazarbus, Church of the Apostles; Anemurium, III 10 C, III 13 C; Balabolu, Necropolis Church; Cennet Cehennem, Temple-Church; Corycus, Churches A, B, D, G, H, I; Çatıkören; Dağ Pazarı, Basilica; Emirzeli, Churches 1 and 2; Hasanalıler; İmamli; Işıkkale; Kanlıdivane, Churches 2 and 4; Manastır

(Mylae); Maraş Harabelerı; Meryemlık, Basilica of St Thecla and 'Cupola Church'; Öküzlü, North Church and South Church; Ovacik; Silifke, Temple-Church; Susanoğlu, Town and Cemetery Churches; Şaha; Takkadın; Ura, Town Church; Yanıkhan, South and North Churches; Yemişkum). Four more churches probably had an eastern passage (Anemurium, Church III 14 C; Balabolu, Churches 1 and 2; Haciömerli). Thus at least 37, and possibly 41, of the known early Byzantine churches of Cilicia had an eastern passage. Future excavations may well reveal that churches where the feature is not presently apparent were also provided with one. The list of Cilician basilicas known to have conventional side-chambers and no passage would actually be shorter.

The discovery of the churches at Yanıkhan has proved particularly useful for the understanding of these passages. For various stylistic reasons the South Church at Yanıkhan must be an early building and if the Matronianus whose donor's inscription on the west door is indeed the Matronianus known from the sea wall at Anemurium, then the church must actually be a fourth century basilica. In any event it is early and its dedicatory inscription tells us that it was a martyrium, whilst it is clear from the position of the church which is close to the centre of the village that this was not a cemetery church. The only other church at Yanıkhan, the North Church, certainly was a cemetery church, and since there is no trace of a third church in the village, which is remarkably well preserved, it is logical to assume that the South Church, as well as being a martyrium, was the parish basilica. Even a cursory glance at the building should convince the most ardent sceptic that the domical chamber at the centre of the east side of the ambulatory passage must have been very important, since it has on its north side an arched niche which apparently contains a sarcophagus, and the chamber was embellished with gilded glass paste mosaics and marble revetments. The chamber either contained the donor's tomb or served as the actual martyrium. The martyrium was certainly contained within the basilica, and it seems reasonable to assume that the special chamber attached to the east side of the church would have enabled the church to function as a martyrium with the least disturbance to its use as a parish church. There are, of course, no proper side-chambers in the South Church at Yanıkhan since the spaces on either side of the main apse provided access to the eastern chambers. The passage had subsidiary apses at its north and south ends, and had two transverse arches which might be argued to have divided it into three chambers, but such arches are a common feature of the local domestic buildings in which they were used to support the floors of upper storeys, and can be seen in the same capacity supporting the upper floors of side-chambers (e.g. Canbazlı, Basilica). To assert that this passage was divided into three bays in order to create side-chambers would involve accepting that the church had both an unsatisfactory passage and unsatisfactory side-chambers. But the importance of the passage is manifest from the provision of a separate access to it along a colonnaded walkway on the south side of the church, and from the elaborate decoration of the central domical chamber.

The North Church at Yanıkhan is so similar to the South Church as to render it likely that the two are very close in date. The North Church stands in the cemetery of the village, and fragments of sarcophagi and grave stelai can be seen lying in the eastern passage. Here, then, the funerary association of the basilica, and more particularly that of its eastern passage, is securely established. There is obviously a close parallelism since the passages of both churches seem to have had a memorial function, but there was an important distinction in practice between the South Church which was the parish church and also the martyrium of a group of named local saints, and the North Church which was the funerary basilica for the ordinary inhabitants of the village.

The variety of eastern passages which is, in effect, a chamber sandwiched between eastward projecting side-chambers is characteristic of the fifth century churches at Corycus, Emirzeli and Öküzlü, and it is possible that in these churches the side-chambers were able to retain some of their individuality because the passage was at the upper level. The walls which contain the subsidiary apses of the Transept Church at Corycus are so thick that it seems likely that there were also subsidiary apses at gallery level. In all churches where the relevant evidence has survived, it is clear that there was an upper storey above the eastern passage. It is not inconceivable, therefore, that some of the functions of the diaconicon, especially its use as a sacristy, could have been transferred to an upper chamber, which would have been a relatively secure point in the building, whilst the preparation of the host, which required privacy rather than security, could have been executed behind the high chancel screen.

There is no discernible pattern in the distribution of eastern passages which were present in parish churches, funerary churches, and monastic churches. If it could be shown that the eastern passages occurred only in buildings with a funerary association, one could argue that they were a Cilician equivalent of the ambulatories which envelop the apse of the cemetery basilicas of the early fourth century which are known to have existed in Rome (e.g. San Lorenzo fuori le mura, Santa Agnese, San Sebastiano: see Krautheimer 1986, 51-4). Three churches took this form (Akören II, Church 2; Anazarbus, Church of the Apostles; Ovacik), and the Church of the Apostles at Anavarza may well be a very early foundation, but not all these churches were funerary. Furthermore, following the example of the South Church at Yanıkhan, it is possible that in churches which are not obviously funerary basilicas, the eastern passage may, nevertheless, have been martyrial in character. This should not be considered surprising since much more famous fourth century basilicas were martyria. I am thinking, of course, of the Constantinian basilicas in Rome and the Holy Land, which did not necessarily contain an actual burial or saint's relic.

It is also very important to consider Meryemlık in this context. It is clear from the account of Basil of Seleucia that the fourth century martyrium of St

Thecla was contained within a basilica, and was itself a centralized structure with an altar set beneath a circular silver ciborium. Egeria defines the sanctuary of St Thecla in the following terms: 'murus ingens, qui includet ecclesiam, in qua est martyrium, quod martyrium est satis pulchrum' (*Peregrinatio* 23, 2). This suggests to me that the martyrium was part of the fourth century church, but retained its architectural independence. Thecla's sanctuary was fully established by the time of Egeria's visit in May 384. Given the evident importance of Meryemlık as a pilgrimage centre by this date, it is surely not unreasonable to suggest that the plan of the South Church at Yanıkhan, may have been modelled on the basilica and martyrium of St Thecla, the fifth century successor of which had an eastern passage. Thus the South Church at Yanıkhan, with its passage and martyrium may well recall the plan of the fourth century basilica and martyrium of St Thecla, which was already by the fourth century, and continued to be, the most important pilgrimage site in Cilicia. If this reasoning is correct, then the relationship of the fourth century martyria in Cilicia with the famous Constantinian pilgrimage churches in the Holy Land becomes all the more compelling, since they, too, were basilicas in which the actual martyrium was an independent unit which was annexed to a basilica (see Krautheimer 1986, 60-3; Forsyth 1968, 17). The peripatetic services which were such a feature of these churches were described by Egeria (*Peregrinatio* 24-5). From her account of the services held in Constantine's church on Golgotha on Sundays, it emerges that crowds gathered in the atrium of the basilica before dawn and were let into the aisles at cock's crow by the bishop. They proceeded down the aisles and into the rotunda of the Anastasis where prayers, readings, and blessings were performed. The group then moved on to the site of the Cross, where another prayer was recited, and thence back through the aisles of the basilica. Mass was read in the basilica in a separate service on ordinary Sundays, although it is clear that special occasions, particularly Easter, were celebrated by lengthy peripatetic services which made full use of the whole building complex. The basilica, therefore, was at once part of the martyrium and also the cathedral of Jerusalem. It was used for the celebration of Mass, and its apse, which contained the bishop's throne, remained its major focus. The aisles of the basilica were used as processional routes which led to the actual martyria which were being commemorated, the Cave of the Anastasis, and the Rock of Cavalry, which were in a courtyard behind the main apse.

At Christmas, of course, the Church of the Nativity at Bethlehem was a major centre in a huge peripatetic service. Its plan conforms to the pattern of the Church on Golgotha. The Constantinian arrangement consisted of an atrium set before a basilica at the east end of which, approached by a flight of steps, was an octagonal chamber surmounting the Cave of the Nativity. Visitors would have proceeded along the aisles, and circumambulated the octagon, at the centre of which was a large hole through which it was possible to look down into the cave. Another relevant Constantinian martyrium is the church at

Mambre (Ramet el Khalil), near Hebron in Jordan (Mader 1957; Wilkinson 1973, 189). Here the turpentine tree beside which Jehovah addressed Moses was enclosed in an ancient precinct wall. Constantine, before 330, ordered the building of a basilica against one wall of the precinct. Thus, once again, a basilica was associated with an object of veneration, but retained its separateness in spite of being part of the same building complex.

The peripatetic services which were such a feature of the Constantinian martyria could also have been performed in the fourth century Cilician churches; indeed such services would seem to be dictated by the plan of the Basilica of St Thecla, if I am correct in suggesting that it contained two martyria. I believe that the site of her miraculous disappearance was venerated above ground, possibly in a chamber associated with an eastern passage, and that the underground cave which was her home during the final years before her disappearance was developed into a separate martyrium underneath the basilica. In the fifth century Basilica at least, there were holes in the floor which would have allowed a view of the Cave Church which could be entered from the south side of the Basilica. Thus at Meryemlık there were recollections of the famous Constantinian martyria of both Jerusalem and Bethlehem.

Even without Meryemlık, the martyrium at Yanıkhan would be sufficient proof of the relationship between the passages in the Cilician basilicas and the plans of early martyria in the Holy Land. But it seems that this type of plan was much more common, and had a much longer history in Cilicia than in any other part of the late Roman world. There are passages in other parts of the early Byzantine world such as Cyrenaica where several churches display the feature, examples being Ras-el-Hilal (Harrison 1964), and Benghazi, Sidi Khrebish (Lloyd 1977, 11-12) in both of which churches there was a baptistery in the northeast side-chamber. There are eastern passages in Lycia too, in the churches on Gemiler Ada and Karacaören Ada which are believed to have been pilgrimage sites (Tsuji 1995, 56-89). But no other area has the concentration of eastern passages which is found in Cilicia and Isauria, and it was to that region, therefore, that Forsyth had to turn in order to find parallels for the plan of the Church in the Monastery at Mount Sinai (Forsyth 1968, 18). The latter is certainly Justinianic, and consisted of a three-aisled basilica, with a series of side-chapels along the north and south sides of the building. These could be compared with the extra chambers so often seen along the sides of the Cilician basilicas, and resemble particularly closely the apsidal side-chapels of the 'Große Armenische Kirche' at Corycus. The semi-dome of the apse at Sinai and the wall above it were adorned with splendid mosaics which represent two events at which Moses, who was closely associated with Sinai, was present, the Transfiguration, and the miracle of the Burning Bush. The former had a double connection with Sinai, since the Prophet Elijah was also present, and the church was actually built around the Burning Bush itself. The apse is flanked by square, apsidal, side-chambers which project eastwards. The small courtyard which was thus defined behind the main apse could be entered by doorways from both side-chambers. This courtyard originally contained the Burning Bush, and was converted into a chapel in the medieval period. The double association of the church with important biblical events compares with both the Constantinian church on Golgotha, and the Basilica of St Thecla. Forsyth's comments on the use of the church at Sinai would fit Cilician basilicas equally well:

'From the entrance of the monastery the route to be followed by pilgrims to the Burning Bush is clearly indicated by the architecture itself. The route leads to the church, then goes along an aisle of the church and out into the former court of the Burning Bush, now the chapel of that name, and then back through the other aisle, thereby completing within the church a circuit in the form of a letter U, around the back of the apse.' (Forsyth 1968, 7)

In considering the antecedents of the plan of the basilica at Mount Sinai, Forsyth first contrasts it with the martyrium of Simeon Stylites at Kal'at Sim'an, and then tries to find parallels:

'The reason why the martyrium of St Simeon would not have been a good model to follow at Sinai seems clear. In the design of the martyrium, as originally conceived in the fifth century, the relic of the Saint was all important while the monks were secondary and obtained only gradually even a subordinate share in the architectural complex. Not until the middle of the sixth century, nearly seventy-five years after the construction of the martyrium, did the monastic buildings reach their full development; and even then the martyrium far outweighed in size and importance the monks' little church. The Mt. Sinai monastery, begun just when the group around the martyrium was completed, picks up the development at that point and carries it much further. The relic is made secondary and the church of the monks dominates. As Procopius states: "Justinian built them a church." So secondary was the relic, the Bush, that he does not even mention it.

In spite of the reversal of emphasis, the Bush had to receive its due share in the plan of the church. Even though reduced in relative importance, it was still a famous object of pilgrimage and loosened generous purse strings for the maintenance of the monks. We have seen that the plan adopted, in order to achieve this compromise, was a basilica in which the nave and main apse were allocated to the services of the monastic congregation, while pilgrims were permitted to follow a circuitous route to the Burning Bush behind the main apse.

Such a scheme, essentially a longitudinal axis inside a U-shaped circulation, had a genealogy going back to Constantine's foundations at the Holy Places of Jerusalem...

Another comparable example, intermediate in date between the Constantinian foundations and the Mt. Sinai church, appears in the Church of St Theodore at Jerash in Jordan, built between 491 and 496. Here the holy object in the center of the court at the left' (i.e. east of the apse) 'is a miraculous well whose water turned into wine yearly at Epiphany. It was approached from the aisles through a porch and flight of stairs on each side of the apse.

These Palestinian examples differ from the Mt. Sinai church in one important respect. They do not give access to the relic or holy object through corner chapels extending outward beyond the apse. Such an arrangement can be found in Cilicia which... was within the orbit of Antioch architecturally. The fifth-century church of St Thekla at Meriamlik, a well-known center of pilgrimage, had two chapels jutting beyond the apse and giving access through doors to a terrace behind it. The purpose of the terrace is not evident... While the Cilician type of plan may have influenced the Mt. Sinai church directly, more likely the type was known in the whole Antiochene area and radiated from there.' (Forsyth 1968, 16-18).

As I indicated previously, Forsyth is here approaching an understanding of the martyrial significance of the Cilician passages, although he did not have the concrete example of Yanıkhan to prove this hypothesis. To misapply Gough's comment (on Forsyth's imprecise, as it turned out, theories on the 'Domed Basilicas'), 'with the evidence now firmly established, who is to gainsay the possibility, or even the probability of this?' (Gough 1972, 205). I am convinced that at Meryemlık the side-chambers and passage (I cannot see why Forsyth ignores the east wall, and calls the passage a 'terrace') contained the martyrium which commemorated the site of Thecla's disappearance. The lavish decoration of the north side-chamber, with its marbles and mosaics, is further proof of the importance attached to this part of the building. I have no hesitation in suggesting that there survived in Cilicia a type of martyrial church plan which was almost forgotten everywhere else, and I consider it most unlikely that this was an Antiochene building type. One searches in vain for eastern passages in Syrian churches, and it is clear that martyria in the immediate orbit of Antioch were centralized buildings, often aisled tetraconches with a central dome. As in most aspects of church planning, Cilicia seems to have maintained a stubborn independence in the planning of her martyria. Any influence Cilicia exerted on the plan of the church at Mount Sinai must, therefore, have been direct.

The church, of course, which is likely to have exerted an influence an architectural thinking outside Cilicia was not the fourth century church of St

Thecla, but the enormous fifth century basilica which replaced it, and which was doubtless part of Zeno's donation to Meryemlık. I think that it is likely that the later church had a tripartite transept in front of the apse, as well as a passage behind it. The south end of the transept either adjoined or contained the entrance to Thecla's cave. I would submit that the much better documented Church of St Demetrius at Thessalonica may also have reflected the kind of architectural thinking about martyria which was common in Cilicia throughout the late Roman period. As it stands, the Church of St Demetrius is a rebuilding of the original church which was burnt down in 1917, but it has been the subject of a thorough modern survey (Soteriou and Soteriou 1952). The Soterious proposed that the church, which may have replaced an earlier fifth century basilica, was erected in the decade of 460-470. Subsequently Cormack (1969, 42-3) has suggested a date at the end of the fifth century. This was accepted by Krautheimer (1986, 128). It would appear, therefore, that the Church of St Demetrius is likely to have been constructed shortly after the completion of the Zenonian Basilica of St Thecla. I should perhaps note that in seeking to find a connection between the architecture of Cilicia and Thessalonica in the late fifth century I would be following Gough who wrote of the West Church at Alahan that 'its architecture bears a considerable family resemblance to that of the Acheiropoeitos (sic) in Salonika, a church generally thought to date to the third quarter of the fifth century.' (Gough 1967/68, 461)

The Church of St Demetrius is a five-aisled basilica with a continuous transept in front of the apse, and a pair of wings, which are almost like side-chambers and project beyond the apse to form two sides of a courtyard which is closed by an eastern wall. The 'side-chambers' are open to the courtyard through triple arches. With both a transept and an eastern courtyard, the church can be closely compared with the Basilica of St Thecla, but these features have never been adequately explained. Krautheimer glosses over the problem of how the martyrium functioned with the comment that:

> 'The grave of the saint is relegated to a crypt: extending below the south transept wing, it was the spiritual but no longer the architectural focus of the building.' (Krautheimer 1986, 126)

But he came some way towards appreciating the significance of the east end of the basilica when he wrote:

> 'Large parts of the decoration and certainly the plan would still seem to date from the fifth century, including a change already during construction: arcades and walls, projecting eastwards on either side of the apse, suggest that at first, instead of the apse, a rectangular chancel enveloped by an ambulatory was envisaged.' (Krautheimer 1986, 128)

With the example of Meryemlık to follow, there is no real necessity to suggest that there was any change in the plan of the church of St Demetrius, and the presence of a form of eastern ambulatory is surely to be seen as an aspect of the vocabulary of Christian martyrial architecture. There is, in fact, some reason to doubt whether St Demetrius was actually buried in this church. The problem is discussed by Mango, who also seems at a loss to explain the plan of the building:

'A particularly well-documented example of a great martyr's shrine is provided by the church of St Demetrius at Thessalonica.... St Demetrius is a large, five-aisled transept basilica provided with a gallery. It is bigger than the Acheiropoietos and was evidently intended for a considerable number of people.

But what precisely were they coming to worship in the fifth century? Here lies one of the problems. It seems that originally St Demetrius belonged to Sirmium, which was the capital of Illyricum until the seat of the prefect was moved to Thessalonica about 442. The cult of the saint may have migrated at the same time. However that may be, there arose a legend that St Demetrius had been martyred at Thessalonica, in the heating plant of the public bath that was next to the hippodrome. This legend must have been known at the time the basilica was planned, for it was built on top of the bath and incorporated the substructure of the latter, which became a kind of crypt under the bema. The strange thing is, however, that the church did not possess any relics of the saint. The main feature of the crypt was a fountain, left over from the Roman bath, which was fenced off by means of a low marble enclosure.

The chief object of veneration in the basilica was not, however, the crypt but a hexagonal silver-sheathed ciborium which was placed on the north side of the nave. This contained a silver object resembling a bed, on which was represented an image of the saint. But even for the ciborium no claim was made that it contained the body of Demetrius. Such were the original arrangements...

We may deduce from the above that, whereas the fifth-century architect went to considerable trouble to locate the church over the spot where St Demetrius was believed to have suffered martyrdom, he did not plan the building so as to give a central position to a cult object. The silver ciborium, which, until the seventh century was the focus of veneration, was placed off center in the nave, like a piece of liturgical furniture and no more. As for the transept, the function of this feature has not yet been ascertained: there appears, in any case to be no reason to attach to it a martyrial significance.' (Mango 1976, 75-9)

I have quoted Mango at length because it seems to me that the 'problems' which he lists can all be resolved by comparison with Meryemlık, and therefore, by extension, find their resolution in the normal practices of Cilician martyrial architecture. Since St Thecla was still alive when she disappeared, there were no relics of her body. This in itself did not prevent the development of Meryemlık as her martyrium. The same observation could be made for the Constantinian martyria in the Holy Land, which commemorated the sites of important events associated with Christ, rather than physical remains.

Mango's plate 82 shows the fine early Byzantine circular marble ciborium in the crypt, but he does not discuss it. By analogy with the circular ciborium which was set up at Meryemlık on the site of Thecla's disappearance, it would be reasonable to suppose that the similar feature at Thessalonica might have marked the supposed position of Demetrius' martyrdom. It is surely more than merely accidental that the ciborium in the Church of St Demetrius stands immediately beneath the courtyard behind the apse. Furthermore, the entrance to the crypt is on the south side of the central bay of the transept. Here, then, is another recollection of Meryemlık, where the entrance to Thecla's cave appears to been related to the transept in the fifth century basilica. Mango compares the ciborium in the nave at Thessalonica to a piece of 'furniture', noting that it contained merely 'an image of the saint'. It is, of course, impossible to determine whether this was an original feature of the church, but, if not, then it could have been an image of the actual martyrium which was contained in the crypt and therefore less accessible for mass devotion. This would be all the more likely, if the foreign feature of the eastern courtyard, which allowed visitors to pass above the site of Demetrius' martyrdom, was not properly understood in Thessalonica. The reason why the architect of the church of St Demetrius should have chosen this plan was presumably because he was seeking a compromise between a martyrium, which he would normally have thought of as a centralized structure, and a basilica which was capable of holding a 'considerable concourse of people'. It would have been quite natural for the recently completed Basilica of St Thecla to come into his mind as an example to follow.

I believe that the case for the eastern passages in Cilician basilicas being martyrial, or at least funerary, in basic purpose can therefore be supported from internal Cilician evidence, and by comparison with martyria in other parts of the late Roman world. The mention of the transepts at Meryemlık and Thessalonica raises the next issue which has to be discussed, for I believe that the inclusion of the eastern passages in the Cilician basilicas was a critical factor which led to the development of the Cilician transepts. There is, in other words a connection in Cilician churches between transepts and eastern passages, and thus, after all, there may have a martyrial association which would explain the transept in the church of St Demetrius.

3

THE TRANSEPT BASILICAS

Cilicia has often been regarded as unimportant by students of early Byzantine architecture. Thus Edwards (1982, 29) referred to Cilicia as 'a cultural backwater' dependent on Syria for architectural inspiration, and Stanzl, though accepting that Cilician 'Domed Basilicas' were important, concluded that their plans must have been slavish copies of buildings in Constantinople: his belief that they could not have evolved locally is evident from his use of the exclamation mark after a comment on domes 'in Kilikien!' (Stanzl 1979, 80). The 'Domed Basilicas' have nevertheless, attracted considerable attention, not least because it now appears that they are not, after all, Justinianic but were constructed in the late fifth century.

I have previously noted that the West Church at Alahan, which has what could be termed a 'proto-transept', could have supported a tower in front of the apse, or a transverse roof across the width of the building. This observation makes the point that the plans of the 'Domed Basilicas' contain the ingredients of a transept, for they include a group of bays in front of the apse, which interrupt the longitudinal thrust of the basilica. In fact the 'Domed Basilicas' and most of the Transept Basilicas form a homogeneous group most or all of which belongs to the late fifth century. The group has plans which evolved locally to suit the unusual architectural problems created by the eastern passage which itself seems to have evolved in response to the Cilician habit of including martyria within basilicas.

Although Alakilise, and perhaps also Köşkerli, have escaped notice, the other 'Domed Basilicas' have received considerable attention. This is not true in the case of the Cilician transepts. Forsyth noted that there was probably a tripartite transept in the Transept Church at Corycus, which he believed belonged to the late sixth century, and wrote:

> 'Its occurrence in the sixth century would not be surprising, since it had appeared in S. Pietro in Vincoli in the previous century, and in various parts of Greece in the fifth and sixth centuries.' (Forsyth 1961, 136, note 29)

Krautheimer accepted that two churches in Cilicia had transepts, and concluded:

'But it is strange to find the type' (cross transept) 'in out-of-the-way towns along the south coast of Asia Minor. It is equally surprising to find in these same places tripartite transepts, well known on the Greek mainland, but as yet unknown on the west coast of Asia Minor.... One is found in the basilica *extra muros* at Korykos.... The other example, a basilica outside (sic) Kanlidivane, presents a tripartite transept incorporated into a basilica with galleries - decidedly a Constantinopolitan or Salonican type, quite unknown on the west coast.... With few exceptions, the available publications have given an all too sketchy picture of the character and chronology of this architecture. This is particularly regrettable since in the sixth century the south coast of Asia Minor seems to have exerted considerable impact not only along the coasts of the eastern Mediterranean, but even as far west as Italy.' (Krautheimer 1986, 110)

I wonder whether Krautheimer would have been quite so confident about the influence of Constantinople or Thessalonica if he had appreciated that a form of transept was included in at least 13 Cilician basilicas, and that all types - continuous, cross, and tripartite transepts - can be attested in Cilician churches which were erected in the fifth century. I have argued above that the plan of the Basilica of St Demetrius at Thessalonica may actually have been strongly influenced by a Cilician prototype. Bittel did suggest that the basilica in the Topkapı Sarayı had a transept, but Mathews has shown that this idea conflicts with the archaeological evidence (Bittel 1939, 179: Mathews 1971, 37). There is, accordingly, no transept in any of the known fifth century basilicas of Constantinople.

The impressive list of transept basilicas could be extended to include the five cognate 'Domed Basilicas', and does not, of course, include any church from Tarsus or Seleucia, although these cities presumably boasted the grandest metropolitan churches of the province. The only churches to survive in a Cilician metropolis (Anazarbus) contained a cross transept (Southwest Church) and a tripartite transept with ambulatory (Church of the Apostles).

Proper appreciation of the significance of the early Byzantine architecture of Cilicia has been bedevilled, as Krautheimer realized, by inadequate understanding of its chronology. The arguments for assigning both the 'Domed Basilicas' and the transept basilicas to the fifth century will be set out below, but for the moment, it should suffice to observe that both groups of buildings are entirely consistent in decorative and architectural terms, and share various striking features which are uncommon in earlier or later buildings.

The Cilician transept basilicas cannot be divided into entirely straightforward categories, since they are variously preserved, and the evidence is often fragmentary, but the following rough guidelines emerge. The West Church at Alahan had an embryonic transept, as did Emirzeli, Church 2. There

were probably tripartite transepts in four basilicas (Anavarza, Church of the
Apostles; Corycus, Transept Church; Kanlıdivane, Church 4; Meryemlık,
Basilica of St Thecla). There was certainly a continuous transept in the North
Church at Öküzlü, and probably also in the Temple-Church at Cennet
Cehennem, the 'Cathedral' at Corycus, and at Köşkerli. The Southwest Church
at Anavarza, and the 'Große Armenische Kirche' at Corycus appear to have had
cross-transepts.

The first point of general import is that of these twelve churches nine also
have an eastern passage, and of the nine only one, the Church of the Apostles at
Anavarza, is an intra-mural church. Most of the others are in cemeteries. One
of the three churches without eastern passages, the West Church at Alahan, is in
a pilgrimage site. Only the Southwest Church at Anavarza is intra-mural, and
appears to have been without a passage, although there are intriguing doorways
in the outer walls at the east end of the church. In other words, there are reasons
to suppose that ten of the transept basilicas were either funerary churches or
martyria. Thus the commemorative associations of the transepts would appear
to be as strong as is the case with the eastern passages. Given this observation,
it is tempting to suggest, on the strength of its ground plan, that the Southwest
Church at Anavarza may have been the martyrium of the Anazarbene martyrs
Tarachus, Probus and Andronicus, who do not appear to have been
commemorated in either of the other major churches at Anavarza. The
commemorative nature of the transept basilicas is in any case fairly certain. By
corollary, it is of interest to note that two of the 'Domed Basilicas' stood in
cemeteries (Alakilise; Corycus, Tomb Church), and two were in important
pilgrimage sites (Alahan, East Church; Meryemlık, 'Cupola Church'). The
nature of the 'Domed Ambulatory Church' at Dağ Pazarı is less clear: Gough at
one time thought that it was extra-mural, and it is very unlikely to have been
used as the parish church rather than the intra-mural Basilica.

Although the transept basilicas are more numerous than the 'Domed
Basilicas', none of them is as well preserved as the East Church at Alahan, and
only in the case of the North Church at Öküzlü is there any precise evidence for
the form of the original roofing system. Forsyth's passionate insistence on
wooden pyramids for the 'Domed Churches' can be compared with his belief
that the tripartite transept of Church 4 at Kanlıdivane was covered 'by a
continuation of the same longitudinal gable roof that covered the galleries
adjoining the nave' (Forsyth 1961, 131). Had he seen the North Church at
Öküzlü, Forsyth might have come to a different conclusion, for there is
preserved a row of windows, above the mouth of the apse, which belonged to
the clerestory of the transept, which must, accordingly, have been covered by a
transverse roof. Windows at a high level in the 'Cathedral' and the 'Große
Armenische Kirche' at Corycus and the high walls in Church 2 at Emirzeli and
the Basilica at Köşkerli suggest that these churches also may have had

transverse roofing systems. Since such an arrangement was possible in at least one building, there is no reason to suppose that it could not have been effected in others.

In most cases where the evidence has been preserved (Cennet Cehennem, Temple-Church; Corycus, 'Cathedral' and Transept Church; Öküzlü, North Church, and, probably, the Basilica at Meryemlık) the galleries did not cross the transept. In Church 4 at Kanlıdivane, however, the transept was divided into three bays by arches between the triumphal arch and the corner of the apse. The gallery floors certainly extended across the transept since the corbels and offset which supported its joists are still visible in the north wall. But the arcading of the gallery was not continued beyond the triumphal arch. The tripartite transept thus became continuous at the higher level. In two churches (Anavarza, Church of the Apostles; Meryemlık, Basilica) there appears to have been a single column between the triumphal arch and the corner of the apse: these may have served as nothing more than the sides of a chancel barrier. There is no evidence at Meryemlık which would suggest that arches sprang across the transept, and it is evident that there was a wooden screen in this position in the transept of the 'Cathedral' at Corycus. It may thus be more correct to think of the arch at Kanlıdivane as part of the sanctuary arrangements. In any event the distinction between continuous and tripartite transepts is blurred, and the latter term should perhaps be applied only to transepts which were divided into three bays by high arches. Since the galleries in the Transept Church at Corycus did not cross the transept, the cruciform piers of the triumphal arch must presumably have supported such high arches. There are similar piers in the Church of the Apostles at Anavarza.

Evidence for cross transepts which were wider than the nave and aisles is much less secure, but is strongly suggested by the ground plans of the Southwest Church at Anavarza, and the 'Große Armenische Kirche' at Corycus. The superstructure of the latter certainly indicates that some form of transept was present in the building. The transept at Cennet Cehennem did not extend beyond the outer walls of the aisles, but its colonnades appear to have turned across the ends of the aisles, rather in the manner of some cross-transepts.

The Cilician transepts seem to combine features from various transept types: this must either reflect the evolutionary nature of the architecture, or else suggests that the typological classifications, which have been established mainly by Krautheimer (1941, 417-29; 1981, 545), should not be applied too rigidly. What is, I think, most significant is that only the central part of the transept, immediately in front of the apse, could be, and was, included within the sanctuary, since the sides of the transepts had to remain available for access to the eastern passage. Since use of the side-chambers, if these were actually present, was also limited by the problem of access to the passage, it would have been very convenient to have an enlarged sanctuary area, suitably screened.

The effect would have been to extend the focus of the basilica from the apse into the nave, or, rather, to the centre of the transept.

In this observation lies the key to understanding the Cilician transepts. It is not necessary to assume that transepts were imported into Cilicia from some more architecturally developed part of the late Roman empire. The transept is a logical response to peculiar local needs, and the stages in its local development can be traced. The regular inclusion of passages across the east end of the basilicas had the effect of destroying the independent nature of the side-chambers, which do not, in any event, appear to have been of paramount importance to Cilician and Isaurian liturgy. Access to the eastern passages could only be through the spaces which would, in Syria, be occupied by the pastophories. Even in Cilician basilicas where there was a corridor, or colonnade along one long side of the church, the side-chambers were still corridors which connected the aisles with the passage. By the fifth century it appears that, even in churches which did not have eastern passages, the side-chambers were not necessarily used as the prothesis and the diaconicon; rather they seem to have served as baptisteries or memorial chapels, and thus tended to bulge outwards from the building lines of the body of the church. A good example of this kind of development can be seen in the church north of Corycus, where the rooms at the southeast corner of the basilica appear to have been a baptistery, and the side-chambers also extended westwards from the mouth of the apse and thus defined a large enclosed sanctuary bay.

This westward expansion of the sanctuary was probably a natural response to the lack of a room for the prothesis, although it might also have arisen from the fact that side-chambers which were used as baptisteries, or whatever, would have been more complicated, and larger, than their simpler Syrian counterparts. Perhaps in response to both factors, the side-chambers certainly tended to move into the eastern ends of the aisles, and it is normal to find that the chancel screen ran across the west walls of these extended side-chambers. Thus was created a triple bay across the east end of the nave and aisles.

In churches without an eastern passage, the side-chambers retained their independence, but it was still possible to insert a triumphal arch to the west of the mouth of the apse. This is exactly what was done in the West Church at Alahan, which thus had what might be termed a 'proto-transept'. In churches where there was an eastern passage, and the side-chambers were mere corridors, with large arches on their three internal sides, the westward extension of these 'side-chambers' was enough to create a transept even without a triumphal arch, and this was the position which was probably reached in the 'Cathedral' at Corycus. It would be an easy step from the plan of either of the churches last mentioned to the inclusion of a full transept with open bays in place of side-chambers, and a triumphal arch on its west side. As has been noted, there are numerous examples of such full transepts in Cilicia, in buildings which can be assigned to the fifth century.

The gestation of the transept can, therefore, be documented in Cilician basilicas from its conception as a response to the inclusion of eastern passages, through the embryonic phase at Alahan, to a viable foetal stage in the 'Cathedral' at Corycus, and birth in such basilicas as the North Church at Öküzlü. The suggestion that the transept, in the forms in which it became popular in the late fifth century, actually evolved in Cilicia, and was exported thence to such centres as Thessalonica, cannot, therefore, be rejected thoughtlessly. It is evident, in any event, that Cilicia, and in particular Isauria, was in the forefront of architectural developments during the latter part of the fifth century.

If my reasoning is sound, there is no reason to follow Krautheimer in categorizing the eastern apartments of the Cilician basilicas as 'formless'. I would propose instead that the unusual Cilician plans represent a sophisticated architectural reaction to some peculiar local problems, and actually had the effect of restoring form in basilicas which were in danger of losing their unity through excessive compartmentalization. The transepts had the effect of concentrating the architectural focus on the bay in front of the apse, which bay was evidently the functional heart of the church since it contained the altar, and also stood at the centre of a cruciform element, consisting of the nave, the transept, and the apse. The architectural focus would have been emphasized by the roofing arrangements, since the transept, like the nave could have been provided with clerestory lighting. It is relevant to note here that it would have been a simple matter to erect a tower over the central bay of the transept. The high arches between the triumphal arch and the mouth of the apse in the Transept Church at Corycus would have supported such a tower very successfully: without a tower they could only have supported walls which would have disturbed the unity of the transept, and which would have risen pointlessly, and inelegantly, to the ridge of the roof.

The arches in the Transept Church at Corycus are the strongest evidence which exists to support the hypothesis that a tower may have risen over the central bay of a Cilician transept, but the fact that such a development can be considered emphasizes the close structural relationship between the Transept Basilicas and the 'Domed Basilicas'. The latter are in a sense the logical culmination of the evolutionary process which produced the Transept Basilicas. In the 'Domed Basilicas' the central sanctuary bay became the dominant architectural element, and, with the loss of the side-bays, gained a strong vertical axis which was emphasized by the addition of towers and special roofing systems. There is no need, of course, to argue that the 'Domed Basilicas' developed from the Transept Basilicas: it would have been possible to have erected a tower over the sanctuary of the West Church at Alahan, and it might even be argued that this was a likely explanation for the inclusion of the triumphal arch in that basilica, the builders of which were evidently not short of funding to support such elaborate schemes. The 'Domed Basilicas' could, therefore, be seen as the destination of an alternative turning taken just before the evolutionary route arrived at the Transept Basilicas. This would explain the closeness of the two groups in detailed terms, since they would be contemporary phenomena.

4

THE 'DOMED BASILICAS'

The expression 'Domed Basilica' or 'Kuppelbasilika' has been applied to certain Cilician churches since Strzygowski first used it to describe the East Church at Alahan (Strzygowski 1903, 110-1). Guyer extended the use of the term to cover the 'Cupola Church' at Meryemlık, and it has seemed convenient to retain the title to define the closely related group of churches which consists of the East Church at Alahan, the Tomb Church at Corycus, the 'Domed Ambulatory Church' at Dağ Pazarı, the 'Cupola Church' at Meryemlık, and the church at Alakilise, although the latter seems to have escaped the notice of recent dome hunters. It is also just possible that the church in the monastery on Mahras Dağı and the church at Köşkerli were 'Domed Basilicas', but this is less than certain. The title 'Domed Basilica' is, accordingly used as a technical term to define a church in which the longitudinal nave was replaced by or incorporated a central square bay which was surmounted by a tower. I use the term advisedly, for as Gough noted:

> 'The very phrase "domed basilica" once had almost the same hypnotic quality in English as "Kuppelbasilika" certainly had in German, to turn a potentially "gentle reader" into a raging fanatic.' (Gough 1972, 236)

The 'Domed Basilicas' have been a subject of controversy since Strzygowski first poured scorn on Headlam's suggestion that there was a wooden roof on the tower of the East Church at Alahan (Strzygowski 1903, 110-1). Guyer's conclusions concerning Meryemlık and Corycus were based more on his own preconceptions than on any objective evidence, and did nothing to resolve the questions of how these churches were roofed, or when they were built. Forsyth demonstrated that the 'Domed Ambulatory Church' at Dağ Pazarı should be included in the group (Forsyth 1957, 233-6), but confused the issue still further by his insistence that all the 'Domed Basilicas' were surmounted by wooden pyramids and were not domed at all. Mango evidently accepted this, for he referred to 'a tower-like structure covered with a pyramidal roof of timber of the kind that was common in Isauria' (Mango 1966, 365, note 26). Gough was at first reluctant to accept Forsyth's conclusions, noting that the architect of the East Church at Alahan 'was familiar with the principles of domical construction' (Gough 1967/1968, 463). But he came out strongly in favour of Forsyth's wooden pyramids in a later article (Gough 1972). Krautheimer appears also to have been converted (Krautheimer 1986, 245). Forsyth, in other words has carried all with him, but his arguments, which are discussed below (see especially the sections on the East Church at Alahan and the 'Domed Ambulatory Church' at Dağ Pazarı), do not stand up to detailed scrutiny.

The question of the date of these buildings has not been a vital issue since Mango first pointed out that the group could be assigned to the reign of the Isaurian emperor Zeno (Mango 1966, 364). This conclusion has been developed by Gough (1972, passim), who has given archaeological weight to the view that Alahan was built under Zeno. This view has been accepted by Krautheimer (1986, 489, note 18). Forsyth assigned both Alahan and Dağ Pazarı to the sixth century, and, as his chronology has been revised, so it is necessary to review his architectural proposals.

The detailed arguments relating to each building are discussed above, and I can state baldly here that each of the five 'Domed Basilicas' was perfectly capable of supporting a masonry dome, and that I am sure there was such a dome at Dağ Pazarı, and consider that it is probable that there was one at Meryemlık. The possibility cannot even be discounted at Alahan. There is insufficient evidence relating to Alakilise to allow any more than a guess, but it is interesting to note that there, as in the three churches previously mentioned, the aisles were covered by barrel-vaults which would have had a strong buttressing effect upon the central nucleus. The Tomb Church at Corycus did not have barrel-vaults over the aisles, and I am convinced that it cannot have had a masonry dome. However, since it is cognate in terms of its plan and decoration with the other 'Domed Basilicas', it has been convenient to include it within the group. One of the reasons which explains why these churches have not been accepted as proper 'Domed Basilicas' has been that architectural historians have felt that such developments should emanate from the capital and not evolve in the provinces. The evolution of the 'Domed Basilica' has already been covered by my analysis of the development of the Transept Basilica within Cilicia, and the argument does not need to be repeated here, but I must emphasize that there are no similar 'Domed Basilicas' amongst the known fifth century churches of Constantinople, or, for that matter Rome or Antioch. In this respect Cilicia stands alone. However, as I have indicated above, Zeno's rise to power in the late fifth century would have had the effect of creating an environment in which the architectural traditions of Constantinople and Cilicia were thrown together, and it is likely that the combination of Constantinopolitan resources and Cilician inventiveness was what gave the final impetus to the emergence of the 'Domed Basilica' as a building type.

It is likely that the case for the Cilician churches having masonry domes in the fifth century will not be accepted until someone discovers an intact, firmly dated, example. I can only wonder why there has been so much fuss. Masonry domes are not in themselves so remarkable. There was one in the eastern chamber of the South Church at Yanıkhan, and the side-chambers of the Chapel of St Mary at Cennet Cehennem both have domes which are still intact. Both churches are likely to be earlier in the sequence of early Byzantine Cilician churches, and may even have been constructed in the fourth century. There is a fine dome, resting on pendentives, in the 'audience chamber' or mausoleum at Akkale, which is probably a late fifth century building. There was a masonry dome over the tetrapylum at the northeast corner of the Transept Church at Corycus, and over the bath to the west of the 'Cupola Church' at Meryemlık: both of the latter structures appear to be contemporary with the churches with which they are associated. The Triconch at Mahras evidently had a masonry dome, since one of its pendentives has survived. All these masonry domes belong to the fourth and fifth centuries, and they were variously set on squinches and pendentives, and even, in the case of the tetrapylum at Corycus, on a combination of both.

It is reasonable to insist, therefore, that by the late fifth century the Isaurian builders were thoroughly acquainted with the processes of domical construction, and with the various methods of setting domes above chambers which were not circular. In fact the Isaurians were famous for their construction of vaults. Thus Isaurians were called in to repair the dome of Santa Sophia in 558 (Theophanes, ed. de Boor, 232: see Mango 1966, 358), and only an Isaurian was able to execute the design of St Martha in respect to the vaulting of her trefoil martyrium in the monastery of Simeon the Younger near Antioch (Van den Ven 1962b, *Vita Marthae* columns 416D-417A: Mango 1966, 361).

By the fifth century, then, the Isaurian builders had considerable experience of domical construction, and in the sixth century their services were in demand for the erection and repair of domes in other provinces. But the mere suggestion that the Isaurians might have erected a dome over one of their own basilicas seems to cause considerable distress to architectural historians. It is not as though the Cilician basilicas were incapable of supporting the weight, or inappropriately planned. This point is discussed in relation to the individual buildings: here it may be more appropriate to mention one building which is astonishingly like the Cilician 'Domed Basilicas', and which is still sufficiently preserved to show that it was surmounted by a dome on pendentives. I refer to the church at Kasr Ibn Wardan (figure 62), which is extremely close in both plan and elevation to the 'Domed Ambulatory Church' at Dağ Pazarı. The overall measurements of the church at Kasr Ibn Wardan (14.8 by 18.5 metres) are somewhat smaller than those of the church at Dağ Pazarı, which is approximately 20 metres square without its narthex. But the nuclei of the two churches are almost identical in size. The domes which surely rose above both of them would both have been about 7.5 metres in diameter. In both cases there was a vaulted fore-choir between the apse and the nucleus. The aisles were also vaulted, although Dağ Pazarı appears to have had barrel vaults, whilst there was a series of cross vaults at Kasr Ibn Wardan. One interesting difference between the buildings is that the piers which would have supported the dome at Dağ Pazarı were 2.2 metres thick, the equivalents at Kasr Ibn Wardan are a mere 1.6 metres thick. In other words the piers at Dağ Pazarı were more than substantial enough to support a masonry dome.

The church at Kasr Ibn Wardan is part of a monumental complex in the Syrian desert which also included a palace and a barracks. Two inscriptions give the dates of 561 and 564, and the whole complex has generally been accepted as an example of the importation of cosmopolitan architecture to a provincial context. Thus Krautheimer wrote:

'At Qasr Ibn Wardan, then, the plan of the 'domed basilica' has been reduced and condensed - one might term it a 'compact domed basilica'. The nave, comparatively long at Meriamlik, has become a mere fragment. Recalling the H. Sophia, the domed bay has been turned into the focus of the entire design. The short arches east and west take the place of half-domes; aisles and galleries open on to the centre bay; even their continuation into a western narthex and gallery recalls the H. Sophia. Indeed, the decorative and the structural vocabulary of Qasr Ibn Wardan is permeated with elements brought from Constantinople.' (Krautheimer 1986, 248)

I am not sure that it is correct to say that the church at Kasr Ibn Wardan was equipped with a narthex, but Krautheimer's description could otherwise be applied as appropriately to the church at Dağ Pazarı, which, however, being earlier, could not recollect Santa Sophia.

Mango noted that some features at Kasr Ibn Wardan were not purely Constantinopolitan:

'The architect of these mysterious buildings was certainly in contact with the metropolitan Byzantine style, yet there are many elements here that are not explainable in terms of Constantinople. First consider the church. The ground plan shows us a rectangle, forty-nine by sixty-one feet, with a projecting staircase tower leading up to the gallery - what is usually, if misleadingly, termed a domed basilica. The flat east wall into which the apse is inscribed is standard in Syria but foreign to the architecture of Constantinople. It is, however, in elevation that the church exhibits its strangest features. The proportions of the inner core of the building are uncommonly tall, and the main structural arches are not semi-circular but bluntly pointed. A Byzantine architect would, furthermore, have placed the dome directly upon the crowns of the great arches; this is not so at Qasr ibn-Wardan. Here a drum, octagonal on the outside, is placed upon the arches, and the pendentives, which reduce the square to a circle, spring within the drum, not below it. In addition the four dome windows that were set on the diagonal were actually cut through the pendentives. No Constantinopolitan architect would have designed such eccentric forms.' (Mango 1976, 151)

The church at Dağ Pazarı, or the Cilician design of which it is one surviving example, might well have been the prototype from which these 'eccentric forms' at Kasr Ibn Wardan were derived. If the cornice which is visible in Headlam's photograph (plate 64) was present on all four sides of the nucleus at Dağ Pazarı and the roofing structure, whether dome or wooden pyramid sat directly upon it, there would have been no room for windows in the tower which were not hidden by the roofing system of the aisles. The same problem exists at Alahan where the tower was surrounded by roofs which rose as high as the level to which it has survived. The addition of a low tambour would resolve these anomalies, and it would not have been at all surprising if Cilician architects had cut arched windows through their pendentives, since this would simply have been an extension of the process which is attested clearly in the tetrapylum at Corycus, where squinch arches were cut out of the pendentives. Even without the archaeological evidence which supports the idea that a dome was present at Dağ Pazarı, a reconstruction along the lines of the church at Kasr Ibn Wardan would be much more satisfactory than Forsyth's gloomy low pyramid.

The piers which support the dome at Kasr Ibn Wardan are more slender than those of Dağ Pazarı, but they are massive by comparison, for instance, with the walls which supported domes of similar diameters on the Kızıl Kilise at Sivrihisar in Cappadocia (Ramsay and Bell 1909, 376-82, figures 300-10), or the triconch sanctuary of the church at Karabel in Lycia (Harrison 1963, 131-5, figure 11, plate XLa). These examples are not chosen entirely at random, since there is some reason to suppose that the Isaurians were active in Cappadocia in the sixth century (Hill 1975, 163; 1977, 20), and I am grateful to the late Martin Harrison for pointing out that it emerges from the Life of St Nicholas of Sion that a person with the thoroughly Cilician name of Conon was in charge of the building works at the Sion monastery, which is probably to be identified with Karabel. This is not, however, the place for analysing the monuments built by wandering Isaurians in the sixth century: the point I am trying to make is that it would actually be surprising if the Isaurians, who had the necessary technical skills, had not put them to use in their home province in the late fifth century when there was an Isaurian emperor on the throne. Since the appropriate technology was available locally, since there is every reason to suppose that financial support was forthcoming, and since there are Cilician basilicas with plans and superstructures which were capable of supporting domes, it seems to me to be arguing against reason to say that all these buildings had wooden roofs. Krautheimer's discussion of the church at Kasr Ibn Wardan follows his consideration of its Cilician relations which sit somewhat unhappily in a chapter entitled 'Standard Building in the Age of Justinian':

> 'It is of course possible that such buildings simply transposed into timber construction a model which was entirely vaulted, with a barrel-vault over the first bay, and a dome over the second bay of the nave - in short a genuine 'domed basilica', to use the accepted term. Such a model may well have existed in Constantinople as early as the third quarter of the fifth century and thus prior to Meryemlık. In all likelihood it existed when, in 524-7, H. Polyeuktos was laid out in the capital. Indeed it has been suggested that the plan for Meryemlık was designed in Constantinople. Certainly the style and quality of the decoration suggest the activity of a workshop imported from the capital. So far no genuine domed basilica has been found in Constantinople prior to the sixth century. Nevertheless it is plausible that it did exist and was carried from the capital to the farthest provinces.' (Krautheimer 1986, 247)

This is surely special pleading. I believe that it is unnecessary to resort to a hypothetical Constantinopolitan prototype, when all the factors required to create the 'Domed Basilica' existed in the province which appears to have been the first to build one. What could have been more natural than that the inventive Isaurian builders would have created the type when one of their countrymen held the imperial purse-strings. Zeno would surely have employed Isaurian architects at the capital, and in that way the 'Domed Basilica' would have become part of the canon of Constantinopolitan architecture. During Zeno's ascendancy, Cilicia would not have been a remote province. If Kasr Ibn Wardan really was built to a design sent from the capital, then it would seem to be possible that the architects' drawings for Dağ Pazarı had survived in the imperial archives for the better part of a century.

If I am correct in proposing that the 'Domed Basilica' was created in Cilicia as part of the response to a variety of peculiar local circumstances, not the least of which were the remarkable specialized skills of the local architects and builders, and the restraints imposed upon them by Cilician church planning, this has several interesting consequences. It is no longer so rash to suggest that there was considerable Cilician input into the development of the transept in the fifth century. More significantly, perhaps, rather than calling Kasr Ibn Wardan, and, by corollary, the Cilician examples 'compact Domed Basilicas', we should be thinking of Santa Sophia as an 'expanded Domed Basilica'. All the experiments needed to create such a grand building, especially the development of the buttressing effects of vaulted aisles and semi-domes on all sides of a central nucleus, and even the inspired idea of introducing a centralized vertical dimension to the basilica, can be attested in Cilician buildings which predate Santa Sophia by as much as 50 years.

5

THE DATING OF THE TRANSEPT BASILICAS AND THE 'DOMED BASILICAS'

The dating of these monuments hinges on the sites of Alahan and Meryemlık. In both cases there is solid evidence to show that that the elaborate building campaigns took place during the reign of Zeno. For Meryemlık there is the explicit statement that Zeno built a μέγιστον τέμενος as a thank-offering at the sanctuary of St Thecla. There has been considerable debate about which of the churches at Meryemlık was actually donated by Zeno. Whilst we may reasonably accept with Hellenkemper (1986) that the 'Cupola Church' is the best candidate, I will set out below my reasons for supposing that such arguments miss the point which is that Zeno must have subsidized the whole scheme, both the great Basilica of St Thecla and the 'Cupola Church', which can no more be separated than the two churches at Alahan, which are more clearly part of a concerted scheme since they were meant to be connected by a colonnaded walkway. It is not necessary to assume that the temenos wall around the Basilica at Meryemlık automatically indicates that that church was Zeno's gift, since the temenos was present at the time of Egeria's visit in the late fourth century, and was almost certainly inherited from a pagan temple. Rather I would submit that the reference to the temenos at Meryemlık should be taken to refer to the whole site, which was, in a similarly collective manner, Thecla's martyrium. A much more important indicator of imperial support is surely the quantity of Proconnesian marble which was lavished on all the churches at Meryemlık, and with which the emperor may have sent a group of expert sculptors.

The dating of Alahan is assured on both epigraphical and archaeological grounds, and Gough has demonstrated that the decorative scheme of the two main churches is entirely consistent, even though the sculpture in the East Church was perhaps more restrained than that in the West Church.

What is surprising is that no serious attempt has been made to find links between these two important sites, although they are there to be found, as they should be if it is correct to assume that they were built simultaneously, and were both in receipt of imperial support. The most important point of comparison has never been noticed, since neither Guyer nor Gough appears to have appreciated the full significance of the basilicas at their sites. Both accepted that the 'Domed Basilicas' were of considerable architectural significance, whilst tending to take the other major churches for granted in architectural terms. But there was evidently a transept in the Basilica at Meryemlık, and there was nearly one in the West Church at Alahan, where a triumphal arch sprang between the west walls of the side-chambers. Both churches may have had roofing systems which were as interesting in their different ways as the roofs of the 'Domed Basilicas'. The great building schemes at Alahan and Meryemlık, in other words, included a Transept Basilica and a 'Domed Basilica'. This exact combination can be seen at Corycus in the adjacent Tomb and Transept Churches, which I believe were contemporary with each other, and probably designed by the same architect.

That there should be three such pairs might be thought to be the result of simple coincidence, but the two intra-mural churches at Anavarza may have formed a similar pair, and the re-used pieces in the 'Cathedral' at Corycus, which evidently originated from two adjacent intra-mural basilicas, suggest that these churches, too, may have been another such pair. This strengthens my argument that the two advanced types of basilica are intimately related, and it is an interesting exercise to take stock of the peculiar features which can be attested in both groups of churches.

I have already noted that no full attempt has been made to compare the churches at Alahan and Meryemlık. The most obvious way to do this would be through an analysis of the sculpture, though to attempt this here at any detailed level would be beyond the scope of the present undertaking. But even a superficial analysis reveals some suggestive points of contact which can be attested not merely at Alahan and Meryemlık, but in a group of Transept Basilicas and 'Domed Basilicas'. The most obvious of these is the presence of animals and, more commonly, birds in the sculpture. At Alahan there were partridges and fish in the cornice of the West Church, and more fish on the corbels of the west door of the West Church. The East Church has inhabited scrolls adorning its doorways, and eagle protomes in the column capitals of the nucleus. The brackets which support the colonettes in the angles of the tower are decorated with rams' heads. The south door of the 'Domed Ambulatory Church' at Dağ Pazarı was embellished with an inhabited scroll. In the 'Cupola Church' at Meryemlık, the column capitals of the narthex and the nave had doves as protomes, and fragments of eagles, a peacock, and a ram's head which were found in the interior have probably fallen from brackets in its tower. The 'Cathedral' at Corycus has a fine capital with a central peacock and ram protomes, which was probably rescued from a fifth century church. Finally Guyer saw a console with a fish at Alakilise.

This list should not be regarded as exhaustive, but it is already suggestive since it includes only Transept Basilicas and Domed Basilicas. The only other church in the province which has animals amongst its sculptural decoration, which, however, appears to be the work of a different school of sculptors, is the Church of the Apostles at Anavarza, which also had a transept. The important point, then, is that such decoration in Cilicia is restricted to the Transept Basilicas and the 'Domed Basilicas'. The identity of subject matter and technique in the sculpture of these churches is highly suggestive of the work of one school of craftsmen, and it is so unlike other Cilician architectural sculpture that one has to consider the possibility that these fine carvings were the work of a gang of master-craftsmen sent from Constantinople by the emperor.

Gough has argued that the mosaics which represent Isaiah's vision of the Peaceful Kingdom belong to Zeno's reign and were encouraged by him as a visual expression of the message in his *Henotikon* (Gough 1972, 210-2). I think that there was probably a further reason which may have caused Zeno to favour the inclusion of animals and birds in decorative schemes. As a native of Isauria, Zeno would have regarded Thecla as his patron saint. His generosity towards Meryemlık can be taken as proof of this. Thecla's sanctuary contained several paradeisoi, some of which were evidently bird sanctuaries and the inclusion of so many birds and animals in the decoration of these churches may have been intended as a direct reminder of what could be seen at Meryemlık. This argument gains support from the mosaic of the southern half of the narthex of the basilica at Dağ Pazarı. Although this was constructed in the narthex of a conventional basilica, it is relevant here since it must have been laid in the late fifth century, and the exotic birds which are depicted at Dağ Pazarı are a re-creation in mosaic of the list of birds which Basil described in Thecla's paradeisos.

Another very obvious sculptural link is formed by a series of impressive pier capitals, examples of which are best seen in the 'Domed Ambulatory Church' at Dağ Pazarı (plate 69) and the Tomb Church at Corycus (plate 43). These have two bands of distinctive spiky acanthus. Their counterparts once existed at Alakilise and in the 'Cathedral' at Corycus, and can still be seen in the North Church at Öküzlü, and in Church 4 at Kanlıdivane. A very stylized variant of this two-banded type of capital can be seen at Kanlıdivane (plate 93): its exact counterpart was formerly in the nave of the Transept Church at Corycus. The type is also found in column capitals at Alahan, Dağ Pazarı, the Transept and Tomb Churches at Corycus, and at Akkale, which I believe may have been a royal palace.

Canopied porches of the type which is best preserved on the north wall of the Tomb Church at Corycus (plate 34) were also present at Dağ Pazarı, Kanlıdivane, the Transept Church at Corycus, and probably also Alakilise and the 'Cupola Church' at Meryemlık, where the very distinctive corbels have been found. There may have been a narrow version of such a porch over the south entrance to the South Church at Yanıkhan, and identical porches on the church north of Corycus. The latter exhibits the extended side-chambers which I have argued are a vital stage in the development toward the inclusion of a transept, and is surely contemporary with the other churches where the canopied porches were present.

Three churches in the group have remarkable fore-courts. There were hemicycles at the west ends of the 'Cupola Church' at Meryemlık and the 'Domed Ambulatory Church' at Dağ Pazarı. The North Church at Öküzlü has a polygonal fore-court. These features are very reminiscent of palatial architecture. I am convinced that a programme of excavations would reveal more of these links, but what is already certain is that this group of important Cilician churches has so many common features in addition to its architectural unity that its members may well be contemporary. The following list emerges: Alahan, West Church and East Church; Alakilise; Corycus, Transept Church, Tomb Church, and the earlier churches whose remains were incorporated in the 'Cathedral'; Dağ Pazarı, 'Domed Ambulatory Church'; Kanlıdivane, Church 4; Meryemlık, Basilica of St Thecla and 'Cupola Church'; Öküzlü, North Church. To this list of churches must be added the complex at Akkale. It would also be possible to add the Basilica at Canbazlı, the church north of Corycus and Church 3 at Kanlıdivane on the grounds that they had variants of the distinctive column capitals. The basic list includes most of the important Cilician basilicas amongst which are the firmly dated churches of Alahan and Meryemlık, and I would suggest that Zeno must have supported more building projects than even Gough envisaged.

At first sight, it would be attractive to suggest that this long list of buildings was erected over a span of time in the fifth and sixth centuries. This seems to be the position adopted by Hild and Hellenkemper in their attributions of dates to the churches. Such a position, however, is not easily reconciled with the literary and archaeological evidence, however incomplete these are, and would not fit the general architectural or historical contexts. To suggest that these Cilician basilicas might have been constructed earlier in the fifth century would put Cilicia in an astonishingly advanced position in architectural terms, but to attempt to move the dating of the group as a whole into the sixth century would involve supposing that the workshops of sculptors could somehow have reformed after the disastrous civil wars which beset Cilicia after the accession of Anastasius. The archaeological record shows clearly that the province never recovered the prosperity which had been so evident in the fifth century.

Cilicia's 'Golden Age' came under Zeno, not Justinian, and the sixth century was a period of urban decline. Cilicia was not naturally a wealthy province, and, with no substitute for Zeno's patronage, its inhabitants in the sixth century could not afford to continue the expensive building schemes which were such a feature of the late fifth century. I can see no escape from the logic that the important buildings which I have been discussing were all constructed during Zeno's ascendancy. Proof, if it were really needed, of the sudden end to the architectural boom which followed Zeno's death is provided by the fact that the grandiose scheme at Alahan was never completed.

6

CONCLUSION

This survey of the early Byzantine churches of Cilicia has revealed that despite the trend towards development and elaboration of the basilical plan, there is a remarkable degree of uniformity in Cilician and Isaurian churches, which are, almost without exception, varying forms of basilica. It is impossible to find any consistent distinction between parish, monastic, funerary or martyrial churches. The only exceptions to the rule that all churches are basilicas are a few small chapels (e.g. Takkadın; Yemişkum, Church 2); the Baptistery and Cave Church, which may also have been a baptistery, at Alahan, and the Chapel of St Mary at Cennet Cehennem which was almost a basilica, since the east end at least was tripartite. Two small buildings had a triconchal plan (Güney Kalesi I 7C; Mahras). Gough thought it likely that the triconch at Mahras was a baptistery, but there is no positive evidence for this, and the function of these triconches remains a matter for speculation.

It would be easy to argue that the basic design of the basilica with the tripartite east end was inherited from Syria, since Cilicia was under the ecclesiastical jurisdiction of Antioch. But from the start the Cilician churches are not straightforward copies of Syrian prototypes, and they develop along quite independent lines. Furthermore it was only the basilical plan which was adopted in Cilicia: there are none of the experiments with circular and polygonal plans which are so characteristic of the Syrian churches, and Cilicia did not adopt the aisled tetraconch plan for its martyria. The overwhelming popularity of basilical plans for the Cilician churches is their single most remarkable feature: I am convinced that it arose out of the fact the most important Cilician martyrium and monastic church, St Thecla's at Meryemlık, was, from the fourth century, a basilica which included a martyrium within its plan, in a manner which recalls the great Constantinian pilgrimage churches of Palestine. The Cilician obsession with the basilica is not, however, evidence of lack of imagination. The basilicas regularly include eastern ambulatory passages as well as displaying every species of transept, and experiments with towers and domes.

All these developments took place before the end of the fifth century. It was always the case that the Cilician economy could not survive without injections of finance from outside the province. These could be seized by piracy and brigandage, earned through mercenary soldiering or building contracts, or presented by a sympathetic emperor. The last circumstance applied only once, and the results, in the latter part of the fifth century, were dramatic, but sadly short-lived. The legacy of the great years of church building in Cilicia can only be found outside the province in the famous churches of the sixth century. This is a fruitful area for further research, and is tied in with the phenomenon of the diaspora of the Isaurian builders from the reign of Anastasius onwards. The Isaurian builders have been followed through the literary record (Mango 1966), and it might be possible to follow their trail by analysis of sculpture. Thus shortly before his death in 1992 Martin Harrison was working up an argument based on comparison of architectural sculpture that the Isaurian builders may have been active in the domed funerary chamber at Karabel in Lycia. If the argument that the 'Domed Basilica' may have evolved in Cilicia and Isauria has any merit, then the other aspect of the broad influence of Cilicia and Isauria is that of the spread of the 'Domed Basilica' and cognate forms in the sixth century. This is a huge subject which is well beyond the scope of the present undertaking, but it may be helpful to conclude with some observations on the continuing inheritance from the flowering of ecclesiastical architecture in Cilicia and Isauria in the late fifth century.

'Domed Basilicas', famously, were constructed in Constantinople during the reign of Justinian, but they were also constructed, albeit less grandly, in other parts of the early Byzantine empire during the sixth century. The various forms evident in Cilicia and Isauria continued as descendants of the more basilical type represented by the East Church at Alahan and the double shell 'domed ambulatory' type represented by the church at Dağ Pazarı. It is interesting to see that by the mid-sixth century the building type had transcended the prototype forms which I have argued evolved in Cilicia and Isauria. Thus in churches such as the Katapoliane on the island of Paros (Mango 1976, 86, figure 123), and St Titus at Gortyn on Crete (Krautheimer 1986, 255, figure 214; Mango 1976, 86, figure 119) the design had developed to include cruciform elements in the ground plan of what have been called 'domed transept basilicas'. The ultimate example of this kind of architectural thinking is represented by Justinian's Church of the Holy Apostles in Constantinople (Procopius, *Buildings*, 1, 4; Krautheimer 1986, 242), which inherited a cruciform plan from Constantine's predecessor, and was surmounted by six domes over the nave, transept and crossing, all supported by massive piers, between which were set the colonnades which separated nave and aisles and followed through round the arms of the transept. The church of St John at Ephesus (mid-sixth century), which has capitals with the monograms of Justinian and Theodore, has a plan very similar to that of the Holy Apostles at Constantinople as that was described by Procopius. Another church which is close to the Cilician and Isaurian types both geographically and in terms of its architecture is the Cumanın Cami at Antalya, which has been thoroughly discussed by Ballance (1955). The sculpture of this church suggests a date in the sixth century, and the plan again incorporates a cruciform element, this time by extending the central bay to north and south at ground level, thus disrupting the longitudinal axis of what remains essentially a basilica. Ballance's reconstruction (1955, figure 2) shows a central tower flanked by gable roofs to north, south, east and west. Regarding the roof of the central bay, Ballance notes the comparison with the Katapoliane on Paros, but favoured a wooden roof over the central tower.

The fertile developments which involve the combination of transept and domes run parallel with buildings which conform more closely to the late fifth century prototypes in Cilicia and Isauria which were constructed in Syria and Asia Minor. Thus Mango has recently drawn attention to the considerable resemblance of the church at Yürme (Germia) on the western borders of Galatia, which he identifies as the pilgrimage centre of the Archangel Michael.

> 'Crowfoot has already noted the resemblance of the Yürme church to the east basilica of Alahan. Apart from the fact that the latter has only three aisles, the arrangement is indeed quite similar: two bays to both east and west, separated by a crossing whose central space is longer than it is wide. ...I think it is very likely that at Yürme, too, there was a central tower surmounted by a pyramidal roof.' (Mango 1986, 125)

In the discussion of the East Church at Alahan above, I have set out my reasons for believing that that church could have supported a dome, and that it is likely that the central tower supported a low tambour, whether or not the surmounting dome was constructed from masonry or timber. The church at Yürme would have been equally likely to have had a low tambour, and it is worth pointing out here that all the sixth century representatives of the building type display such a feature. Mango's comments on the roofing of the church at Yürme are intriguing.

> 'The church was a masonry vaulted basilica with a gallery, nearly 50 m. long and 27m. wide, not counting the corner towers.... It is evident that the roof of the nave, which I assume to have been barrel-vaulted, generated considerable lateral thrust and that elaborate measures were taken to shore up the sides of the building by thickening walls and doubling arches. Indeed the visible remains represent at least two and possibly three phases, and it seems likely that the original church collapsed and was reconstructed.' (Mango 1986, 119)

One is immediately reminded of the reconstruction of the roofing system which is apparent in the East Church at Alahan, and it is clear from Mango's account that, if the church at Yürme was the subject of major reconstruction, then excavation there would be no more likely to find the remains of a masonry dome than it was at Alahan, where such evidence would have been removed in antiquity at the time when repairs to the building were conducted.

Mango's plan (Mango 1986, figure c - printed in reverse) shows the church at Yürme as having the Anatolian feature of towers at the north and south ends of the narthex, but the un-Anatolian features of side-chambers beside the apse. Given the other points of contact with Alahan, it is difficult to avoid feeling that the Isaurian features of the church at Yürme are more than accidental. The architectural sculpture would seem to support the idea of possible involvement of Isaurian builders, for in the courtyard of the mosque at Yürme are examples of capitals which closely resemble types found at Dağ Pazarı and Meryemlık. Such a capital is illustrated by Mango (1986, plate 7). His photograph also shows a large corbel of the type which may have been used to support the squinches in the towers of the East Church at Alahan and the 'Cupola Church' at Meryemlık.

The dating of the church at Yürme is problematic. The architectural sculpture would sit happily in the late fifth or early sixth century, but Mango (1986, 124-5) draws attention to the *Miracles* by Pantoleon, in which it is stated that the patrician Studius rebuilt and adorned the church.

> 'Since this is a text of Constantinopolitan origin no earlier than the middle of the 9th century, its authority is not very weighty. On the other hand, we have no reason to reject it and it may not be entirely coincidental that the masonry of what I take to be the earlier phase (in the crossing) resembles that of the Studius basilica at Constantinople, which has five consecutive courses of brick alternating with three of stone. If the role of Studius is accepted, we would have a date of c. 460, perhaps for the building of a large and impressive church on the site of a humbler one. The presence in the village of a large impost capital bearing the monograms of Justinian and Theodora... may indicate a second rebuilding in the years 527-48. It should also be noted that all our evidence concerning Germia, both textual and archaeological, points to the early Byzantine period.' (Mango 1986, 124-5)

If the church at Yürme could have been constructed as early as 460, then the potential time-scale for the development of the 'Domed Basilica' in Cilicia and Isauria would also be extended into the reign of Leo, which is not, of course, at all an unlikely possibility, especially since Zeno the Isaurian was Leo's son-in-law and Magister Equitum.

The most obvious example of a direct descendent of an Isaurian building, Kasr Ibn Wardan, built in north Syria in 561-4, has been discussed above in the context of the 'Domed Ambulatory Church' at Dağ Pazarı which it resembles extremely closely. The importance of the church at Kasr Ibn Wardan for the present discussion is the simple observation that part of its masonry dome survives, supported by a structure which is less massive than some of our

Cilician and Isaurian buildings. The same point has to be made about the Kızıl Kilise in Cappadocia where a masonry dome is still supported on a tower which has the same overall measurements, but slighter walls than the East Church at Alahan.

It is not until we come to the case of the great churches erected in Constantinople in the sixth century that masonry domes have been generally accepted by architectural historians. The 'missing link' between the Cilician and Isaurian examples and the Justinianic 'Domed Basilicas' of Constantinople is Anicia Juliana's church of St Polyeuktos at Saraçhane which was excavated and published by Harrison (1986 and 1989). Harrison believed that this church was constructed in the years 524-7. For the purposes of the present discussion, it is enough to note that the church was certainly completed at the beginning of Justinian's reign, but important research on the brickstamps of Constantinople, which is currently being conducted by Jonathan Bardill, is likely to demonstrate that the building programme began substantially earlier than was formerly believed. Since only the foundation of Anicia Juliana's church survive, the evidence for the presence of a dome in this church is circumstantial: archaeology has revealed a squat plan with massive footings which are far more substantial that would be required in a conventional basilica, and the dedicatory inscription of the church (preserved as *Palatine Anthology* 1. 10: see Harrison 1986, 5-8) contains a flowery account of the building which is highly suggestive of domical architecture. The scale of the church of St Polyeuktos was enormous, and Harrison's proposed dome would have sat on a central bay which measure about 18 metres square. The church as a whole would have had a considerable resemblance to the 'Cupola Church' at Meryemlık, in that to the west of the central domical bay there was a short section of nave which was presumably covered by a barrel-vault. It may not be an accident that this was the only major sixth century foundation in Constantinople to be equipped with proper side-chambers.

Three major domical foundations in Constantinople survive from the time of Justinian. The church of Sts Sergius and Bacchus (finished by 536) is not, of course, a basilica, but its plan with an domed octagon set within a square show how the double-shelled type of 6th century church is a development of the 'Domed Ambulatory' type seen at Dağ Pazarı where the basilical origins of the type are ignored in favour of carrying the colonnades of the central bay across the west side of the church. San Vitale in Ravenna (finished in 546-8), where the octagon takes over the entire plan, can be seen as a variant of the same type. The exact form of Justinian's church of St Irene (begun in 532) is obscured by the major re-building after the earthquake of 740, but the ground floor of the building largely retains its Justinianic form, and it is clear that this church, like St Polyeuktos, was closely related to the 'Cupola Church' at Meryemlık, having a domed bay flanked to west and east by a barrel-vaulted nave and choir, and supported by vaulted aisles and galleries.

It was Justinian's Santa Sophia (532-7) which transcended the by then established form of the 'Domed Basilica'. It was far bigger than anything previously attempted, being 71 by 77 metres overall with a central domed bay which measured 100 Byzantine feet (about 32 metre) square. The plan preserves the tripartite east-west arrangements of the basilica, but the insertion of the hemispherical vaults which rise over the western and eastern parts of the nave, supporting the still higher central dome, mean that the eye of whoever enters the church is inevitably drawn upwards. The vertical axis is at least as dominant as the horizontal. This is not the place for a lengthy architectural analysis of Santa Sophia, but it is appropriate to note here that Justinian had to call in Isaurians to make the dome of the Great Church secure in 558 (Mango 1966, 358).

Whilst its scale and hemispheres marks Santa Sophia apart, the church is still part of the exciting development which was happening in early Byzantine architecture in the late fifth and sixth centuries and it is appropriate to end by returning to the Cilician and Isaurian context which led to the full development of the 'Domed Basilica' type as it is represented by Santa Sophia. The dramatic developments in church planning in Cilicia and Isauria arose out of the happy combination of the peculiar constraints imposed by the local obsession with the basilica for all ecclesiastical purposes and the undoubted skills of the Isaurian builders and architects. All the developments in church planning in the region were influenced by the constraints imposed on the sanctuary arrangements by the need for access to the eastern passages through spaces which would otherwise have been reserved for use as pastophories. It is clear that the nucleus in the East Church at Alahan served as a sanctuary, since it was surrounded by screens and contained four altar-like podia. In the 'Cupola Church' at Meryemlık the ambo stood on the west side of the nucleus which must also, therefore, have been used as the sanctuary. In the Tomb Church at Corycus a semi-circular colonnaded exedra projected westwards from the west side of the nucleus: its plan is suggestive of the developments which were to follow in hemispherical vaults of Santa Sophia, but the great significance of the exedra at Corycus is that the chancel screen, like the chancel itself, had become an integral part of the architectural scheme. The next logical step in this progression was taken at Dağ Pazarı where the nucleus had a colonnade on its west side, as well as the north and south sides. Here the precedent for the type of church represented by Sts Sergius and Bacchus was established.

We have seen that the 'Domed Basilicas' in Cilicia and Isauria are closely linked with the Transept Basilicas in the same region. The building types manifestly belong to an era of intense architectural experimentation: this explains why the roofing systems of the East Church at Alahan, the church at Yürme, and Santa Sophia itself had to be repaired or replaced. Two building types are deeply significant. The design of the 'Cupola Church' at Meryemlık is the prototype of St Polyeuktos and thus of the great sixth century 'Domed

Basilicas'. The 'Domed Ambulatory Church' at Dağ Pazarı, with its transverse, barrel-vaulted, western 'aisle' is a building type which was certainly domed, but hardly a basilica though it grew out of a strongly basilical tradition: it is the prototype for such double-shelled buildings as Sts Sergius and Bacchus and San Vitale. Both types stand at the end of a dynamic line of local architectural development in Cilicia and Isauria, and, through their association with Zeno and the capital, at the head of the exciting architectural developments which occurred in Constantinople under Justinian.

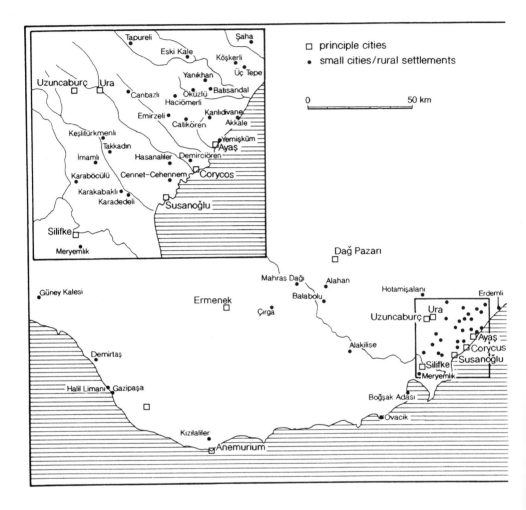

Map, Cilicia and Isauria.

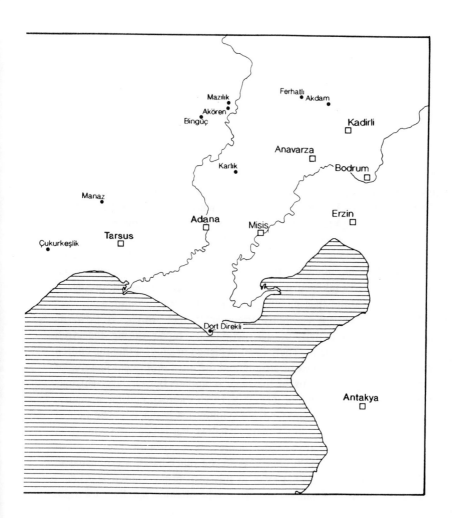

Mazılık
Ferhatlı • Akdam
Akören
Bingüç
Kadirli
Anavarza
Karlık
Bodrum
Manaz
Erzin
Adana
Misis
Tarsus
Çukurkeşlik
Dört Direkli
Antakya

CATALOGUE

ADRASSUS see BALABOLU

AKDAM, Basilica[1]
This church was first reported in l982 by Edwards who visited the site in 1979. Akdam Köy is situated 25 kilometres to the northeast of Kozan on the road via Bucak. The extensive ancient settlement covers an outcrop to the north of the modern village. Apart from a few cisterns, the church, which occupies the crown of the settlement, is the only identifiable monument. The other ruins consist of coursed rubble, mainly Cilician grey limestone, but with occasional fragments of brick and pink sandstone. The church itself is poorly preserved with only a fragment of the apse standing substantially above ground level.

The plan of this church is highly irregular, a fact which, as Edwards observes, may reflect a pattern of destruction and repair during the Arab occupation of the Cilician plain. There is no evidence to suggest that the church was ever equipped with a narthex or atrium, and the most prominent features of its plan are the squat dimensions of the nave (compare Batısandal), which is considerably broader than it is long (15.25 x 18.75 metres), and the eccentric positioning of the apses, which are far from symmetrically placed. The first of these features would be unique in a Cilician basilica, but is common enough in southern Cappadocia, especially in the immediate environment of Kayseri (Caesarea in Cappadocia). Multiple apses, on the other hand, are unusual in Anatolia, but normal in Cilicia; but even in this respect the church at Akdam hardly conforms to the Cilician norm. The only obvious parallels for such irregular positioning of the apses are themselves to be found in the Taurus district: one may compare the arrangements here most closely with the South Church at Tomarza in southern Cappadocia, or perhaps with the monastic church on Mahras Dağı in the highlands of Isauria, which also provides the nearest parallel for the proportions of the church at Akdam. The simplest explanation, however, for the overall proportions of this church may be that it

---

[1] Edwards 1982, 29-32, figures 1 and 3, plates 6-8; Hild, Hellenkemper and Hellenkemper-Salies 1984, 202; Hild and Hellenkemper 1990, 165.

had four aisles, or, more likely, a passage along the north side of the building, such as was provided in Anemurium III 10 C.

The walls of the main part of the church consist of coursed limestone blocks (averaging 34 centimetres in length, and 19 centimetres in height), pointed with lime mortar, which face the rubble and mortar core. The blocks are roughly rectangular, with the mortar pointing showing very obviously. By contrast, the walls of the apse are much more carefully built, with both interior and exterior faces consisting of larger, more regular, smooth ashlars (averaging 60 centimetres in length, and 39 centimetres in height). The core of the apse wall is considerably thinner than that in the rest of the building. Edwards concluded from these observations that the nave and apse represent different building phases, with the apse belonging to the late fifth or the sixth century, and the rest of the church belonging to a somewhat later date. It is reasonable to suppose that some of the minor annexed structures may be later constructions, but superiority of construction technique in the building of the apse may be regarded as a normal feature of the early Byzantine architecture of both Cilicia and Anatolia in areas where stone is the normal building medium. The churches at Corycus and Yanıkhan provide some particularly striking examples of this very feature which is the simple explanation for the fact that, in Cilicia, the apse of a late Roman building is regularly preserved long after the rest of the structure has disappeared.

It is the plan of this church which is particularly remarkable. As has been noted, the overall proportions of the nave are broader than they are long, and there is no sign of the existence of either narthex or atrium. There is a tiny chamber (measuring 2 metres by 1 metre internally) attached to the outside of the west wall of the church, almost at its southern end. This was entered through a door in its own south wall, and does not appear to have communicated with the main body of the church. Edwards was not able to determine the position of doorways. His suggestion that this church was a basilica arises from the presence of a column base in the north half of the nave. This consisted of a block 50 centimetres square forming the plinth, torus, and base of the column. The arrangements at the eastern end of the church are particularly striking. The main apse, which measures a little over 6 metres at its chord, is not central to the church, but displaced slightly to the south. Other features of the main apse are normal: it presents a polygonal exterior face, pierced, almost certainly, by three windows, the northern of which survives. There are at least two side-chambers to both north and south, consisting on each side of a smaller apsidal chamber immediately beside the main apse, and a larger, roughly rectangular outer chamber, which, in the case of the southernmost side-chamber, projects beyond the building-line of the south wall of the south aisle. The northern apsidal side-chamber consists of little more than a niche on the east side of what is, in effect, a passage leading to the northernmost side-chamber, whilst the southern side-chambers are considerably larger, and, seemingly, more intimately connected.

Little survives of the decoration of this basilica. Apart from the column base mentioned previously, there is a simple moulding visible around the arch of the existing window in the apse, and Edwards reported the existence of a fragment of relief sculpture near the apse which 'is quite oblong in shape and could not have been a capital'. The appearance of this relief is consistent with the possibility that it formed part of a screen, either across the chancel, or between the colonnades of the nave.

Edwards at no point discusses the questions of whether this church had galleries, and how its roof was arranged. In the absence of a programme of excavation, it may not be possible to answer such questions, but the proportions of the plan are unusual, and it seems reasonable at least to speculate that some form of centralized roofing structure may have been most appropriate on a building of this shape. In the case of the monastic church on Mahras Dağı, which this church resembles, it is also possible to make a case for such a reconstruction.

AKÖREN[2]

Two sites lie in the Taurus foothills above the Cilician Plain, some 12 kilometres southsoutheast of Karşantı. Four important early Byzantine churches in two ancient village settlements (Akören 1 and Akören II) were first briefly described by Hild and Hellenkemper (1990, 168, plates 29-48). Hellenkemper (1994) has recently published plans and further photographs of the churches, though with no further accompanying text. The locality is currently the subject of a survey project directed by Gabrielle Mietke and it is anticipated that her work will refine our understanding of the monuments at this important site very considerablu (Mietke, forthcoming).

AKÖREN I, Church 1[3]

This church stands on the edge of the settlement. It measured about 30.80 by 22.30 metres overall, and was a three-aisled basilica with side-chambers, narthex and an unusual outer passage which extended round the north, west, and south sides of the building. The passage had five openings with four columns on each side and was about 5 metres wide on the west side and 2.5-3 metres wide on the north and south sides. The building was obviously restored in the medieval period. Nave and aisles were separated by two rows of seven columns. The published photographs reveal that only the apse stands to any height. It has a polygonal external face, and was flanked by side-chambers,

[2] Hild and Hellenkemper 1990, 168-9, plates 29-48; Hellenkemper 1994, figures 14-22; Mietke 1995.
[3] Hild and Hellenkemper 1990, 168, plates 31-5; Hellenkemper 1994, figure 17.

both longer on the north-south than the east-west axis, which are shown on Hellenkemper's plan as bonded to the east ends of the external passage and the aisles, but butting against the external face of the apse. The southern side-chamber only had a projecting polygonally faced subsidiary apse. The side-chambers could be entered through doorways at the east ends of the aisles, and the southern side-chamber had an additional doorway leading from the southern external passage. The south side-chamber, with its extra doorway and apse, was presumably a room of considerable significance, perhaps a baptistery. Doorways between the outer passage and the church proper were provided at the central point of each wall, and there were three windows in the south wall of the church. The triple-arched window of the main apse has a running moulding following the upper edge of its window arches, and a straight heavy moulding forms a continuous window sill. A heavy cornice ran round the exterior of the apse at a higher level in a manner similar to those which decorate the exteriors of the apses at Bodrum. The church was constructed from well formed ashlars though these become smaller above the level of the springing of the apse semi-dome. Relief crosses decorate the corner stones at either side of the mouth of the apse. A heavy limestone impost capital with shallow geometric decoration (Hild and Hellenkemper 1990, plate 35) could hardly be earlier than the second half of the sixth century.

AKÖREN I, Church 2[4]

This much-ruined church is reported by Hild and Hellenkemper as a small basilica (about 18 by 14.10 metres), perhaps with no narthex, standing close to the domestic remains of the settlement. A limestone console by the south door of the church gives the date AD 553 (572 in the Anazarbene era). Hellenkemper's plan (1994, figure 17) shows a simple basilica with curved apse flanked by side-chambers with walls following the outer face of the apse, and a flush east wall to the whole building. The main entrance appears to have been on the south side of the church and was approached through a vestibule attached to a long corridor running parallel with the main axis of the church.

AKÖREN II, Church 1, Church of the Holy Cross[5]

Hild and Hellenkemper report this remarkable building as a three aisled basilica measuring about 32 by 20.5 metres, dedicated to the Holy Cross 32. The church appears to have begun as a simple basilica with two rows of eight columns, galleries, and no side-chambers. To this basic church were added a narthex at the west end with doorways at its north and south ends, a colonnaded walkway along the south side of the building and a side-chamber on the south side of the apse. Hellenkemper's plan shows doorways on either side of the apse, but only

---

[4] Hild and Hellenkemper 1990, 168, plates 37-8; Hellenkemper 1994, figures 14-16.
[5] Hild and Hellenkemper 1990, 168-9, plates 39-42; Hellenkemper 1994, figures 18-20.

one side-chamber on the south side. The main west door of the church is flanked by a niche. There are remains of an ambo, and various inscriptions around the doors, as well as one on the outer face of the apse which gives the date of 525. The remarkable decorated piers at the south end of the narthex may be attributed to the sixth century.

AKÖREN II, Church 2, Ambulatory Church[6]
This was a substantial basilica (28 by 15.50 metres) with an ambulatory apse of the type known from the Church of the Apostles at Anavarza, with the inner apse marked by an exedra with a curved arcade of eight arches supported by seven columns. There was no narthex. A large apsidal side-chamber against the eastern half of the north side of the church was entered through openings from the aisle and from the northwest corner of the apse ambulatory: it had a single arched window in the apse. As with the other churches at Akören, fenestration was concentrated on the south side of the building. The construction is of limestone blocks which are relatively roughly coursed. There is a pronounced horse-shoe elevation to the arch at the mouth of the apse of the north pastophory.

AKYAKA (Mandane)
Hild and Hellenkemper (1990, 340-1) report an early Byzantine basilica in the remains of Mandane (31 kilometres east of Anemurium, 18 kilometres west of Celenderis).

ALAHAN[7] (Apadnas?) (figures 1-3)
The building complex at Alahan is now the most famous of the early Christian monuments of Isauria. This is, in a way, surprising, since in antiquity it can in no way have rivalled the marble splendour of the exactly contemporary buildings of the much more renowned pilgrimage shrine of St Thecla at Meryemlık. The buildings at Alahan are, of course, much better preserved than those at Meryemlık, but the popularity of Alahan probably owes as much to the wildly romantic nature of its setting as to its unquestionable claims to architectural significance. The site has attracted travellers since Evliya Çelebi, who visited Alahan in 1671-2 (MacKay 1971), and was first brought to the attention of western scholars by the Count Leon de Laborde, who visited the site in 1826. In 1890, Headlam, with his colleagues Hogarth and Ramsay, planned the site, which was then almost ignored until it became the subject of the detailed studies of Michael Gough from 1952. Various scholars, especially Verzone and Forsyth, have subsequently published accounts of the monument,

---

[6] Hild and Hellenkemper 1990, 169, plates 47-8; Hellenkemper 1994, figures 21-2.
[7] Mary Gough 1985; Headlam 1890; Hild, Hellenkemper and Hellenkemper-Salies 1984, 254-63; Hild and Hellenkemper 1990, 193-4; Hill 1981, 31; Hill 1994, 141-4; Mango 1991; Verzone 1956.

but Gough must be regarded as the main authority. His early death in 1974 left his work at Alahan unfinished, and was, of course, the major factor contributing to the delay in the appearance of the final report on Alahan. The task of editing and completing this report was undertaken by his widow, the late Mary Gough. The volume which she edited was, in her words (1985, xiv), 'quite different from the one which Michael Gough might have written'. The book 'is designed to be a handbook to Alahan Monastery.... The wide field of review and comparative examination must be left to future Early Christian archaeologists'. We have, then, a careful description of what Gough found at Alahan, but there is another book to be written, which will be able to make fuller use of the surviving excavation records which are currently held by the present author. The account of this complicated site which follows here is necessarily limited: it is mainly restricted to discussion of matters which affect architectural conclusions and I shall not attempt to describe properly the richly decorative sculptural features.

Hild and Hellenkemper (1990, 193-4) accept the identification of Alahan as the μοναστήριον εἰς τὸ ᾽Απάδνας ἐν ᾽Ισαυρίᾳ which was restored by Justinian (Procopius, *Buildings*, 5, 9, 33). This would provide a convenient historical context for the repairs to the tower of the East Church, which, along with Gough and Mango, I believe was constructed during the reign of Zeno (474-91), but I state immediately that for different, but complementary, reasons, neither Cyril Mango (1991, 298-300) nor the present author (Hill 1984, 141-2) is convinced that Alahan began its existence as a monastery. The complex has no obvious trapeza for communal eating, but it does contain two major churches, both with a synthronum, a baptistery, a bath house, a ceremonial walkway and assorted elaborate tombs and shrines. In other words there are at Alahan all the necessary elements for a pilgrimage shrine and the argument for this identification is clinched by an inscription which records the presence at the site of ἀπαντητηρία (guest-houses) and a παραμονάριος (custodian). This raises the interesting question of who was being honoured by the building of the complex. Gough (1962) suggested that the West Church, which has figures of the evangelists on its west door, might have been dedicated to the evangelists. Mango (1991, 300) favoured the possibility that the pilgrimage centre as a whole was a healing centre devoted to the archangels. Hellenkemper (1994, 221) has recently advanced the view that the site might have been dedicated to the local saint, Conon, but his appeal to a graffito carved on a window divider in the narthex of the East Church (Harrison 1985, 24) does not seem to offer very strong supporting evidence. I offer a simpler possibility. There are at Alahan two important tombs of Tarasis the elder and Tarasis the younger: even though the latter was never occupied, the possibility must be considered that the site was dedicated to one or other Tarasis, or both. The status of the younger Tarasis as a local saint is firmly attested by the reliquary which was found at nearby Çırga (Gough 1955), and, if Harrison (1981) is correct in suggesting that

Tarasis was Zeno's original name, then this could offer a potential explanation for imperial interest in sponsoring the site.

The major importance of Alahan for this study rests in the fact that, in spite of Hellenkemper's recent indecision (1994, 221), it can be confidently assigned to the late fifth century, more precisely to the reign of the Isaurian emperor Zeno (474-91). The arguments to support this conclusion can be considered under four heads: epigraphical, architectural, archaeological, and historical. These have been aired at various times by Gough (see especially Gough 1972), and are reconsidered by Harrison in the final report (Harrison 1985), but they are worth summarizing here.

There are at Alahan two funerary inscriptions commemorating residents named Tarasis, one apparently the son of the other (Gough 1955b, 115-7). Tarasis the Elder died on 13 February 462, and is described as ὁ κτίσας τα ἀπα[ντη]τηρία. The ἀπα[ντη]τηρία are presumably guest-houses, and may well be a reference to the 'Two-Storeyed Building' cut into the rock face to the east of West Church. The second inscription records that Tarasis the Younger became παραμονάριος (custodian) in 461, and lived at Alahan for a number of years for which an unfilled blank space was left. It is impossible to guess how many years Tarasis the Younger actually lived at Alahan, but the probability is that he neither died, nor was even buried there. The silver reliquary which was found in the church at Çırga, across the Göksu valley, near Balabolu, was evidently originally intended for St Conon, but has a pricked inscription which post-dates the manufacture of the box, and reads ὑπὲρ ἀναπαύσεως τοῦ μακαρίου Ταρασῆς δίς. Taken together, the two inscriptions at Alahan suggest that the development of the complex as a centre for visitors was under way by 461, and that occupation of the site continued into the later fifth century. But it appears that Tarasis the Younger may have left Alahan before the end of his life.

The architectural arguments for dating the buildings are concerned with the relationship of the East Church at Alahan to other buildings of the 'Domed Basilica' type in the province (see Forsyth 1957; Gough 1972; Hellenkemper 1986) especially the 'Kuppelkirche' at Meryemlık, which must be part of the building campaign which Zeno supported at Meryemlık after 476 (Evagrius, *Historia Ecclesiastica*, 3, 8). Comments on finds of pottery and coins are very rare in Gough's preliminary reports, and one is merely left with a vague impression that the excavations yielded little by way of stratigraphical information. Little more is done to explore the stratigraphy in the final report, but it appears that nothing emerged which would appear to have conflicted with the proposed attribution of the building programme at Alahan to the late fifth century. One observation of a structural nature may, however, be of critical importance, since it bears on the question of how to find an appropriate historical context for such an elaborate building scheme. In his Fifth Preliminary Report Gough published clear evidence to show that the colonnaded walkway which linked the two churches was begun at the east end, completed as far as the shrine which stands opposite the tomb of Tarasis the Elder, but was left unfinished for the greatest part of its length (Gough 1968, 164-5). A small hoard of eight Anastasian coins (Harrison 1985, 27) was found in an unfinished drain at the west end of the walkway. The shrine itself must also be considered unfinished, since although its upper courses show Mary and John the Baptist flanking the empty throne of the second coming in a highly elaborate architectural setting, the carving on its lower courses is merely drafted. Gough concluded from this evidence, taken together with an analysis of the development of the sculptural decoration of the two main churches, that it was likely that the West Church commenced building before the East Church, and that the building programme was meant to be completed by the construction of the baptistery and the colonnaded walkway (see particularly Gough 1967a, 45-7). But, as well as providing an interesting clue to the order of events in the building programme, the fact that the walkway was never finished, in which respect we may also note the striking lack of decorative sculpture in the baptistery, suggests that the building campaign must have stopped precipitately, presumably because funding had dried up.

We are thus driven to look for a suitable historical context which would explain the provision of so much finance and its abrupt withdrawal. The late fifth century provides the ideal solution. From 474 to 491 there was an Isaurian emperor on the throne, who based his position on the support of the Isaurian military faction, and used his home province as a place of refuge and retreat, and also for the incarceration of political enemies. This is where the possible personal connection with Alahan on the part of Zeno is significant. Harrison has demonstrated that his original name was probably Tarasis, son of Kodisas, and Jones (1971, 214, 441) had previously argued that Zeno might have originated from the city of Coropissus, which has traditionally been identified with the ruins at Dağ Pazarı (Hild and Hellenkemper 1990, 313-4), 16 kilometres to the east of Alahan. Now, however, Hellenkemper (1994, 213) identifies Dağ Pazarı as Dalisandus (without explanation), and following Harrison (1981, 27-8) the idea of Coropissus being Zeno's birthplace is also questionable. Whatever the truth of all this, the presence at Alahan of two characters with the same name as Zeno (i.e. Tarasis) may well have been enough to attract his interest to the building project. In any event Zeno was certainly born in the territory of some city in Isauria (in the village of Rosoumblada), and it may reasonably be expected that Cilicia and Isauria would have benefited financially from Zeno's goodwill during his tenure of the imperial throne. This benefit would have ceased in 491 with the accession of the hostile Anastasius, and the occasion of bitter civil wars in the province from 492 to 498. Such a historical scenario appears to fit the sequence of events at Alahan perfectly, and to attempt to find an alternative chronological context is fraught with difficulty. Owing to the epigraphical evidence, it is difficult to propose a date for the commencement of the building scheme much more than ten years before the critical date of 461. In other words it seems unlikely that the main building programme at Alahan can have commenced much before the reign of Leo (457-474), during which reign Zeno established himself as Magister Equitum in the east, and as head of the imperial Isaurian guard. But unless it is possible to push the date of the building programme well into the first half of the fifth century, we are faced with the problem of explaining why building should have ceased so abruptly during Zeno's ascendancy. To find a later date, say in the sixth century, is still more difficult, since this would involve proceeding well into the century to reach a point when the province could be expected to have recovered from the wars under Anastasius, and, to judge by the lack of growth in other centres in the province during this period, it is doubtful whether such complete recovery ever occurred. Furthermore, the sculpture at Alahan, particularly the exuberant and animal-rich sculpture of the West Church, would seem wholly inappropriate in the sixth century.

The last word on this matter of dating is something of an argument based on silence. It might well be objected that it would be surprising to find buildings of such marked architectural originality in so obscure a province, when there are not even any comparable contemporary buildings known in Constantinople. The reply to this could be that Constantinople continued to prosper in the sixth century, whilst Cilicia did not. If Zeno did commission any buildings of the order of the East Church at Alahan in the capital, they must be assumed to have been replaced by such centralized basilicas as those dedicated to St Polyeuctus, and to Sts Sergius and Bacchus in the earlier part of the sixth century. In any event Constantinople had a very much longer Christian architectural history than Cilicia. The latter region has consequently preserved a higher proportion of its early Byzantine buildings, and it has to be admitted that the developments which can be detected in the Cilician churches suggest that the building types which survive at Alahan could perfectly well have evolved in the province independently.

ALAHAN (Apadnas?), Cave Church (figure 1)[8]

This small church (7.5 metres wide and 7.7 metres long) is part of the three-storey cave complex which must belong to the early phases of activity at Alahan. It is situated beside the rock-cut cells at the very western end of the terrace, and is certainly earlier than the present West Church since the narthex of the latter building, which was one of its primary features, was constructed in such a way as to avoid interfering with the apse of the earlier building. The Cave Church consists of two narrow aisles, which are divided by a row of columns. The north aisle is entirely cut into the rock face, and has a rectangular

---

[8] Bakker 1985, 76-80, figures 14-19, plates 5-6; Gough 1967a, 44-5; Hill 1981, 30; Hild and Hellenkemper 1990, 194.

recess at its east end, into the northeast corner of which is sunk a circular pit. The south aisle has an eastern apse, with a raised floor. The southern half of the apse wall, and the south wall of the church were free-standing, built of coarse limestone masonry. The interior of this church was plastered and painted. Gough suggested that the northern aisle may have been provided for catechumens, and that its pit may have served as a font. This is a more plausible suggestion than Gough perhaps realized, for the plan of the Cave Church, with its twin chambers, may be compared with those of other baptisteries in Cilicia, and was subsequently reproduced in Alahan's free-standing baptistery at the centre of the terrace. The position, at the north end of the narthex, is also typical for the region and may be compared with the dispositions in the Basilica at Dağ Pazarı, and the church at Şaha. The Cave Church could presumably have been used as the baptistery at Alahan until its successor was completed. It may even have been created as the first baptistery on the site, at the northwest corner of the original West Church.

The Cave Church must be one of the earliest structures at Alahan, but there is no objective reason to suggest that it was created earlier than the arrival of Tarasis the Elder, and it may well have been constructed just after the middle of the fifth century, when the usage of the shrine at Alahan had expanded to a level which justified the creation of a baptistery.

ALAHAN (Apadnas?), West Church ('Church of the Evangelists')[9] (figure 2; plates 3-5)

This church is the earliest of the main surviving buildings at Alahan, and also the largest, measuring 36.5 by 16 metres overall, with the internal measurement of the nave plus aisles being 22 by 14.5 metres. We owe our understanding of its complexities entirely to Gough's excavations (conducted in 1955, 1961, 1962, and 1967). The church has been fully and helpfully described by Bakker (1985, 80-102), and the reader is referred to his description: the account which follows concentrates on broad points and areas of Bakker's analysis which require amplification. Earlier visitors to Alahan had not recognized the existence of this building: indeed Headlam and his colleagues thought that the impressive western doorway of the church was the main external entrance to a monastic precinct (Headlam 1892, 10-11). This doorway has been much discussed (Gough 1955, 119-22; Gough 1962, 180-1; Grabar 1970, 23-8); for present purposes it is sufficient to note that it is easily the most elaborate to survive in a Cilician or Isaurian church, and is an example of early Christian art in its most exuberant phase. The lintel has a bust of Christ in a wreath supported by flying angels. These are flanked by two busts, and there are two

---

[9] Bakker 1985, 80-102, figures 19-43, plates 7-30; Gough 1962, 175-84; Gough 1963, 105-12, figure 1; Gough 1964, 187-9; Gough 1967a, 42-3; Gough 1968, 159-63, figure 1; Grabar 1962; Headlam 1892, 10-11, figure 1; Hill 1981, 31; Hild, Hellenkemper and Hellenkemper-Salies 1984, 255; Hild and Hellenkemper 1990, 194.

more busts set in the scrollwork which decorates the fronts of the jambs. It was these four busts, and the tetramorph showing the four symbols of the Evangelists in the Vision of Ezekiel which prompted Gough to suggest that this basilica was dedicated to the Evangelists. The insides of the door-jambs show archangels apparently trampling on pagan demons. The exuberance of the west door is reflected in the rest of the decorative scheme: the cornice of this building, for instance, had a very striking design which includes crossed pairs of fishes.

The plan of the church is of considerable significance, since it stands at an important transitional stage in the development towards the transept, and demonstrates at least three phases of construction and occupation. Following Gough's terminology, these will be referred to as Primary 1, Primary 2, and Secondary. The Secondary phase consisted of a much reduced single-chambered chapel, the walls of which were founded on the stylobates of the original nave colonnades (Bakker 1985, figure 41). Although no positive dating evidence for this structure is offered, Gough evidently considered that it might have been occupied as late as the Selcuk period. That Gough's Primary 2 phase may have lasted until the seventh century, albeit on a reduced scale, is suggested by finds of the so-called 'Monastic Ware' (Gough 1964, 190; Williams 1985, 41-7). It would be remarkable if it could be demonstrated there was continuous occupation from the seventh century to the Selcuk period, but Williams writes rather about 'some re-occupation of the site in the twelfth to fourteenth centuries' (1985, 52). In practice, the Secondary Church which resembles similar reductions such as that in the Necropolis Church at Anemurium, is likely to have been a product of the late sixth or seventh centuries.

Various local considerations affected the original planning of the West Church. It has already been noted that the narthex did not extend to the full width of the church in order to avoid disrupting the apse of the Cave Church, but there are discrepancies in the published record relating to the southwest corner of the basilica. Bakker's plan of the basilica (1985, figure 19) shows a small narthex consisting of a central porch outside the west door of the nave which did not extend to be in line with the south wall of the basilica. The published reconstruction drawings (Bakker 1985, figures 23-5), however, show a wider narthex extending to the south side of the church. As this corner of the building has been damaged since it was first excavated, it is hard to establish the truth on the ground, but it seems clear from the beginnings of an arch visible in Bakker's plate 7 and from the southward return from the west door of the narthex which appears in the overall site plan (Bakker 1985, figure 71) that the 'entry to the narthex of the Basilica was through an arched portal with trabeated openings to either side' (Bakker 1985, 80). That said, the trabeations, rather than arcades are unusual, and the extra doorway to the south of the narthex entrance shown in Bakker's figure 25 is even more so.

The arrangements for fenestration were also unusual. The north side of the Basilica was deeply cut into the cliff face and could presumably have admitted no light. Nor was there normal fenestration through the south wall. Here, instead, were three 'doorways', which cannot actually have been used as entrances since their thresholds are 3 metres above ground level. Although these 'doorways' were perhaps taller than conventional windows, they were not so numerous that they can have admitted very much light to the side-aisles. It is most likely that at this altitude considerations of comfort were more paramount than considerations of lighting, and these openings were accordingly designed to be closed with heavy wooden shutters in the winter months (Bakker 1985, 81). Gough found fragments of window dividers in the fill of the Secondary walls: these must have originated from clerestory windows, which with the double window in the apse, must have been the main source of light in this church.

The floor of the south side of the Basilica is supported on massive substructures, and it is quite possible that there was a crypt, since there is a door at a low level in the south wall. There is also provision of slit windows at the base of the south wall, but Gough was disposed to the theory that 'these might have afforded light to builders examining the church foundations' (Gough 1963, 106).

Nave and aisles were divided by two rows of ten columns in a double order. Fragments of voussoirs from the arches of the lower order had been incorporated in the walls of the Secondary Church, and were found to have been stuccoed and painted (Bakker 1985, 93-4). The lower parts of the columns from the gallery were slotted to receive a wooden parapet. It is unclear how access to the galleries was gained, especially since, in the absence of the full narthex, which would have communicated between the north and south galleries, it would presumably have been necessary to provide two staircases. It would appear, in fact, that access to the south gallery can only have been through one of the southern side-chambers: the equivalent arrangement may have applied on the north side, although here there also exists the possibility of access from the outside at a high level since the church is set so deeply into the rock face.

The arrangements at the eastern end of the church have been clearly discerned. This end of the church is better preserved than the west end, because it is here more deeply cut into the rock, a fact which resulted in the floors of the side-chambers to the north of the apse being at a higher level than the rest of the building. The floor of the easternmost north side-chamber is so high that it is at gallery level. The apse forms a slightly stilted semi-circle on the inside, and does not project beyond the eastern wall of the church since two side-chambers flank it on both sides. These chambers are not arranged in an entirely symmetrical manner, and it is noticeable that whereas the outer face of the apse wall is curved in the northern side-chamber, it presents itself as a flat tangent in the southern chamber. The apse has a double window, and is provided with a three-tiered synthronum the central section of which is raised. In the Primary 1 phase this bench simply filled the curve of the apse, but in the Primary 2 phase the synthronum was extended westwards into the chancel area, entirely blocking the doorway between the chancel and the north side-chamber. The floor of the apse, and of the area immediately to the west of it is raised above the level of the rest of the church, and approached from the nave by a flight of three steps, at the top of which, on the northern side of the bema, stood the altar. Removal of the walls of the Secondary church revealed the interesting fact that the sanctuary area did not consist merely of this raised bema area, but extended to include the first three bays of the nave. Slots cut in the four eastern columns, and in the stylobate which runs between them prove that chancel slabs were set across these intercolumniations. The fourth intercolumniation seems to have provided access between the aisles and the chancel, and screens originally projected obliquely into the aisles to accentuate these doorways. The fifth intercolumniation was again blocked by a screen. It is possible that the stylobate would have been carried across the nave of the church between the two sixth columns, but the flooring of the Secondary Church has destroyed the relevant evidence. There also appears to have been a screen across the nave between the first pair of columns, immediately in front of the bema.

The most important features of this eastern part of the church is, however, one upon which Gough and Bakker never commented. There are cruciform piers at either end of the bema steps, with half-round engaged pilasters on the sides which flank the chancel. These would serve no purpose unless we assume that there was a triumphal, or fore-choir, arch at this point. Thus, although the West Church at Alahan must be included in the group of Cilician churches in which the side-chambers are set to the west of the apse, and thus enclose a chancel area (compare, e.g. Kanlıdivane, Church 1; Canbazlı), the presence of what is, in effect, a triumphal arch at this point places the West Church at a unique transitional point in the story of the emergence of the transept in the fifth century basilicas of Cilicia. Here it is necessary to give some consideration to Bakker's proposed reconstructions (1985, figures 22-5). The arrangements which he proposes for the east end of the church are not entirely convincing, for he shows the roof running uninterrupted from nave and aisles to the extreme east end of the church. This involves creating an inaccessible void above the apse, extending the clerestory to the end of the church, and also running the slope of the aisle roof over the southward projection of the south side-chamber. An alternative reconstruction, which would not involve the unparalleled void above the apse, would be to assume that the clerestory stopped at the mouth of the apse where the east wall of the nave would have risen to provide a gable end. The apse and side-chambers could then have had sloping roofs draining to the east. There is the further possibility that the triumphal arch in front of the apse could have risen as the west wall of a transept-like structure. This would make more sense of the fact that the side-chambers project to north and south of the line of the aisles, since a transversely roofed unit running across the entire width of the east end of the building would accommodate the otherwise awkward angles in the long façades of the building. Such an arrangement would also accommodate the cornice with rams' heads along the top of the south wall of the church (Bakker 1985, 83, figures 23, 29-30), since this could have terminated against the projecting side-chamber rather than disappearing under its roof. The high window which appears in Bakker's figures 20 and 25 would make good sense as the means of lighting a staircase at this point in the building, but looks very squashed beneath the proposed southward sloping roof of the side-chamber. Bakker was committed to the assumption that the West Church had a clerestory running for the entire length of the building: he accepts that his reconstruction is problematic in the area of the south side-chamber, but says that any reconstruction with a higher south pastophory would have meant that 'the resultant shape of the Basilica would have been very ungainly. This arrangement would have been certainly less attractive in appearance.' (Bakker 1985, 85). My suggestion of a transverse architectural unit would overcome all these objections and would restore to the building the architectural complexity which its plan suggests.

There is a further unresolved issue relating to this church. This is the question of why it was erected in such a cramped and inconvenient position, requiring so much quarrying and so many substructures to create its platform. Bakker also observed the church was not rectangular. 'These inconsistencies with a plan that is normally orthogonal are probably due to faults or weak seams in the bedrock which prevented its orientation' (Bakker 1985, 80). It was also presumably felt desirable to set this basilica as close as possible to the Cave Church, thus providing a link with the earliest phases of worship at the site. But I wonder if there was not perhaps a more immediate reason even than that. I have previously referred to the parallelism of Alahan and Meryemlık: the great basilica of St Thecla was built directly over an earlier church, beneath which was her cave, which could be entered through a door on the south side of the later Basilica. The position of the West Church at Alahan would have been much more suitable for a smaller building, and it is tempting to wonder whether here, too, that smaller church, or the cave or cell which it had contained, was preserved as the crypt of a later, more elaborate basilica. This would make much better sense of the undercroft than Gough's suggestion that its doorway and windows were purely for the use of masons. The same considerations may have led to the inconvenient siting of Church 4 at Kanlıdivane, and the Basilica at Mazılık.

ALAHAN (Apadnas?), East Church ('Koca Kalesi')[10] (figure 3; plates 7-12, 15-16)

This building is the most famous and most well-preserved of all the Cilician churches. So well has it survived, in fact, that it is almost true to say that it would be possible to put the roof back on the structure. Again the reader is referred to Bakker's full description of the building (1985, 102-20). Measuring approximately 23 by 15 metres (without its eccentrically aligned narthex), it is considerably smaller than the West Church at Alahan, and is the smallest known example of a Cilician 'Domed Basilica'. Arguments about the precise way in which the nuclei of these churches were roofed has beset scholars since Strzygowski, who never visited Alahan, first ridiculed Headlam's innocent suggestion that the East Church at Alahan probably had a wooden roof (Strzygowski 1903, 51; Headlam 1892, 12). Later scholars, notably Forsyth and Gough, have supported Headlam's proposal against Strzygowski's implied suggestion that the tower at Alahan supported a solid, masonry dome, but the discussion has often been more rhetorical than objective (Forsyth 1957, 223-36; Gough 1972, 202-3).

For all the novelty of its superstructure, it is important to remember that the East Church at Alahan remains a basilica, and retains the division into nave and aisles. But, even at the west end of the nave, there is the very real distinction that repeated arches across the short axis of the nave give the visitor to the church an impression very different to that gained from the long parallel rows of columns which are found in the traditional early Byzantine basilica. It could even be argued that the western part of the East Church contains a pair of transept-like bays. As was the case in Church 4 at Kanlıdivane, the galleries continue across the bay: the architect who designed this church has not turned the gallery to match the cross-axis at the west end, although that is exactly what was done in the Tomb Church at Corycus. Though the presence of the central tower gives the building a surprising vertical axis, it could still have been used for the same liturgical performances as might have been executed in the West Church. The sanctuary has been highlighted by the central tower, but the basilican plan has survived, and the galleries which run from west to east retain some of the feel of the standard basilica at first floor level

It is the superstructure, then, of this building which is so remarkable, since the central nucleus also dominates the vertical composition. The effect of the presence of the central nucleus, which was marked off by a parapet and railings, was, as has been noted, to increase the size of the sanctuary at the expense of the nave. Since there was a very similar arrangement in the West Church, this might have been particularly convenient in pilgrimage churches where the

---

[10] Bakker 1985, 102-19, figures 44-54, plates 31-49; Forsyth, 1957, 230-3; Gough 1958a, 244-8; Gough 1964, 185-7; Gough 1967, 45-7; Gough 1967/68, 461-3; Gough 1968, 165; Gough 1972, 202-3; Headlam 1892, 11-19; Hellenkemper 1986, 74-7; Hill 1981, 31; Hild, Hellenkemper and Hellenkemper-Salies 1984, 258-63; Hild and Hellenkemper 1990, 194.

ordained monastic community surrounding the site is likely to have outnumbered the lay visitors. Four podia stood within the central nucleus, two facing each other in the western half, the other two on the eastern side of the nucleus under what is, in effect, the triumphal arch as well as the support for the eastern wall of the tower. The altar almost certainly stood at the top of a flight of two steps which led up to the raised floor of the apse. As in the West Church, the apse was pierced by a double window, and equipped with a synthronum which was at some date extended westwards across the entrances to the side-chambers from the chancel. Low benches also stretched between the columns across to the western side of the central bay. There are again double side-chambers, but here they are more regularly shaped, and aligned west-east. There is a cupboard-like recess in the southwest side-chamber. Unusually, the east ends of the aisles are marked by apsidal recesses through which doorways give access to the side-chambers.

Although the stone floor of the central nucleus could be shown to have been repaired at several points, Gough (1964, 186; 1968, 165) took the absence of fallen voussoirs to mean that there was never a masonry dome on the tower. This argument is similar to Guyer's unacceptable proposal that the great Basilica at Meryemlık had no galleries in its original scheme, because he found no traces of the upper order. Since the floor of the Basilica at Meryemlık was repaired, and the columns of the arcades were encased in or replaced by massive piers, it is likely that the roof fell in and repairs had to be effected. If the gallery fell too, then its masonry would simply have been cleared away. Similarly, if a masonry dome had fallen at Alahan, its debris would have been removed if the building continued in use, and a simpler timber and tile roof would probably have replaced it. This is exactly what appears to have happened in the 'Domed Ambulatory Church' at Dağ Pazarı, and Alahan is one of the few sites in the region where there is some reason to believe in continued occupation into the early medieval period. If there is any sense in Headlam's suggestion (1892, 18), now revived by Hild and Hellenkemper (1990, 193-4) that Alahan might be Apadnas, which, according to Procopius (*Buildings* 5, 9) was restored by Justinian, then Justinian's restoration could have taken the form of replacing a fallen dome with a simpler construction. The evidence for the repairs to the floors of the nucleus, the nave, and the apse, which was found by Gough (1964, 186) would then support this hypothesis.

Even so, Bakker (1985, 112) seems to take it for granted that the tower of the East Church at Alahan did not support a dome. The tower does have an appearance of lightness and delicacy, with its upper walls seeming thin, and weakened by the insertion of triple-arched windows on the north and south elevations. The topmost interior corners of the tower are filled with elegant squinch arches supported on slender colonnettes (plate 11). These are highly ornamental, and have been thought to be too insubstantial to support heavy masonry. Because of the rectangular proportions of the tower, Forsyth asserted positively that the roof of the tower was capped by a wooden pyramid. Gough was prepared to accept this, but wrote:

> 'Rather than being domed, the tower may have been capped by a pyramid of timber, which could have been accommodated on the oblong base, would have exerted little thrust, and, once fallen, would have left no trace after the lapse of centuries. Nevertheless, when all is said and done, the use of squinch arches at the angles of the tower strongly suggests that the architect was familiar with the basic principles of domical construction' (Gough 1967/68, 463).

Gough's second sentence here seems to me to be most significant: my own feeling is that a pyramid would sit most unhappily on the elegantly curved squinch arches, and I am not entirely convinced that the oblong nature of the tower would have proved an insurmountable obstacle to a dome-builder. It would have been a simple matter to create a wooden circle over the squinch arches, and I can see no reason why the tower of the East Church should be any less capable of supporting a wooden dome than a wooden pyramid. Since the structure would in any case have had to be protected by tiles, the external appearance, whether pyramid or dome, would have been identical, but a wooden dome, seen from the inside, would have been much more satisfactory aesthetically. This may be the most plausible resolution of the problem of the tower's roofing system, but I would like to set out my reasons for suggesting that a masonry dome was at least a technical possibility.

Forsyth produced a drawing (1957, 231) of his proposed wooden pyramid which was never questioned by Gough, although it is misleading in two ways. In the first place, at no point is there a cornice surviving on the tower: we cannot therefore be certain that it survives to its full height, or that there was no tambour. Secondly, and much more seriously, Forsyth takes no account of the corbels which project from the north and south sides of the tower (frontispiece). These have flat tops, and can only have supported the wooden tie beams of roofs which rose at least as high as those against the east and west sides of the tower. It would appear, therefore, that roofs on all four sides of the tower rose to a greater height than was actually necessary to protect the rest of the building, and would have covered all the existing windows. The most obvious explanation is that this roofing system was designed to buttress a tower which was under stress. The apparent delicacy of the tower is an illusion which is created by the complete absence of the roof; when the church was intact, very little light could have entered since all the windows would have been underneath the roofing system: this might actually suggest that the tower rose to a greater height, perhaps as a tambour with windows. In fact, the walls are 65-80 centimetres thick, and thus more substantial than those of the tetrapylum at Corycus, which were not buttressed by a surrounding roof system and yet were adequate to support a masonry dome. The masonry dome of the Kızıl Kilise near Sivrihisar in Cappadocia rises over a rectangular tower: it is supported by walls of equivalent thickness, and its tambour sits on squinches of equivalent size to those of the tower at Alahan, even though the dome of the Kızıl Kilise is not buttressed by an enveloping roofing system (Ramsay and Bell 1909, 376-86; Restle 1979, 57-63). I would not wish to appear to be stating categorically that there was a masonry dome on the East Church at Alahan, but I think it is important to note that Forsyth's arguments against one are less than watertight, and that the whole articulation of the tower suggests a domical roof, and was strong enough to have supported one. In fact, I suspect that the roof over the nucleus was, after all, wooden. This observation does not arise from a consideration of the tower itself, but from the fact that, unlike the towers at Meryemlık and Dağ Pazarı, it was not buttressed by a surrounding vault: the ceilings and gallery floors of the aisles at Alahan were supported by a simple timber construction which rested on corbels and can have had little effect in terms of strengthening the tower. But, if there was a wooden roof over the nucleus, this might nevertheless, if only for reasons of fenestration, have sat on a low tambour, and it is, therefore, altogether more plausible that it would have been domical rather than pyramidal.

The narthex of the East Church was highly irregular, being 4.5 metres wide at its north end, and only 2.5 metres wide at its south end. This disposition allowed the architect to disguise the fact that the East Church did not meet the colonnaded walkway at a right angle. The disembodied capitals which are so prominent a feature of the present east façade must originally have supported the upper floor of the narthex: in this case it would have been possible to pass between the north and south galleries without the need to provide separate staircases. Since the church was cut deeply into the cliff on the north side, it was possible to provide a doorway into the church at gallery level. Parts of this doorway can still be seen at the north end of the narthex: it had a high threshold which was presumably designed to deflect rainwater. Fragments of window columns found in the vicinity of the narthex show that its upper floor was fenestrated: windows at this level would have enabled the architect to restore some symmetry to the west façade, which, seen from ground level, would have appeared somewhat irregular, owing to its relationship with the colonnaded walkway. If, as seems likely, the area between the major churches, behind the north wall of the walkway, was a monastic enclosure normally not open to the public, only the upper floor of the narthex would have been seen by outsiders, and then only from afar, so that the architect may have been quite content so long as the façade was imposing at a high level.

The south façade, which was the other front of the building visible from a distance to visitors, was lightened by the gallery windows. External pilasters were also applied, which enliven the appearance, but at the same time serve to give extra structural support to the tower.

Sculptural decoration in the East Church is limited, essentially, to those parts of the building where it has the most immediate effect. The three doorways into the church proper are decorated with especially handsome inhabited scrollwork, and the east wall of the narthex is further enlivened by the inclusion between the doors of arcuate stoups. Some of the capitals of the columns in the centre of the nave have splendid animal protomes, and there is a further burst of animal decoration on the consoles which support the colonnettes under the squinch arches. By normal standards this building is very richly decorated, but it seems almost austere beside the much more lavishly decorated West Church.

ALAHAN (Apadnas?), Baptistery[11] (figure 1, plates 13-14)

This is the only free-standing building in the province which can be identified as an early Christian baptistery. Such grand provision for baptismal purposes might be thought surprising in a monastic environment, but since the baptistery seems to have been the latest major building to have been erected at Alahan, we must assume that the increasing number of visitors rendered such accommodation necessary.

The main part of the baptistery consists of two aisles which are aligned east-west. This section of the building belongs to the primary phase of the complex and measures overall 11.25 by 8.6 metres. On the south side of the building was added a range of two rooms which are three metres wide. Gough thought that there had originally been a colonnade in the same position as the south wall of the added southern rooms. Each of the primary aisles has an apse lit by a single arched window. The south aisle was plainly furnished with a secondary bench along its south wall, Gough suggested that this simple room may have been used for instruction and for changing. The north aisle contained the font, which consists of a tank in the form of a Greek cross set into the floor of the west half of the aisle (plate 13). Three steps in each arm lead down to the plaster-lined, central square tank. The font was served with water directly from the aqueduct to the north of the building, was equipped with a drainage system. The curve of the apse is provided with a simple synthronum. The altar base survives at the chord of the northern apse and in front of it, in the eastern part of the aisle Gough found two column stumps in secondary use. Demolition of secondary walling yielded fragments of four small Corinthian columns, which Gough suggested may have formed a ciborium over the font. Gough was not able to prove that the two aisles were originally divided by a colonnade, although this must be considered likely. In the secondary phase three coarse masonry piers were employed for this purpose, the easternmost of which stood uncomfortably close to the engaged column between the two apses. The inner

[11] Bakker 1985, 129-34, figures 61-5, plates 50-2; Gough 1963, 112-5, figure 5; Gough 1964, 188-9; Hild, Hellenkemper and Hellenkemper-Salies 1984, 263.

faces of the walls of the baptistery were originally plastered and painted to resemble verde antico marble slabs.

The building is rather plain in comparison with the two basilicas at Alahan: it is likely that like the shrine and the colonnaded walkway, it was left unfinished. The lack of elaborate mouldings, and the lumpish simplicity of the engaged capital between the two apses is certainly a far cry from the elaborate detail of the sculpture in the two large churches.

ALAKILISE, Basilica[12] (figure 4)

The remains of a very substantial basilica were noted at this site by Guyer in 1906. He returned in 1907, accompanied by Herzfeld, and subsequently published some preliminary notes on the building, which were never followed up by a later, lengthier report. The site was originally discovered by Heberdey and Wilhelm, who proposed that it should be identified with the ancient settlement of Pracana, though this identification is not accepted by Hild and Hellenkemper (1990, 385). Alakilise lies about 33 kilometres westnorthwest of Silifke, on the west side of the Göksu (Calycadnus) valley. In 1906 it was still a substantial Greek settlement, and the villagers had, 50 years previously, erected a modern church over what was probably the atrium of the ancient basilica. Various pieces of spolia from the earlier church had been built into the new church. Now little remains to be seen at the site apart from a large mound of rubble.

In Guyer's time only the northern half of the main apse was standing well above ground, and his plan is, accordingly, very sketchy in respect of all other parts of the building. Guyer, nevertheless, was able to make some very interesting observations about this important, if subsequently neglected building. The apse was constructed from enormous squared ashlars of local limestone, and there were visible, some 23 metres west of the mouth of the apse, the remains of another wall, aligned north-south, constructed in an identical manner. There were sufficient hints of foundations in the area to the west of this wall for Guyer to suggest that a more modern church stood within the original atrium. From the standing section of the apse, and part of the east wall of the north aisle, Guyer was able to prove the existence of galleries in the original building, and concluded that these were supported by barrel-vaults which covered the aisles. The apse was pierced by a double window, and had rectangular side-chambers to north and south. Guyer also described various fragments of architectural sculpture, often carved from white marble, which he attributed firmly to the fifth century on grounds of style. Kautzsch (1936, 95) subsequently attributed the pier capital from Alakilise to the second quarter of the sixth century: whilst this dating is surely too late, Kautzsch did make the

---

[12] Heberdey and Wilhelm 1896, 117; Guyer 1909-10; Hild, Hellenkemper and Hellenkemper-Salies 1984, 252-3; Hild and Hellenkemper 1990, 170; Kautzsch 1936, 95.

appropriate observation that the capital may be compared to pier capitals in the Funerary Church at Corycus, and he could have added the pier capitals in 'Domed Ambulatory Church' at Dağ Pazarı. The end of Guyer's article is devoted to speculation about the conceivable reconstruction of this building. He points out that the building does not appear to have been a regularly roofed basilica, and concludes that Alakilise may, like the recently excavated 'Cupola Church' at Meryemlık, have been a species of domed basilica. Guyer presumably intended to pursue this argument at a later date, and it is worth attempting to do so now.

The shape of the nave is basically square. It is, in fact, marginally wider than it is long, being approximately 22 metres from east to west (not including the apse), and 25 metres from north to south. The church appears to have measured approximately 28 metres overall from east to west. These measurements approximate quite closely to the equivalent measurements in the 'Domed Ambulatory Church' at Dağ Pazarı. Both churches had barrel vaults over the aisles, as does the East Church at Alahan. The pilaster capital from Alakilise (Guyer's plate 6) is, as has been seen above, remarkably similar to the pier capitals at the mouth of the apse in the church at Dağ Pazarı. It also corresponds closely to the pier capitals at the springing points of the arches at the centre of the Tomb Church at Corycus which is also cognate in plan. Guyer's plate 8 shows a console from Alakilise which he says was decorated on its side with a fish motif. Consoles are relatively rare in Cilician basilicas, but the parallels are again to be found in the same very suggestive group of buildings. The acanthus decoration of the front on the console found at Alakilise is very similar to that on the consoles which support the canopies over the entrances of the Tomb Church at Corycus, but it is more likely that this console originally performed the same function as the consoles which support the small columns under the squinch arches of the tower of the East Church at Alahan. One can compare also the consoles which were found in the rubble blocking the centre of the nave of the 'Cupola Church' at Meryemlık. In the case of both Alahan and Meryemlık the consoles are decorated with animal motifs: fish were represented on the cornice of the West Church at Alahan.

There is, therefore, quite powerful evidence to link the church at Alakilise with the well-known group of 'Domed Basilicas', which include the 'Kuppelkirche' at Meryemlık, and the East Church at Alahan, both of which are convincingly dated to the reign of Zeno in the late fifth century (474-91). On grounds of both architecture and sculpture, then, this church must also be assigned to the late fifth century.

ANAVARZA (Anazarbus)[13]

Anazarbus was an important city in the upper Plain, and from the reign of Theodosius II was the metropolis of Cilicia Secunda. The site preserves the remains of a variety of important buildings. As well as three churches, there survive parts of a baths, a stadium, an amphitheatre, an impressive Roman aqueduct, and the double circuit of late Roman city walls. The importance of Anazarbus as a Christian centre was doubtless accentuated by the deaths in the amphitheatre in AD 304 of the three martyrs, Tarachus, Probus, and Andronicus.

The monuments of Anavarza were noted by Langlois, and its churches were first described by Gertrude Bell, whose visit to the site in Spring 1905, was troubled by floods and snakes. In 1949 Michael and Mary Gough spent four months at the site surveying its monuments. The early Byzantine remains comprise three churches, two within the central area of the ancient city, and one outside in the southern necropolis, on the slopes leading up to the original site of the acropolis on the great rock which overshadows the city-site on the east side. On this rock was constructed the great Armenian fortress, in which can still be seen the Chapel of the Armenian Kings: the remains of an apse to the north of the Armenian chapel may, however, be earlier in date.

ANAVARZA (Anazarbus), Church of the Apostles[14] (figure 5)

This church was built on the site of an earlier structure, which was, in all probability, a pagan temple: Gough noted its wall footings at the bottom of a pit dug by treasure hunters in the area of the chancel. The cornice which ran along the top of the south wall was re-used from the Classical building. Since the church stands at the centre of the ancient street system, it was suggested by Gough that it may have been the cathedral of Anazarbus. The identification of the church is given by an inscription which runs round the outer face of the apse and can be completed to read [T]ΩN AΠOCTO+ΛΩN TOY X[PICTO]Υ.

This is a large building, measuring overall 56.2 by 28.1 metres, with an unusual plan. The apse is strongly horse-shoed in plan, and is set 5 metres in front of the east wall of the church. There was no narthex, and no side-chambers, although provision of the latter is almost invariable in Cilicia Pedias. Instead the east wall of the church follows the curve of the apse from where it leaves the north wall of the church round to its junction with the south wall. The east wall is curved on its inner face, and presents five sides of a dodecagon on the exterior. This arrangement has the effect of creating a circular ambulatory passage round the outside of the apse. The presence of a passage at the east end of a Cilician church is not, in itself, remarkable: it is the curved

---

[13] Gough 1952, Hild and Hellenkemper 1990, 174-85.

[14] Bell 1906a, 15-19, figures 9-16; Gough 1952, 116-8, figures 7-8; Hellenkemper 1984, figure 26; Hild, Hellenkemper and Hellenkemper-Salies 1984, 198, 201; Hild and Hellenkemper 1990, 182, plates 63-4.

shape of the passage which makes this building remarkable, but the arrangement can be paralleled at Akören and Aphrodisias. The passage is very similar to the ambulatories which envelop the apses of fourth century cemetery basilicas in Rome, but nothing suggests that this church, which stood at the centre of the city, was funerary, or that it should be dated so early.

Other aspects of the plan also deserve comment. Gough noted in his first, longer, article on Anavarza that:

'The opening into the apse was flanked by a pair of black granite columns, which lie across the opening, probably exactly as they fell.' (Gough 1952, 118).

From the presence of these columns Gough concluded simply that the western part of the church was divided into nave and aisles by a colonnade. However, in 1955, he wrote:

'Inside the building, towards the east end and not far from the opening of the apse, stood two cruciform piers, inside each of which a monolithic shaft of gray granite has fallen inwards. This, in effect recalls part of the interior of the Transept Basilica extra muros at Corycus in Cilicia Aspera' (Gough 1955, 205).

This second observation appears to be at odds with the more simple arrangement suggested by Gough's original description. My own inspection of the site confirmed the existence of the cruciform piers to the west of the mouth of the apse, as well as the presence of the fallen granite columns of Gough's first description. Assuming that these columns are lying just as they fell, since it seems improbable that anyone would have moved them, it is necessary to assume that they stood between the mouth of the apse and the eastern returns of the cruciform piers of the triumphal arch, and formed the central supports of double arches on either side of the chancel area, thus splitting the 'transept', into three bays, and creating a tripartite transept. This line of argument, of course, precludes the possibility, presented in Gough's earlier publication, that the two surviving granite columns formed parts of the nave colonnades. It is not, however, necessary to abandon the idea that the western part of the church was basilical in form, since the western returns on the cruciform piers and the pilasters engaged with the west wall of the church provide ample support for the proposal, which, even without such support, would be likely enough. Acceptance of the idea that there may have been a triumphal arch in front of a three-bayed chancel area actually removes one of the difficulties posed by this church. I have noted that the absence of side-chambers is remarkable in so large a basilica in the Cilician Plain: the possibility must be considered that the side bays of the chancel served for at least some of the normal functions of the pastophories. But it seems logical to assume that from time to time occasions arose when it was felt necessary to process from the aisles around the back of the apse. The suggestion that the side bays of the chancel may have had to serve as pastophories in both the Church of the Apostles at Anavarza and the 'Cathedral' at Corycus would appear to contradict this suggestion, but it is perhaps more than coincidental that both churches provide for communication between the main apse and the eastern passage, and also that in the north and south walls at Anavarza, and in the north wall at least at Corycus, doorways admit into the eastern passage from outside the building. There is, furthermore, at Anavarza a doorway in the south wall of the church at the east end of the nave which could presumably have been used in conjunction with the southern entrance to the ambulatory passage in order to by-pass the sides of the chancel. Hellenkemper (1994, figure 26) has recently produced a new plan of the Church of the Apostles. This serves to complicate the issue still further since he shows rows of 17 columns along the stylobates of the nave and completely omits the cruciform piers which were reported by Gough. Hellenkemper's plan does, however, contain the useful information that the internal apse was an open exedra with three columns which presumably supported four arches.

If the plan of the Church of the Apostles provides considerable ground for speculation, we are, at any rate, on firmer ground when considering the original appearance of the façades of the church. The apse stands to the level of the windowsills, and the south wall, which appears to have been damaged by an earthquake, fell as one piece. It was, therefore, possible for Gough to suggest convincing reconstructions of the east and south faces of the building, and it is reasonable to assume that the north wall will have corresponded closely to the south wall. A doorway was positioned in the south wall towards the east end of the nave, and was flanked by four windows to the west, and three windows to the east. A simple string course ran over the arches of the windows, but stopped against the jambs of the doorway, which was itself of trabeate construction, with acanthus consoles positioned at either end of its lintel. The three windows which pierced the eastern sides of the apse were taller than the nave windows, and, therefore, carried the string course round the eastern end of the church at a higher level. The string course was punctuated at various points by the addition of crosses in raised relief. There was further decoration on the corner stones of the outside of the apse just below the levels of the window-sills. All four angle stones were adorned with wreaths which encircled a cross. The fields thus created within the wreaths are filled variously, with fish, small birds, lambs, and in the case of the fourth, now lost stone, Bell recorded two peacocks standing on cups. At the centre of the outside of the apse, at a slightly lower level was carved another wreath encircling a cross which supports the alpha and the omega. The dedicatory inscription honouring the Apostles, already mentioned, runs over the top of this central wreath. The windows of the apse are also more elaborately decorated than those along the side. The arches of all three were embellished with vegetable scrolls, that of the central window being inhabited by birds. The sides and apse of the church were capped by the re-used Classical cornice. This has occasional lions' heads in its sima. The cornice stops towards the western end of the north side, and was presumably not carried across the pitched roof-lines of the west end. The details of the west façade are uncertain, but it is clear that there were three doors, one into the nave, and one each into the aisles, and that, unusually in so large and ambitious a basilica, there was neither narthex nor atrium. Bell and Gough both express the view that this church was built during the reign of Justinian with considerable confidence, but it is hard to find any solid evidence for this conclusion which is based essentially on vague stylistic analysis of the sculpture. According to Procopius (*Secret History* 18, 10), Anazarbus was devastated by two earthquakes in the sixth century during the reigns of Justin and Justinian after each of which the city was rebuilt and duly renamed Justinopolis and then Justinianopolis. Against this story, which would presumably support a sixth century date for a major church at the centre of Anazarbus, must be balanced Procopius' unreliability in reporting such events, and the apparent almost total dearth of sixth century remains in the city. It could as easily be argued that this church, with its scarcely weathered south façade, may actually have fallen in one of the earthquakes in the first half of the sixth century, and should therefore be attributed to an earlier century. Such a proposal would make better sense of the extensive usage of Roman spolia, and what Gough terms 'the Classical style of the architectural embellishment' (Gough 1952, 118). Lastly, the tripartite transept in this church finds all its Cilician parallels in churches built during the fifth century. The caption to Hellenkemper's published plan also attributes the church to the late fifth century.

ANAVARZA (Anazarbus), Southwest Church[15] (figure 6)
This church is described only by Gough, who wrote: 'Of this building it is difficult to give any fuller description than an idea of the ground plan, since the walls nowhere stand higher than a metre or so above ground level' (Gough 1952, 113). Since 1948 the church, which is closest to the modern village, has suffered so heavily from stone-robbing that, by 1976, only one door-jamb was visible above ground level, and, without excavation, it would now be impossible to recover even the ground plan. It is, thus, impossible to add anything to Gough's description.

The church measured 51.8 by 37.3 metres, and was broadly cruciform in plan with an extremely shallow apse projecting only 2 metres beyond the east wall of the church. There was no sign of a narthex, nor any remains of the internal divisions of the church. A loose Corinthian pilaster capital, and the footings of pilasters in the cross arms and against the northern section of the west wall suggested that the interior must have been divided into naves and

---

[15] Gough 1952, 113-4, figure 6a; Hild, Hellenkemper and Hellenkemper-Salies 1984, 201; Hild and Hellenkemper 1990, 182.

aisles by colonnades, although no such pilasters were evident against the east wall beside the apse. The apse was probably lit by three windows, and the church had no less than eleven doors, five each along the north and south sides, and one in the centre of the west wall. Gough considered that the central northern door was actually the main entrance, since the posts and lintels of this doorway were embellished with simple mouldings, and its lintel was decorated with acanthus. The floor of an area extending for 4 metres in front of the apse was raised above the level of the rest of the church, and the northeast and southeast doors let into the church at this level. In the northeast corner of the church was a small room which Gough thought might have served as the priests' vesting room. Gough saw fragments of a coloured mosaic pavement with a running scroll border at the west end of the south arm. This had red, blue, and white tesserae. There also appeared to have been a plain white tesellated pavement outside the southeastern end of the church.

Gough's plan shows dotted lines running along the axes of the church which are meant to indicate the lines of the original colonnades. These dotted lines are shown petering out just before the raised platform at the east end of the church. The existence of this platform, combined with the more suggestive fact of the absence of pilasters against the eastern wall would seem to suggest that the colonnades on the east-west alignment may well not have extended through the full length of the church, but may have terminated either in line with the eastern colonnade on the north-south alignment, or, which is perhaps more plausible, in line with the eastern walls of the cross arms. These suggestions are too hesitant to allow the admission of any precise local parallels, but the church must have been similar to the 'Große Armenische Kirche' at Corycus, and also perhaps Church A at Perge in Pamphylia, where the nave colonnades stop short of the apse at a cross transept, which projects beyond the walls of the nave and aisles (Rott 1908, 47; figure 19). The Southwest Church at Anavarza may thus have had a cross transept. This feature may reasonably be accepted alongside the tripartite and continuous transepts as part of the repertoire of early Byzantine church planning in Cilicia.

The very shallow projection of the apse may be compared with the plan of several Cilician churches (e.g. Bodrum and Kadirli), but in all other cases the feature is associated with the presence of side-chambers. Since these do not feature in this church, there is at least a possibility that the apse was set to the west of the east wall, or was represented by a semi-circular colonnade on the east side of the transept.

The dedication of this church is not known, but its plan suggests strongly that it was a martyrium. It is quite likely, therefore, that this church may have been dedicated to the Anazarbene martyrs Tarachus, Probus, and Andronicus.

ANAVARZA (Anazarbus), Rock-Cut Church[16] (figure 7, plate 18)

This church, which is described by both Bell and Gough, stands well up the slope of the approach to the acropolis rock. It is situated near the cemetery area to the south of the city, and is flanked by graves to its west and south. Almost nothing remains by way of masonry structures, but because the east end of the building was cut deeply into bedrock, parts of the plan are still clearly discernible.

The interior width of the church was 29.2 metres, and it was at least 43 metres long. It was, therefore, in terms of ground area, the largest of the three main churches known at Anavarza, but since it was the only church of the three to be equipped with a narthex, the area devoted to the nave was actually smaller than that in either of the other churches. In this church the apse is rounded on both interior and exterior faces, and a small stone bench was provided round the inside. A scatter of glass tesserae across the site shows that the church was decorated with expensive glass wall mosaic, which was presumably likely to have adorned the apse. The apse was pierced by three windows, below which (at measurements of 62 centimetres and about 1 metre below the sills) were two rows of sockets which Gough conjectured might have related to arrangements for curtains. The apse is so deeply cut into the rock that it is possible to reconstruct the exact dimensions of the windows, each of which was 3 metres high, 1.85 metres wide, and stood 1.8 metres above the stone bench. The two central piers between the three arched windows had acanthus capitals, and the spandrels of the arches were embellished with crosses in relief. One of the window blocks carries an inscription which gives the date for the foundation of the church in the 535th year of the Anazarbene era, that is AD 516. The curved appearance of the apse is unusual in Cilicia Pedias, and it also appears that, in its original form, the church was not provided with side-chambers. The small apsidal chamber measuring 12 by 5 metres at the southeast corner is of a different, more flimsy, build than the rest of the church, and appears to have been a later addition. No part of this small room was rock-cut.

Pilasters engaged in the east wall of the nave show that the church was divided into nave and aisles. An Ionic pilaster capital and a column base found by Bell would seem to confirm this, although it should be noted that this would be the only example of the Ionic order being used in a Cilician church. The proportions of the nave and aisles are also unusual, with the nave, which is 16.5 metres wide, being well over twice the width of the aisles (6.5 metres).

The plan of the west end of the building is still easily discerned, and shows quite clearly that this was the only church at Anazarbus to be equipped with a narthex. This structure, uniquely in Cilicia, has the tripartite form which is most common in the basilicas of southern Anatolia, especially in the province of

---

[16] Bell 1906, 21, figures 17-19; Gough 1952, 115-6, figure 6b; Hild, Hellenkemper and Hellenkemper-Salies 1984, 201; Hild and Hellenkemper 1990, 182.

Lycaonia (see Bell and Ramsay 1909, passim). The reason so often offered to explain this feature in Anatolia may also be relevant here: since there were originally no side-chambers at the eastern end of the church, it is possible that these western rooms were used for the same purpose. In this church there may also be a simple practical reason for this arrangement: it may well have been felt that the labour involved in quarrying out the native rock in order to build the apse was not justified in the case of the less important pastophories. The arrangement of the west end of the Rock-Cut Church at Anavarza serves as a reminder that the city was firmly in the upper plateau of Cilicia Pedias, and was likely to be influenced by Anatolian architecture, rather than submitting unreservedly to influences from Syria.

ANEMURIUM (Eski Anamur)[17]

The site of the ancient city of Anemurium was first described by Beaufort, and has been the subject of a major Canadian survey and excavation project directed by Professor James Russell in recent decades. Russell's excavations have added very considerably to the information derived from the survey project directed by Elizabeth Alföldi-Rosenbaum in the 1960s. The city stood on the east side of a rocky promontory which is the most southerly point in Asia Minor. It had a long history from the Hellenistic period through to the seventh century AD, but was never very important. All the remains of buildings can be dated to the second century AD or later: they include four churches which have been positively identified, and some other buildings which may also have been churches. All the known churches were basilicas: they belong to the period from the late fourth and through the fifth century, when the city was at its greatest extent. The Necropolis Church probably belongs to the late 4th century, and the other churches were probably constructed after 408 and before about 450. It is very clear from the study of the churches which have been excavated that the city was well into decline in the second half of the 6th century, and that the churches appear to have stood disused, and subject to stone robbers, for some time before they collapsed. The secular re-use of the Church of the Apostles has been demonstrated as happening during the late sixth century.

ANEMURIUM (Eski Anamur), Basilica[18]

The first mention of a basilical church at Anemurium was made by Strzygowski, who noted a small church with a nave measuring 10.6 by 5.6 metres, with a horse-shoed apse which projected 3.1 metres from the east wall of the church, and was 4.1 metres wide at its chord. These measurements do not correspond with any of those in the plans published by Alföldi-Rosenbaum and

---

[17] Alföldi-Rosenbaum et al 1967, 1-17; Hild, Hellenkemper and Hellenkemper-Salies 1984, 269-73; Hild and Hellenkemper 1990, 187-91; Russell 1980a; Russell 1989.

[18] Strzygowski 1903, 53.

Russell, Strzygowski's basilica being considerably smaller than any of those visible today.

ANEMURIUM (Eski Anamur), Basilica II 16, Church of the Apostles ('Seaside Church')[19]

This building appears on Alföldi-Rosenbaum's general site-plan, but she did not identify it as a church, since only its west end was visible. Russell decided to excavate the building, starting in 1976, after illicit gravel-extraction from the beach had already removed a large section of its mosaic.

Excavation has uncovered traces of a basilica, which is the only one at Anemurium known to have been provided with an atrium. The whole complex measures approximately 40 by 16.5 metres, with the church proper being about 27 metres from east to west. The narthex was formed by the eastern arcade of the atrium peristyle. The entirety of the church, including the atrium seems to have been decorated with fifth century mosaics, which were at some time repaired by a Christian confraternity (φιλιακὸν). The narthex floor had a series of interlocking loops containing at its centre, in front of the entrance to the nave, a tabula ansata with an inscription which dedicates the church to the Holy Apostles. The border of the mosaic in the main part of the church consists of a chain of guilloche circles and ovals which enclosed single birds and pairs of birds, a design which may be compared with that of the floor mosaic of the northern half of the narthex mosaic in the Basilica at Dağ Pazarı. The east end of the church has suffered seriously from erosion, and was relatively difficult to study, but Russell's plans do not indicate the presence of pastophories or an eastern passage associated with the round apse.

The sea wall of the city had to be reduced to foundation level in order to construct the atrium of the Church of the Holy Apostles, but the line of the sea wall could be seen as an area of mosaic raised above the level of the rest of the floors which had settled in antiquity. The church must therefore be later than the construction of the sea wall under Matronianus in the 380s, and the presence of early fifth century pottery under the floor of the south corridor of the atrium suggests a date for the construction of the church around 425. The church was in secular re-use by the late sixth century, and in the seventh century, as is attested by a series of late floors, fills, and rough walls in the atrium where the south and probably the north arcades were blocked to make rooms.

ANEMURIUM (Eski Anamur), Basilica III 10 C[20] (figure 10)

This poorly-preserved church was a basilica which measured approximately 21 by 11 metres, but with an additional narrow eastern passage extending 1 metre

---

[19] Hild, Hellenkemper and Hellenkemper-Salies 1984, 269; Hild and Hellenkemper 1990, 190; Russell 1977, 8; Russell 1980, 5-7; Russell 1986, 180; Russell 1989, 1624, figure 9.

[20] Alföldi-Rosenbaum et al 1967, 15, plan 1, figure 9; Hild, Hellenkemper and Hellenkemper-Salies 1984, 269; Russell 1977, figure 1; Russell 1986, 179-80, figure 3; Russell 1989, 1624.

beyond the eastern face of the apse, and a chamber along the north side of the church. There was a narthex which could be entered only through a doorway at its south end, as the west wall of the narthex had no doorways (compare Kanlıdivane, Church 3). Steps leading upwards immediately inside the doorway were necessary since the floor of the church was at a higher level than the entrance to the building. Three doorways provided communication between the narthex and the main part of the church. Nave and aisles were divided by three pairs of columns and the nave was paved with re-used marble slabs. The apse was semi-circular in plan, flanked by pastophories entered through doorways on either side of the mouth of the apse. The north pastophory had a separate wall with a doorway on its south side, to distinguish it from the narrow eastern passage, whilst the south side-chamber simply continued into the eastern passage. A secondary wall was inserted at some stage blocking the eastern passage and, in effect, separating the pastophories. A chamber or passage, approximately 4 metres wide, ran along the eastern half of the north side of the basilica, ending in a small room at the northeast corner of the church, which was entered through a doorway in the north wall of the north side-chamber. A short distance to the southwest of this church is a small square building containing a triconch (Building III 6 A). This is similar to the triconch on Mahras Dağı, but, given the lack of entrances on the west side of Church III 10 C, it is relatively unlikely that the triconch building could have been part of an architectural complex which also included the church.

ANEMURIUM (Eski Anamur), Central Church (Cathedral?) III 13 C[21]

This basilica is also very poorly preserved, and is known mainly from Russell's excavations, which commenced in 1982. It stands at the centre of the settlement, and measures roughly 31 by 17.5 metres overall. Its position led Russell to suggest that this could have been the cathedral of Anemurium, and the fact that this is the largest of the churches at Anemurium combined with the discovery of a baptistery in the south pastophory would tend to support that conclusion.

The main entrance to the church, as in the Church of the Holy Apostles, was at the south end of the narthex. The interior was divided into nave and aisles by two rows of seven columns which supported the second row of columns for the gallery. An elaborately sculpted chancel screen ran across the east end of the nave just to the west of the piers which received the ends of the arcades. Fragments of chancel screen left behind by the stone robbers include a piece with the rear legs of an animal, and a fine almost complete two-sided limestone panel with a Maltese cross in low relief. There was a two-tiered synthronus round the inner face of the apse, with a cathedra at its centre, and the

---

[21] Alföldi-Rosenbaum *et al* 1967, 15, plan 1; Hild, Hellenkemper and Hellenkemper-Salies 1984, 269; Russell 1977, figure 1; Russell 1986, 174-8, figures 1-2, plates 1-3; Russell 1987, 155; Russell 1988, 134; Russell 1989, 1626, figures 4-5, 11-12.

rectangular altar stood at the centre of the apse, slightly to the east of its chord. A Corinthian window capital presumably fell from the double window of the apse.   There were doorways halfway along the southern and northern outer walls, the northern of which was at some stage blocked, and an entrance through the north wall was also provided at its east end, just west of the pastophory wall.

Pastophories which followed the curve of the apse were entered through doorways on either side of the apse, and were marked from the eastern passage by transverse arches springing between the apse and the east wall of the church. The north pastophory and much of the eastern wall had fallen away, but their plan is clear from the preserved opus sectile pavement of the north side-chamber, and the tesellated mosaic floor of the passage. The south pastophory contained a cruciform free-standing font (like that in the Baptistery at Alahan) which was surmounted by a vaulted ciborium supported by four columns. Copious fragments of glass-paste mosaics, which included human figures, possibly of saints, showed how the ciborium had been decorated.

Russell attributed the church to the second quarter of the fifth century. The roof collapsed around 650, but by then the church had stood in disuse long enough to allow systematic removal of the finer sculptural elements.

ANEMURIUM (Eski Anamur), Basilica III 14 C[22]

This basilica is also very poorly preserved. It stands about 60 metres to the east of Basilica III 13 C, and measures roughly 25 by 10 metres overall. Alföldi-Rosenbaum noted that the apse was 'enclosed within a rectangle'; this was, presumably, an eastern passage.   Although it is not marked on Alföldi-Rosenbaum's plan, it is just possible to make out the traces of the east wall of the narthex on the ground.

ANEMURIUM (Eski Anamur), Church A II 1, Necropolis Church[23] (figure 8)

This is the best preserved of the churches, although it is only the apse which survives to any height above ground. The basilica, which has been excavated in its entirety since 1976, stands towards the northern end of the site, outside the city walls in the area of the necropolis.

The building has had a somewhat complicated architectural history: it seems to have started as a small basilica first built in the 4th century, was considerably altered and enlarged during the fifth century, but was never properly rebuilt after being severely damaged in the sixth century, perhaps by the earthquake

---

[22] Alföldi-Rosenbaum et al 1967, 15, plan 1; Hild, Hellenkemper and Hellenkemper-Salies 1984, 269.

[23] Alföldi-Rosenbaum et al 1967, plan 1; Hild, Hellenkemper and Hellenkemper-Salies 1984, 270-3; Hild and Hellenkemper 1990, 190; Russell 1975, 126, figure 19; Russell 1977, 6-8, figures 3-5; Russell 1980a, 37, figure 5; Russell 1989, 1626-8, figures 6-8, 10.

which struck Anemurium around 580. In the seventh century a small chapel was set up in the east end of the nave, and the rest of the church was used as part of the cemetery. The church, like the rest of the city, was abandoned by about 660. Russell was also able to demonstrate that the church stood on the site of an earlier building complex, which is still visible in the form of an arcade which runs in front of the west side of the church at a slightly different alignment.

In its first two phases the church was essentially basilical in plan, based on the core of the fourth century church which measured 18.5 by 12.7 metres for most of its extent. After the fifth century alterations the church expanded to 21.5 by 17 metres through its main extent. The nave was 5.65 metres wide, and was separated from the aisles by two rows of six columns. There was a narthex across the west end of the church, which, like that of Basilica III 10 C, was entered from the south by a flight of steps which in this case led downwards into the church. There were three doorways from the narthex into the nave and aisles, one from each bay of the narthex.

The apse was semi-circular in internal and external plan, and was flanked by irregular side-chambers. Its semi-dome is still standing, and is, like the rest of the building, constructed from limestone rubble and mortar with very coarse facing stones. It is lit by two arched windows, and some of the plaster rendering still adheres to its inner face: curved window glass found during the excavations presumably came from the apse fenestration. The bema occupied the east end of the nave, and in the fifth century its floor was raised above that of the western part of the nave, and a chancel screen was inserted. Russell found parts of a mosaic on the raised bema floor which showed a leopard and a kid on either side of a palm tree with an inscription giving a partial quotation from Isaiah's vision of the Peaceful Kingdom, beneath this was found the simpler primary mosaic, which had been damaged at the centre of the mouth of the apse, possibly by the collapse of some of the apse roofing material. The primary mosaic of the bema contained a mosaic inscription marking its donation by a Protector. The association with this church of a senior military figure supports Russell's conclusion that the original church was built in the 380s when Anemurium had a military garrison.

On the south side of the apse are the foundations of two chambers. The easternmost chamber, which belongs to the period of alterations in the fifth century, is apsidal, and projects to the east well beyond the main apse. This southern side-chamber is also eccentrically aligned towards the northeast as compared with the main apse. To the north of the apse is another side-chamber which is squared off by a nub of wall which hides the point of junction with the outer face of the main apse. A corridor, which was 3.35 metres wide, was added in the fifth century along the north side of the north aisle, and seems to have communicated with it through an arcade of four arches. At the western end of this corridor was a square, open, vestibule which Russell thought had

originally consisted of four arches. At the eastern end of the northern corridor
was a small L-shaped chamber which served as a baptistery, since it contained a
simple rectangular font sunk into the floor. Russell (1989, 1628) suggested that
the northern aisle/corridor may have served as a catechumenon for novices,
although it seems to have had very open access to the rest of the church. The
presence of a second baptistery in Anemurium is intriguing. In view of its
position in the necropolis, this church cannot have been a second (say,
Monophysite) cathedral, and one is therefore tempted to wonder whether, like
the complex at Alahan, which was also provided with a baptistery, it had a
pilgrimage function in a city which claimed to have been visited by Barnabas
(Lipsius 1907, 282-3, 296-7).

The archaeological evidence suggested strongly that the main phase of
occupation of the Necropolis Church belonged to the second half of the fifth
century, and, as Russell observed, the presence of a Peaceful Kingdom mosaic
would tend to confirm this if we accept Gough's argument that these mosaics,
several examples of which are known in Cilicia, can be associated with the
reconciliatory religious policies set out in Zeno's *Henotikon* (Gough 1972, 210-
2). The Necropolis Church had been severely damaged by the end of the sixth
century, and was not properly repaired. Instead, a small chapel about 8 metres
long was created by enclosing an area at the east end of the nave immediately in
front of the apse with secondary walling. This chapel had a single entrance in
the centre of its east wall. The remainder of the church was cleared of its
sculpture and taken over as part of the cemetery. The burials which it contains
must presumably belong to this phase of the occupation of the building, since
there is no evidence to suggest that any part of the site of Anemurium was
occupied after about 660.

APADNAS see ALAHAN

APHRODISIAS see OVACİK

ARSINOE see MARAŞ HARABELERİ

AYAŞ ('Ayash') (Elaeussa-Sebaste),[24]

The site of the ancient city of Elaeussa at Ayaş, 4 kilometres east of Corycus is
well known. It was an important settlement in the Hellenistic period and the
early centuries of the Roman empire, and controlled the village settlements at
Çatıkören and Kanlıdivane. The city was the seat of a bishop in Cilicia I, but
Elaeussa appears to have gone into decline by the fourth century, and in the late

---

[24] Feld 1965, 132-3; Gough 1954, 55-64, figures 3-5; Gough 1955a, 202-3; Gough 1972, 210-
2; Heberdey and Wilhelm 1896, 61-7; Hild, Hellenkemper and Hellenkemper-Salies 1984, 205;
Hild and Hellenkemper 1986, 69-71; Hild and Hellenkemper 1990, 401; Keil and Wilhelm 1931,
220-8, figure 176, plate 55.

Roman period was completely overshadowed by Corycus. This may have been the result of the progressive silting of the harbour and resultant loss of trade to Corycus.

The first lengthy account of the ruins at Ayaş was published by Heberdey and Wilhelm, who recorded many of the inscriptions on the heroa and sarcophagi in the necropolis. Keil and Wilhelm, who visited the site in 1925, published plans and descriptions of some of the major buildings. As well as producing a plan of the temple-church, they mentioned the existence of a five-aisled 'Bischofskirche' on the headland to the east side of the settlement, which was in antiquity the island on which King Archelaus set up residence (Keil and Wilhelm 1931, 220). It was Archelaus who gave the city its alternative name of Sebaste in honour of Augustus. Recent descriptions have been published by Feld (1963, 132-3) and Hild and Hellenkemper (1986, 69-71). From these descriptions it seems unlikely that the 'Bischofskirche' was indeed a church, and Hild and Hellenkemper also describe two other three-aisled basilicas, 'B' and 'C' (1968, 70), the orientations of which suggest that they, too, were not churches.

AYAŞ ('Ayash') (Elaeussa-Sebaste), Temple-Church[25] (figure 11)

The temple of Ayaş stood on the summit of the headland on the western side of the city overlooking the west side of the ancient harbour. It was built in a distinctive Corinthian order, and was a peripteral temple with twelve columns by six standing on a stylobate which measures 17.6 by 32.9 metres. Since the visit of Keil and Wilhelm, and Gough's excavations, which were carried out in 1952 and 1953, the building has become a confused heap of rubble, possibly as the result of earthquake damage.

Conversion of the temple into a church involved major structural alterations, and, in the event, only a small part of the temple platform was actually used for the church proper which measures 11.35 by 7.3 metres. The temple was orientated in such a way that the corners of its platform point to the four cardinal points of the compass. The apse of the church, which is a right angle to the alignment of the temple, therefore points northeast. All the columns of the southeast façade, and the first three columns of the long sides at the south and east corners were removed. The apse of the church was then constructed against the next four columns of the northeast side. Here, although at least three of the columns were left in position, they were cut to take the shape of the corners of the church, and the curve of the inner face of its apse. The columns from the rest of the northeast side were replaced by a solid wall with a short return on the northwest face to provide one jamb for a gateway in the first intercolumniation of the northwest façade. The remaining columns of the northwest and southwest sides were probably left in position, but with the

[25] Feld 1965, Gough 1954, 55-64; Gough 1972, 210-2; Hild and Hellenkemper 1990 401.

intercolumniations on the northwest side filled with masonry. Gough found traces of a continuation of the southwest wall of the church across the northwest end of the temple platform. It seems likely, therefore, that the southwest colonnade was left open to serve as an extended portico along the southwest side of the church. The part of the platform to the northwest of the church was an enclosed area which could be entered through a door in the northwest wall of the church, or through a doorway at the north end of the northwest façade of the temple. Gough notes that the 'priests' quarters' may have been found in this area, but does not offer any evidence to support this idea. The main door of the church was evidently that on the southwest side. The southeast end of the temple platform was left completely open and devoid of columns, and seems, from the provision of steps on its northeast and southeast sides, to have served as the public approach to the church.

Evidence for the interior arrangements of the church is limited, owing to the poor nature of its preservation, and to the fact that the nave was never completely excavated. The presence in the fill of the nave of a small column base and fragments of small capitals suggests that the church was divided into nave and aisles. There were side-chambers next to the apse, but these were only 1.2 metres deep, and Gough found no evidence to suggest that they could have been entered. The nave was floored with flagstones as far as the bema which extended 1.8 metres in front of the chord of the apse. On the raised floor of the bema Gough found a mosaic which possibly represents the paradise prophesied by Isaiah (Isaiah 11, 6-7). In his main article on Ayaş Gough contented himself with the observation that this mosaic conformed 'to the pattern-book style prevalent among Antiochene artists during the late fifth and early sixth centuries' (Gough 1954, 203). Gough later developed his argument to suggest that the mosaic might be one of a group, including also the pavements of the 'Cathedral' at Corycus, and the church at Karlık, which he suggested might have been designed in the context of the aftermath of the publication of Zeno's *Henotikon* in 482 (Gough 1972, 210-2). To this group of mosaics may be added the pavement in the Necropolis Church at Anemurium (Russell 1977, 6-8; figures 3-5). On stylistic grounds alone, the attribution of the mosaic to the fifth century seems entirely reasonable, but we do not have to suppose that the building of the church belongs to the same period. It is more likely, as Gough believed, that the conversion of the temple took place at a considerably earlier date. 'The position of the church, inside the temple, suggests that it was the immediate follower of its pagan predecessor' (Gough 1954, 63).

AYAŞ ('Ayash') (Elaeussa-Sebaste), Basilica A[26]

This church lies on the east side of the ancient settlement. It was first reported by Hild and Hellenkemper and was probably a three-aisled basilica with an apse

---

[26] Hild and Hellenkemper 1986, 69.

which measures 8.55 metres wide and has wall thicknesses of 0.97 and 1.05 metres. The building was constructed from large limestone blocks. The foundations of the east side of the building have fallen into the sea. A synthronus is visible in the apse, which was flanked at least on the south side by a pastophory which was 4.34 metres wide. Hild and Hellenkemper suggest an overall width of about 20.5 metres with a length of about 35 metres including a narthex, but they note that in the western parts of the building walls are not preserved above ground level, though foundations probably survive under the turf. Fragments of Proconnesian marble may be seen in the vicinity of the church.

AYDINCIK (Celenderis)[27]
During his survey and excavation work at Aydıncık Zoroğlu found and conserved a fragment of opus sectile pavement which probably came from a fifth century church.

BAHÇE DERESİ see İMAMLİ

BAKA (Feke)[28]
Langlois first reported a very old church in this village near Kozan in Eastern Cilicia. Hild and Hellenkemper saw fragments of mosaic from the nave and apse of a church in a field of Eski Feke about one kilometre southwest of Feke. Parts of the church, including the apse are visible under a house. Hild and Hellenkemper attribute the mosaic to the first half of the fifth century.

BALABOLU (Adrassus), Intra-Mural Churches (Churches 1-3)[29]
There has been only a limited amount of fieldwork conducted at Balabolu and information on the internal churches is mainly limited to a few notes in Alföldi-Rosenbaum's Necropolis Report:

> 'We noted three apsed buildings in the ruins of the city, two of which are certainly churches, while the third is not strictly orientated, and thus might be a secular building: 1. an apse a little above the fountain on the slope of the city hill; 2. a little higher up the same slope, an apse, with a chord of 6.50m., encased in a rectangle, not strictly orientated; 3. just below the top of the city hill, an apse, externally enclosed (it is impossible to state, without excavation, what kind of enclosure this was but it looks as if it might have been polygonal), with portions of walls on

---

[27] Hild and Hellenkemper 1990, 298; Zoroğlu 1987, 412, plates 16-17; Zoroğlu 1988, 138, plates 18-19.

[28] Hild and Hellenkemper 1986, 98-9, plates 151-5; Hild and Hellenkemper 1990, 208; Langlois 1861, 408.

[29] Alföldi-Rosenbaum 1980, 53; Feld 1963/64, 95; Hild, Hellenkemper and Hellenkemper-Salies 1984, 273; Hild and Hellenkemper 1990, 159.

either side extending to the west. Six courses of ashlar are visible here, but as facing only, the core of the visible walls consists of rubble and small stones; the walls are very thick; there might have been a window in the apse.' (Alföldi-Rosenbaum 1980, 53, note 125)

Feld's notes add a few details. He identified all three buildings as churches, but notes in the case of Churches 1 and 2 that only the apses were visible, and that he saw no traces of pillars or columns. He does add a few details to the account of Church 3.   He records that it was a small church, the apse of which was constructed of well-cut limestone ashlars and measured 3.1 metres wide, and 2 metres deep. There was evidently an architecturally defined chancel area since walls ran westwards from either side of the apse, through which doors (73 centimetres wide, and 60 centimetres west of the mouth of the apse) led into the side-chambers.

These meagre hints do not give a very precise picture of the early Byzantine monuments of Adrassus, but it is at least clear that they conform to the familiar norms of the region in having the eastern passage enclosing the apse (Churches 2 and 3), and at least one example (Church 3) of an extended chancel area defined by setting the side-chambers in front of the mouth of the apse.

BALABOLU (Adrassus), Necropolis Church (Building 9)[30]

A 'summary ground plan' and some cursory comments on this building constitute Section V of the Introduction to Alföldi-Rosenbaum's Necropolis Report. Both the plan and the attendant discussion are unsatisfactory, and there is little in either to suggest that the author had any real interest in this building, which is dismissed as being 'of a conventional type that does not need any discussion' (Alföldi-Rosenbaum 1980, 56).

The Necropolis Church appears to have been larger than any of the intra-mural churches. The horse-shoed apse measures 6.5 metres at its mouth, and the church as a whole measures 29 metres from east to west (without either narthex or eastern passage), and 17 metres from north to south. Sufficient foundations could be seen immediately to the west of the apse to establish that the church was divided into nave and aisles: this observation is reinforced by the presence of an acanthus pilaster capital. The positions of the three doorways in the west wall of the church could be positively determined from the simply moulded doorjambs which were still in place. The presence of a narthex is indicated, but no details of its width or outside appearance were noted, because of the difficulty of the terrain. One interesting feature in the narthex is the presence just north of the central doorway into the nave of a semi-circular niche containing a bowl on a pedestal. The niche, pedestal, and bowl are carved from one block of limestone. This caused Alföldi-Rosenbaum some problems of identification: 'I have not found anything like this in other roughly

---

[30] Alföldi-Rosenbaum 1980, 52-6, figures 1, 7-8, plates 52-7; Feld 1963/64, 95.

contemporary churches, and I cannot offer any explanation for the purpose of this basin in a niche, which reminds one distantly of medieval baptismal or holy-water fonts' (Alföldi-Rosenbaum 1980, 55). The presence of what is surely a stoup in the narthex of a church which has no atrium, and, therefore no fountain, is hardly surprising, and may be compared, for example, with local examples in the East Church at Alahan and the North Church at Yanıkhan.

Study of what can be seen of the east end of this church reveals that it is not as uninteresting as Alföldi-Rosenbaum would have us believe. She suggests, somewhat hesitantly, that there may have been side-chambers, and there seem to be no grounds to doubt this. Certainty on this point can be reached not merely on the evidence of the flimsy wall which is shown to the north of the apse, but from the surviving indications of the sanctuary arrangements which are imperfectly understood by Alföldi-Rosenbaum. She notes in her text that the first bay to the west of the mouth of the apse was blocked on both sides of the nave, although, following the conventions she lays down for her plan, the latter would appear to cast doubt on this matter. It can, in fact, confidently be assumed that this church, like the intra-mural Church 1, had side-chambers which sit forward beyond the mouth of the apse, and communicated with the chancel area at the east end of the nave. The plan and text also indicate the course of a north-south division crossing the nave between the first pair of piers or columns to the west of the apse. At its north end this runs up against 'a kind of console' on the second support in the nave. Alföldi-Rosenbaum observes sadly: 'Here again, we cannot give an explanation'. By combining the information in her figure 8 (detail B) and plates LIV 3, LV, and LVI, with the confused indications in the text, it is possible to conclude that this church was probably fitted with a chancel screen very similar in appearance and position to that fitted in the Funerary Basilica extra muros at nearby Dağ Pazarı (figure 29). Further support for this idea may be derived from the fragments of decorated screens which Alföldi-Rosenbaum publishes in her plates which are, as she herself observes, similar in appearance, if inferior in execution, to the fragments of chancel screen found in the West Church at Alahan. The apse is described as being enclosed in a rectangle. On the main plan of the church (figure 7) a gap of less than a metre is shown between the outside of the apse and the east wall of the church. On the general plan of the necropolis (figure 1) the gap is much larger. It is most likely, therefore, that this church was equipped with an eastern passage.

BATISANDAL, Basilica (plates 19-21)[31]
Batısandal is a small village which stands on the road to Öküzlü just after the left turning off the road from Limonlu to Canbazlı, which is taken 2 kilometres

---

[31] Hild and Hellenkemper 1986, 78-9, fig. 12, plates 101-4; Hild and Hellenkemper 1990, 212; Hill 1984, 189-91.

south of Yanıkhan. The ruins at Batısandal consist of some domestic buildings, the basilica which stands immediately to the north of the road on the east side of the village, and a necropolis with sarcophagi on the southwest sides of the village.   Only the east end of the church is preserved above ground, but sufficient of this survives to allow some useful observations. The church was of squat plan (somewhat similar to Akdam), with overall dimensions of about 14.5 by 14 metres without the narthex which was originally provided. The apse, which is 4.15 metres wide is very well preserved, although three large blocks have fallen from the centre of its semi-dome.

The plan of the east end of this church may be compared with that of the West Church at Alahan and Church 1 at Kanlıdivane, in that the apse is contained within the east wall of the church, which is also the east wall of the side-chambers. These side-chambers project beyond the mouth of the apse, but, as at Kanlıdivane, the walls of the side-chambers are set slightly to the outside of the sides of the apse so as to define an area which is wider than the mouth of the apse. There were niches in the walls of the side-chambers against the apse. The western sides of both side-chambers have fallen, and it is impossible to determine whether there were doorways between the aisles and the side-chambers, but it seems most likely that, as is shown in the plan drawn by Hild and Hellenkemper, the side-chambers were, in effect, open extensions of the aisles. In this church the side-chambers were rectangular, whereas in Church 1 at Kanlıdivane the walls between the apse and the side-chambers follow the curve of the apse. The Basilica at Batısandal originally had galleries over the aisles, and an upper floor over the side-chambers. The apse was lit by a double arched window, and there are small rectangular windows in the east wall of the church, which once lit the side-chambers. The building techniques employed in this church are typical of the region: the apse is constructed from large, well-dressed, ashlars; other surviving parts of the building consist of small stones facing a rubble and mortar core. Columns which had been re-cut for use as water-troughs could be seen in the village, and may have originated from this basilica.

This basilica would seem to belong to the group of Cilician basilicas in which the side-chambers are set forward from the mouth of the apse in order to define the area of the sanctuary. There is one important peculiarity which must be mentioned in this respect, although we have no means of telling whether it is a primary feature of the church. At the same level as the window sills, set into the north side of the curve of the apse just at its mouth, are two sockets (plate 20): the inner socket is rectangular, but the outer one takes the form of a slot shaped like an inverted L. It would have been possible to insert a beam into this slot horizontally, and then secure it into position by dropping it down into the bottom of the rear part of the slot. The arrangement was evidently designed to fix a wooden screen, or supports for curtains across the apse on a semi-permanent basis. If, as is commonly the case in Cilician basilicas, the altar stood on the chord of the apse, an arrangement to provide curtaining off of the altar at critical points in the service could have been an extremely useful church furnishing.

Hild and Hellenkemper (1986, 79) suggested a date in the sixth century on the basis of the decoration of the window-capitals, although they later (Hild and Hellenkemper 1990, 212) suggest either the fifth or sixth century as a possibility. The resemblance of the window capitals to capitals from Church 4 at Kanlıdivane leaves a date in the last quarter of the fifth century the earliest plausible suggestion for a date for this building.

BEY ÖREN[32]

This ruin-field lies well to the east of the road from Silifke to Uzuncaburç, about 7.5 kilometres northeast of Silifke. Keil and Wilhelm reported the existence here of a very ruined three-aisled basilica with a narrow narthex and a beautifully carved main door. They published a dedicatory inscription of one Photinos from the lintel of the door into the north aisle. The existence of this basilica was also noted by MacKay but it can no longer be seen.

BIÇKICI KALESİ[33]

This site, about 3 kilometres northnorthwest of Gazipaşa is mentioned briefly by Alföldi-Rosenbaum as probably being a 'fortified monastery'. She considered the church here to be medieval, and noted that it had a cistern, which was a late addition, under the east end of the north aisle. Hild and Hellenkemper confirm the monastic identification of the site, but consider that the original building of the church, which displays three building phases, may be attributed to the sixth century. The church, which is constructed from roughly coursed small limestone blocks, stands at the centre of the complex and is a three-aisled basilica with a narthex and a rounded apse. Nave and aisles were separated by piers, and there were galleries and side-chambers. The aisles were covered with barrel vaults in the manner of the Church J (the Monastic Church) at Corycus.

BİNGÜÇ[34]

Hild and Hellenkemper report a ruined early Byzantine church at Bingüç on the road from Adana to Çatalan, 15 kilometres southwest of Çatalan. The church is indicated by a column, worked stones and fragments of mosaics.

---

[32] Hild and Hellenkemper 1990, 214; Keil and Wilhelm 1931, 30; MacKay 1968, 821.
[33] Alföldi-Rosenbaum 1967, 68; Hild and Hellenkemper 1990, 215, plates 140-3.
[34] Hild and Hellenkemper 1990, 215.

BODRUM (Hierapolis Castabala)[35]

From being the capital of the Tarcondimotid dynasty in the late Hellenistic period, Hierapolis declined in importance under the Romans, and was quickly overshadowed by Anazarbus. As the name suggests, Hierapolis owed its importance to the shrine of Artemis Peraia, which was its major monument. The Christian remains at Bodrum, although of impressive proportions, reflect the gradual eclipse of the city, since both churches are entirely built of Classical spolia, most of which can be assigned to the third century. The site was first reported by Davis, who was there in 1875. It subsequently attracted various scholars, notably Bent, Heberdey and Wilhelm, and Bell. Dupont-Sommer and Robert have published a study of the cult at Hieropolis, which contains some photographs of the churches. More recently, Feld (1986) has analysed the two churches and Hellenkemper (1994) has produced new plans of them.

BODRUM (Hieropolis Castabala), North Church (Town Church)[36] (figure 12, plate 22):

The North Church or town church (measuring 33 by 17 metres) of which only the apse now stands is in most respects very similar to the South Church. The external appearance of both must have been virtually identical, a fact which may be verified from the presence in both churches of the curious, and hardly elegant, rows of large, square blocks which are such a feature of the east façades above the level of the windows. The same arrangement of a nave flanked by side-aisles which lead into the side-chambers which also communicate with the apse is present in both churches. The North Church was certainly equipped with galleries over the aisles. Gough observed traces of a courtyard on the north side of the building. The planning of the apse was identical. Here, however, all four sets of pier capitals, though still spolia, do match. In this church almost all the architectural sculpture consists of spolia from an earlier building. The exception is a window capital (Gough 1961, 171, plate 23) which has a central peacock and a pair of snakes on its upper edge. A date in the latter part of the fifth century would be reasonable for this piece.

What does distinguish this church from the South Church is that at some stage its interior was remodelled. Bell's plan clearly shows two pairs of cruciform piers which divided the nave into three bays with broad arches, in an arrangement somewhat reminiscent of Basilica A at R'safah (Krautheimer 1986, 155-6, figure 111), although here the eastern piers in the nave block part of the

---

[35] Bell 1906a, 4-6; Bent 1891, 233-5; Davis 1879, 128-34; Dupont-Sommer and Robert 1964; Feld 1965, 141; Feld 1986; Gough 1976, 392; Heberdey and Wilhelm 1896, 25-6; Hellenkemper 1994, figures 23-5; Hild, Hellenkemper and Hellenkemper-Salies 1984, 194-7; Hild and Hellenkemper 1990, 293-4.
[36] Bell 1906a, 4-6, figure 1; Feld 1965, 141; Feld 1986; Gough 1955a, 203, note 6; Gough 1961, 171, plate 23; Hellenkemper 1994, figures 23-4; Hild, Hellenkemper and Hellenkemper-Salies 1984, 194-8.

apse in a most unfortunate manner. The arches supported by the piers contained bricks: it is hard to think of another example of such construction in Cilicia, except in bath-houses and cisterns.

BODRUM (Hieropolis Castabala), South Church[37] (figure 13, plate 23)

This church stands outside the ancient settlement to the south. Its plan was first published by Heberdey and Wilhelm (1896, figure 3): a new, slightly revised, plan has recently been published by Hellenkemper (1994, figure 25), but there is no text with his new plan. A fuller discussion has been published by Feld (1986). The basilica measured 31 by 19 metres, excluding the narthex, and was a perfect example of a type of basilica common in Syria, and which was probably much more common in the Cilician Plain than the few surviving examples would suggest. The church consisted of a narthex across the west end, which was almost unrecognisable even when Heberdey and Wilhelm saw it, a nave with aisles separated by two rows of ten columns, and a semi-circular apse flanked by side-chambers, which are entered at the ends of the aisles and through doorways from the apse itself. There appears to have been a window at a high level immediately south of the mouth of the apse, and it is, therefore, likely that there were galleries over the aisles. The apse is polygonal on the outside, with three sides, each pierced by an arched window, projecting slightly beyond the main eastern building line of the basilica.

The most striking feature of this church is its complete lack of new building material. This is particularly noticeable in the east façade where all the mouldings, and the capitals which support the window arches are re-used stones, probably from a third century building. One particularly unfortunate aspect of this systematic re-use of spolia is that the two outer pier capitals on the apse do not match the inner pair, even in size. Given the conventional plan and the lack of newly carved decoration, it is hopeless to try to date this building, but it seems likely that it was contemporary with the other church, and that a date in the second half of the fifth century is therefore most likely.

BOĞŞAK ADASI (Nesulion)[38]

Byzantine remains on this island were first reported by Guyer and Bean and Mitford. Hild and Hellenkemper report domestic structures and a three-aisled early Byzantine basilica with apse and narthex, constructed from large and small limestone ashlars with a tiled roof. A window column with acanthus capital which probably belonged to the apse window is attributed by Hild and Hellenkemper to the second half of the fifth century. On the northeast side of the church, and communicating with it, is the small cross-shaped domical

---

[37] Bell 1906a, 4-6; Feld 1965, 141; Feld 1986; Heberdey and Wilhelm 1896, 25-6, figure 3; Hellenkemper 1994, figure 25; Hild, Hellenkemper and Hellenkemper-Salies 1984, 198.

[38] Bean and Mitford 1970, 195; Guyer 1950, 59, 69; Hild and Hellenkemper 1986, 37; Hild and Hellenkemper 1990, 367.

building with a projecting circular apse which was planned by Guyer (1950, figure 11b). The apse was lit by a double window (now much damaged) divided by a window column. Hild and Hellenkemper attribute this small chapel to the early sixth century. The central bay, which was originally covered by a dome on pendentives, is flanked by four vaulted arms, each 2.82 metres wide. On either side of the mouth of the apse, facing north and south under the vault in front of the apse, there are rectangular niches, and smaller semi-circular niches were set in the east and west walls of the north and south side-arms. Traces of the interior plaster may be seen. The purpose of the domical chapel is unknown and it is unlike any other early Byzantine church in Cilicia, though it may be compared with the domical structure at Akkale. Following Edwards' suggestion for Akkale (Edwards 1989), one is tempted to suggest that the chapel at Boğşak Adası was of funerary significance.

CACİK[39]

This ruin-site in the Taurus near the Cilician Gates (probably now Asar Kaya in Cacik Dere) is mentioned by de Jerphanion who recorded the presence here of three small churches (15 by 15 metres, 10 by 6 metres and 8 by 6 metres). All are described as having the same plan: there is a single door in the west wall, and a semi-circular apse is contained within the east wall which extends north and south to create side-chambers. There is no indication as to whether these structures were divided into nave and aisles, but this can hardly have been achieved in the smaller chapels.

CAFARLI[40]

Hild and Hellenkemper report two three-aisled early Byzantine basilica constructed from mortared limestone at this ancient settlement some 22 kilometres northnorthwest of Kadirli. One had traces of a round apse and a side-aisle with mosaic fragments.

CALOCORACESIUM see SUSANOĞLU

CANBAZLI

The village of Canbazlı, the ancient name of which is unknown, stands 7 kilometres southeast of Ura (Olba) on the ancient road from Corycus to Olba. The village was probably a dependency of the latter city. The site was first recorded by Bent. The major remains are the necropolis, which contains several handsome heroa, and the basilica, which stands on the southern side of the village. This last was the subject of study by Eyice. Keil and Wilhelm reported a second smaller basilica on top of a ridge on the north side of the settlement.

---

[39] Hild and Hellenkemper 1990, 220; De Jerphanion and Jalabert 1911, 299.
[40] Hild and Hellenkemper 1990, 221

CANBAZLI, Basilica[41] (figure 14, plates 24-7)

This building is one of the best preserved early Christian basilicas in Cilicia. The cornice at roof level survives on most of the outer walls of the church, and the arcade of the south gallery is still in position, although all the masonry has fallen from above it. The basilica stands in the centre of the north end of a precinct which is approximately 75 metres square. This was almost certainly the precinct of a Classical temple, and the basilica, which contains quantities of spolia, is constructed from the material of the pagan building.

The church measures approximately 29 by 22 metres overall, although the internal width of the nave plus aisles is 14.5 metres. This inconsistency is due to the unusual shape of the narthex, which will be discussed below. Nave and aisles were divided by two rows of six columns which supported arches. The pilaster capitals at the ends of the arcades may have been re-used, but the column capitals appear to have been cut for the building. Feld suggested that these very stylized acanthus capitals should be dated to the early sixth century, but this has rightly been questioned by Eyice, who wishes to give them an earlier date (Feld 1963/64, 98-9: Eyice 1979, 8). A date after the middle of the fifth century seems to have been accepted by Hild, Hellenkemper and Hellenkemper-Salies (1984, 252), though Hild and Hellenkemper state rather more cautiously (1990, 223) that the church is no later than the first half of the sixth century.

The south arcade survives at both ground and gallery level, and it is clear from slots in the lower parts of the gallery columns that a wooden parapet was originally provided at this level. The floors of the gallery and the first floors of the narthex and side-chambers were wooden: their joists rested on consoles which project from the outer walls. Transverse arches across the side-chambers were presumably meant to provide extra support for the floor joists of the upper storeys of these rooms. There was a wooden staircase at the north end of the narthex.

The apse was lit by a double arched window. Its central pier has fallen, but Eyice found a column of the correct size in the nearby cemetery: this had holes for the fixing of window grills. A single-tiered stone synthronum was set in the curve of the apse. The east wall of the building contains the apse, and as the side-chambers are rectangular, parts of the east wall are extremely thick. The bema extends for 2.2 metres in front of the apse, and is raised slightly above the level of the nave floor. In this church the side-chambers are also set forward from the mouth of the apse, so that their walls define the north and south sides of the chancel. The moulding at the base of the gallery colonnade runs right up to the mouth of the apse, and proves that in this building there was no triumphal

---

[41] Bent 1891, 219; Eyice 1979; Feld 1963-64, 98-9; Forsyth 1961, 135; Hill 1981, 29; Hild, Hellenkemper and Hellenkemper-Salies 1984, 250-2; Hild and Hellenkemper 1990, 223; Keil and Wilhelm 1931, 36-9, figures 62-3, plates 58-61.

arch at the mouth of the chancel. The side-chambers have doors which connect with both the aisles and the chancel. The south side-chamber projects further south than the aisle, and is, therefore, larger than its northern equivalent; it is also distinguished by the provision of a cupboard in its north wall in the thickness of the wall against the apse. Both side-chambers are lit by windows in the east façade; the south side-chamber also has a south-facing window. Apart from a door into the middle of the north aisle, the north wall, presumably in deference to the climate in winter, was left completely plain, but there is a mass of windows in the south elevation, where three single windows pierce the wall at ground level, and five pairs of windows light the gallery. The doorways and windows in this church are remarkable for their lack of decoration, and are all trabeated. Only the main doorway into the nave was enlivened by having a cross carved above it.

It is clear that the entire church was covered by a simple timber and tile roof. Parts of the cornice are still present on the tops of the east and west façades, and these show that there were low-pitched gables at both ends of the building. The east wall of the church rises above the apex of the semi-dome of the apse, which is simply included under the main roof.

In essence, then, this is a three-aisled basilica with narthex and side-chambers, but there is a striking peculiarity in its plan, which puzzled Keil and Wilhelm. Without excavation it is not possible to determine to what extent the church-builders re-used earlier foundations, but it may well be that some of the oddities in planning, including the eccentric orientation, could be explained as the result of such activity. The major peculiarity is the shape of the narthex which extends beyond the outer walls of the aisles, and has entrances from east and west at its north and south ends in addition to the arcaded central part of the west façade. Furthermore, the northern end of the narthex is wider than the southern end (7 metres as opposed to 5 metres). Keil and Wilhelm showed the west wall of the narthex bending to take account of this reduction in width, and this curious feature is reproduced by Eyice, who passes over it without comment. Feld, however, did query the suggestion made by Keil and Wilhelm, in support of which no precise evidence is adduced, that the narthex was a later addition to the church. The proposal was contradicted emphatically by Eyice (Eyice 1979, 8). Feld's point is that the re-used pilaster capital in the narthex matches those at the both ends of the south aisle, which could hardly be in a secondary position. This evidence, whilst it may support the argument that this church was provided with a narthex when it was built, does not demonstrate conclusively that the narthex, as presently constituted, has exactly the same plan as when it was first erected. Here the point about the possible re-use of earlier foundations assumes critical importance. It is, of course, particularly unfortunate in this respect that the central section of the narthex has fallen, not least because its rubble chokes the area where the plan is in doubt, but it is nevertheless possible to see the remains of a wall which once ran across the narthex in continuation of the line of the stylobate of the south arcade inside the church. Part of this footing continues beyond the present west wall of the church, and there is the stub of a return northwards visible just at the point where it comes into line with the northwest corner of the narthex. There was, therefore, at some stage a separate chamber at the southwest corner of the church which was narrower than the main part of the narthex to the north of it. This southern chamber is virtually intact, and in its floor can be seen what appears to be the top of a cistern, or water tank. It is at least possible that this southern chamber was used as a baptistery, which could be entered from the narthex, from the south aisle, or even directly from outside the building. Considerations of symmetry may have dictated the northern extension of the narthex, but in this building, where the south side-chamber is similarly eccentric, such considerations would not appear to have been paramount. A more practical reason may, therefore, be more likely. The narthex must have been two storeys high, since the doors at the west ends of the galleries are still preserved. Access to these was gained by way of a wooden staircase set at the north end of the narthex. Since this was already truncated at its south end by the chamber which I have suggested may have been the baptistery, it would have been entirely logical for the architects to have decided to extend the north end of the narthex, so as not to reduce accommodation for catechumens even further. The original appearance of the west façade may thus have been somewhat lop-sided, with the narthex displaced northwards from its normal central position. We cannot guess what the original provision of entrances may have been, and it is even very difficult to work this out for the secondary phase of the narthex, when the west wall was re-aligned. Keil and Wilhelm's plan shows a mixture of piers and door-jambs ranged along a dotted lines, and they give vague indications in their text that there might have been two wide arches flanking a central doorway. This is hardly likely on aesthetic grounds, and in any event Keil and Wilhelm are trying to make architectural sense out of what is probably nothing more than a coarse secondary infill thrown up after the original west end of the basilica had been damaged. The simplest explanation of the surviving arrangements at the west end of the church is that there were three doorways, corresponding roughly to the nave and aisles, set into a wall in which spolia, including pier capitals, were re-used haphazardly. The presence of the pier capitals which can hardly be in their original positions, even in terms of the architectural history of the church, suggests the original northern portion of the narthex façade may well have been arcaded in the normal Cilician manner. If the capitals are in their correct positions, there must surely have been five arches in the narthex portal. Eyice published drawings of three hypothetical reconstructions of the west façade (Eyice 1979, 4-5, figures 7A-C x). These are not entirely satisfactory since the west façade is drawn as a straight line, and, since he overlooks the evidence of the reconstruction of the narthex, Eyice's drawings are certainly meant to refer to the second phase of the narthex, when its west wall was crooked. Eyice's figure 7A shows a system of five arches: as I have suggested this is the most obvious explanation of the existing pier capitals, but Eyice considers this possibility 'peu probable', and goes on to say that 'Cette disposition n'est point representée ici, en Cilicie'. But there was a five-arched portal in the Tomb Church at Corycus, and there was probably one on the Basilica of St Thecla at Meryemlık. The five-arched portal is the only solution which suits both the pier capitals, and the jambs at the centre of the portal which would rest conveniently against the central arch. Eyice's two other solutions are much less likely, although he himself prefers his drawing 7C in which there are three high arches, with a free-standing architrave occupying the central part of the central arch.

To attempt to date this building precisely is probably a hopeless undertaking. Feld's suggestion of a date in the early sixth century is open to the objection that this seems an inappropriate historical context in this particular province. His date, indeed, would seem altogether more appropriate for the apparently bodged repairs to the west end of the church. Given the good state of preservation of the precinct wall, which can hardly be later than the third century, and might well be earlier, and the extensive re-use of building materials in the church, one is actually tempted to suggest that the basilica at Canbazlı might have been built somewhat earlier, perhaps in the fifth century, but such a suggestion is based on little more objective evidence than was Feld's. It is, in any event, unnecessary to follow Forsyth in saying that the church cannot be earlier than the sixth century because of the advanced nature of its planning. This is in fact less advanced that the similar design of the West Church at Alahan, which is firmly dated to the late fifth century. Eyice noted that the few decorative elements of the church were all of types which had a long currency, but felt that in order to accommodate the capitals of the narthex the church should be assigned to the second half of the fourth, or to the fifth century (Eyice 1979, 8).

CANBAZLI, Small Church[42]
Keil and Wilhelm reported a small church (14.4 by 8.6 metres) constructed from large blocks about 100 metres east of the large basilica. There was an apsidal nave flanked by a single aisle on the north side. Hild, Hellenkemper and Hellenkemper-Salies (1984, 252, figure 29) publish a plan drawn from Keil's sketchbook, which shows doorways in the south and west walls of the nave, and a single column separating the nave and north aisle.

---

[42] Eyice 1979, 2; Keil and Wilhelm 1931, 39, plate 16; Hild, Hellenkemper and Hellenkemper-Salies 1984, 252, figure 29.

CANBAZLI, Cemetery Church[43]

A church of reasonable size with a narthex (17.5 metres long overall) was found by Keil and Wilhelm in the cemetery on the northeast side of the settlement (1931, 34, 36). The walls were partly built of polygonal masonry, and there was a synthronum in the apse. Eyice reported that only a part of the curve of the apse was visible in 1973 (1979, 2). Hild, Hellenkemper and Hellenkemper-Salies report that the church is now buried.

CANYTELA see KANLIDİVANE

CARALLIA see GÜNEY KALESİ

CASTABALA see BODRUM

CELENDERIS see AYDINCIK

CENNET CEHENNEM (Corycian Cave)[44], (Cenet Deresi)

The Corycian Cave is situated 5 kilometres to the west of Corycus, 1 kilometre inland from the little harbour of Narlikuyu. The cave, which is a natural collapsed limestone cavern, was famous in antiquity as the prison of Typhon, and had a temple of Zeus on its lip. The cave was also famous as an ideal habitat for the crocuses, the saffron from which was exported from Corycus. In the late Roman period, the temple at the lip of the cavern was converted into a church, and a second church was constructed in the bottom of the cavern, actually in the mouth of the underground cave proper. To the west of the Temple-Church can still be seen extensive traces of domestic buildings of the late Roman period.

CENNET CEHENNEM (Corycian Cave), Temple-Church[45] (figure 15, plates 28-30)

The first detailed reports on this building were published by Bent. Unfortunately the structure suffered considerably at his hands, since in his zeal to collect inscriptions he enthusiastically demolished what he termed the 'late, Christian addition'. Later epigraphers were to doubt quite how scrupulous Bent was in identifying even the pagan masonry, and there is no reason to doubt that Bent's actions have destroyed vital evidence concerning the east end of what has turned out to be an unexpectedly complicated church.

---

[43] Eyice 1979, 2; Keil and Wilhelm 1931, 36, plate 16; Hild, Hellenkemper and Hellenkemper-Salies 1984, 252.
[44] Hild and Hellenkemper 1990, 314-5.
[45] Bell 1906, 29; Bent 1891, 214; Keil and Wilhelm 1931, 216-7, figure 167; Feld and Weber 1967, 254-78, figures 1-5; Hild and Hellenkemper 1990, 314-5.

The building has been described by Keil and Wilhelm, and, more recently by Feld and Weber, but its complexities are still not fully understood. The church measures approximately 39 by 23 metres overall, and it is clear that a new south wall was built on the foundations of the old peribolus wall, but that the north wall of the cella was incorporated in the church. The incorporation of this northern wall is demonstrated most dramatically by the change from large dressed ashlars to coarser small stones in its highest courses. The apse was constructed between the antae of the temple, and a further east wall was constructed 1.8 metres beyond the outer face of the apse. It was this last eastern wall which suffered particularly badly at the hands of Bent. No columns survive from the interior of the building, but traces of the stylobates, especially that of the south colonnade have been reported, and it is clear that the basilica was divided into nave and aisles. Beam-holes in the north wall show that there were galleries with timber floors over the aisles. There was no narthex, but since the precinct wall of the temple was retained 17 metres to the west of the church, there was, in effect, some provision for a fore-court. Three doorways in the west wall let into the nave and aisles.

Arrangements at the east end of the basilica are less clear. A passage ran across the outside of the apse. One corbel which is still in position, and more corbels and beam-holes which were seen by Bell in 1905, show that this passage had two storeys. There is no trace of walls which could have divided this part of the building to provide separate side-chambers, although the arches which sprang from east to west across the passage would have had some slight compartmentalizing effect. A small door in the north side of the apse allowed communication between the apse and the eastern passage. The apse was not provided with windows, but did have a single-tiered synthronum around its inner face.

The main problem with this building is that of the interpretation of the dispositions in the area of the chancel. Keil and Wilhelm and also Feld and Weber clearly show the stylobate of the south colonnade stopping short some 5.5 metres west of the apse. Feld and Weber were also able to show the north-south element shown in Keil and Wilhelm's plan was in fact the basis of a chancel screen placed across the nave between the ends of the colonnades. Keil and Wilhelm planned a southern return to the stylobate, which Feld and Weber confirmed. In the latters' plan, this appears as a heavier foundation than the chancel-screen, and has a square base resting on it 1.5 metres south of the end of the east-west stylobate. Feld and Weber do not explain this feature, and seem to have been somewhat puzzled by this part of the church. There are, however, two other features of this part of the building which can here be adduced in order to produce a coherent picture. There is a row of beam-holes for the supports for the floor of the south gallery which stop at the same point in the church as the southern colonnade (plate 30). Furthermore, there is no sign in the surviving parts of the east walls of the church that the colonnades ever came up against them. It is evident, therefore, that this church was equipped with a transept over 5 metres wide in front of the apse. The base at the end of the south aisle suggests that the colonnades in the nave may have turned through 90 degrees to meet the outside walls of the building. If this was the case, then the plan would have been similar in many ways to that of the Southwest Church at Anavarza, although this could not be categorized as a cross transept since there are no arms which project beyond the outer walls of the aisles. Keil and Wilhelm were inclined to attribute the conversion to the fourth century: the idea is attractive since in places the masonry may be closely compared with that of the alterations to the temple at Ayaş. Feld and Weber considered that a date at the end of the fifth century was more likely, and this was accepted by Hild, Hellenkemper and Hellenkemper-Salies.

CENNET CEHENNEM (Corycian Cave), Chapel of St Mary[46] (figure 16, plates 31-2)

This charming small church (12.4 by 6.7 metres) is perfectly preserved in the very mouth of the Corycian Cave. Tchihatcheff reported that the building was in use as a mosque in the 1850s. For a period in the 1970s the building was used as a tea-shop. A quatrain inscribed over the entrance still records the dedication of the church to the Virgin by one Paul (Hicks 1891, 242), revised by Keil and Wilhelm (1931, 219):

῞Ωσπερ Θεὸν ἐδέξω τὸν ἀχώρητον Λόγον,
χαίρουσα μεικροῖς ἐνκατώκησον δόμοις,
οἷς Παῦλος ἀνήγειρε θεράπων ὁ σὸς καμών,
τὸν παῖδα τὸν σὸν Χριστὸν ἐκμιμουμένη.

Hicks, for whatever reason, thought that the dedication was probably made in the fourth century.

The first serious attempt to record the building was made by Gertrude Bell in 1905. She, however, was insistent that it was originally provided with a stone barrel-vaulted roof. Bell was able to confirm the observation originally made by Tchihatcheff, that there were wall-paintings in the apse, which she identified as the Virgin flanked by rows of saints. The site abounds with masonry debris since the church is built on, and from, the Hellenistic wall which once blocked the mouth of the cave, but there is absolutely no evidence to suggest that this church once had a stone roof which has fallen down. Keil and Wilhelm proved this point very laboriously, and produced a plan and an elevation of the building. Their plan has been revised by Eyice.

---

[46] Bell 1906, 30-1; Bent 1891, 212-3; Eyice 1971, 330-1, figure 4; Feld 1963/64, 102-3; Hicks 1891, 242; Hild, Hellenkemper and Hellenkemper-Salies 1984, 225-6; Hild and Hellenkemper 1990, 314; Keil and Wilhelm 1931, 217-9, figure 171; Tchihatcheff 1854, 127-34.

This church provides the only certain instance in Cilicia of a single naved church with a tripartite east end (one of the churches at Cacik may have had a similar plan). The side-chambers, uniquely, are roofed with domical vaults (plate 32). These domical vaults, like the semi-dome of the apse, sit on simple triangular blocks of masonry which serve in place of squinches or pendentives. The effect is most striking in the apse where, at 2.2 metres above ground level, the triangular block suddenly converts the rectangle to a semi-circle. The nearest surviving parallel for such an arrangement is to be found on the other side of the Taurus in the great monastic church of Mahalaç, on the summit of Kara Dağ (Ramsay and Bell 1909, 241), but the dome of the eastern chamber in the South Church at Yanıkhan was supported in the same way. Immediately above these awkward triangular infills sits a heavy moulding which runs round the curve of the apse, turns onto the east wall of the nave and then stops. The apse displays a further eccentricity at its mouth. Monolithic piers provide jambs for the doors into the side-chambers from both the nave and the apse, as well as supporting the horse-shoed semi-dome of the apse. Rows of six small arcaded windows are set in the north and south walls. By virtue of its position, the church is naturally gloomy, but these tiny windows do little to increase the amount of light reaching the nave. The windows in the south wall are in fact quite pointless in this sense since they look directly into the depths of the cave. It must be assumed, therefore, that the windows are intended to be decorative rather than functional. The same appears to be true of the cornice which runs round the top of the north, west, and south walls of the church. The upper side of this is perfectly smooth, and shows no sign of ever having supported a roof of either masonry or timber. The former is out of the question, since it is inconceivable that it could have left no trace of its former presence: even a wooden roof would have been awkward because of the change of levels at the mouth of the apse, and there is no trace of anything ever having rested against the east wall of the nave. In practice, a roof would neither have been necessary nor desirable. The church is well protected from the elements by the overhanging roof of the cave, and any form of roofing would have blocked out what little daylight percolates to this depth.

Many of the elements of this church can reasonably be classified as primitive: the plan, and some of the details, particularly the lines of arched windows, would have been quite at home in Syria, and the simple supports for the domes find their nearest parallel in a fourth century building. It may, therefore, be relevant to note that Butler once drew attention to the similarity between early Byzantine basilicas in Syria, with their tripartite east ends, and a group of temples of which that at Is-Sanamen is probably the most famous example (Butler 1906, 413-23). The superstructure of the church at Cennet Cehennem is actually closer to the temples than any of the Syrian examples cited by Butler, since it shares with them the feature of having the raised roof over the apse, which caused Butler to wonder whether the main parts of the temples were left unroofed. The point Butler wished to make was that it would be foolish to assume that churches with advanced plans (i.e. the tripartite east ends) had to be later than more simply planned churches. This point seems all the more relevant to this particular church, and causes one to feel that Hicks' early date may well be correct. Hild, Hellenkemper and Hellenkemper-Salies (1984, 226), however, opt for a date in the sixth century on the evidence of the windows and their arcaded moulding.

CIVIKLI[47]

Hild and Hellenkemper report an early Byzantine church with a decorated limestone door-frame and part of an apse mosaic which they attribute to the sixth century at Cıvıklı, 10 kilometres northeast of Baka and southwest of Saimbeyli.

CORASIUM see SUSANOĞLU

CORYCIUM ANTRUM see CENNET CEHENNEM

CORYCUS (Kızkalesi)[48]

The site of the ancient city of Corycus preserves more important early Byzantine basilicas than any other site in Cilicia. The city evidently prospered in the late Roman period, though it seems to have been relatively obscure in the early Roman empire. Now a small village which has been developed as a tourist centre, the site has had a very long continuous history since it was occupied in the medieval period, when, as Curco, it was visited by the Crusaders. Its two castles are ample testament to the importance of Corycus in the late Roman and Armenian periods. The complicated history of the city is well documented by its churches and chapels.

Although the site is so well-known, and so convenient of access, it is very imperfectly published and understood. Gertrude Bell, who rushed through in 1905, was the first to describe the churches in any detail, and her work was followed up in 1907 by Herzfeld and Guyer, who conducted a season of survey and excavation at the site. Their publication, which eventually appeared in 1930, is, unfortunately riddled with inaccuracies and is particularly bedevilled by Guyer's considerable ignorance of the early Christian architecture of the rest of Rough Cilicia. This leads him to various impossible conclusions about the dating of the churches. Worse still, it is often impossible to verify Guyer's descriptions of parts of building which still survive: the kindest explanation for

[47] Hild and Hellenkemper 1986, 99, plates 156-7; Hild and Hellenkemper 1990, 228.
[48] Bell 1907, 7-22, figures 1-20; Herzfeld and Guyer 1930, xi-xii, 90-189, figures 86-204; Forsyth 1957, 225-8, figures 5, 7; Forsyth 1961, 132, 136-7; Hellenkemper 1994, 215; Hild, Hellenkemper and Hellenkemper-Salies 1984, 209-22; Hild and Hellenkemper 1990, 315-20; Keil and Wilhelm 1931, 120-213.

this would be to suggest that confusion set in during the 23 years between fieldwork and excavation, but it sometimes appears that Guyer's too firmly fixed preconceptions led him to look only for evidence which supported his architectural theories. Herzfeld and Guyer worked in collaboration with Keil and Wilhelm who conducted an epigraphical survey of the cemeteries of Corycus.

Apart from Forsyth, who has made a few brief comments, modern archaeologists and architectural historians appear largely to have ignored Corycus, and the site receives relatively brief treatment in the various publications of Hild and Hellenkemper. The early Christian churches here, which are generally still well preserved, display every variation in basilical planning known to the highly inventive early Christian architects of Cilicia, and, although they are not considered here, the medieval chapels are also of interest since they serve as a canon with which other undatable small chapels in the region may be compared. A thorough new survey of the monuments at Corycus would represent a major contribution to our understanding of early Byzantine ecclesiastical, domestic and defensive architecture.

CORYCUS (Kızkalesi), Church A, ('Cathedral')[49] (figure 17, plate 33)

This church stands on the higher ground to the northeast of the Land Castle. Only the northern half of the apse and part of the north wall can be seen today, but it is likely that excavation would reveal much more of the church since it is buried by at least 2 metres of rubble. Guyer conducted limited excavations, and has described the church at some length, although he did not adequately examine or understand the east end of the building.

This was a large basilica, measuring approximately 45 metres from the west wall of the narthex to the outside of the apse, and 21 metres from north to south. There was no atrium as such, but there does seem to have been a large open space to the west of the church.

The narthex followed the conventional Cilician pattern, but with the addition of a small apse at the north end, which Guyer suggested was a secondary feature. It is certainly the case that this abuts the north wall of the church, but its masonry is identical, and there is nothing to suggest that the north wall of the narthex has at any point suffered a secondary breaching. Since the basilica is cut into the rock on its north side, it is inconceivable that there could have been a doorway in this position, and I think that it is most likely that this little apse was an original feature. There is an apse, after all, at the southern end of the narthex of the Tomb Church at Corycus, which appears to have contained a water tank. The apse in the narthex of this church may also have been a large stoup, served perhaps by the cistern immediately north of the church. Guyer

---

[49] Forsyth 1961, 135, 137; Gough 1972, 211; Herzfeld and Guyer 1930, 94-108, figures 87-107; Hild, Hellenkemper and Hellenkemper-Salies 1984, 210-2; Hill 1981, 33.

recorded foundations which ran across the narthex in line with the colonnades of the nave. He suggested that the narthex might, therefore, have been divided into rooms in the Lycaonian manner, but Herzfeld's plan shows narrow pilasters, on the line of these foundations, against the east and west walls of the narthex which must, accordingly, have been open for its full length. Foundations in the Roman buildings are often constructed across openings, and it is no surprise to find them here.

The body of the church was divided into nave and aisles by rows of Proconnesian marble columns which supported limestone acanthus capitals. This slightly surprising combination suggests that the columns may have been in secondary use. The nave was 9 metres wide, exactly twice the width of the aisles. Guyer reported confidently: 'Sicher war diese Kirche flachgedeckt; von Emporen hat sich nichts vorgefunden' (Herzfeld and Guyer 1930, 97). During the long time lag between excavation in 1907 and publication in 1930, he appears to have forgotten the depth of overburden in this church. The doorways in the apse walls are buried in rubble up to the height of their lintels: the floor of the apse must, therefore, be at least 2 metres below present ground level. The apse, which is high by any standards, is thus quite out of proportion to a church without galleries or a clerestory. The north wall is similarly buried, and, allowing for the fact that the nave floor was lower than that of the apse, the long slot in the inner face of the north wall, which is about 1.5 metres above current ground level, must be around 4 metres above the original floor, in exactly the position which would suggest that it was intended to take the joists of the floor of the gallery above the north aisle. Even if a gallery was included, the height of the apse is such that it could have accommodated a clerestory over the nave.

Guyer's interpretation of the plan at the east end of the nave cannot be reconciled with the surviving remains. Herzfeld and Guyer found a pier in the eastern part of the north arcade, standing 5.8 metres to the west of the apse. Between this pier and the east wall of the nave they found one stone, which they suggested was a column base. Since this was off centre, they proposed that there must have been a matching pier against the east wall, and that there were two arches at the east end of the north arcade separated from the rest of the arcade by the free-standing pier. Only the north arcade was excavated, and whilst the free-standing pier is clearly shown on Herzfeld's excavation plan, the proposed eastern one is merely indicated by a broken line on the reconstruction drawing of the apse (Herzfeld and Guyer 1931, figures 87 and 90). An irregularity in the east wall of the nave which appears on the reconstruction drawing, at the point where the eastern pier would have been attached, might be thought to support Guyer's proposal were it not for the fact that this section of wall is still standing, and is perfectly smooth. Furthermore, at precisely the point where Guyer's pier should be attached, there is a square hole at the same height as the slot in the north wall which evidently supported the floor of the gallery over the north aisle. Close examination of Herzfeld's plan suggests that the continuation of the stylobate beyond the free-standing pier was as hypothetical as the eastern pier, and suggested only by the oddly positioned stone which was interpreted as a column base. It could equally well have been the base of a wooden upright which would have supported the wooden beam which apparently ran into the face of the east wall of the nave. The simplest explanation of these features would be to suggest that the arcades stopped at the free-standing pier, and that there was a transept in front of the apse. The wooden beam between the pier and the east wall of the nave could then be explained as part of a screen which enclosed the chancel area in front of the apse. Herzfeld and Guyer found parts of the stylobates of a chancel screen which ran across the nave between the free-standing piers (i.e. on the west side of the transept): it would also have been necessary to screen off the north and south sides of the chancel since the church had a passage around the back of the apse, and there were presumably occasions when crowds of people would have proceeded through this section of the basilica. The eastern passage, which is discussed below, was not recorded by Herzfeld and Guyer, but its presence, and that of a transept, explains another inconsistency in the published plans. In the excavation plan (Herzfeld and Guyer 1930, figure 87), and the detailed plan of the apse (Herzfeld and Guyer 1930, figure 90), a small return is shown against the north side of the free-standing pier. This surely indicates that a wide arch sprang across the east end of the aisle, dividing it from the transept, and supporting the end of the gallery floor. However, in the reconstruction plan which covers the whole building doorways are shown which correspond to those on the east side of the transept, which provided access to the eastern passage (Herzfeld and Guyer 1931, figure 88: this is reproduced without comment as Forsyth 1961, figure 22). There was obviously no evidence for the doorways north of the piers, and they would only make sense as entrances to side-chambers, but even in the reconstruction proposed by Herzfeld and Guyer these 'side-chambers' were open to the nave through double archways.

The inclusion of a continuous transept would resolve another of the problems in this building. A vertical face in the surviving section of wall beside the north corner of the apse, which commences at the level of the sima, appears to be one side of a window. It is far too high to have been a doorway, and is not directly above the doorway into the eastern passage. Symmetry would suggest that this may have been the south jamb of a window with three arches which was set above the level of the roof of the eastern passage. The position of this window corresponds to one which lit the transept of the 'Große Armenische Kirche' at Corycus. Its presence indicates that the roof over the transept must have been higher than the roof over the galleries, and., therefore, that the building must have had a transverse roofing system, which in all probability rose over a clerestory.

One problem which was noted by Forsyth remains: 'excavations... have revealed no cruciform piers such as would be necessary in order to support a triumphal arch between the nave and choir' (Forsyth 1961, 135). The absence of such piers is not entirely conclusive, since the return which supported the arch across the north aisle was butted against the pier at the east end of the arcade. Similarly, the supports for the triumphal arch in the Transept Church at Corycus stand against the piers of the arcades, and were interpreted by Guyer as the terminal elements of the chancel screen. If there was no triumphal arch in this church, the transept would have lost none of its transversality, and the beam which would have been required to support the roof in this part of the church would not have had to be any longer, or stronger, than those which spanned the nave.

The floor of the north aisle was decorated with opus sectile. There was a coloured, tesellated, mosaic pavement in the bema (ie the centre of the transept), which was raised a little above the nave. The central section of this mosaic included geometric patterns, but in the southern part of the bema and the apse Guyer found fragments of a depiction of the 'Peaceful Kingdom' of Isaiah. This section of the mosaic was laid facing south rather than west, an arrangement which is particularly awkward in the apse. In the southwestern part of the chancel was found the dedicatory inscription which is discussed below. The altar probably stood on this mosaic just west of the centre of the mouth of the apse. Guyer found four small column bases arranged in a square which perhaps supported a ciborium over the aisle.

A feature which Guyer interpreted as a synthronum ran round the inner face of the apse and across the doorways into the eastern passage. It cannot, therefore, be attributed to the first period of use of the church. Guyer also found slight foundations of walls which extended westwards from the mouth of the apse, and which he considered belonged to a late chapel which was erected within the nave against the original apse. Guyer's plan shows the western wall of this secondary chapel running across the chancel, but this position is purely conjectural, and it seems much more likely that the chapel would have extended further to the west. It is quite likely that Guyer's synthronon was in fact a secondary facing to the apse, which belonged to the later reduced chapel, and may have supported a lower semi-dome, perhaps after the original one had fallen. The primary apse was so tall that if the secondary chapel proposed by Guyer was actually built against it the walls would have been much taller than they were wide.

The original apse, which had no windows, was semi-circular on the inside, and polygonal on its outer face. Doorways in the walls of the apse led into the eastern passage. The walls of the apse stand much higher than any other part of the church, and show most clearly that it was constructed from re-used materials. The inner face of the apse is irregular, especially at the northern corner, and there are square holes throughout the surface. Guyer thought that these had been sockets for the supports for marble cladding, but the holes form no regular pattern, and the handsome capital beneath the sima moulding at the corner of the mouth of the apse is almost flush with the ashlar surface. It is clearly in re-use since it was originally a pilaster capital, and has its third face buried in the apse wall. A thin layer of plaster would have brought the surface up to the level of the capital, but it must nevertheless have looked slightly awkward with no pilaster to support it. This capital is carved from marble, unlike those of the nave, and has a central peacock flanked by rams' heads at the corners. Animal protomes are known from Alahan and Meryemlık, and it would be logical to expect this superior capital also to have belonged to a building of the late fifth century.

It is now impossible to determine the precise arrangement of the east end of the church, but the published plan is misleading. The north wall of the church continues eastward beyond the mouth of the apse, and there is a wall on a north-south alignment 3.5 metres to the east of the apse. The outer face of the apse, which is faced with small stones is polygonal in plan: Guyer noted that this was unusual, but thought that it must be an early feature. Since he could adduce no Cilician parallels his argument lacks authority. In the 'Cupola Church' at Meryemlık and Church 4 at Kanlıdivane, the outer face of the apse has flat angled sides. In both churches the passage followed the plan of the apse: excavation might thus reveal that here, too, the passage followed the shape of the apse. In any event, it is clear that this church did not have enclosed side-chambers at ground level.

Guyer thought that the Church was built early in the fifth century, and believed, because of its early date and central situation, that this must have been the Cathedral where the bishop of Corycus officiated (Herzfeld and Guyer 1930, 108). Guyer's proposed dating was based on his unconvincing ideas about the shape of the apse, and, more specifically, on the dedicatory inscription which he found in the mosaic floor of the chancel. This inscription records the gift of him οὗ τὸ ὄνομα ὁ κύριος γινώσκι and gives the date ↑ΜΑ. Guyer took this to mean that someone called Theognost made the dedication in the year 741 of the Seleucid era, that is AD 429/30. The case for deriving a name in this cryptic fashion is thoroughly dubious, since the formula is well known from several churches in the area (e.g. Dağ Pazarı Funerary Church), and Forsyth has demonstrated that the number is actually 941, therefore AD 629/30 (Herzfeld and Guyer 1930, 107-8: Forsyth 1961, 137, note 32). The problem is also discussed by Hild, Hellenkemper and Hellenkemper-Salies (1984, 211), who come down in favour of a fifth century date for the church on stylistic grounds. But the problem with the mosaic inscription is a crucial one since, if the seventh century date were correct, instead of standing fairly early in the history of Cilician ecclesiastical architecture, the 'Cathedral' at Corycus would be the latest positively dated basilica in the province.

Forsyth's reinterpretation of the date of the building would also appear to cast serious doubt on Guyer's suggestion that this was the Cathedral. 629/30 is precisely the year in which the Persians evacuated Asia Minor and Cilicia (Foss

1975, 744). It is not unreasonable to suggest that this church was built to replace an earlier Cathedral of Corycus which was sacked by the Persians, and includes whatever building materials could be usefully salvaged from the earlier building. These included the ashlars from which the apse is constructed, and also much of the decoration of the church. I have noted the odd combination of marble columns and limestone capitals in the nave, and also the oddly positioned fine marble capital at the north corner of the mouth of the apse. It is very likely that these have come from the earlier church. More surprisingly, perhaps, it would appear to be possible that the mosaic floor of the sanctuary has been moved. In this church it is the wrong way round, and it fits the apse extremely awkwardly, especially in relation to the synthronum. Its subject is one which appears to have been popular in the reign of Zeno (Gough 1972, 211), and as Hild and Hellenkemper indicate a fifth century date would be appropriate for the pavement. When we combine this observation with the evidence of the capitals which are so reminiscent of Alahan and Meryemlık, and the use of Proconnesian marble, there is a case to justify suggesting that the earlier 'Cathedral' may have been one of the products of the great building campaign in Cilicia during Zeno's reign. The late date and insecure historical context of this church might explain the absence of the triumphal arch, especially if relatively unskilled artisans were trying to reproduce, in haste, the fifth century cathedral.

The scanty remains of three basilicas can be seen immediately to the south of Guyer's 'Cathedral'. The southern of these (Church D) was referred to by Guyer as the 'Kirche uber der Zisterne', and very briefly described. Guyer never mentions the largest basilica (Church C) which stood between the other two. Churches C and D both had larger apses than Guyer's church, and one of them, therefore, may well have been the original Cathedral of Corycus.

CORYCUS (Kızkalesi), Church B (plate 45)

The apse of this church, which is not mentioned by Herzfeld and Guyer, is preserved about 25 metres south of the 'Cathedral'. The debris from this building covers an area of 20 by 50 metres. It is possible that excavation would uncover the full plan of the church, since its platform has been used as a base for cairns of small stones picked up during field clearances. The apse, which is 4 metres wide, was semi-circular on the inside, and inscribed within the eastern wall. It was probably lit by a double arched window, and there is an arched doorway in its north side which presumably led into a side-chamber. It is likely that there was a similar doorway on the south side. The semi-dome of the apse still retains an extensive covering of plaster and traces of painted figures can still be discerned.

A dripstone moulding runs across the outer face of the apse above the level of the window arches. Foundations of a wall 3.5 metres to the east of the outer face of the apse, and of the southeast corner of the building, show that there was an eastern passage.

CORYCUS (Kızkalesi), Church C

This stands about 20 metres south of Church B. Although it is extremely badly preserved, and has been largely covered by a greenhouse, it is possible to make out the rough outline of a large basilica. Numerous fragments of Proconnesian marble columns and capitals are strewn across the site, the latter being exact replicas of the capitals which Herzfeld and Guyer found in the sanctuary of the Basilica of St Thecla at Meryemlık (Herzfeld and Guyer 1930, 24-7; figures 24-7, 29-30). At the east end of the building traces of two apses can be seen. The lowest course of the north apse, which is 6 metres wide, and of a central apse, 10 or 12 metres wide and slightly to the west, have survived. There is a large deposit of rubble covering the probable site of the south apse. The plan of these apses would suggest that there were originally apsidal side-chambers flanking the main apse. Amongst the rubble which encumbers the central apse can be seen a large marble pier capital, decorated on two faces, and very similar to the pier capitals of the nucleus of the Tomb Church. This capital must have fallen from the angle at the mouth of the apse.

The site of the church has been extensively dug over, and the soil contains quantities of tesserae, presumably from mosaic pavements. The irrigation trenches which are cut through the building show that there is a deep build-up of masonry debris, and a thick black destruction layer, which suggests that the church may have been destroyed by fire. The question arises of whether this church or the Church B was the source of the re-used materials in the 'Cathedral'. Church B is closer, and may have been the source of the limestone capital in the nave, but most of the decorative details of the 'Cathedral', notably the marble columns and the peacock capital, are reminiscent of the surviving pieces of architectural sculpture of Church C. The seventh century builders of the 'cathedral' probably used the remains of both churches indiscriminately.

It is clear that there were at least four important basilicas at the centre of Corycus, two of which appear to belong to the fifth century. The quantities of Proconnesian marble, and the general richness of the sculpture of these churches is very reminiscent of the Sanctuary of St Thecla at Meryemlık. That complex certainly enjoyed imperial support, and it would not be surprising if a city as important as Corycus had also enjoyed preferential treatment.

CORYCUS (Kızkalesi), Church D ('Church over the Cistern')[50] (figure 22)

This church was situated about 70 metres south of the 'Cathedral', close to the south side of the modern road. It appears on Herzfeld's and Guyer's site plan to the north of the road, but there can be no doubt about its position, since the

---

[50] Herzfeld and Guyer 1930, 109-10, figure 108.

substructures which Guyer planned are still preserved. Guyer paid little attention to the building although he did provide a plan of the apse, which was 5 metres wide, and the substructure upon which it stands. Concerning the apse he noted merely that it was semi-circular in plan and lit by three arched windows. Only one block, at the north corner of the apse, has survived.

The substructure, however, is still well preserved. There is a roughly apsidal chamber measuring 3 by 4 metres immediately beneath the apse, and a larger chamber (9 by 7.5-6.75 metres) to the west. The larger chamber has a row of piers running centrally along its length. The barrel-vaulted roof consists of rectangular blocks supported by rib-arches, and is still intact. A similar substructure immediately to the south was one bay wide, and has lost its roof. Guyer noted an apsidal shape in the outer face of the west end of the substructures.

Guyer identified the substructures as a cistern. Traces of painting on the north wall of the larger chamber suggest, rather, that it was an undercroft or crypt. There is a wide arched opening at the west end of the northern substructure which leads into a passage which is choked with rubble. The two surviving substructures are also interconnected. The rambling plan of these inter-connected chambers is more suggestive of undercrofts than cisterns. Since the northern substructure so closely reflects the shape of the building above it, it is likely that the trapezoidal shape of the southern substructure, and the large apsidal curve at the west end also reflect the plans of walls which were once above them. The passage leading from the west side of the undercroft suggests that there was a further chamber, or chambers, to the west. The apsidal curve has a diameter of approximately 10 metres, and from the evidence of Guyer's plan alone, it would be possible to suggest that a large basilica once stood here, and that the apse seen above ground by Guyer was originally a subsidiary apse at the northern end of the eastern passage. The conclusion is strengthened by the fact that the area to the west is a level field which contains fragments of limestone columns and capitals.

CORYCUS (Kızkalesi), Church E[51]

Herzfeld's general plan of Corycus shows two churches just inside the walls in the northern part of the ancient city. Guyer mentions these very briefly, noting merely that in both churches the side-aisles ended in apses.

Church E is sited almost due north of the 'Cathedral'. This part of the ancient city is now intensively cultivated, and the church has been ploughed away to such an extent that it is now impossible to make out any details of the plan. It appears on Herzfeld's and Guyer's plan as a rectangular church, presumably a basilica, measuring about 25 by 15 metres, with three apses at its east end, and a narthex.

---

[51] Herzfeld and Guyer 1930, 110, figure 86.

CORYCUS (Kızkalesi), Church F[52]

This stands approximately 100 metres to the east of Church E. On the general site plan it is shown as a three-aisled basilica with three apses, measuring about 30 metres by 17 metres. The nave and aisles are now a lemon grove, but the central and southern apses are partially preserved. Several courses of the semi-dome of the central apse are still in position. There were no windows in the apse, and no moulding at the level of the springing of the semi-dome. As in Churches 2 and 3 at Kanlıdivane, there is a horizontal row of regularly spaced sockets in the inner face of the apse, just below the level of the springing of the semi-dome. At the corners of the mouth of the central apse can be seen the pilaster responds for the nave arcade: the eastern springing of the first arch of the south arcade is still in position.

The aisles terminated in apses, but there appear to have been no side-chambers as such. Several courses of the southern apse remain from which it can be seen that the sketch published by Herzfeld and Guyer is inaccurate. The southern apse is semi-circular on the inside, but is inscribed within a flat eastern wall which is keyed into the outer face of the main apse, which extends further to the east.

CORYCUS (Kızkalesi), Church G, Transept Church extra muros ('Querschiffbasilika extra muros')[53] (figure 18, plates 34-7)

This basilica is the most eastern of the churches on the road through the cemetery on the northeast side of Corycus. This is the street which Herzfeld and Guyer called the 'Via Sacra' or 'Graber Strasse'. Immediately to the northeast of the church can be seen the single remaining pier of a four-way arch which stood over the road. This was briefly described by Guyer, who considered that it marked the beginning of the cemetery on the approach to Corycus, and was contemporary with the Transept Church (Herzfeld and Guyer 1930, 124-6; figures 128-9). The Tetrapylon is exactly aligned with the east end of the Transept Church, and the two buildings appear to have been part of a single architectural scheme. This is an important point, since the Tetrapylon was covered by a masonry dome. Herzfeld discussed the archway separately in a later publication:

' ...pyramidal pendentives are but a variant of the spherical. The Muhammedan architects preferred them, because they have the advantage of occupying only part of the quarter circumference, while the spherical pendentive becomes awkward unless it is full.

[52] Herzfeld and Guyer 1930, 110, figure 86.
[53] Bell 1907, 3-10, figures 1-7; Forsyth 1961, 136, note 29; Herzfeld 1943, 55-6, figure 25; Herzfeld and Guyer 1930, 111-24, figures 109-27; Hild, Hellenkemper and Hellenkemper-Salies 1984, 216-7; Hill 1981, 33.

Figure 25 supports this strange thesis by an exceptional spherical pendentive, whose radius is not the diagonal radius of the room. It is the remains at Corycus, Cilicia[57] of a tetrapylon over a street leading from the east gate of the town to a number of churches and tombs.

Not a square pillar only, but two short sides of a right angle, ending in pilasters for the four archivolts, form the supporting piers. The radius of the pendentive, therefore, is determined by the "extrados" of the archivolts, and they would not touch the corners of the room in the diagonal, but would have at the level of the imposts of the archivolts an unsupported, triangular undersurface and would need a cylindrical support, filling the former between the pilasters from the floor up. To avoid this inconvenience, a niche has been hollowed out of the pendentive, which reduces the suspended undersurface to almost nothing. They function like corner niches over an octagonal transition dome, that is to say this rare solution is a hybrid crossing between the spherical pendentive and the octagonal transition dome.'

Footnote 57:

'See E Herzfeld and S Guyer (Meriamlik and Korykos.... Only the illustrations in that book are mine, the text is entirely Guyer's. It is unimportant, but to avoid the reproach of discrepancy between Guyer's description and mine, I must remark that I believe the two stones, visible to the right of my sketch to be a stone dome, while he assumes a wooden roof.' (Herzfeld 1943, 55-6).

It is ironic that Guyer, who was obsessed with masonry domes, should have suggested that the tetrapylon had a wooden roof, but this is one of the many errors which crept into his text in the decades between the fieldwork and publication. The surviving pier is important as evidence of the fact that the late Roman architects were so accomplished in designing domes that they could not only handle squinches and pendentives, but could also, when occasion demanded, combine the two. The point is of great importance for the understanding of the Cilician 'Domed Basilicas'. In this context it is of interest to note that here the masonry dome of a bay which was 9 metres square was supported by L-shaped piers which were only 51 centimetres thick.

The Transept Church was first described by Gertrude Bell who saw it in 1905, and it was studied in greater detail by Herzfeld and Guyer in 1907. It appears that parts of the church had deteriorated in the short period of time between their visits. Bell saw the capital of the west end of the north arcade in position. This capital, which was the exact counterpart of one at the east end of the south arcade in Church 4 at Kanlıdivane (plate 93), is neither illustrated nor mentioned by Herzfeld and Guyer. Bell's photographs also show more masonry in position in the southeastern part of the church, and it is clear from her text, that the northern pier in front of the apse was in a better state of preservation (Bell 1907, 4-6). Herzfeld and Guyer carried out very limited excavations, and published only a few new photographs. Their major contribution was a more detailed plan, but in respect to the piers which stand in front of the apse, Bell's plan still remains more useful.

The basilica measures approximately 60 by 20 metres overall. Herzfeld and Guyer established that the foundations seen by Bell at the west end of the complex were those of a small atrium. The atrium was the exact width of the church, and, together with the narthex, which serve as its east side, formed a perfect square. There were butt joints where the atrium met the west wall of the narthex, and it seems likely that the atrium had fallen into disrepair whilst the church was still in use, since there were buttresses against the south and west walls of the narthex, the latter being on the north stylobate of the atrium colonnade. There were entrances and colonnades on all three outer sides of the atrium. The east side consisted of the arcaded portal of the narthex. Guyer conjectured that the square chambers at the west end of the atrium might have supported towers: there are similar foundations at the north side of the atrium of the 'Cupola Church' at Meryemlık, but in both cases there is no evidence for the superstructure.

The narthex was entered through a triple-arched portal, and was certainly double-storied. The beginning of a stairway can still be seen climbing round the north end of the narthex. Three simple doorways communicated between the narthex and the interior of the church. The central doorway is larger than the others, and has a very shallow relieving arch above its lintel.

Nave and aisles were definitely divided by arcades supported on seven columns. Both bases of the pilasters at the ends of the arcades can still be seen on the west wall of the nave. There is no definitive evidence for galleries over the aisles, but their presence must be considered likely, since there were upper stories at both ends of the church. The south wall is much better preserved than the north wall and shows most of the articulation of doorways and windows at ground level. Two doorways were evenly spaced along the length of the south aisle, and had a triple arched window between them, and double-arched windows on either. Guyer noted that the window at the east end of the aisle was wider, but all the double-arched windows in the south wall are shown as being the same size in Herzfeld's plan (Herzfeld and Guyer 1930, 114; figure 109).

The most important features in the plan of this church are the piers which terminate the nave arcades. Their west faces stand 6.7 metres from the mouth of the apse. Guyer thought that these were T-shaped, and, as well as receiving the nave arcades, supported arches across the aisles, and across to the mouth of the apse. He found parts of the chancel screen which ran between the piers, and defined a choir in the area immediately in front of the apse. This seems to have consisted of a low parapet with an arched doorway at its centre. Part of a stylobate between the north pier and the mouth of the apse shows that the choir was no wider than the nave. Guyer thought that a pair of bases which stand against the piers, and convert them into a cruciform shape, were nothing more than the terminal elements of the chancel screen. He was puzzled by their size, and devised two ingenious theories to account for this, suggesting that they might either have been parts of a double ambo which was incorporated into the chancel screen, or else martyr's monuments (Herzfeld and Guyer 1930, 114-8; figure 116). In either event, Guyer was positive that there was no triumphal arch, and, presumably because he could see no pilasters against the mouth of the apse, that the piers must have supported the west springing of high arches which marked off the continuations of the aisles on either side of the choir bay in front of the apse.

Guyer's reconstruction thus includes a sort of primitive transept, which he thought was similar to that of the 'Cathedral' in having no triumphal arch, but with the distinction of open side-bays (Herzfeld and Guyer 1930, 114). Forsyth has taken the reconstruction a stage further:

'The question arises whether a fully developed tripartite transept can be found.... I know of only one church in the vicinity which may qualify, namely the "Transept Church extra muros" at Korikos. Its excavators believe that it had transept arms which opened out through large arches to left and right of the choir and which were higher than the aisles, but they are convinced that no triumphal arch divided the nave from the choir . . . We have seen the importance of a triumphal arch in defining the transverse space of a transept and in supporting the independent roof over it: a developed tripartite transept is hardly conceivable without such an arch. In the Korikos church are two large blocks which project into the nave. They are applied to the piers, now almost demolished, at the entrance to the choir and certainly seem designed to carry a triumphal arch. Since they are decorated with relief carving, however, Herzfeld and Guyer believe that they are the terminal elements of a chancel rail which divided the nave from the choir. Yet the massiveness of the blocks, which are as thick as the nave walls, is so inconsistent with a merely decorative purpose that the excavators themselves are puzzled to explain their size. Moreover, my own inspection of the blocks convinced me that they are earlier than the chancel rail, because the carved ornament on their faces has been partially destroyed by cuttings to receive the rail, and therefore that they were not intended as its terminal elements. A reasonable conclusion is that they were intended as bases for a triumphal arch, in which case the church probably possessed a fully developed tripartite transept' (Forsyth 1961, 136, note 29).

This 'reasonable conclusion' was reached by someone who had not seen the much better preserved elements of the transept at Öküzlü, which must dispel any lingering doubts that Cilician architects could design such things. The conclusion derives further support from Gertrude Bell's plan, for she shows the inner sides of the piers to have been rounded. This shape seems most appropriate for the lower courses of the triumphal arch, and, since the north pier at least was better preserved when she saw it, Bell's drawing of this detail deserves respect. The insertion of the chancel screen is not the only alteration in this part of the church. Guyer published a drawing of a section of opus sectile which was laid in new plaster over the original stylobate of the penultimate intercolumniation of the south arcade (Herzfeld and Guyer 1930, 120; figure 118). It is, then, highly likely that this church had a transept, into which a chancel screen was inserted, perhaps at the same time as the re-laying of the floor. It is interesting to note that the north and south bays of the transept were not included in the choir: this suggests that access to whatever lay to the east was, or became, more important than the architectural integrity of the transept. The purpose of the high arches between the triumphal arch and the mouth of the apse is unclear to me. They are presumably the elements which cause Forsyth to define the transept as 'tripartite', although it does not exactly meet Krautheimer's definition, 'a centre bay continuing the nave together with wings, as high as the nave or lower, but always separated from the centre bay by colonnades' (Krautheimer 1986, 521). It was thus the chancel screen rather than the high arches which gave this transept its tripartite character. That the arches were not essential can be seen from Öküzlü, and it is difficult to see how they would have related to a gabled transverse roof. There is at least a possibility, therefore, that these arches might have supported a wooden pyramid over the centre of the transept.

Guyer's account of the east end of the basilica is decidedly sketchy. His opening exclamation, 'Und nun die Ost-Teile!', effectively conveys the extent to which he was confused by the plan and the constant changes in the masonry in this section of the church. The main apse stood against the east side of the transept, and was semi-circular on its inner and outer faces. Only a small section of its northern half survives to any height. It was pierced by wide arched windows, and flanked by side-chambers which communicated with the transept through wide arches. The side-chambers project eastwards beyond the extremity of the main apse, and also project slightly beyond the lines of the north and south walls of the aisles. Both side-chambers terminate in small apses which are contained within the thickness of their east walls. An excrescence on the north side of the northeast corner was a sort of porch with an inner and outer door which led into the north side-chamber. Guyer found a splinter of glass mosaic in this room, which may thus have been richly decorated (Herzfeld and Guyer 1930, 122). Both subsidiary apses have arched windows with external dripstone mouldings.

Guyer appears to have been puzzled by various aspects of the construction of the east end. Firstly he noted, 'Abschluss fanden die Pastophorien in gleicher Weise wie einige merkwürdig massiven Mauer sitzen' (Herzfeld and Guyer

1930, 122). Confronted with a similar phenomenon in the Tomb Church, Guyer suggested that there must have been a passage behind the apse at gallery level which was supported by the mighty east walls of the side-chambers (Herzfeld and Guyer 1930, 137). The same reasoning could presumably have been applied here, where there was certainly an upper floor over the north side-chamber, as is proved by the beam-holes in the surviving section of the apse. Given the extraordinary massiveness of the east walls of the side-chambers, I think it is also likely that there were subsidiary apses at the higher level.

The apparent jumble of different building techniques in this part of the church so confused Guyer that he was forced to suggest that alterations were carried out on a grand scale by the Armenians. Gertrude Bell's remarks concerning this east façade are rather more helpful.

'The wall which connected the two small apses with one another was of a different and poorer style of building than that employed in the rest of the church; moreover it was separated by straight joints from the masonry on either side of it. It is conceivable that it was a later addition, in which case the two inner walls of which there were some traces (they are indicated tentatively on the plan), connecting the interior angles of the small apses with the central apse, would have to be taken as forming originally the sides of a bay, open along all its width to the east and closed by the curve of the main apse to the west. This is, however, highly improbable. The significance of straight joints is not great in Asia Minor, nor do they necessarily imply addition to the original structure. An abrupt and apparently meaningless change in the character of the masonry is not unusual; it has already been noticed in the first basilica at Kanytelideis' (Kanlıdivane) 'and will be noticed again in the second basilica at Corycus,' (the Tomb Church) 'in both of which instances it seems to be attributable to the vagaries of the builders. At any rate, if there has been reconstruction in the three churches I believe that it followed exactly the lines of the original building and in no respect altered the original plan. In the present example the traces of interior walls connecting the small apses with the main apse are more likely to have been merely the remains of the arches that carried the roof of the passage behind the central apse (cf Kanytelideis, Basilica No 2).' (Bell 1907, 6-7)

Bell's insistence on the contemporaneity of the differing sections of masonry is much more convincing than Guyer's recourse to medieval Armenians, although I do not accept that the changes in construction are 'meaningless'. There is total uniformity in the foundations which are consistently built from large square ashlars, as are the semi-domes: small stone masonry is only used for parts of walls which do not support or contain vaulting. The east façade consequently now looks very uneven, but there is no break in the foundations, and surviving patches of plaster show that the present appearance is misleading, since the whole building was covered with stucco.

The east façade exhibits another peculiarity which Guyer passed over without comment. The massive walls of the side-chambers are twice reduced in thickness as they rise. These reductions take place at the top level of the footings, and again above the apse windows, that is at the level of the springing of the semi-domes. The very top levels of the east wall, above the semi-dome, were built with small stones. This was surely a sophisticated method of altering the strength of construction according to the varying stresses in different sections of the wall: more economical methods were used in less important areas. The eastern wall of the passage has been reduced somewhat since 1905, and its top course is now at the same level as the higher reduction in the walls of the side-chambers. Gertrude Bell's photograph of this façade of the church (plate 34) shows that although the passage wall was in small stones rather than ashlars, it, too, was reduced at this level, as would have been necessary if the east wall was to appear uniform after the application of stucco.

The east end of the north wall preserves a feature which rarely survives in the Cilician basilicas. At the very top of this section of the church four heavy corbels are still in position. These must have supported a cornice which would have carried the tile and timber roof well beyond the walls, with the result of throwing rainwater well away from the stonework..

The north and south façades of the church were enlivened by the generous provision of windows and doorways. Three projecting bosses can be seen above each of the surviving doorways in the south façade (plate 34). These appear to be the supports for attached wooden porches with gabled roofs. The last surviving window of the north wall is still surmounted by a fragment of dripstone moulding: since these mouldings are also present in the east façade, it is most likely that they were provided throughout the church. The Transept Church would thus originally have been very similar in appearance to its neighbour, the Tomb Church, where the façades are more fully preserved.

The Transept Church and the Tomb Church were very similar in other ways. The arrangement of apses and side chambers was the same in the original schemes of both buildings. The disposition of windows and doorways in the south walls of both churches is almost identical. Both have an atrium with three entrances. Perhaps most significantly, both are highly ambitious in architectural terms and include important developments in early Byzantine architecture. So many small details appear in both churches that it seems likely that they must be the work of the same master architect. I believe that the Tomb Church must belong, with the other Cilician 'Domed Basilicas', to the late fifth century. I can see no reason why the Transept Church should be any later. This observation has important consequences, since the Transept Church is remarkably similar to Church 4 at Kanlıdivane, and to the church at Öküzlü. These three churches form a group of Cilician 'Transept Basilicas' as important in their way as the group of 'Domed Basilicas', and are all situated within 10 kilometres of each other. I have already noted that the capitals of the north arcades of the Transept Church at Corycus and Church 4 at Kanlıdivane are identical: pier capitals at Kanlıdivane and Öküzlü are also identical, and, furthermore match the pier capitals of the Tomb Church at Corycus and the 'Domed Ambulatory Church' at Dağ Pazarı. Thus we may conclude that the 'Domed Basilicas' and the 'Transept Basilicas' are closely related groups. If the high arches in the Transept Church were in fact structural, and intended as supports for a wooden pyramid then there would have been an extremely close relationship. This last observation, of course, reinforces my conviction that there were very strong ties linking the Transept Church and the Tomb Church at Corycus, both of which, I believe, were erected in late fifth century.

CORYCUS (Kızkalesi), Church H, Tomb Church extra muros ('Grabeskirche extra muros')[54] (figure 19, plates 38-44)

This is the most completely described and most fully preserved basilica in Corycus, but it remains the most perplexing. The title 'Tomb Church' is Guyer's, and relates to his untenable theory that the nucleus of the church was originally a free-standing tomb. Since Guyer did find sarcophagi in front of the apse, and, since the church is sited in the midst of the necropolis, it has seemed convenient to stick by Guyer's descriptive name for the building.

The church was first described by Gertrude Bell, who noted the presence of a square nucleus at the centre of the building in what would normally be the nave. Guyer put trial trenches through the church, and published a long account of its architecture. Since Guyer's trenches have been back filled by debris, it is impossible, without further excavation, to supplement his description. But Forsyth has largely demolished Guyer's conclusions concerning the interpretation of the building (Forsyth 1957, 225-8). Forsyth's article contains a lengthy summation of Guyer's arguments, and an equally lengthy dismissal of them. It would be pointless, accordingly, to offer another review of Guyer's argument here, so I shall set it out very briefly. In short, Guyer thought that the central nucleus of this church was originally a free-standing quatrefoil tomb, around which a sort of basilica developed. This tomb, he thought, had a domical or pyramidal roof over its centre and semi-domes over the flanking exedrae. Guyer never resolved the question of whether this edifice was covered by the roof of the church, or somehow incorporated within it. The walls do not survive to a sufficient height to offer any evidence which might elucidate the nature of the superstructure, and it is, therefore, difficult to find anything to add to Forsyth's observations on the subject.

---

[54] Bell 1907, 10-16, figures 8-14; Forsyth 1957, 225-8, figures 5-7; Hellenkemper 1994, figures 6-7; Herzfeld and Guyer 1930, 126-50, figures 130-58; Hild, Hellenkemper and Hellenkemper-Salies 1984, 212-6; Hill 1981, 33; Hill 1994, 140.

This is the largest of the churches at Corycus, measuring nearly 80 by 30 metres. A large part of this area is taken up by the atrium and narthex which together are over 35 metres long. The atrium was entered through a doorway in the centre of each of its outside walls and had a peristyle around three sides. The two-storeyed narthex formed the east side of the atrium, and was entered through a five-arched portal. This portal is, in effect, a grandiose version of the normal three-arched Cilician narthex entrance, but it displays two other peculiarities which Guyer and Forsyth do not explain. There were two additional arched openings at the north and south ends of the west wall of the narthex which communicated with the peristyle, and the south end of the narthex terminated in an apse. It is possible that this apse contained a fountain or at least a water tank since there are fragments of a marble basin lying beside it. There is a square foundation in front of the west portal of the narthex which looks as though it could be the head of a cistern. This feature is shown on Herzfeld's plan, but Guyer did not comment upon it. The apse in the narthex could thus have been used by visitors for ablutions before they entered the church proper. The wide arch at the east end of the south side of the peristyle would have provided a convenient point of access to the fountain. Similarly, the wide arch at the north end of the west wall of the narthex allowed immediate access to the stairway which led up to the narthex gallery.

The centre of the church was entered through three doorways which are placed unusually close together. The central doorway is remarkable for being much taller and wider than the side-entrances. Thus the beam holes which held the joists of the floor of the upper storey of the narthex rest directly on the massive lintel of the central doorway, whilst there is room for six courses of masonry above the relieving arches which surmount the lintels of the side-doors.

The western part of the church proper was occupied by two aisles which ran across the building on a north-south alignment and were separated by a colonnade. Everyone who has written about the church has accepted that these aisles had no galleries, and rose through the full height of the building. The evidence for the great height is clearly the vertical scar at a high level in the west end of the north wall, but it is less easy to be certain that there was no gallery, at least over the west aisle. The joists for such a gallery would presumably have run across the shorter (east-west) width of the space, and absence of beam-holes in this part of the north wall of the church is thus irrelevant. The transverse colonnade and its upper order are missing, and the evidence from the east wall of the narthex is uncertain, since its top three surviving courses are different in character to the rest of the wall. Guyer thought that there was a row of windows in the upper part of this wall, but the surviving pier at the north end of the wall supports the arches of openings which would have risen from floor level in the narthex gallery, and therefore have more the character of doorways. There is a further, aesthetic consideration which may be relevant here: if it was intended that there was to be a transept at the west end of the church, then a double order of columns running along its length could only have detracted from its effect. If, however, there was a gallery over the west transverse aisle, then the colonnade would have had some structural meaning. I would suggest, therefore, that the case for a gallery over the west transverse aisle is stronger than the case for its absence. It is much less likely that there was a gallery over the east transverse aisle, since this would have interfered with the west exedra of the nucleus.

This nucleus is the most striking feature of the church. It is defined by four L-shaped piers which are surmounted by pier-capitals very similar to those of the 'Domed Ambulatory Church' at Dağ Pazarı, and the Basilica at Alakilise. Only the two northern capitals are still in position. They presumably supported the ends of the triple arcade which is likely to have defined the north side of the nucleus. The exedrae which Guyer wished to append to the north and south sides of the nucleus would, as Forsyth observed, come much too close to the doorways in the outer walls of the church, and their semi-domes would have been higher than the beam-holes in the north wall which evidently supported the floor of a gallery to the north of the nucleus. The nucleus is constructed from larger blocks than those of any other part of the building, which suggests that some special superstructure was perhaps intended, but this must have had a wooden roof, since the outer walls of this church are even less substantial than those of the East Church at Alahan.

In the original plan of the church, the apse stood against the west side of the nucleus, flanked by apsidal side-chambers which extended eastwards. A wall between the ends of the side-chambers enclosed a small courtyard behind the main apse. Thus, as Guyer and Forsyth observed, the original appearance of the east end of the church was very like that of the Basilica of St Thecla at Meryemlık: it resembled even more closely the east end of the nearby Transept Church. Guyer noted the massive nature of the walls of the subsidiary apses, and suggested that, in the original form of the church, these may have supported a passage behind the main apse at first floor level. At some later date the main apse was moved eastwards into line with the east walls of the side-chambers.

The side-chambers were connected by doorways to the central nucleus, and also to the aisle-like chambers to north and south of it. The south side-chamber contains the entrance to a cistern which fills the area beneath the central apse and the choir in front of it. Guyer found two fragments of a trefoil or quatrefoil marble piscina inside the cistern (Herzfeld and Guyer 1930, 145; figure 157). Khatchatrian identified this as a font (Khatchatrian 1962, 100; figure 130). It is possible, therefore, that the south side-chamber may have been used as a baptistery. The fact that there is a quatrefoil basin, which was probably a font, in the south side-chamber of the 'Cupola Church' at Meryemlık provides corroborative evidence for the idea, since the churches are in other respects so similar. On the northeast and southeast corners of the Tomb Church are long rectangular chambers which Herzfeld and Guyer did not investigate. Forsyth suggested that these chambers may have contained ramps to provide access to the upper floors of the side-chambers, and to the galleries to north and south of the nucleus. This is a sensible suggestion, since such access would have been needed at the east end of the church if there was no connecting gallery over the east transverse aisle at the west end, and thus no possibility of using the stairs in the narthex. Forsyth's suggestion does, however, ignore Guyer's observations relating to the southeast chamber. Guyer found traces of water pipes at the east end of the south wall, and proposed that there might have been a curative baths at this corner of the church. This is perhaps unlikely, but Guyer's observation would seem to strengthen the suggestion that this corner of the church was used for baptismal purposes. In the original scheme, if there was, indeed, a passage at gallery level, there would have been need for only one stairway, which could have been in the northeast chamber.

Although the atrium presents a somewhat fortress-like appearance, this church is remarkable for the lightness and interest of its façades. The central parts of the north and south walls are pierced by series of arched windows over which runs a dripstone moulding, and the seven external doorways are all enlivened by canopies which rest on projecting consoles. Again, there is a very close similarity here with the appearance of the Transept Church.

The outstanding problem, as I have indicated, is the question of how this complicated building was roofed. The simplest answer is to say, with Forsyth, that there must have been a tower at the centre of the church, as was also the case in the East Church at Alahan, the 'Domed Ambulatory Church' at Dağ Pazarı, and the 'Cupola Church' at Meryemlık. I would add the Basilica at Alakilise to this group, which has other features in common. thus I would draw attention to the close similarities between the pier capitals in the nuclei, and the canopies over the exterior doorways, at Corycus and Dağ Pazarı. Forsyth was troubled by one aspect of the plan of the Tomb Church:

> 'For the central square with exedras at the end and arcades on the sides, I find no nearby parallels. It is interesting, however, that this is the basic scheme of St Sophia at Constantinople' (Forsyth 1957, 228).

From this I conclude that Forsyth must have thought that there was a semi-dome over the west exedra. I think that it is rather more likely that a high arch sprang across the gap between the western piers of the nucleus, and that the west exedra was, in effect, a sort of chancel screen. This would restore some of the openness to the design of the building, and would give some point to the provision of an upper floor in the narthex and a gallery in the west aisle. Without an intervening semi-dome, anyone standing in the gallery would have had a fine view of whatever was in the nucleus, which was clearly the focus of the building. On the other hand, a semi-dome would have looked most curious under the higher roof of the church. It may also be relevant to note that there are western apses in the churches at Meryemlık and Dağ Pazarı: in both cases these were at the west end of the atrium, but they do provide some degree of parallelism for the plan of the Tomb Church.

If there was no semi-dome over the west exedra, this would go some way towards resolving another of Forsyth's worries about this church.

> 'Viewed as a whole the plan of the "Tomb Church" is unlike our usual idea of a church. It suggests, rather, a domestic complex composed of numerous apartments to which individuals penetrate, passing through many doors and ascending narrow stairs. No space, no axis dominates; there is no openness; and the group is enclosed by a forbidding wall like a compound. The seven outer doors seem designed to admit individuals, one at a time, and no great portal welcomes a populace. The general effect of the plan is monastic in the extreme. This great church seems more suited to the needs of a laura than a parish, more expressive of private devotions than of congregational worship.' (Forsyth 1957, 227-8).

I feel that this is an unsympathetic reaction to a building in which the nucleus is a completely dominant space, and which was so generously provided with doorways and windows. The atrium has three entrances, when one is more common in the region. The five arched portal in the west side of the narthex is grander than any other example in the province, and supplemented by extra wide arches to north and south. There are doorways, too, in the north and south walls of the church proper. The church may well have been monastic, but it seems that lay people must have been admitted if it was indeed provided with a baptistery. The western aisles alone provide as much floor space as a normal basilica, and I see this church as a successful attempt to combine the capacity of the basilica to hold crowds of people with the more specialized demands of commemorative churches in which there is a strong focus on a central shrine or sacred object. Forsyth is doubtful about the relevance of Guyer's sarcophagi, but I am inclined to agree with Guyer that this church was surely an important martyrium.

Openness was provided at gallery level. If I am correct in supposing that there were no semi-domes other than the main apse projecting from the central nucleus, then the generous provision of galleries would have enabled the maximum number of people to view whatever occupied the central floor space, and to witness whatever ceremony was performed there. If Guyer is correct in suggesting that there was a passage behind the apse at first floor level, then it may even have been the case that liturgical ceremonies were enacted in the galleries. The extra doorway at the north end of the narthex, which led directly to the stairway, may also be an indicator of the unusual significance attached to the upper floor of this church.

As has been indicated previously, this church is one example of the Cilician group of 'Domed Basilicas'. There can be little doubt that it belongs, with the others, to the late fifth century, more particularly to the reign of Zeno. Because of its close relationship with its neighbour the Transept Church, which may have been designed by the same architect, the Tomb Church is also an important link in the argument which shows that the Cilician 'Domed Basilicas' are contemporary with the Cilician Transept Basilicas.

CORYCUS (Kızkalesi), Church I ('Große Armenische Kirche extra muros')[55] (figure 20; plates 46-48)

Gertrude Bell described this remarkable church as 'the most perfect example of a system of a double row of apses' (Bell 1907, 19). Guyer thought such schemes so bizarre that they could not possibly be late Roman, and must therefore be Armenian (Herzfeld and Guyer 1930, xii). As a result the church was given the cumbersome and misleading title of 'Große Armenische Kirche'. It is clear that both Herzfeld and Guyer had little enthusiasm for the building. Herzfeld's published plan is merely a reproduction of his field sketch in which the features are not shown at any consistent scale, and in which the horse-shoed apses of the main range have acquired a curious ovoid shape (Herzfeld and Guyer 1930, figure 160). Guyer, punch-drunk with the rich decoration of the churches at Meryemlık, and the three more famous churches at Corycus, wrote of 'die geradezu beispiellose Dürftigkeit der Gliederung' (Herzfeld and Guyer 1930, 153). This was not the only occasion when Herzfeld and Guyer had recourse to the Armenians as the explanation for buildings they could not understand, but it is perhaps the most dramatic. The record has been put straight by Hild, Hellenkemper and Hellenkemper-Salies who attribute the building to the sixth century and provide a full plan of this complex basilica (1984, 218-21, figure 15). Their plan reveals the church as a symmetrical structure with a basilica (plus narthex) at its core, but enveloped by structures on all sides. On the west side there was a small atrium with two square chambers at its northeast and southeast corners. There were long thin passages terminating in small apses on the north and south sides of the church. An ambulatory with two subsidiary apses at the east end of the church communicated with 'side-chambers' at the northeast and southeast corners of the whole building. Even the main aisles terminated in apses, providing the church with a grand total of seven apses.

Only the east end of the church has survived, but parts of this survive to a considerable height. The main apse, which is 6.2 metres wide at its chord, is flanked by two small apses which stood at the ends of the north and south aisles. Bell and Guyer both assumed that the interior was divided into nave and aisles

---

[55] Bell 1907, 19-22, figures 20-2; Herzfeld and Guyer 1930, 150-4, figures 160-3; Hild, Hellenkemper and Hellenkemper-Salies 1984, 218-21.

because of the presence at the mouth of the main apse of stones which might have received the ends of the arcades, but both seem to have found these stones puzzling. Gertrude Bell referred to them as 'brackets' rather than capitals, and noted that their decoration was similar to that of the piers which supported the triumphal arch in the Transept Church (Bell 1907, 21). Guyer described one of these stones as 'ganz einfach gebildete Kämpfer' (Herzfeld and Guyer 1930, 153). These stones have fallen, and are not visible in the published photographs. It is, however, still possible to see the scar of the bracket which was inserted between the main apse and the south apse. It is quite clear that the stonework here has been hacked out, and that the bracket must have been in secondary use. This would explain why it so puzzled Bell and Guyer. The simplest explanation would seem to be that these stones were not intended to receive the ends of the nave arcades, for they were set too low for such a purpose, but really were brackets, intended, perhaps, to support a wooden screen across the east end of the nave. Guyer suggested that the nave arcades must have been supported on piers because he found few fragments of columns in the area to the west of the apses. Since 1907 this part of the church has had a track constructed through it. Nevertheless, there are sufficient broken columns in the vicinity to suggest that the basilica must have had colonnades, and the plan produced by Hild, Hellenkemper and Hellenkemper-Salies marks the position of part of the stylobates for supporting the colonnades.

The main apse was pierced by a double arched window, and by doorways in its north and south sides which led into the eastern passage.. Two arches sprang from the semi-circular outer face of the apse across to the eastern wall of the passage. The northern of these arches is still standing. The east passage is itself equipped with two apses which are 3.29 metres wide and positioned symmetrically opposite the spurs of wall connecting the western range of apses. The passage was lit by three windows which alternate with the subsidiary apses. Bell was puzzled that the only access to the east passage appeared to be through the doorways in the main apse, and speculated that ruins immediately to the north and south of the church might prove to have been side-corridors linking the various parts of the basilica, and thus allowing the processions which were possible in other churches with passages. Herzfeld and Guyer were able to confirm this. They showed that there were corridors, roughly 4.5 metres wide, along both long sides of the basilica. They also found traces of a sixth apse inside the north corridor some 8 metres to the west of the main line of apses. Guyer therefore suggested that both corridors may have contained apsidal side-chapels. All these features have been confirmed by Hild, Hellenkemper and Hellenkemper-Salies, whose plan shows doorways at the east ends of the aisles to communicate with the eastern side-chambers and the ambulatory passage.

Guyer observed that there had been an upper floor above the east passage. This is clear from beam-holes which are visible in the outer face of the main apse, and in the west face of the outer wall of the passage, above the arches of the subsidiary apses. Guyer does not consider the question of whether there were also galleries over the aisles. If these were absent, this would be the only Cilician basilica with a two-storied eastern passage in which this was the case. Unfortunately the masonry above the mouth of the apse at the end of the north aisle has fallen since 1907. There is therefore no surviving evidence relating to this problem (Herzfeld and Guyer 1930, figure 161). But in 1907 there was sufficient masonry still in position to preclude the possibility of a doorway at the east end of a hypothetical north gallery. There is, in any case, a problem of levels, since the apex of the north apse is slightly higher than the beam-holes visible in the east wall of the passage. It seems inevitable, therefore, that if there was a gallery over the north aisle, it cannot have communicated with the upper floor of the passage. It is not, however, necessary to conclude that there were definitely no galleries over the aisles. Two possibilities remain. It is just conceivable that there were galleries over the side-corridors. I think that this is very improbable since this would require a free-standing double order of colonnades between the nave and aisles. It is, however, not inconceivable that this church had a transept, and such a feature would help to explain the advanced position of the apses of the north and south corridors. In such an event there would have been no need of doors in the west walls of the upper floor of the passage (though windows might have been provided), and the absence of returns for nave colonnades at the mouth of the apses would be explained. The presence of a transept would be much less surprising than the absence of galleries in this particular basilica. It is, furthermore, possible that the transept was wider than the nave and aisles. There is a possible Cilician parallel for such an arrangement in the Southwest Church at Anavarza, but it may well be that this church was more similar to Basilica A at Perge in Pamphylia (Rott 1908, 48; figure 19). The brackets beside the mouth of the apse, which puzzled Bell and Guyer, are most likely to have supported wooden screens similar to those which surrounded the central bay of the transept in the 'Cathedral' at Corycus.

There remains the vexed question of when this church was built. Guyer was convinced that this was a medieval building: it is therefore necessary to examine his argument.

'Die Technik - kleine nur dürftig zugerichtete Quadern - ist die bei armenischen Bauten übliche. Auffallend ist bei der Grösse und regelmässigen Plangestaltung des Baus die geradezu beispiellose Dürftigkeit der Gliederung. So ist z. B. von Kapitälen überhaupt gar nichts zu sehen; an ihre Stelle treten bei den Apsisbogen ganz einfach gebildete Kämpfer. Nur am Boden liegend fand sich ein zu einem Altarziborium oder einer ähnlichen Klein-Architektur gehörendes korinthisches Rundkapitäl as weissem Marmor (Abb. 163); sein flaues relief und sein langgestrecker Habitus könnten vermuten lassen, dass wir es mit einer Kopie nach einem byzantinischen Vorbild zu tun haben. Auch Gesimse sucht man an diesem Bau vergebens; die Hochwände der Apsiden gehen ohne jede Vermittlung (!) direkt in das Kuppelrund über. Alle diese Beobachtungen zeigen uns, dass dieser Bau unmöglich in der byzantischen Zeit entstanden sein kann; er wird erst während der Epoche der kleinarmenischen Herrschaft, d.h. im hohen Mittelalter erbaut worden sein.' (Herzfeld and Guyer 1930, 154).

I shall take Guyer's points in turn. I see nothing inferior about the masonry: nor did Bell, who wrote 'the character of the masonry throughout was remarkably good' (Bell 1907, 22). Small squared stones were used in Cilician architecture throughout the Roman period. It is hardly surprising that they are found in Armenian constructions, since the materials for these were normally quarried from ancient buildings. I would agree that the plan is grand and regular: it would be all the more remarkable if it was medieval, since in the rest of the region it is impossible to find a medieval church which is more than a single chambered chapel with perhaps an extra lean-to annex. The poverty of the decoration might result from the fact that so little of the building as a whole has survived, but even if it could be proved that there never was any, this would not, in itself, justify assigning the church to the medieval period. Even if we were to accept Guyer's argument about the white marble column, one such surface find is of very little significance. The exclamation mark inserted into Guyer's remarks about the lack of a moulding at the springing of the semi-dome merely betrays his ignorance of local architecture. Examples of such apses are plentiful: Guyer could reasonably have been expected to know that there was one nearby at Şaha since Gertrude Bell had published a photograph of it the year before he worked at Corycus (Bell 1906b, 387; figure 2). There are no such mouldings in the fourth century South Church at Yanıkhan, and some reason, therefore, to suppose that this feature is actually an indicator of earliness. It follows that I have no doubt that this is a late Roman edifice. I would be surprised if it were earlier than the latter part of the fifth century, or later than the early part of the seventh.

CORYCUS (Kızkalesi)), Church J, Monastic Church ('Klosterkirche')[56] (figure 21, plates 49-51)

This monastic complex stands on the west side of the road through the ancient necropolis, a short distance to the north of the northeast corner of the city walls. It has been described by Bell and by Herzfeld and Guyer. The limited excavations of the latter did little to elucidate the nature of this complicated and imperfectly understood building. Herzfeld and Guyer were of the opinion that it had a long history of occupation stretching from the late Roman to the

---

[56] Bell 1907, 17-19, figures 15-18; Herzfeld and Guyer 1930, 154-61, figures 164-73; Hild, Hellenkemper and Hellenkemper-Salies 1984, 221; Hill 1994, 140.

Armenian period. The nucleus of the monastery covers an area of at least 40 metres by 25, and it is still possible to make out a precinct wall which encloses part of the cemetery to the north and east.

Bell saw the complex 'deep under corn' (Bell 1907, 18): the monastery is now planted out with lemon trees, and the trenches of Herzfeld and Guyer have long since been levelled. Without undertaking a major campaign of excavation, one is, therefore, obliged to take Herzfeld and Guyer's plan and description largely on trust, although there are a few minor amplifications of details of the construction which can be added.

The excavators considered that the earliest buildings on the side were the apses they termed A, C, and G, and the chapels in front of the latter two apses. Apse A is now buried under rubble, but examination of C reveals that its barrel-vaulted fore-choir was only 1 metre wide, and the foundations which extend for a further 3.5 metres to the west are those of a later chapel tacked on to the original apse. Herzfeld and Guyer also concluded that the apses they termed D, E and F were inserted between apses C and G. The priority of G is somewhat doubtful since the strangely aligned wall which links apses F and G is clearly secondary to both of them.

Herzfeld and Guyer excavated an area to the west of apses C and D in which they discovered part of a stylobate which had supported round columns. Guyer was thus able to argue that there had been a basilica at the centre of the complex which was constructed by creating nave and aisles to the west of apse C, and appending the apsidal chambers B and D as side-chambers which projected slightly to the east of apse C. Since he found two types of column bases, Guyer suggested that the basilica had originally been equipped with galleries. Apse A was retained at the end of a passage along the north side of the basilica. In Guyer's reconstruction the main apse would have a remarkably deep fore-choir which would seem inconsistent with the presence of galleries, but since the solid walls to the west of apse C, and the barrel-vault which they supported, were a secondary addition, we can reconstruct the plan of a conventional basilica at this point in the church.

The nave and aisles had doors at the west end which communicated with a narthex which had the characteristic triple-arched portal so common in this part of Cilicia, but beyond which was an exo-narthex. Exo-nartheces are not common in Cilicia, but there was perhaps another one in Church C at Tapureli, which was also probably monastic. The west wall of the exo-narthex is still partially preserved, and shows unequivocally that there were two storeys at this end of the building. A row of beam-holes in the outer face of the west wall suggests that there may even have been a porch against the exo-narthex.

The southern part of the building complex is particularly remarkable. Here the apses D, E and F are still standing. In front of them is a tripartite fore-choir covered by three barrel-vaults. The three bays are separated by double arches which spring from small impost blocks on ugly square piers. This gives something of the impression of a miniature nave and aisles. Apse D was, in effect, subsidiary to both apses C and E, and it is inconceivable that it was not built at the same time as apse E. It would appear, therefore, that at the time when the basilica which had C as its main apse was created, two additional apses were included at the southeast corner which almost had the effect of creating a double basilica. To the west of the 'nave' in front of apse E was a square chamber which was flanked to the south by the apsidal chamber G. Further west still was a range of small rooms which included a cistern head. This provision of water tempts one to suggest that a baptistery was included at this point in the church, especially since the structure bears some comparison with the secondary phase of the Baptistery at Alahan, where two aisles were separated by arches which sat on a large square pier.

Guyer observed that the rooms to the west of the southern apses might have been living quarters. The cistern would have been as useful for domestic purposes as for baptismal ones, and I suspect that this may be the correct explanation for the jumble of rooms uncovered by Herzfeld and Guyer in the southwest corner of the building. The complex has obviously had an extended history of occupation. It appears that at some stage a small chapel was constructed against the apse of the central basilica. This reduction in size is most likely to have taken place between the seventh century (as happened in the Necropolis Church at Anemurium) and the Medieval period (as in the West Church at Alahan). Since the barrel-vaults of the southern apses are still intact, these must always have been available for use as chapels. Thus we may assume that in the later period of occupation of the monastery there would have been a row of chapels along the east side of the establishment; perhaps an open area at the centre in what had been the west end of the nave of the basilica; and a range of rooms in the west and south parts of the building which may have been used as monastic living accommodation.

There can be no doubt that this building was well-established in the late Roman period, but it is clearly reasonable to follow Guyer's suggestion that it was still occupied in the Armenian period. Apart from the central basilica, very little of what survives in this building is entirely suggestive of the late Roman period. Barrel-vaulted fore-choirs did occur in Cilician churches of that period, the most notable example being that of the 'Domed Ambulatory Church' at Dağ Pazarı, but such constructions are much more characteristic of the medieval churches of the region. There are good examples of them in Churches K and M in the Land Castle. But if the barrel-vaulted fore-choirs of the Monastic Church were built in the Armenian period, then this is the most ambitious ecclesiastical building of that date to survive in Cilicia. Without a detailed programme of archaeological study, and in the face of so much evidence of continuous alterations, it would be foolish to attempt any more precise analysis of the dating of this building.

CORYCUS (Kızkalesi), Church K, Northwest Church inside Land Castle[57] (figure 23, plate 52)

This was the largest church within the Land Castle. It is of particular interest since it is a good example of a late Roman basilica which was converted into a single-naved chapel in the medieval period. The apse, which is 6 metres wide, is the major surviving part of the early church. Herzfeld and Guyer were able to uncover enough of the foundations to establish that the nave was 17.6 metres long, the nave was 7 metres wide, and the aisles 2.35 metres wide. The overall size of the church must have been somewhere in the region of 26 by 14 metres, which is considerably smaller than the other basilicas of Corycus. Guyer believed that the first church was divided into nave and aisles by piers whose bases are built into the secondary walls. Whilst these are helpful for establishing the former existence of an arcade, they could as well have supported columns as piers. The apse was lit by a single arched window, which at some date was filled in and plastered over. Beneath the window can still be seen the beam-holes for wooden seating for the clergy. The north side of the apse was pierced by a doorway which presumably led into a side-chamber. The outer face of the apse has two tall buttresses which, as Guyer observed, give it something of the appearance of the apse of the Basilica of St Thecla at Meryemlık. The west springing of a barrel-vault can still be seen between the buttresses. This rests against the outer face of the apse, and is clearly the successor of a wooden roof which once covered a single storeyed passage at the east end of the church.

The secondary chapel was built against the mouth of the apse. Its walls, which follow the lines of the stylobates of the nave arcades, extend westwards for 5.95 metres. As seems to have been typical of these medieval chapels, it was covered by a barrel vault. The supporting walls for this roof encase elements from the earlier building, and the barrel-vault itself appears to have been constructed inside and against earlier masonry. This method of reconstruction may be compared with what was done inside Church 1 at Binbirkilise, although here, of course, the later barrel-vault replaced an earlier one (Ramsay and Bell 1909, 42-5; figure 5). It is possible that sections of the original clerestory are still preserved in the upper parts of the medieval walls, since there are larger blocks in the highest courses, and a window at a high level not only has a dividing column which resembles those of the Transept Church, as Guyer observed, but also the dripstone moulding which is still such a prominent feature of the Tomb Church, and a small fragment of which can still be seen on the north façade of the Transept Church. Against this idea, it must be noted that there are stubs of masonry which project to north and south from the mouth of the apse. If these are not simply buttresses, they may be relics of

---

[57] Herzfeld and Guyer 1930, 181-5, figures 195-9; Langlois 1861, 212.

the east walls of galleries, in which case the clerestory would have been at a higher level.

The later chapel was divided into three bays by pairs of pilasters against the side-walls which supported the rib arches of the barrel-vault. Blind arches spring between the piers against the side walls of the chapel. The secondary west wall has fallen, but the footings of its central doorway can still be seen. This may have been similar in appearance to the doorway in the western bay of the south wall, which has a relieving arch over the lintel. The interior wall surfaces were plastered and painted. Langlois reported seeing figures of Armenian saints: Herzfeld and Guyer illustrate two small sections of wall-painting with arabesque patterns.

CORYCUS (KIZKALESİ), Church L[58]
Hellenkemper reports a 'church within the city, next to the sea wall'.

East of CORYCUS (Kızkalesi), Funerary Chapel (plates 53-4)
The remains of this church stand on the edge of a low cliff between the modern road and the sea in an ancient cemetery about 1 kilometre east of Corycus. The northern half of the apse, and a fragment of the east end of the north wall are all that survive above ground level. This was a small building measuring 16 by 9.5 metres. The apse was semi-circular on both faces, and projected from the east wall. The northern side of a double-arched window is still in position in the apse. The foundations at the west end of the church show that there was a narthex with a single opening at the centre of its west and east walls. It is likely that there was an open arch on the west side of the narthex, and there was certainly a doorway between the narthex and the nave. The floor of the nave was paved with limestone slabs. No fragments of columns or capitals can be seen near the building, and, in view of its smallness it is possible that this was a single-chambered chapel. However, the building compares in size with the Cave Church at Meryemlık, and is actually larger than the Temple Church at Ayaş, thus the possibility that there were aisles cannot be entirely discounted. The church is built throughout with small square stones facing a rubble and mortar core except in the semi-dome of the apse where larger blocks are employed above the sima moulding. The surviving part of the north wall still has small patches of plaster, and displays a random pattern of putlog holes, some of which were filled with broken tiles and mortar.

Although this may not have been a basilica, there can be little doubt that it is a late Roman building. The masonry is entirely consistent with an early date, as is the plan which included a narthex, and in which the apse does not fill the full width of the east wall. Both features would be unusual in a medieval Cilician chapel, which would normally have been covered with a barrel-vault. It is

---

[58] Hellenkemper 1994, 215.

likely that this was a small extra-mural funerary chapel. It is surrounded by a cemetery on all sides, and the southeast corner of the church is actually built over an ancient barrel-vaulted hypogaeum. A continuation of the east wall of the chapel runs southwards over the tomb chamber.

North of CORYCUS (Kızkalesi) (Demirciören)[59] (figure 24, plates 55-8)

This church lies 4 kilometres north of Corycus, a short distance to the east of the ancient paved road to Canbazlı. It stands on the northeast side of the ancient settlement, is surrounded by a cemetery, and to the west, beside the road, are very ruined late Roman houses. Keil and Wilhelm thought that the site was monastic, but it has the character of a small village. The church has been very briefly described by Keil and Wilhelm, and still more briefly mentioned by Feld, who simply reports the discovery of a column capital.

This church is fairly well-preserved: the plan is still discernible, and the north wall survives to first floor level. There was a two-storied narthex at the west end which had a three-arched portal which occupied almost the entire width of its west face. This portal has fallen, but the width of the south wall of the narthex is taken up by a wide opening with an arch which is still in position. This springs from simple impost blocks on which is carved a round medallion with a Maltese cross. Beam-holes in the east and west walls of the narthex show that the floor of its upper hall was supported on cross-joists.

Three doors led from the narthex into the nave and aisles. The central doorway was wider and taller than the other two. Keil and Wilhelm report that the body of the church was divided into nave and aisles by two rows of five columns. These appear as dotted outlines on their plan and they publish no photographs of the interior of the church. There are no visible signs of the colonnades today apart from the column capital (figure 59), which bears a very close resemblance to one found in the Tomb Church at Corycus (Herzfeld and Guyer 1930, 142; figure 151). I suspect that Keil and Wilhelm could see no more evidence relating to the colonnades than is visible today, that is the piers at the west end, and the consoles which received the eastern arches at the mouth of the apse. They seem to me to have been over-generous in their proposed allocation of columns which would have resulted in an intercolumniation of only 1.4 metres. Furthermore, it can be seen from the position of the consoles beside the mouth of the apse, that the arches of the arcade, being so narrow, would have been very low in relation to the floors of the aisle galleries. Four columns rather than five would seem to give the interior of the church a more satisfactory articulation. A peculiarity which is not adequately shown on the plan published by Keil and Wilhelm is that whilst the east ends of the nave arcades rested on consoles which project directly from the walls beside the

---

[59] Hild and Hellenkemper 1986, 67; Hild and Hellenkemper 1990, 237; Feld 1963/64, 101; Keil and Wilhelm 1931, 119-20, figure 148, plate 149.

mouth of the apse, the western arches were supported by massive piers which were created by doubling the thickness of the wall between the nave and the narthex at this point. The galleries over the aisles are attested by small consoles which project from the north wall, and which presumably supported a wooden plate on which the cross-beams of the gallery floor rested.

A peculiarity of this church is that access to the galleries was gained by way of a stone stairway in the west end of the north aisle. This stairway was 1 metre wide, and rose towards the upper hall of the narthex. The three lowest steps are still in position, and there is a clearly visible stain on the north wall which shows where the rest of the stairway must have rested against it. This arrangement must have been very awkward at gallery level, since the west end of the north gallery would have been excessively narrow. The stairway is in no way supported by the north wall, but merely butts against it. It is possible, therefore, that the stairway was a secondary insertion, but there is no sign that there was ever a wooden staircase in the north bay of the narthex; nor, due to the width of the western portal, is there really enough room. The north wall of the church is sufficiently well preserved to show that there was no doorway at a high level which could have been approached by an outside staircase. There is, however, another deficiency in the published plan which may be relevant to this problem. The north opening between the narthex and the nave was not in fact a doorway, but a wide archway. Since this was as wide as the north aisle, it took more account of the congestion caused by the stairway than would have been the case if there had been a narrower doorway in this position. The archway was evidently an original feature of the church, since the masonry of the north wall is undisturbed, and if this archway was provided in order to take account of the stairway in the north aisle, then it would appear that that stairway was also an original feature. The heavy pier at the west end of the north arcade can now be seen to serve a useful purpose in buttressing the west wall of the nave at the point where it terminated. It was presumably thought necessary to build a similar pier on the south side in order to keep the arcades symmetrical. It could still be argued that the wide arch would have the effect of weakening the west wall at precisely the point where it had to support the massive weight of a stone staircase. The answer to this must surely be that the upper part of the staircase must have been wooden, as is suggested by the substantial beam-holes in the north wall where it meets the west wall of the nave. An entirely solid staircase would surely have left more trace. Similarly, there would surely be more traces if the upper part of the stairway had been supported on some arched substructure. It is quite possible that the galleries of this church were constructed entirely of wood: in this case, the pier at the west end of the north arcade, and the beam-hole above it could be compared with the piers beside the mouth of the apse in the North Church at Yanıkhan.

The north wall, which has no windows, has a central doorway which was protected by a rounded stone canopy which was supported by projecting consoles. There was a similar door in the south wall, which was flanked by double arched windows with dripstone mouldings. The south façade was thus a version in miniature of the façade of the Tomb Church at Corycus.

The east end of the church is substantially preserved, with parts of the semi-dome of the main apse and the south apse still in position. This part of the building is choked with rubble and secondary dry-stone walls. The main apse is lit by a double window with pronounced horse-shoe arches. This window, which is surmounted by a dripstone moulding, projects very slightly from the main building line of the east wall of the church, but the projection is flat and does not follow the outer curve of the apse (plate 57). Neat round holes which were drilled in the inner face of the apse at the level of the bottom of the window may have held brackets, perhaps for lamps. The central apse is flanked by side-chambers which project westwards to define a chancel area. Doorways connected the side-chambers with the aisles and with the chancel. The side-chambers terminate in apses which have small square windows. There are rectangular niches in the north and south faces of the main apse which must have served as cupboards in the side-chapels. Beam-holes at a higher level in the outer face of the apse show that the side-chambers had upper floors.

There is a range of extra small rooms at the southeast corner of the church (plate 58). The south room of this complex contains a well-head, and it is likely that the suite of rooms was once a baptistery. The complex had its own separate entrance through what was, in effect, a small narthex, since the west room against the south wall of the church was entered through a wide archway. This vestibule had doorways which communicated with the southern chamber, and with a rectangular chamber equivalent to the south side-chamber to which it was connected by a wide arched opening. This has the effect of creating a double chapel on the southeast corner of the church which communicates with the main church as well as having an independent access. If this was a baptistery, the double chamber may be compared with the free-standing baptistery at Alahan, and the complex as a whole is similar to the Necropolis Church at Anemurium, although there the Baptistery was on the north side of the church. The south side-chamber of the 'Cupola Church' at Meryemlık was almost certainly used as a baptistery, as probably was the south side-chamber of the Tomb Church at Corycus.

The masonry is consistent throughout the building, including the southeast chambers. All visible foundations consist of heavy ashlars. Large blocks are also used in the apses, and for corners and piers. The masonry of the remaining walls consists of smaller stones facing a rubble and mortar core. The walls have frequent putlog holes. These are particularly noticeable in the north wall where the ancient system of scaffolding can easily be worked out (plate 55). Occasional traces of plaster show that all walls were rendered on both inner and outer faces.

The relationship of this church with the Tomb Church at Corycus is sufficiently close to suggest that the two churches must be contemporary. They share a distinctive type of column capital, and the same details appear in the articulation of their façades. It seems likely then that this church should also be attributed to the late fifth century.

ÇAMLICA (Philadelphia)[60]

The site of Philadelphia lies at the location known as Çamlıca near İmsi Ören about 11 kilometres east of Ermenek. Bean and Mitford reported the presence of a terrace with the foundations of a large church which Hild and Hellenkemper identify as early Byzantine.

ÇANLI BOĞAZI[61]

About ten kilometres south of Uzuncaburç, the road forks; the left fork leads to Uzuncaburç, and Kirobaşı, and the right fork to Canbazlı. A short distance up the latter road, in the hillside immediately to the north, Keil and Wilhelm spotted with their binoculars what they thought was a well-preserved church ruin, which they did not have time to visit.

ÇATIKÖREN, Basilica (figure 25, plates 60-1))[62]

The site of Çatıkören was first visited by Bent: Keil and Wilhelm were the first to record its name. It lies, as Bent observed, three miles west of Kanlıdivane, but is best approached by the ancient paved road which leads from Ayaş, and lies about 10 kilometres inland. In recent times the site has been visited by Gough and Feld. Feld published a plan and a few notes on the church. Gough mentioned the site twice in his publications but never described it, although his notes survive with the rest of the Gough papers and include a sketch plan of the church. The basilica stands in an ancient cemetery on the south side of the valley. It was first reported by Bent who considered that it was built on the foundations of an earlier building, which was presumably an ancient temple. The church measures 34.4 by 14.8 metres overall, including the narthex and the eastern passage. The nave is 20.9 by 14 metres internally. The church was a three-aisled basilica with galleries, narthex, and an eastern passage with a subsidiary apse at its south end. The west wall of the narthex is almost completely destroyed: it is, therefore, impossible to reconstruct its form. The nave had two orders of Corinthian columns, which supported an arcade which seems to have sprung directly from the east and west walls. Hild and

---

[60] Bean and Mitford 1970, 216; Hild and Hellenkemper 1990, 378.

[61] Keil and Wilhelm 1931, 31.

[62] Bent 1891, 210-11; Eyice 1981b, 208; Feld 1963/64, 104-7; Gough, Manuscript notes; Gough 1954, 52; Gough 1955a, 204; Heberdey and Wilhelm 1893, 66; Hild, Hellenkemper and Hellenkemper-Salies 1984, 227; Hild and Hellenkemper 1986, 76-7, figure 11, plates 94-5; Hild and Hellenkemper 1990, 224-5.

Hellenkemper (1986, 77) postulate six pairs of columns in the nave arcades. Surviving monolithic columns are 2.77 metres high and 0.41-0.45 of a metre in diameter. Beam-holes throughout the church show that there were galleries over the aisles, and a second floor over the eastern chambers. Gough noted consoles which project from the west wall of the church to support the upper storey of the narthex. The arrangements at the east end are somewhat idiosyncratic: doors at the east ends of the aisles provide access to side-chambers which communicate with the eastern passage through wide arches. These 'side-chambers' are not large, but Feld's sketch plan make them appear smaller that they actually are. The narrow eastern passage itself is 1.22 metres wide and has an apse measuring 2.68 metres at its chord set at its south end, an arrangement which may be compared with that in the Basilica at Dağ Pazarı. The main apse, which is 6.5 metres wide, had no windows, and is enclosed in straight walls which form three sides of a hexagon. The arches which supported the upper floor of the passage, and perhaps marked off the side-chambers, sprang directly from the outer face of the apse to the outer wall of the church. The masonry, small stones facing a rubble and mortar core, is consistent throughout most of the building. Exceptions to this are the main apse, which is constructed from larger, finely dressed, ashlars, and the lower courses of the south wall and the southwest corner of the narthex. These latter anomalies, which were noted by Gough, must be the earlier foundations mentioned by Bent. Gough also noted that unofficial local excavations had revealed that the floor of the basilica was the native bedrock. Gough considered that the capitals could be dated to either the fifth or sixth centuries; Feld favoured the first half of the sixth century. A large mausoleum stands just outside the subsidiary apse, and the church is surrounded by sarcophagi and graves.

ÇIRGA[63]

This yayla, which lies one hour's ride to the south of Balabolu was the find-spot of a silver reliquary originally dedicated to St Conon, but bearing a secondary pricked dedication to St Tarasis. Gough, who published the description of the reliquary, did not visit Çırga, but reported that the site was said to have 'kemerli bir kilise - a church with arches'. The discoverer of the reliquary claimed that it was found at the end of a church in a stone container, the lid of which was flush with its top, and had to be prised open with a pick.

ÇOK ÖREN see SUSANOĞLU

ÇOLAKU see ŞEYTAN DERESİ

---

[63] Gough 1958, 244-5.

ÇUKURKEŞLİK[64] (figure 26)

The presence of a church in this ruin-field which lies 15 kilometres northwest of Mersin was first noted by Heberdey and Wilhelm: the only published account of the building is that of Liesenburg, who did not visit the site. He published a plan he had been given in order to back up his argument that there was an intimate relationship between the early Byzantine churches of Cilicia and Egypt. The only detail which Liesenburg's text adds to the plan is that there were galleries over the aisles in this church. The plan shows a three-aisled basilica with a narthex, which measures 26 by 14 metres overall. The apse is six metres wide at its chord. The arrangements at the east end of the church are remarkable, since the plan shows side-chambers which are set well forward from the mouth of the apse linked by a wall which runs straight across the nave, and has a door at its centre. This wall is shown as being as substantial a feature as all the other walls of the building. In the absence of any more detailed information, it is impossible either to confirm or deny this feature, but it is most likely that there were the footings for a chancel screen at this point which have been misunderstood. If so, the basilica at Çukurkeşlik would fall into the group of churches in Cilicia where the side-chambers are set forward in order to define a chancel area. This church appears to share with the basilica at Batısandal, and Church 1 at Kanlıdivane the feature that there is a slight return to north and south at the mouth of the apse before the inner walls of the side-chambers. A further odd feature which is shown on the plan is the provision of doors into the side-chambers not only from the chancel and from the aisles, but also from outside the building. The vague indications of the form of the narthex are particularly unlikely to inspire confidence, since the west façade of the church appears lop-sided. It seems most reasonable to assume that this church probably had a triple arcade in the west wall of the narthex, as was the case in so many other Cilician churches.

DAĞ PAZARI[65]

The first modern visitor to Dağ Pazarı, E. J. Davis, reported that the village, which he called Kestel, after the mountain to the west of the upland plain in which it stands, had been founded about six years before his arrival in June 1875. The next visitors were Ramsay, Headlam and Hogarth in 1890. Headlam wrote 'the site is not of great importance', but published a very useful photograph of the major surviving monument, the 'Domed Ambulatory Church'. Ramsay proposed that the site as probably being the ancient city of Coropissus, and the Armenian fortress of Sibilia, and until recently it has been accepted that the identification with Coropissus was probably correct. Wilson's

---

[64] Heberdey and Wilhelm 1896, 40; Hild and Hellenkemper 1990, 231; Liesenburg 1928, 109-11, figure 30.
[65] Davis 1879, 325-36; Forsyth 1957, 233-6; Gough 1976, 256; Headlam 1892, 20-1; Hill 1979, 8-12; Ramsay 1890, 366, 369; Sykes 1915, 538-9; Wilson 1895, 181-2.

Handbook, published in 1895, contains a short, but tantalizing account of the site from which it appears than in his day the ruins were much more extensive, and included remains of public buildings in the area to the southeast of the 'Domed Ambulatory Church', a colonnaded street apparently running on a north-south alignment through the settlement, and ruins of many houses. Wilson also reported visible remains on the southern side of the site of another church. It would appear, therefore, that this small ancient city had at least four churches. Sykes, who passed through in 1913, seems to have thought even less of Dağ Pazarı than Headlam, describing it as 'a village where no village ought to have been'. Forsyth visited Dağ Pazarı in 1954, and, although trusting Headlam's misleading plan of the 'Domed Ambulatory Church', was the first to appreciate that that church was not, as Headlam had pronounced, 'later and of a more conventional type than that at Koja Kalessi'. Proper realization of the significance of the site finally came with Gough's work there in the years 1955 to 1959: unfortunately, he died in the middle of plans to return for another season of excavation, and had at that time published little more than preliminary observations on his findings. What follows is therefore dependent to a considerable extent on Gough's field-notes and his scattered published material. Unlike his predecessors, who saw more remains at the site, Gough described Dağ Pazarı as 'a large and impressive site' (Gough 1976, 256).

The identification of Dağ Pazarı as the site of ancient Coropissus is not accepted by Michael Ballance (private communication). He has long held that Dağ Pazarı should be identified as the site of the ancient Isaurian city of Dalisandus, and although Hild and Hellenkemper (1990, 313) accept the probability of the identification with Coropissus in the *Tabula Imperii Byzantini* for Cilicia, Hellenkemper has recently (1994, 213) identified Dağ Pazarı as Dalisandus, though he offers no explanation for this. Inscriptions found at Dağ Pazarı prove conclusively that the site was a city, and in due course a bishopric. The city was occupied in Classical times, but it seems to have gone into decline during the sixth century, when there do not appear to have been sufficient funds for the repair of public buildings, and was depopulated by the eighth century. There was medieval re-occupation under the Selcuks and Armenians, but the site was then unpopulated until 1875 when the modern village was established by Bulgarian Turks. The name Dağ Pazarı ('Mountain Market') suits the village's role as a centre of population in a very sparsely occupied district. The main source of revenue for the modern village is timber: this was a major export of ancient Cilicia, and it is likely that, as the ancient site has been re-settled, so the ancient industry has been re-established. The broken pattern of settlement here throughout the historical period shows how marginal the environment really is. Only in antiquity was arable farming attempted on any large scale at this altitude.

DAĞ PAZARI, Monastery[66]

In his entry in the Princeton Encyclopedia of Classical Sites, Gough writes: 'As a bishopric, Dağ Pazarı almost certainly boasted a monastery (now destroyed)'. He does not give any evidence for this, and I have not been able to find any reference to such a monument in his papers, but it is possible that Gough was referring to the church which Wilson saw somewhere south of the 'Domed Ambulatory Church'. Hild and Hellenkemper offer the plausible suggestion that the decorated free-standing doorway with a cross on its lintel which survives close to the south circuit of the city walls may belong to this church.

DAĞ PAZARI: Basilica[67] (figure 27, plates 62-3)

The existence of this church was first revealed by the discovery of a mosaic floor by a villager who was building a stable over what turned out to be the narthex. Gough excavated the building in 1957 and 1958, and attempted some repairs to the narthex mosaic. He never published any lengthy report on his work, and within twenty years, the site has become virtually built up, with the mosaic floor almost totally destroyed. Gough's excavation, which was hampered by the modern hut over the narthex, and a house over most of the north side of the nave, consisted of a series of soundings, and, since he never wrote up his findings, and it is very unlikely that it will ever be possible to re-excavate the site, it is probable that the full complexity of the plan of this basilica will never be unravelled. This is particularly unfortunate since the Basilica demonstrates at least four building phases, and has unusual elements in its plan at both east and west ends. In essence this church was a three-aisled basilica with an inscribed apse, side-chambers, and an eastern passage with a central subsidiary apse. At a later date a narthex was added, and, later still, a baptistery was constructed at the northwest corner of the building. The church was divided into nave and aisles by two rows of seven Corinthian columns which probably supported a horizontal cornice. The columns were stuccoed, and had vertical slots which suggest that there were wooden screens between the nave and aisles. There was no evidence for a second order of columns, and it therefore appears that this church did not have galleries. The floors of the aisles were embellished with a simple opus sectile design. The church was burnt down, probably in the sixth century, and never rebuilt, although a small chapel was created in the narthex. Excavation in the area of the nave produced charred timbers (up to 20 centimetres square) and broken tiles from the roof, as well as elements of the church furnishings which included two large marble basins, a fragment of a stone eagle, and a bronze lamp chain, with a cross in place of the central link. Carbonized pieces of the door at the west end of the

---

[66] Gough 1976, 256; Hild and Hellenkemper 1990, 314, plate 246; Wilson 1895, 182.

[67] Gough, Manuscripts and drawings (1957/58); Gough 1958c, 644-6; Gough 1959a, 8; Gough 1959b, 3-4; Gough 1960b, 3; Gough 1965a, 410-11; Hild, Hellenkemper and Hellenkemper-Salies 1984, 265-7; Hild and Hellenkemper 1990, 313; Hill 1979, 9-12; Hill 1981, 29, figure 5.

south aisle were also found, along with its iron studs and door-plates, and even a key.

The presence of a modern house over the northern half of the nave and the northern side-chambers precluded full exploration of the plan of the eastern part of the church, but it seems likely that the arrangements discovered on the south side of the building would have been duplicated on the north side. At the east end of the church was a stilted semi-circular apse flanked by side-chambers. On the south side at least there was a doorway between the apse and the side-chamber, which also had doorways allowing access to the south aisle, the eastern passage, and through the south wall. The eastern passage was 2.2 metres wide, and provided with a small projecting apse immediately behind the main apse. The ambulatory passage did not run further south than the south jamb of the entrance to the southern side-chamber. Gough considered that the whole church east of the narthex was of one build, but never explained some oddities which emerge from his own findings. The alignment of the primary part of the building is northwest-southeast. There was no evidence for the presence of galleries, a fact which seems very remarkable in a Cilician church of this size (about 50 by 16.5 metres). The nave and aisles were divided by colonnades which had very Classical Corinthian capitals, and were probably trabeated. At the west ends of these colonnades were found the foundations of half-columns engaged against short wall footings, which showed returns for a stylobate which ran across the west end of the nave. The precise arrangement at the east end is more difficult to discern, but here the most important peculiarity is the presence of a vertical join between the east wall of the nave and the rubble core of the apse, the outer side of which is not faced. Gough also found a square stone base at the south side of the mouth of the apse which he thought might have supported a column, as was the case in the extra-mural basilica at Dağ Pazarı. Gough's plan also reveals a confused mass of foundations in the side-chamber and the ambulatory. From these he concluded that the southern side-chamber was divided into two unequal bays, the western being the larger, but he ignored the foundations which ran transversely across the ambulatory in the area behind the main apse. The vertical joint and change of building technique in the build-up of the main apse, combined with the unnecessary foundations in the side-chamber and ambulatory are surely conclusive evidence that there must be at least two building periods here. The most likely solution is that the Christian basilica was a conversion of an earlier basilica in which the colonnades were present on at least three sides of the interior, and which probably had a projecting rectangular tribunal at its southeast end. This explanation would make sense of the extra foundations, and the curious arrangement of the stylobates, as well providing a reason for the eccentric orientation, since the building might well have been constructed to serve secular purposes. This primary function of the building would account for the Classical nature of the capitals, and the trabeation would also conform to a dating in the

Roman period. This explanation of the architectural problems would also provide a context for several early fourth century coins which were found in the basilica. The conversion of the building to Christian usage may not have been effected until the beginning of the fifth century, since Gough found a coin of Arcadius (395-408) under the southwest corner of the floor of the church.

The suggestion that the church is essentially a conversion of an earlier building does not destroy Gough's point that the narthex was an addition to the basilica, but it is perfectly possible that the narthex was nevertheless an original feature of the church. The narthex deviates from the alignment of the basilica to a marked extent: this brings it more close to the east-west alignment which we would expect for a church. The Christian architect may, therefore, have deliberately included the narthex in his conversion not merely for utilitarian reasons, but also in order to compensate at least to a small extent for the inconvenient alignment of the structure with which he was dealing. The narthex presents another problem in addition to that of its relative position in the building scheme, which is that of the original appearance of its west wall. The donkey stable over the north end of the narthex re-used the ancient footings, and it was, therefore, possible to recover the walls of only the southern half of the narthex. Here Gough found the footings of a substantial doorway opposite the doorway into the nave, and also a simpler opening which corresponded roughly to the entrance to the south aisle, but was displaced slightly to the north. The central part of the west wall of the narthex was composed of irregular large blocks of spolia, and was unlike any other part of the building in terms of its construction. Gough also reported that an apse had been inserted into the north end of the narthex over the debris which marked the destruction of the basilica. He thought that this little chapel might be as late as the seventh century, and would have fulfilled the religious needs of the much reduced population of that period. The irregular appearance of the west wall would seem most appropriate to this late phase of the occupation of the church, and although Gough proposed that there were originally three doorways in the west wall of the narthex, it is perhaps more likely that there was originally an open colonnade, spolia from which was incorporated into a later closed façade.

The main feature of interest in the narthex is its mosaic floor. This covered an area measuring nearly 17 by 5 metres, and was of very high quality. As found, it consisted of two parts, the southern half being a repair to the original mosaic which had filled the whole narthex. The earlier, northern, section of the floor contains an inscription recording the dedication of the narthex and its floor under Bishop John Elpidius in a fifth indiction. This section of the mosaic has a design of interlinked roundels containing birds which alternate with sacks of fruit and chalices. The southern half of the mosaic shows an elaborate vine scroll issuing from a chalice. Two fat-tailed sheep face each other on either side of the chalice, and the scroll is inhabited by a great variety of birds, and one hare. Immediately above the central chalice is a roundel containing an inscription which records the restoration of the mosaic by Bishop Longinus. The period of neither Bishop's tenure can be determined, but it seems likely that the earlier mosaic should be attributed to the same period as the conversion of the basilica into a church, most probably the first half of the fifth century. Gough considered that the second part of the mosaic might well belong to the late fifth century, but offered no particular reason for this. The date would suit stylistic considerations since the mosaic is similar in feeling to the range of mosaics depicting animals and birds which were being produced in the region at that time, and would also suit the archaeological evidence, since the latest stratified coins which could be attributed to the occupation of the whole church were sixth century issues. The various birds depicted in the later part of the mosaic, which include a swan, a crane, a goose, doves, and pheasants, represent all the species which Basil of Seleuceia described in the bird park at Meryemlık (Dagron 1978, *Miracula* 24, 25-8). This may well be more than merely accidental, and, given Zeno's undoubted involvement with the sanctuary at Meryemlık, it may not be illogical to suggest that the bird mosaic here, and others like it, have as strong a flavour of the late fifth century as that proposed by Gough for the paradise mosaics which contain quotations from Isaiah, and which Gough wished to relate to the publication of Zeno's *Henotikon* in 482 (Gough 1972, 210-2).

The baptistery was a secondary addition to the church at the north end of the narthex. It was about 13 metres square, and had the foundations of an apsidal structure on its southeast side set one metre west of the outer wall. Using this evidence Gough suggested that the baptistery originally took the form of a small basilical chapel with a passage behind the apse. Since only foundations were found for the apse, and no trace of stylobates emerged to prove that there were once aisles, it must be considered more likely that the apsidal foundations were nothing more substantial than those of a priests' bench, which need not have stood as much as a metre above floor level. The font was a monolithic octagonal limestone block which stood slightly to the west of the centre of the mouth of the apsidal foundation. It was stuccoed and painted, and had steps in four of its sides: there were two steps on the north and south sides, and one step on the east and west sides. The intra-mural Basilica was easily the largest of the three churches known at Dağ Pazarı, and is likely to have been the cathedral of the bishopric. Its history is probably an accurate reflection of that of the city in which it stood. It seems to have been built during the third or early fourth century, possibly as a secular basilica. It was converted to Christian use during the fourth century, or, at the latest, during the early years of the fifth; was partially damaged by fire in the second half of the fifth century and carefully restored; but when a more serious fire wrecked the building at some point in the sixth century, no attempt was made to restore it. Instead a miserable chapel was created out of the debris of the narthex, and even this seems to have abandoned during the seventh century. During the brief centuries of re-occupation during the Selcuk period, a small child was buried in the late chapel.

DAĞ PAZARI, 'Domed Ambulatory Church', Standing Church[68] (figure 28, plates 64-70)

This is the best preserved of the monuments at Dağ Pazarı, but also the most perplexing. Gough conducted a limited excavation inside the building in 1958, and clarified some of its problems, but his trenches were not extensive for reasons which appear in the manuscript of a public lecture which he entitled 'Dağ Pazarı and its Churches'.

> 'The excavation of the church planned by Headlam has not been easy, as a minor engineering operation was needed to clear the areas to be dug of huge blocks of masonry which have fallen from above, from the vaulted aisles and the dome and, later, from the walls.'

The first visitors to the site, Davis and Headlam, both dismiss it as being a very ordinary church, but their brief descriptions contain some useful points. Davis describes it in the following terms:

> 'The highest point in the city was occupied by a church of the usual form, viz. a nave, two aisles, and a stone-vaulted apse. All the roof except at the apse has fallen in; a line of arches on either side separated the nave from the aisles. At the sides of the apse, and inner side walls, are pilasters with Corinthian capitals, taken from some earlier building. The west façade has fallen into utter ruin; there was a wide, open, paved space in front of it.' (Davis 1879, 325)

Headlam wrote:

> 'It has the appearance of having been built on foundations dating from an earlier period, perhaps those of the temple that it succeeded, and was surrounded by a large peribolus wall. Although probably early - being not later than the time of Justinian - it has no features of great interest. The plan is simple. At the west end was a structural narthex. From this the church was entered by three doors. It consisted of a nave with two aisles. The nave ends in a bema and apse which is partly external, the aisles in side chambers. There was no ornament of any interest. The church seems certainly later and of a more conventional type than that at Koja Kalessi.' (Headlam 1892, 20)

---

[68] Davis 1879, 325; Forsyth 1957, 233-6; Gough 1959a, 8; Gough 1960b, 3-4; Gough 1972, 203-8; Headlam 1892, 20-1; Hild, Hellenkemper and Hellenkemper-Salies 1984, 264-7; Hild and Hellenkemper 1990, 3134; Hill 1979, 9; Hill 1981, 32.

Some inconsistencies in the coursing of the surviving east end of the south wall lend credence to the suggestion made by both Davis and Headlam that the church may include spolia from an earlier building, but there is now no trace of a surrounding wall. Headlam's most useful contribution was his photograph of the east side of the church which clearly shows a wall which originally rose above the mouth of the apse, and was capped by a flat cornice (plate 64). It also appears that in the nineteenth century it was still possible to make out the traces of an atrium on the west side of the church, and of a precinct. What is most clear of all is that both Davis and Headlam regarded this as a conventional basilica with nave and aisles divided by colonnades. Although, as will be seen, this was no ordinary basilica, certain of its features are conventional. The church measures approximately 27 by 20 metres overall, and has a semi-circular apse, which was lit by three arched windows: the southern dividing column and southern arched window of which can still be seen. An unusual feature is the slight projection of the apse which may be compared with the Town Church at Ura, but would be more normal in the Plain. Gough's excavations in 1958 revealed the two-tiered synthronum around the inside of the apse, and a mass of glass tesserae which suggest that the semi-dome was originally adorned with a figured mosaic. The chord of the apse is 4.5 metres wide and immediately to the west is a chancel area which is 4 metres deep. Barrel-vaulted side-chambers survive to north and south of the apse and choir. These side-chambers were provided with doorways into the choir, and into the aisles. The aisles were single-storeyed and barrel-vaulted. There are doorways at the centres of the outer walls of both north and south aisles. These doorways were once provided with hooded porches supported on consoles, and the jambs of the south door, which may have been the main entrance, were decorated with an inhabited scroll. Gough found traces of a courtyard on the south side of the church. To either side of the exterior doorways on the inside of the aisle walls were set semi-circular niches, the purpose of which has not been determined. The church had a narthex with a single entrance in its west wall, and three doorways leading into the main part of the church. Pairs of niches set between the doorways in the east wall of the narthex were probably stoups. The outer wall of the narthex had three shallow buttresses on either side of the doorway. Between these buttresses stone benches were provided. There was almost certainly an atrium on this side of the building: this had an apse, of approximately the same dimensions as the eastern apse, on its west side. Although the exterior is relatively devoid of sculptural ornament, the church was enlivened by the presence of buttresses on the north, west, and south faces, and by the unusually generous provision of windows at ground level. The windows beside the doorways in the north and south walls are arched and have simply moulded springing stones, but most of the remaining windows are plain rectangles. Another feature which enlivens the articulation of the façades is that the surviving doorways have open relieving arches above their lintels. The interior of the church appears to have been much more lavishly decorated than the exterior. There are particularly elaborate capitals at the mouth of the choir (plate 69), and Gough found rich acanthus column capitals in the fill of the nave. The semi-dome of the apse probably had a mosaic with glass tesserae, and the floor of the apse had a geometric pattern in opus sectile. The small areas uncovered by Gough's sounding revealed that the aisles and the narthex had tesellated mosaic pavements with guilloche patterns of high quality. The niches in the inner faces of the north and south walls would have increased the decorative effect of the complicated articulation of the outside walls.

It was not until Forsyth visited Dağ Pazarı in 1954 that the full significance of the plan of this church started to emerge. Forsyth, with only Headlam's plan to follow, pointed to the close similarities between this church and the 'Kuppelkirche' at Meryemlık, the Tomb Church at Corycus, and the East Church at Alahan. Forsyth argued strongly that all these churches had a tower-like central bay which was roofed by a wooden pyramid. He pointed to the flat-topped wall visible above the apse in Headlam's photograph as being the eastern wall of such a tower at Dağ Pazarı. Forsyth did not, however, question Headlam's plan, and therefore assumed that this roof was oblong in shape. He wrote, in relation to the arches which sprang from the mouth of the apse:

> 'We may note that the upward sweep of the north and south springs is far more steep than that of the eastern ones, as befitting the much greater span of the north and south arches. Turning now to Headlam's photograph, we realize that the crown of the eastern arch of the nucleus would be lower than the roof of the choir, but the crowns of the north and south arches, being a couple of meters higher, would have risen nearly to the level of the cornice at the top of the nucleus. Consequently, no room is left for a vault or dome to spring above the north and south arches, and the only alternative is a wooden roof, which would probably have had a pyramidal rather than a gable form, for the cornice of the nucleus was clearly horizontal all around and no evidence of a ramping cornice is visible in the photograph.' (Forsyth 1957, 235)

Forsyth's argument is less than watertight. The distinction between the angle of inclination of the arches to which he refers is not at all clear to the eye since there are only one or two springing stones of the north and south arches surviving, and as will be seen, Gough's excavations have proved that all four arches had the same span. Also Forsyth's argument does not preclude the possibility that a gable could simply have fallen from above the cornice visible in Headlam's photograph. Such a gable could have supported a normal longitudinal roofing system. Whilst I have been unable to trace whether Headlam's field notes or, better still, further photographs survive, the 1890 field-notes of his companion, Sir William Ramsay, are preserved, along with Ramsay's other papers, in the Ashmolean Library. The first 17 pages of the notebook for 1890 relate to Dağ Pazarı, and on page 12 appears 'perpend section through apse', which shows a triangular gable sitting on the cornice of the wall above the mouth of the apse. This establishes clearly enough that at least one member of the 1890 expedition thought that the church had a longitudinal basilical roofing system. This is, of course what would be expected from the building as it appears in the plan published by Headlam. Pages 10 and 11 of the same notebook contain a rough sketch of the plan of the nave and some relevant measurements. Among this information appears the observation that there was a pier on the south side of the nave 15.3 metres west of the pilaster at the mouth of the apse. Ramsay noted that there were two arches to the east of this pier, and one to the west. This conforms perfectly with the plan as it was published in Headlam's monograph, and we must surely assume that the plan represents what was visible at the time. There is no indication in Ramsay's sketch that there were similar pier bases visible on the north side of the nave, and we can presume that these were included in the plan for reasons of symmetry. It must, therefore, be accepted that Davis and Headlam saw exactly what they said they saw, that is a basilica divided by arches into nave and aisles. If so, they must have seen the last vestiges of a secondary plan, which was in all probability basilical, although it is even possible that what they saw was some form of medieval repair which could have supported a simple roof which need not necessarily have covered the whole building. Gough's limited excavations certainly produced enough evidence to show that the building was in some way occupied in the medieval period, as he stated in the lecture which was referred to above.

> 'The dating of this church has so far proved extremely difficult since in the time of the Karamanoğulları it was probably still in use as a han or a shelter for animals. Even today the pastophories are store rooms for straw. The stratification so far encountered has been of layers of dung, interleaved, as it were, with yellow clayey earth, representing presumably periods of time when the church was entirely abandoned, since the number of small finds is, practically speaking, nil. At the top is a metre's accumulation of masonry blocks and rubble - the result of eighty years of stone robbing.'

The last sentence is particularly important since it contains the key to the puzzling final sentence of the previous quotation from this lecture. It is clear that the stratigraphical record revealed two destruction levels in this building: one contained masonry characterized as coming 'from the vaulted aisles and the dome'; a second, later, destruction level, which was found above the medieval occupation levels, contained materials which Gough assumed came from the 'walls', and had been deposited recently. The simplest explanation of the stratigraphy is to assume that the dome and vaults of the church fell in antiquity, and were levelled, and partly re-used, either in antiquity or in the medieval period, when some attempt was made to cover the building with a simple timber roof. The building still showed traces of this secondary phase when seen by Davis and Headlam, but stone-robbing in the first half of this century removed the traces of the secondary building. Ramsay's notebook contains many measurements giving heights of walls in 1890, and it appears that the walls were very little better preserved then than they are today. The newly deposited debris found by Gough would, therefore, best be explained as the rubble from the demolition of the secondary patching. Although the details of Forsyth's argument are unconvincing, his suggestion that the church at Dağ Pazarı had a tower over the nave was to be confirmed by Gough's soundings in 1958. Gough found very substantial L-shaped piers in the western part of the nave, which formed two corners of a central nucleus 10.8 metres square (plate 70). He also found the bases of two columns which supported the arcade between these piers across the west side of the nave. Since the spaces between the western piers and the pilasters at the mouth of the apse is identical, Gough suggested, reasonably, that there would have been two columns along both north and south sides of the nucleus which would have supported the arches which start to spring from beside the mouth of the apse. The remains give no precise answer to the question of how this nucleus was roofed, but Forsyth's objections to the suggestion of a masonry dome have all been shown to be invalid. There certainly remains a great mass of fallen masonry choking the centre of this building. Gough evidently thought that the church had had a dome while he was excavating it, but his recantation came in 1972 when he published his thoughts on the 'Domed Basilicas' at Alahan, Meryemlık, and Dağ Pazarı:

'At Dağ Pazarı, I carried out a sounding in the church in 1958, and this established beyond reasonable doubt that its nucleus was of exactly the same pattern as those at Meryemlık and Alahan. Even with Headlam's hypothetical plan, and no more, to help him, Forsyth remained convinced that the eastern bay of the nave was roofed with a timber pyramid, and with the evidence now firmly established, who is to gainsay the possibility, or even the probability of this?' (Gough 1972, 205)

But Gough is surely being naive to think that the firm establishment of the evidence for the tower nucleus in any way supports Forsyth's arguments about its superstructure. I have tried to show that the reverse is true, and that Gough's discoveries actually undermine Forsyth's histrionic arguments in favour of the wooden pyramid. I would propose, indeed, that the case for the masonry dome is a very strong one. The previous existence of a masonry dome would explain two aspects of this building which do require explanation. Firstly, the debris from such a structure accounts for the depth of the overburden of broken masonry which chokes the building. Secondly, it is much more likely that the collapse of a masonry dome would have also brought down the barrel-vaults which buttressed it, than that a lighter, wooden, roof would have done so; and we have seen that the later repairs to the building involved re-roofing the aisles as well as the nave. It could even be argued that it might well have been the stresses imposed by the weight of the masonry superstructure which caused the surrounding barrel-vaults over the aisle and the western bay of the nave to fail in the first place, and that the dome, as it were, fell under its own weight. It is more than likely that the dome here was supported by pendentives, since what appears to be the base of one can still be seen at the south corner of the mouth of the fore-choir, where the joint between the high arches of the nucleus is not quite vertical (plate 67). The appearance of this church may thus have been very similar to that of the church at Kasr Ibn Wardan, which is very similar in plan and size (figure 62).

The dating of this building has been discussed by Forsyth and Gough, and largely depends on the interpretation of the plan. Forsyth pointed to a basic similarity of plan linking this church with the other 'Domed Basilicas'. Forsyth noted that the capitals in the apse windows at Dağ Pazarı and Alahan are nearly identical, as are the pier capitals of the nuclei at Dağ Pazarı and Corycus. Forsyth wanted to date the church at Dağ Pazarı to the sixth century, but Gough in 1972 extended his argument to show that there were good reasons for attributing the building of the group as a whole to the reign of Zeno (474-91). The group of 'Domed Basilicas' in Cilicia is more closely related than Forsyth or Gough realized. It will be useful here to outline the points which are relevant to Dağ Pazarı. The unusual hooded canopies over the doors at Corycus were originally also present at Dağ Pazarı. Dağ Pazarı and Meryemlık share the feature of having a western apse. Dağ Pazarı and Alahan both have slender buttresses which enliven the articulation of their façades.

Alahan and Meryemlık are securely dated: there can be little doubt that the 'Domed Ambulatory Church' at Dağ Pazarı is so closely related to them that it, too, should be assigned to the reign of the Isaurian emperor Zeno.

DAĞ PAZARI, Funerary Basilica extra muros[69] (figure 29, plates 71-74)

Gough published a lengthy account of his findings in this church, which he excavated in 1958 and 1959, and which has subsequently been quarried almost out of existence. The plan is relatively simple, but it is worth summarizing Gough's description here, since, owing to the circumstances of its abandonment, the basilica preserved rare evidence relating to the sanctuary.

The church stands outside the western circuit of the city walls on a terrace just above the north bank of the Kavak Gözü. There is an area of rock-cut tombs approximately 100 metres to the northwest, and Gough, therefore, suggested that this might have been a funerary church. The existence of the

---

[69] Gough 1959a, 8; Gough 1960a, 6-7; Gough 1960b, 3-4; Gough 1965a, 410; Gough 1965b, 233; Gough 1975, 147-63; Hill 1979, 12.

basilica was first reported in 1952 after one of the villagers, who was robbing stone from the site, found a bronze thurible. Gough dated this to the fifth century along with the original mosaics of the church. He concluded that a fire destroyed the north aisle at some point in the sixth century, and that it was not subsequently repaired. The church which is cut into the rock on the north side was soon afterwards buried under debris from the hillside, probably during a landslide. This double catastrophe meant that there can have been little chance to rescue the furnishings of the church, and some of these were buried with it.

The church is in plan a three-aisled basilica with a narthex, probably an atrium, and a projecting apse without side-chambers. The basilica measured 25.87 metres in overall length, and its internal width was 14.85 metres. The narthex extended across the full width of the church and was 3.2 metres wide, with walls 0.64 and 0.68 of a metre thick. The narthex had one doorway in its west wall, and three in its east wall leading into the nave and aisles. The doorway into the northern aisle was blocked and plastered over: Gough does not comment upon this closure, but it seems possible that the room thus created at the northern end of the narthex might have covered some of the functions of the absent pastophories. Parts of a simple mosaic survived on the floor of the southern half of the narthex. Two arcades with seven columns separated nave and aisles. The squat columns were 2.25 metres high and spaced 2.04 metres apart. They would, therefore, have supported high arches. The limestone columns were originally stuccoed and painted, and a least one had had an inserted metal cross as decoration. The capitals were very simple, with vestigial foliage, and a cross at the centre of the top of one side. A sanctuary area was defined at the east end of the nave by a screen which ran across the church between the penultimate pair of columns. The choir was defined by a low parapet at the centre of which was a doorway. The parapet supported four columns, which Gough suggested carried three arches, the central of these being the entrance to the sanctuary. He published a reconstruction drawing (figure 74) of such a system with capitals on the small columns to match those of the nave colonnades, and the whole screen reaching 3.5 metres high (the approximate height of the nave arcades), but he found no architectural fragments which could have come from higher than the small columns of the screen, other than a small voussoir block with a suspension ring for the broken sanctuary lamp and chain which had fallen in the doorway between the nave and the bema. Immediately in front of the chancel-screen, just north of the doorway into the bema, Gough found the foundations of the ambo which stood in the nave at the end of a short solea passage. The circular base of the ambo had sockets for wooden uprights, and probably had a wooden floor and superstructure. This is the only recorded example of such an arrangement in Cilicia, although one may compare the circular marble ambones found at Meryemlık (Herzfeld and Guyer 1930, 69, 75-6). A small column base found at the beginning of the solea, on the line of the parapet of the chancel-screen, which must have been open at this point, was perhaps the support for a lectern. The western part of the nave, and the length of both aisles, were paved with limestone slabs, but the area of the bema, behind the chancel-screen, was covered with a coloured mosaic in three panels. The central panel had a pair of does facing each other across a fountain, the side panels had geometric patterns based on a central cross. Gough was convinced that the mosaic in the bema should be dated to the fifth century. The area of the apse is the only part of the church where there is evidence of more than one building phase, since it had three separate floor levels. The apse was horse-shoed in plan, its diameter being 6.02 metres, and its chord 5.8 metres. Gough found two column bases on either side of the mouth of the apse, which he suggested might have been supports for a fore-choir arch, although he noted the incongruity of having columns smaller than those in the nave colonnades supporting an arch which was nearly three times as wide. The apse projected 3.77 metres beyond the east wall of the church and was originally lit by a double window. Its northern foundations were rock-cut. The first apse floor was at the same level as the bema, and was covered by a mosaic, the dedicatory panel of which was preserved beneath the altar. The second floor was laid immediately above the first and consisted of a pattern of interlinked roundels with a scale border. In the third phase a thick layer of crushed limestone was laid as bedding for heavy limestone slabs. This third period was the only one to have a synthronum. The position of the altar, just east of the centre of the chord of the apse, does not seem to have altered during the use of the building. Its base was found in situ with even the reliquary, which contained a silver box and a broken glass vessel, intact under a circular white marble cover. The altar top, which was originally supported on four wooden legs, and was a piece of red and blue Isaurian marble, had been carefully laid, face down, over the altar base. The building was constructed throughout of rubble and mortar faced with small stones, and had a tile and timber roof, and probably a clerestory. With the exception of the unexplained detail of the small column bases at the mouth of the apse, its plan is simple and unremarkable. But the evidence for the liturgical provision inside this basilica is very important for the understanding of the clues for such arrangements in other Cilician churches.

DELELİ[70] (figure 30)

This ruin-site in the Taurus near the Cilician Gates is mentioned only by de Jerphanion who described three buildings there, two of which were churches. One, which measured approximately 15.75 by 8.8 metres, had a semi-circular apse contained within the east wall of the building between two side-chambers. There was no narthex, and the west doorway of the church was the only part of the building standing above ground level. The second church measured 21 by

---

[70] De Jerphanion and Jalabert 1911, 302-3, figure 11.

11 metres: it had the same plan at the east end, but also had a narthex. Again it was only the doorways which survived above ground, there being one each in the west walls of the narthex and the nave. The doorway between the narthex and the nave had corbels which de Jerphanion suggested might have supported ornamental pillars. The site stands on the border between Cappadocia and Cilicia, and may well technically belong to Cappadocia (Hild and Hellenkemper 1990, 220), but the side-chambers are typical of Cilician church planning.

DEMIRCIÖREN see North of CORYCUS

DEMİRTAŞ, (Syedra)[71]
Bean and Mitford noted the presence of a large church among the ruins of the ancient city of Syedra, but gave no description of it.

DEVECİLİ[72]
Hild and Hellenkemper report a three-aisled basilica in this ancient village site one and a half hours north of Kanlıdivane.

DİKİLİTAŞ[73]
Hild and Hellenkemper report the ruins of a church which was probably early Byzantine at Dikilitaş, 13 kilometres southsouthwest of Kozan. One standing column has given the site its name.

DIOCAESAREA see UZUNCABURÇ

DOMUZTEPE[74]
Hild and Hellenkemper report a three-aisled basilica (about 26 by 15 metres) with a sixth century mosaic depicting animals at the village of Çerçioğlu near Domuztepe (22 kilometres southeast of Kadirli, 17 kilometres northeast of Osmaniye).

DÖRT DİREKLİ (Megarsus)[75]
This site was noted by Gough as having a basilica of conventional type for the Cilician Plain, with nave, aisles, narthex, and an external apse flanked by side-chambers. Hild and Hellenkemper list various churches, but these are of either medieval or unspecified date.

ELAEUSSA-SEBASTE see AYAŞ

---

[71] Bean and Mitford 1962, 191-4.
[72] Hild and Hellenkemper 1990, 238.
[73] Hild and Hellenkemper 1990, 238.
[74] Hild and Hellenkemper 1990, 242.
[75] Gough 1955, 204; Hild and Hellenkemper 1990, 335-6.

ELBEYLİ ('EL BOJLI')[76]

This small ruin-field was reported 6 kilometres north of Kızılgeçit by Keil and Wilhelm who saw the remains of a miserable church at its highest point. This is presumably the building which Hild and Hellenkemper refer to as 'eine Kirche(?)'.

EMİRZELİ[77]

Only very brief notices have appeared concerning this extensive ancient village with an Olban tower and Roman and late Roman houses and cemeteries which lies northwest of Çatıkören about 11 kilometres northnorthwest of Corycus. The overall site plan published by Hild, Hellenkemper and Hellenkemper-Salies (1984, figure 51) shows three large basilicas between about 28 and 40 metres long, and apparently associated in a compound marked by a wall on its north side.

EMİRZELİ, Church 1[78]

The westernmost basilica appears to have courtyards to west and south, and there was a narthex at the west end. The church was clearly a basilica, though the interior arrangements are not discernible. The apse, with its triple arched window is relatively well preserved, and it appears from Hellenkemper's photograph (1994, figure 9) that there were galleries over the aisles. As in the North Church at Yanıkhan the lower parts of the apse were constructed from large well cut ashlars and the upper parts have smaller squared stones. Flanking the apse are two eastwards projecting apsidal side-chambers with intermediate eastern chambers in the manner of Öküzlü North Church and the Transept-Church at Corycus.

EMİRZELİ, Church 2[79]

This is the smallest of the three basilicas at Emirzeli. On the west side it has a conventional basilical plan with a narthex, and the interior divided into nave and aisles by arcades supporting galleries. The east end of the church is remarkable. The circular apse was unbroken by windows because it was completely enclosed by the eastern apartments of the church. Whilst there was definitely no transept in front of the apse, the side-chambers rose to such a height that it is possible that there was a transverse roofing element which covered the building

---

[76] Keil and Wilhelm 1931, 93-4.
[77] Eyice 1981b, 208, plates 87.3, 89; Hellenkemper 1994, figures 9-10; Hild, Hellenkemper and Hellenkemper-Salies 1984, 228, 294, figure 51; Hild and Hellenkemper 1990, 249, plates 166-71.
[78] Hellenkemper 1994, figure 9; Hild, Hellenkemper and Hellenkemper-Salies 1984, figure 51.
[79] Hellenkemper 1994, figure 10; Hild, Hellenkemper and Hellenkemper-Salies 1984, figure 51, Hild and Hellenkemper 1990, 249, plates 166-7.

at this point. The appear to be high external corners which would have risen above the pitched roof of the aisles on both the north side-chamber (Hellenkemper 1994, figure 10) and the south side-chamber (Hild and Hellenkemper 1990, plate 166). Beyond the side-chambers and communicating with them through wide arches (as in Kanlıdivane, Church 4) were two further apsidal chambers between which was a square chamber immediately east of the apse.

EMİRZELİ, Church 3[80]

This is shown on the plan published by Hild, Hellenkemper and Hellenkemper-Salies as standing immediately to the northeast of Church 2 and connected to it by a slanting which joined the northwest corner of Church 1 with the narthex of Church 3. From the plan it appears to be a simple basilica with narthex. No side-chambers are shown on the plan, but Hild and Hellenkemper (1990, 249) seem to indicate that all the churches at Emirzeli had pastophories and the spurs which project eastwards from the church on the plan would seem to support the view that this church too had side-chambers.

EPIPHANEIA see ERZİN

ERÇELİ ('Bagh-Oeren')

Heberdey and Wilhelm reported a ruined chapel in a valley near Erçeli which they called 'Bagh-Oeren'.

ERDEMLİ (Calanthia)[81]

The first reference to a church at Eski Erdemli was made by Heberdey and Wilhelm, who noticed that the village mosque was converted from an early Byzantine church of remarkable size. The mosque is still in use, but it is now possible to make out only a small section of the original building. More appears to have been visible at the time of Feld's visit, and he was able to obtain some measurements which fully substantiate Heberdey and Wilhelm's claims for the size of this building. The apse was approximately ten metres wide at its chord and, if a marble column seen by Feld to the west of the mosque was originally part of the narthex, then the church would have been somewhere in the region of 39 metres long, and must presumably have been equipped with the normal Cilician narthex with two columns and a triple arcade. The apse did not project beyond the east wall of the church which also defined the east side of the side-chambers. Feld found one column base (46 centimetres in diameter) which probably came from the nave colonnade. The surviving masonry of the apse

---

[80] Hild, Hellenkemper and Hellenkemper-Salies 1984, figure 51; Hild and Hellenkemper 1990, 249.

[81] Heberdey and Wilhelm 1896, 46; Feld 1965, 137, Hild and Hellenkemper 1990, 281.

consists of large limestone ashlars. Ancient tombs can be found immediately to the east of the mosque, and about 100 metres to the west: the church must accordingly be assumed to be funerary in nature. It is a great pity that more information cannot be obtained concerning this church, since its great size is particularly remarkable for a church in what was the cemetery of an ancient village. Hild and Hellenkemper suggest a fifth/sixth century date for this church, and also report a small church on the road to Şaha.

ERGENUŞAĞI, Akkilise[82]

The church known as Akkilise gives its name to a locality near the village of Ergenuşağı (28 kilometres northwest of Kozan). The church is a relatively well preserved example of the eastern Cilician type of basilica constructed from large limestone blocks with its façade strongly articulated with horizontal mouldings which run over the window arches and a modillioned cornice. The building is heavily encumbered with rubble, and no plan has been published. Hild and Hellenkemper comment that the church belongs in an east Cilician group along with Bodrum, Kadirli, Ferhatlı, Akdam and Mazılık, and consider that it was occupied in the medieval period.

ERZİN (Epiphaneia)[83]

Gough records the presence of two churches at this site, which was first visited by Heberdey and Wilhelm, whose notes on one church are reported by Hild, Hellenkemper, and Hellenkemper-Salies who publish a plan, based on Heberdey's sketchbook, of a three-aisled basilica without side-chambers measuring 36.35 by 23.60 metres overall without the apse. Although there is a problem about side-chambers, Heberdey's church, with a rough stone apse, is presumably to be identified with the one which Gough described as a conventional Cilician basilica with narthex, nave and aisles, and side-chambers flanking an inscribed apse. The church was created out of spolia, including granite columns, probably from a temple. The second church was created by the addition of a brick apse to an earlier building, probably a temple, but, according to Gough, showed no sign of ever having possessed a narthex, side-chambers, or even colonnades which divided it into nave and aisles. Gough thought that this 'rough and ready' conversion of an existing building might well be one of the earliest churches in Cilicia (Gough 1955, 203). The use of brick is extremely uncommon in Cilician churches, at least until the Armenian period, but is characteristic of Roman buildings up to the third century. Thus its appearance here may serve to support Gough's suggestion. However, in his

---

[82] Hild and Hellenkemper 1986, 98, plates 145-50; Hild and Hellenkemper 1990, 251.

[83] Gough 1955, 202-4; Gough 1976a, 315; Hild, Hellenkemper, and Hellenkemper-Salies 1984, 194-5; Hild and Hellenkemper 1986, 103; Hild and Hellenkemper 1990, 250.

entry for Epiphaneia in the *Princeton Encyclopedia of Classical Sites* Gough wrote, 'There are two ruined churches, both apparently of the 5th or 6th c.'

ESKİ KALE see YENIYURT KALE

EVZENDİ[β-]

The village of Evzendi is in the mountainous area to the west of Ermenek, about 5 kilometres to the west of İmsi Köy. Heberdey and Wilhelm saw a ruined church with late graffiti carved on the door frame. Bean and Mitford report 'an admirably carved fish'.

FEKE see BAKA and KARAKİLİSE

FERHATLI[85]

A significant portion of the apse and parts of the north and south walls of this basilica stand near the village of Ferhatlı (8 kilometres northeast of Kozan). The apse was 7.9 metres wide and was five-sided externally, with a horizontal base moulding and a projecting string-course at the level of the springing of the windows. Inside the apse are the remains of a synthronum and cathedra. Hild and Hellenkemper attribute the church to around 500, and observe that it was subsequently reduced to a single-naved church with extra newly-built apses.

FLAVIAS see KADİRLİ

GAVURKIRILDIĞI[86]

A 'ruined church, apparently of late Roman date', was reported on this hill in the upper Cilician Plain by Alkım.

GAZİPAŞA (Selinus)[87]

The ruins of the ancient city of Selinus lie on the northern slopes of a promontory near the village of Selinus. This was one of the minor cities of western Cilicia, most famous, for being the place where the emperor Trajan died. The site was surveyed by Alföldi-Rosenbaum, who noted the presence of three churches, only one of which, building 10 C, she described in any detail.

---

[84] Bean and Mitford, 1970, 220; Heberdey and Wilhelm 1896, 129; Hild and Hellenkemper 1990, 254.

[85] Hild and Hellenkemper 1990, 254-5, plates 175-6.

[86] Alkım 1950, 556-7.

[87] Alföldi-Rosenbaum et al 1967, 29-35, plan 3· Hild and Hellenkemper 1990, 407-8.

GAZİPAŞA (Selinus) Church 10 C[88] (figure 31)

This church stands just below the summit of the site. As it survives it consists of a single-chambered chapel, measuring 12 by 6 metres, with a water-tank and hypocaust room annexed to its southeast corner. The apse is still standing, and parts of the north and south walls of the chapel survive to the level of the springing of the barrel vault which covered it. The chapel represents the remodelling of an earlier basilica, which was approximately 14 metres wide. Alföldi-Rosenbaum does not actually indicate whether there was any trace of foundations to the west of the later chapel, but the original basilica cannot have conformed to normal Cilician proportions since the site is constricted by the rocky outcrop at the southwest corner of the building. The stumpy proportions of the early church may be compared with the proportions of the early basilica at Meryemlık. After remodelling this church would have resembled the secondary phase of the Necropolis Church at Anemurium. The north and south walls of the chapel are not of identical construction, and it is, therefore, possible, that the reduction from basilica to chapel took place in two stages. The eastern end of the south aisle survived as a southern chamber to the chapel, but only the foundations of the north wall of the north aisle indicate its former presence. The barrel-vault of the chapel was strengthened by two rib arches, which divided the nave into three bays. There were doorways in the two eastern bays of the north wall, and one in the western bay of the south wall. There were also two, eccentrically placed, doorways in the west wall. There was a rectangular niche in the central bay of the north wall of the nave, and similar niches were cut into the south wall of the southern chamber. The most unusual feature of the chapel is the provision of a water tank beyond the southern chamber at the southeast corner of the building. This was lined with pink, waterproof plaster, and served with water by a terracotta pipe coming from the south. To the east of the tank is an irregular room, the floor of which is 2 metres above the level of the later nave. Part of this discrepancy in levels is accounted for by the provision in the southeastern room of a hypocaust floor system. The hypocaust room was approached by a flight of steps rising behind the outer curve of the apse.

The apse, which is slightly horse-shoed, and measures approximately 3.5 metres at its chord, is the main surviving element of the original basilica. A semi-circular niche to the south of the mouth of the apse may also be part of the original scheme, since it is blocked by the secondary south wall.

Alföldi-Rosenbaum suggested that the original basilica might be identified with the sanctuary of St Thecla which Basil of Seleucia describes as being on the summit of the hill at Selinus (Dagron 1978, *Miracula* 27, 30-48). Basil relates a story of how St Thecla appeared to the citizens of Selinus, and instructed them to build a house for her at the summit of their city in a position

---

[88] Alföldi-Rosenbaum et al 1967, 33-5, 66-8, figure 25; Hild and Hellenkemper 1990, 407.

from which it could be seen from far away, so that enemies would be terrified by the prospect, and security would be restored to the city. The citizens built Thecla's sanctuary which was still effective in Basil's day. The position of Church 10 C exactly suits Basil's description, and it is, therefore, possible that this was, as Alföldi-Rosenbaum suggested, a pilgrimage centre from an early date.

Alföldi-Rosenbaum's argument then follows a more questionable line (Alföldi-Rosenbaum et al 1967, 68). She points to the common association of pilgrimage churches with cisterns and bath-houses, and then states baldly:

> 'The chapels with cisterns recorded by us all belong to the medieval period, and in the examples of Selinus and Biçkeci Kalesi they were built at a later stage in the history of the churches to which they belong.'

We must assume that Alföldi-Rosenbaum thought that the secondary phase of this church was medieval, but the argument is surely syllogistic, besides which the basic assumption that all churches with cisterns are medieval is quite untenable. Numerous parallels of early date could be cited from Cilician examples, but two, which are particularly apposite, will suffice. It must be relevant to note that the two best-known pilgrimage centres in Rough Cilicia, Meryemlık and Alahan, both had cisterns and bath-houses. Baths were an essential feature of Thecla's miraculous cures at Meryemlık, and the presence of a bath here would seem to strengthen the suggestion that the church at Gazipaşa was dedicated to her. All this would seem to constitute strong support for the argument that there was a pilgrimage church at Selinus. As to its date, one can only note that the structure is remarkably similar to the secondary chapel in the Necropolis Church at Anemurium, which is firmly dated to the late sixth or early seventh century. Alföldi-Rosenbaum does not offer any structural evidence to support her dating, and in a sense the similarities between the construction of the walls of varying phases, all of which, including the primary apse, consist of mixed sandstone and limestone ashlars, are more striking than the differences. Accordingly, I would suggest that Church 10 C must be regarded as displaying signs of its occupation from the fourth or fifth century through to the seventh, until more conclusive evidence for a later date is produced. The excavation of this building should prove most instructive.

GAZİPAŞA (Selinus), Church 11 C[89]

This church stands outside the city on a terrace to the west of the necropolis, and is described by Alföldi-Rosenbaum as being a basilica 'of comparatively large dimensions' with a nave and two aisles, belonging to the fifth or sixth century.

---

[89] Alföldi-Rosenbaum et al 1967, 29, 66-7.

GİLİNDERE see AYDINCIK

GÖREKEN YAYLA[90]

Hild and Hellenkemper report the remains of two early Byzantine basilicas which were heavily re-modelled in the Armenian period. Church A, which was reduced to a single-aisled church in the medieval period, was 25.5 metres long with a nave 7.6 metres wide. Church B, known as 'Kırkkapı' was about 27.2 by 16.2 metres without a narthex. New curved moulding for the window heads were carved at the time of the re-modelling.

GÖRMEL [91]

Bean and Mitford reported various ruins in the vicinity of this village which is 14 kilometres southeast of Ermenek. Just above the village, on the path to the yayla, which is 5 kilometres to the east, the ruins of a church and a monastery were pointed out to them, and another church, which they did not visit, was reported at a locality close to the yayla, which was called simply 'Ören'.

GÜNEY KALESİ[92]

The site at Güney Kalesi was thought by Alföldi-Rosenbaum to be that of the ancient city of Antiocheia ad Cragum, and she accordingly included a description of the site in *A Survey of Coastal Cities in Western Cilicia*. Bean and Mitford subsequently suggested that Güney Kalesi was the site of Cibyra Minor, a city of Pamphylia (Bean and Mitford 1970, 59-66), but Mitford then proposed an identification with Carallia (Mitford 1980, 1254). Now Hild and Hellenkemper (1990, 191) have reverted to the identification of Güney Kalesi as Antiocheia ad Cragum. The only account of the buildings of Güney Kalesi is Alföldi-Rosenbaum's survey. The site preserves at least nine churches and chapels, most of which appear to have been occupied in the medieval period. Only three of these churches appear to have belonged originally to the early Byzantine period.

GÜNEY KALESİ, Church I. 15[93] (figure 32)

This church stood in a cemetery to the west of the city. Alföldi-Rosenbaum published a plan with only a few comments, although this was clearly a complex building which underwent considerable alterations. She interpreted the complex as being a single-chambered chapel built on the foundations of an earlier rectangular building with colonnades. She does not suggest that the earlier building was a basilica, but her plan would be consistent with the view

---

[90] Hild and Hellenkemper 1990, 262, plates 188-90.
[91] Bean and Mitford 1970, 208; Hild and Hellenkemper 1990, 262.
[92] Alföldi-Rosenbaum et al 1967, 18-29, plan 2; Bean and Mitford 1970, 59-66; Hild and Hellenkemper 1990, 191-3; Mitford 1980, 1254.
[93] Alföldi-Rosenbaum et al 1967, 27-9, figure 22.

that here was originally a basilica 23 metres long, and perhaps 12 metres wide, on the site of which a single-naved chapel was created by building infills in the north colonnade, and a new wall along the south stylobate. Alföldi-Rosenbaum considers that the apse was a secondary feature since it was built from the same materials as the secondary walls, and was distinct from the superior ashlar work of the foundations. If so, it seems likely that the apse occupies the same position as an earlier one, since the plan shows what appear to be the foundations of the north side-chamber, or the north end of an eastern passage. There must be some doubt about the phases of the building, since differences between the masonry of foundations and walls could almost be regarded as normal in Cilician basilicas. The plan also shows what appears to have been a narthex at the west end, which may have been wider than the rest of the building. A hall of this size is unlikely to have been built against a single-chambered chapel, whether this was created in the seventh century, or during the medieval period. The apse was paved with limestone flags, beneath which was found a small corridor and an underground chamber. It is not stated whether this was a cistern, or may have been a crypt. That this was a memorial church is likely from its position in the cemetery, with a substantial tomb about 20 metres to the southwest of the apse.

GÜNEY KALESİ, Basilica I. 11C[94]
This stood in the eastern part of the central area of the city. Alföldi-Rosenbaum's plan shows merely the apse, indications of the outer wall, and one door jamb at the west end. The basilica measured at least 24 by 14 metres, and was cut into the sloping site. Substructures on the south side contained broken columns.

GÜNEY KALESİ, Triconch I. 7C[95]
This structure stands in the centre of the ancient city, immediately north of the colonnade which ran through the site on an east-west alignment. It is not certain that this was a Christian building, but it is oriented, and has a western entrance, and its position at a relatively late date in the history of the city is assured since we are told that 'Two columns belonging to the arched entrance obviously were taken from the colonnades, as were large blocks, one of them a base, on the south-west corner' (Alföldi-Rosenbaum et al 1967, 18). The plan consists of a rectangle (8 by 6.5 metres), with apses set centrally in the north, east, and south walls. Alföldi-Rosenbaum's plan shows the east apse to be 3 metres wide, while the south apse is only 2 metres wide. There appears to have been a hall (5 metres deep) with an arched entrance on the west side. Unfortunately, no trace of the roofing system has survived.

---

[94] Alföldi-Rosenbaum et al 1967, 20, figure 13.
[95] Alföldi-Rosenbaum et al 1967, 18-19, plate XX 1.

GÜVERCİN ADASI[96]

Hild and Hellenkemper report a small early Byzantine church and architectural fragments amongst the ruins on this island 11 kilometres southwest of Taşucu.

HACIÖMERLİ[97]

This site lies 11.5 kilometres inland from Ayaş. Hild and Hellenkemper report a small three-aisled basilica in an ancient settlement with about 50 houses. The church had a narthex and galleries, The decorated jambs of the main doorway into the nave still stand. Nave and aisles were separated by columns 44-45 centimetres in diameter. The apse was 5.35 metres wide and lit by a double-arched window. The apse was flanked by side-chambers and a monolithic cruciform font probably belonged in the northern side-chamber, which presumably served as a baptistery and may have had a subsidiary apse. Doorways from the side-chambers suggest the presence of an eastern passage. Two-zoned capitals from the nave and the broad-leaved capital from the apse window suggest a date early in the sixth century.

HALİL LİMANI[98]

A large basilica with a nave 31.3 metres long and 19.8 metres wide was reported by Hild and Hellenkemper at Halil Limanı between Aidap (Iotape) and Gazipaşa (Selinus). Their plan shows a basilica with narthex and two large side-chambers which are not bonded to the apse. The northern side-chamber (9 by 11 metres) is substantially larger than the southern side-chamber. There is probably a cistern under the narthex (as in the South Church at Yanıkhan). The internal arrangements are not visible since only the apse (6.5 metres wide) is preserved to any height. It is constructed from uncoursed mortared rubble, with tile courses and arches, and was lit by a double-arched window. The height of the spurs of wall attached to the apse allow the assumption that the church had galleries. Hild and Hellenkemper report foundations for floor mosaic and traces of glass-paste wall mosaic. The material of the church contains significant amounts of spolia including granite columns. Hild and Hellenkemper make no comment on the fact that the apse is displaced to the south of the centre line of the basilica by about 4 metres. The most likely explanation for this phenomenon is that the church was equipped with a passage along its north side.

---

[96] Hild and Hellenkemper 1986, 33; Hild and Hellenkemper 1990, 264.
[97] Hild and Hellenkemper 1986, 78, plates 96-100; Hild and Hellenkemper 1990, 266.
[98] Hild and Hellenkemper 1986, 120-2, figure 20, plates 183-4; Hild and Hellenkemper 1990, 286.

HASANALILER, Basilica[99] (figure 33)

The village of Hasanalıler stands on the site of a late Roman settlement on the ancient road from Cennet Cehennem to Ura (Olba). Ruins of houses and a basilica were first reported by Sykes. The church was described by Feld, who visited the site in 1962, and at first merely noted that it was one hour north of Cennet Cehennem. He gives its name, Hasanalıler, in a footnote to his article, co-authored by Weber on the Temple-Church at Cennet Cehennem. Hild and Hellenkemper have subsequently published a plan and fuller descriptions of the church.

In essence the church was a three-aisled basilica measuring 28.5 by 18.5 metres overall (including northern and eastern passages). It had a narthex across the west end, which probably had the characteristic Cilician façade with a central triple arcade, since Feld reported two columns lying behind its ruins. The nave was flanked by aisles and galleries, and its foundations were cut out of the rock on the south side. The southern nave arcade still stands: its arches are supported on monolithic piers. The apse was 5.17 metres wide at its chord, and flanked by a subsidiary apse (2.1 metres wide) at the end of the north aisle: it had no windows since it was completely surrounded by a two-storeyed eastern passage. There was a two-storeyed side-chamber on the south side, whilst the north aisles terminated in an apse. A wall 2 metres beyond the outside of the apse enclosed an eastern passage which could be entered through the south side-chamber, and through a doorway in the north side of the curve of the apse, and from the northern passage The plan of the basic church is somewhat irregular since the north aisle is 3.9 metres wide and the south aisle only 3.2 metres wide. The northeastern part of the church is built over vaulted substructures which project eastwards beyond the line of the eastern passage. The substructure to the east of the apse at the end of the north aisle is itself absidal and has a niche in its northern façade. Hild and Hellenkemper consider that this church should be attributed to the sixth century because it had piers rather than columns supporting the nave arcades. The argument is not utterly convincing, and it may be safer to follow Feld and assume that the church belongs either to the fifth or sixth centuries. Given the complexities of the eastern apartments of the building it may in any case be the product of an extended building programme.

HIERAPOLIS CASTABALA see BODRUM

HOTAMİŞALANI (Mairamlık)[100]

This small site is 5 kilometres south of Kirobaşı (Mağra) on the east side of the road to Uzuncaburç, (Diocaesarea). Sterrett, who knew the site as 'Mairamluk'

---

[99] Eyice 1988, 22; Feld 1963-64, 103; Feld and Weber 1967, 271 note 9; Hild, Hellenkemper and Hellenkemper-Salies 1984, 226; Hild and Hellenkemper 1986, 64-5, figure 7, plates 67-70; Hild and Hellenkemper 1990, 270; Sykes 1915, 543-4.

[100] Sterrett 1888, 6-7.

observed that this is 'the name given by the Turks to a place sacred to the Virgin Mary'. The name Mairamlık is still used by local farmers. Hotamişalanı is, therefore, a name of dubious antiquity, although MacKay suggested that it might preserve the ancient name of Kirobaşı (Otanas or Ortanada?). Sterrett reported: 'three arches, belonging possibly to the substructure of a church, are still standing. A Corinthian capital also is still to be seen.' Sterrett also published an inscription on a font which was dedicated by one Theodosius. Only the battered column capital was still present in 1975. It was of a (probably fifth century) type with stylized acanthus leaves with a broad, flat central spine very similar to the pier capitals at the mouth of the choir in the 'Domed Ambulatory Church' at Dağ Pazarı. Sterrett's arches have gone, but a terraced platform which must have been the foundation for a basilica is still clearly visible. The church stood on a rocky outcrop. To the west, and below it, can be seen fragments of sarcophagi.

İMAMLİ, Basilica[101] (figure 34, plate 77-78)

The village of İmamli stands halfway between Silifke and Uzuncaburç, and is overshadowed by the Hellenistic fortress of Meydankalesi. Heberdey and Wilhelm reported seeing ruins which included a church immediately to the west of the road to Uzuncaburç, a short distance north of Döşeme. These ruins can be identified with some foundations which are still visible just south of İmamli. The village is referred to as Meydan by various travellers, but this name is no longer used except for the fortress. Gertrude Bell published a description of the church, which she visited in 1905, but referred to the site, very imprecisely, as 'Olbia'. The ruins stand immediately beside the modern road, and have been heavily quarried for hard-core as well as building materials for İmamli. Only the lowest courses of the main apse have survived, and Bell's description is therefore the only evidence for the original appearance of the church. There is a cistern just to the west of the church which has been kept in repair: two of the pier capitals from the church have been hollowed out to make water troughs, which stand beside the cistern. A large square stone block which forms the well-head on top of the cistern has possibly been created by drilling through the bottom of a simple early Byzantine font.

The church was a basilica with a narthex, and eastern passage, measuring 25 by 11 metres overall. Bell does not describe the narthex, nor is it visible in her photographs, but her plan shows a large space at the centre of its west wall, and it seems likely that it had the normal triple arcade. The narthex also had a doorway at its north end. Three doorways led from the narthex into the nave and aisles. The nave colonnades were supported on rectangular monolithic piers, and there had been square impost capitals on the engaged piers at the east end of the arcades. The apse, which measured 3.5 metres at its chord, was semi-

---

[101] Bell 1906, 26-8, figure 26; Hild and Hellenkemper 1990, 274.

circular on both faces and was lit, unusually, by a single rectangular window, the lintel of which was formed by the moulding which ran round the apse at the level of the springing of the semi-dome. There was a deep eastern passage which was entered through a doorway at the end of the north aisle. The south aisle was slightly shorter than the north aisle, and ended in a blank wall which was set forward slightly from the mouth of the apse in order to accommodate a doorway on the south side of the eastern passage. The passage had two subsidiary apses, both approximately 2.4 metres in diameter, one positioned centrally, the other at its south end. All three apses were constructed from much larger blocks than the rest of the church. There was a doorway in the south side of the central subsidiary apse. This doorway, and also the doorway at the end of the north aisle, had monolithic lintels with flat bottom sides and curved upper faces. Bell also found traces of a doorway on the north side of the church in line with the east wall of the narthex, and conjectured that there had once been a passage along the north side of the church. The north aisle of the church is visible in Bell's photograph, which shows what may be two fallen columns along the north side of the aisle; parts of small columns can still be seen at the site. These columns cannot have originated from the nave colonnades, and it is therefore possible that the north corridor and the north aisle were connected by an open colonnade, as was the case in the Necropolis Church at Anemurium.

İMSİ ÖREN (Philadelphia)[102]
The probable site of the ancient city of Philadelphia lies on a hillside above the village of İmsi Köy, eleven kilometres east of Ermenek (Germanicopolis). The identification was proposed by Bean and Mitford, who reported the presence amongst the ruins of a terrace with the foundations of a large church.

IŞIKKALE[103]
Işıkkale is the site of a small ancient village near Karakabaklı, about 11 kilometres northeast of Silifke. The site contains the remains of a three-aisled basilica with narthex and eastern chambers. Nave and aisles are separated by arcades supported by monolithic columns with fine acanthus capitals similar to those in the large church at Canbazlı. Both north and south arcades survive at ground level. On either side of the apse were large two-storeyed side-chambers which joined to form an eastern passage.

---

[102] Bean and Mitford 1970, 216; Hild and Hellenkemper 1990, 378.
[103] Eyice 1981b, 207; Hild and Hellenkemper 1990, 276, plates 201-3.

KADİRLİ (Kars Bazaar) (Flavias), Ala Cami[104] (figure 35, plates 79-81)

The identification of Kadirli with the ancient city of Flavias has never been confirmed epigraphically, but must be regarded as certain, since there is no other serious candidate in the northern part of the Cilician Plain which suits the historical evidence so well, or which preserves so many traces of Roman occupation (Gough 1952, 94-5, Hild and Hellenkemper 1990, 378).

The surviving early Byzantine church, was in use as a mosque, the Ala Cami, at the time of Davis' visit in May 1875, and was still in a good state of repair in 1905 when seen by Gertrude Bell. In her photographs, and in those of Bossert and Alkım which were taken in 1947, it stands in isolation, to the east of the village, surrounded by an open cemetery. The spread of Kadirli has now encompassed the Ala Cami. The building has had a varied history, and shows at least three phases of construction, the walls of all of which include spolia from Classical buildings. This confused Davis and Bent to such an extent that they interpreted the building as a monastery with a small church with cells beside it at the eastern end of a precinct. It was Gertrude Bell who first pointed out that the whole building was originally a basilica, and that in the medieval period, after the collapse of the roof, a small chapel had been tacked onto the west side of the apse, and that what had been interpreted as 'cells' had been created by roofing over the eastern ends of the aisles and the original side-chambers.

Gertrude Bell's servants had left with her baggage before she found the old church, and she felt obliged to follow them rather than stopping to measure the church. Bossert and Alkım published a plan of the southern half of the church with the following apology:

> 'Unfortunately at the time we did not have the means to make a more detailed and complete plan but are nevertheless satisfied that the present will serve to give the reader a general idea.' (Bossert and Alkım 1947, 19)

This last is somewhat over-optimistic, since their plan is little more than a sketch, which gives a very misleading impression of the arrangements at the east end of the building. Their plan shows the southern side-chamber, which is rectangular, as following the curve of the apse, when there was a triangular section of masonry which filled the angle between the apse and the east wall of the side-chamber. The apse is also shown with a curve which would come to a point at its eastern extremity if it was reproduced on the north side of the church. They omit the stilt of the apse, and the short sections of the east wall of the nave between the side-chambers and the corners of the mouth of the apse. A further error in their plan is that it shows a doorway into the southern end of the narthex. There is no suggestion of this in Gertrude Bell's photograph, and she

---

[104] Bayliss 1996; Bell 1906, 10-12, figures 6-7; Bent 1890b, 233; Davis 1879, 124-5; Bossert and Alkım 1947, 18-20, figure 167, plates 2-18; Feld 1965, 139, figures 5b-5d; Hild, Hellenkemper and Hellenkemper-Salies 1984, 201-2; Hild and Hellenkemper 1990, 378-9, plates 332-5.

states positively in her text that the end of the narthex was 'without openings'. I stress this last point, since Bossert and Alkım print a long quotation from Bell's description which actually omits the whole phrase concerning the south wall of the narthex, and therefore gives the impression that she saw doorways in it. This confusion may explain why Bossert and Alkım have distorted the proportions of the church, making it seem shorter than it is. Thus they show the church as being approximately 35 metres long, when in reality it is nearer 40. Although they show the correct number of openings in the south wall, it would appear that they have moved one of them into the end of narthex as an effect of their own erroneous copying of Bell's description. The plan which is offered here is based on sketches found in Michael Gough's papers: it does not take account of the excavation of Halet Çambel which uncovered steps at the western end of the church and a passage leading to an underground chamber beneath the Armenian chapel. This chamber may have been a crypt approached by a passage from the west end of the church as was the case in the Church of St Polyeuktos in Constantinople (Harrison 1989, 64, figures 53-6).

The first church was a basilica with nave and aisles separated by colonnades. There were galleries over the aisles, and upper floors over the side-chambers. The apse, which was stilted and semi-circular on both inside and outside, was flanked by small side-chambers, which were shorter on the east-west axis than on the north-south axis. The church was covered with a tile and timber roof which rested on a modillioned cornice and which, if the cornice which runs round the apse is in its original position, was hipped over the semi-dome of the apse. The apse is preserved to a sufficient height to show that no attempt was made to fill in the corner between its wall and the east wall of the church above the level of the ceiling in the upper side-chambers, although a small masonry infill was provided to square off the corners of the side-chambers themselves. The apse is lit by three arched windows which are set into its shallow projection. The piers which support the window arches are decorated with applied double columns which support extremely battered acanthus capitals. A string moulding runs continuously over the arches. The keystones are decorated with crosses in small medallions. The arrangement is very reminiscent of churches in north Syria. A smaller version of the modillioned cornice which crowns the walls of the church runs round the outer curve of the apse as a sort of drip-stone moulding immediately above the windows.

The rest of church was unusually well provided with doors and windows. On the long sides there is a line of six rectangular windows which lit the galleries, and a seventh rectangular window, at a slightly lower level, which lit the upper side-chamber. At ground level, a central doorway, which had a lintel surmounted by a flat relieving arch, is flanked by two arched windows to the west, and three arched windows to the east. A continuous moulding, which matches the string course over the apse windows, runs over the arches of the windows of the north and south walls, giving an appearance somewhat similar to the south façade of the Church of the Apostles at Anavarza as it appears in Gough's reconstruction drawing (Gough 1952, 117). There were also two doors at the east end of the south wall. One of these, which was at a higher level, allowed access to the side-chamber, the other was at the end of the south aisle.

The precise arrangement of the original interior is impossible to determine because of the medieval remodelling of the church in order to create the single-chambered chapel which included the original apse. The inserted chapel was built from the spolia of the earlier building, but a distinctively medieval moulding decorates the arch of its doorway. The conversion involved not merely the insertion of walls on the line of the original stylobates and across the nave, but also the alteration of the east ends of the aisles, which were covered over. The cross-beams between the chapel and the outside walls of the original church were supported by corbels rather than being inserted into beam-holes. Corbels on the west wall of the chapel show that it must also have had some form of porch. Beam-holes which took the joists of the original gallery floors run for the whole length of the side walls. The original east wall of the nave had a decorated cornice running across it at the level of the capitals which are placed at the corners of the mouth of the apse at the springing of the semi-dome, and the walls of the medieval chapel butt against the decorated moulding on the east wall of the nave. The oddly proportions of the side-chambers, which could not have been extended westwards beyond the mouth of the apse.

The narthex, as Bossert and Alkım observed, was a later addition. The resultant butt joint in the south wall is clearly visible in Bell's photograph which was taken while the south end of the narthex was still standing. The same observation can also be made concerning the north end of the narthex, which has also been disrupted by the addition of a minaret. The west wall of the narthex has three doorways, the central of which is wider and taller than the other two. All three doors are trabeated and have moulded jambs and lintels which were probably brought from an earlier building. The west wall of the nave has disappeared, probably to provide building stone for the minaret, but the south jamb of a doorway into the south aisle is still in position and suggests that the east wall of the narthex also had three doors into the nave and aisles. Beam-holes over the doorways in the west wall of the narthex show that at some point there must have been a porch, or even an atrium, at the west end of the building. The secondary nature of the narthex is a little surprising but it is likely that the nartheces of the churches at Bodrum were also secondary features. Since the only narthex at Anavarza is the unusual tripartite narthex of the Rock-Cut Church, which is dated to the year 516, it would appear that the known early churches of the upper Plain may all have lacked a narthex when first built.

In view of the major alterations to the church, it is hardly surprising that none of its furnishings have survived. Bossert and Alkım found fragments from a chancel, the upper part of a marble post, and a section of a decorated slab, in the garden of a house at Kadirli, but could not establish whether these had originated from the Ala Cami. There were mosaic floors in the nave and the side-chambers.

The church is the subject of cuurent study (Bayliss 1996); meanwhile it is difficult to date, but the decorated façade, though not the plan, of the apse may be compared with those of Syrian churches of the late fifth century, and it is difficult to argue with Hild and Hellenkemper's proposal that the church should be attributed to the late fifth or early sixth centuries.

KADİRLİ (Kars Bazaar) (Flavias), Church of the Fullers[105]

During their visit to Kars Bazaar Bent and Hicks were shown a mosaic which was being used as the floor of a reed hut. They had this washed and were able to copy a mosaic inscription recording the dedication of a church by the Guild of Fullers.

'KALE PUNAR' see MAHRAS DAĞI

KALINÖREN (Titiopolis)[106]

The probable remains of Titiopolis lie at Kalınören, about eight kilometres north of Anemurium. Hild and Hellenkemper report the remains of three basilicas with galleries and side-chambers constructed from uncoursed mortared rubble.

KANLIDİVANE (Canytela)[107]

The settlement, which was never a city, was part of Olban territory in the second century BC, and under Elaeussa-Sebaste in the Roman period. The village was built around a great cavern in the limestone, which measures 200 metres across and 60 metres deep. The site seems to have had strong religious associations: there was a sacred precinct in the bottom of the cavern, and it is likely that Church 4, which sits on the very edge of the cliff, occupies the site of a second temple.

This religious association evidently survived into the Christian period since no less than five early Byzantine churches are known to have been built around the cavern.

KANLIDİVANE (Canytela), Church 1[108] (figure 36, plates 82-4)

The east and west ends of this basilica are relatively well preserved. Although very little trace of the interior arrangements survives, it is clear that this was a standard example of the Cilician basilica, with narthex, nave and aisles, galleries, and an inscribed apse flanked by side-chambers. The basilica

---

[105] Bent 1891, 233; Hicks 1891, 1; Hild and Hellenkemper 1990, 379.

[106] Hild and Hellenkemper 1990, 447-8, plate 395.

[107] Bell 1906b; Eyice 1977; Hild and Hellenkemper 1990, 285-6, plates 205-14

[108] Bell 1906b, 405-8, figures 11-16; Eyice 1977, 423-5, figures 11, 17-19; Feld 1965, 134, plates 1d, 2a; Hild, Hellenkemper and Hellenkemper-Salies 1984, 208; Hill 1981, 29.

measures 31 by 18.4 metres overall. The church stands about 50 metres west of the cavern, and was probably a joint foundation with Church 2, which is 28 metres to the north, since a wall linked their east ends (plate 84), and there seems to have been a courtyard between them.

Eyice has pointed out that there was an atrium on the west side of the basilica: only occasional foundations of this can be seen, and the most impressive surviving part of the church is now the narthex, which is preserved to the height of the springing of the arch of its gallery window (plate 82). The lowest courses of the narthex are constructed from well-dressed limestone ashlars, whilst the rest of the wall consists of rubble and mortar faced by small square stones. This should not be seen as evidence of multiple periods of construction, since a similar phenomenon is manifest in the east wall of the church where the apse is constructed from large ashlars, but the higher courses of the side-chambers, and the courses of masonry above the apse window are in small stones. In both cases the transition to smaller stones comes where there is less stress on the masonry. Thus the architects of this church have used ashlars for the foundations, and for those parts of the building which supported the semi-dome of the apse, but have used cheaper methods in less critical places. The practice of varying the method of construction, which is clearly seen in the North Church at Yanıkhan, might almost be regarded as normal in Cilicia.

The normal Cilician triple-arched entrance to the narthex is here seen intact, although the capitals which support the arcading may be spolia from an earlier building. Above the entrance was a single, wide, arched window. The west wall of the narthex contains many putlog holes, which show how the scaffolding used by the builders was arranged in five spans on six vertical supports, and indicate that the building was stuccoed.

Three doors lead from the narthex into the main part of the church. The central door is much taller than the others, and has a cross carved at the centre of its lintel. All three doors have moulded jambs and lintels which are surmounted by semi-circular relieving arches. The tympanum over the doorway into the nave is open, but those over the aisle doorways have been filled in with masonry.

Nave and aisles were separated by colonnades. This is proved by the presence of several columns which have been re-erected in the area of the north aisle. Eyice has computed that there must have two rows of five columns supporting six arches, but has not excavated the stylobates to check this hypothesis. The south wall of the church has been badly damaged, but enough survives to show that there was a doorway at the centre of the south aisle. This lacks mouldings, but still has the relieving arch filled with masonry over the lintel. The north wall, which is preserved to a greater height for most of its length, has a similar doorway towards its west end, but was otherwise not pierced by windows. The west end of the north wall survives to a sufficient height to show the beam-holes for the joists which supported the floor of the gallery.

A row of slots at a lower level to the east of the north doorway has never been explained, but it is possible that there was a secondary roof over the aisle which ran up to, but not beyond, the north door. Similar slots can be seen at the same level in the outer faces of the apse walls. The columns from the nave arcades have at some stage been re-erected in a line running across the church from a point immediately to the east of the north door, which is exactly where the slots in the north wall stop. 5 metres to the east of the row of re-erected columns there is a rough foundation aligned north-south. Since this includes fragments of window dividers which may well have originated from the clerestory, it can hardly be interpreted as the bema of the original church. The simplest explanation of these features would be that they are the remains of a secondary remodelling of the church, which would have been very similar in plan to the secondary phase of the Ala Cami at Kadirli. It seems likely that a single-chambered chapel was annexed to the west side of the original apse, but only extended for half the length of the original nave. A porch on the west side of the chapel was supported by the re-erected columns from the original arcades, and the eastern parts of the original aisles were covered with low roofs.

The apse is well preserved, with nine courses of its semi-dome still in position. It is horse-shoed in plan, being 7 metres in diameter, and 6.7 metres wide at its mouth. It is lit by a double arched window, and is contained within the eastern wall of the church, which is also the eastern wall of the side-chambers. Capitals at the corners of the mouth of the apse support a simple cornice from which springs the slightly horse-shoed semi-dome. Feld considered that these capitals should be dated to the late fifth century. The side-chambers are irregularly shaped since no effort was made to disguise the outside curve of the apse wall. The pastophories extended 2.5 metres forward from the mouth of the apse, thus defining a sanctuary area at the east end of the nave. Arched doorways connected the side-chambers with this sanctuary area, and with the east ends of the aisles. The inner walls of the side-chambers were offset slightly from the corners of the mouth of the apse, in line with the stylobates of the arcades, the eastern arches of which were supported by engaged capitals on the corners of the side-chambers. These capitals are similar to those at the mouth of the apse, but at a lower level. Beam-holes in the east wall of the church, at a higher level than the slots in the outer face of the apse, show that the side-chambers had rooms at gallery level. The joists for the floors of these rooms therefore ran from east to west and were strengthened by arches which sprang across the side-chambers in line with the mouth of the apse. The upper side-chambers were lit by rectangular windows in the east wall.

The east façade of the church is flat. Its plainness was relieved by the double window of the apse, which is surmounted by a drip-stone moulding, and by the rectangular windows of the upper side-chambers, the northern of which is still intact. A considerable drop in levels between the floor of the apse and the base of the outer face of the east wall accentuates the distinction which has been mentioned between the ashlars of the lower courses of the east wall and the small stones of its upper courses.

Gertrude Bell saw a single-storeyed chamber which was annexed to the north side of the north side-chamber. This was the same length as the side-chamber, and was entered through a doorway in its western wall. The wall which connected Churches 1 and 2 ran from the northwestern corner of this extra chamber. The main north-south street through the ancient town runs between the apses of Churches 1 and 2 and the wall at the edge of the cavern. The fine doorway which is preserved just to the north of Church 1 may, therefore, have been an important entrance to the complex. Like the main doors in Church 1, this doorway has moulded jambs and lintel, with a cross at the centre of the lintel, which is surmounted by a semi-circular relieving arch, with masonry filling the tympanum.

KANLIDİVANE (Canytela), Church 2[109] (figure 37, plates 85-6)

This church is the least well preserved of the surviving basilicas at Kanlıdivane, and, in many respects, the most puzzling. It was first recorded in 1905 by Gertrude Bell, who was able to produce only an approximate plan owing its the ruinous state. The church has suffered from considerable re-building at its east end since Bell's visit, in the course of which the rest of the church has been used as a stone quarry. The southern half of the apse has been entirely removed for this purpose. Eyice has re-surveyed the building, but his published plan is confusing, since it includes all the modern alterations, which are not distinguished from the ancient walls.

Church 2 stands 28 metres to the north of Church 1 with which it seems to have been a joint foundation. The two churches are identical in construction with well-cut ashlars used for the apse and foundations, and rubble and mortar faced with small square stones for the rest of the walls. The ashlar foundations are still clearly visible on the south side of the north wall. The wall between the churches joins Church 2 at the southwest corner of the chambers to the east of its passage. The northern half of the apse, and a section of the north wall are the only substantial remains, but it is fairly easy to gain some idea of the original appearance of the western part of the basilica. Church 2 measures 41 by 18.6 metres overall, the internal measurements of the nave being 21 by 17 metres. Eyice reports seeing traces of a narthex. The church was divided into nave and aisles by two rows of columns, fragments of which remain within the building: Eyice's plan shows two rows of five. From the pilaster foundations against the mouth of the apse it is clear that the north aisle was 2 metres wider than the

---

[109] Bell 1906b, 409-10, figures 17-18; Eyice 1977, 425-6, figures 13, 20; Feld 1965, 134, plates 2b, 2c; Hild, Hellenkemper and Hellenkemper-Salies 1984, 208.

south aisle. The west door and the apse are, therefore, placed slightly to the south of the centre of the building. This peculiarity is repeated in Church 4, where the proximity to the cliff may have dictated the arrangement, but it is hard to see any such reason for the wider north aisle of Church 2. There was only one door in the west wall, the lintel of which was decorated with a medallion. The doors in the north and south walls were arranged in exactly the same way as those in Church 1 with the northern door being set further to the west. Bell and Eyice do not consider whether there were galleries, but since Bell's photograph shows that there was an upper floor above the eastern passage, it must be considered likely that there were also galleries above the aisles. The apse is horse-shoed in plan, being 6 metres in diameter, and 5 metres wide at its chord. No attempt was made to disguise its outer curve. A simple projecting moulding runs round the apse at the level of the springing of the semi-dome. Beam-holes round the inner face of the apse must have supported benches for the priests. There is a row of small square sockets spaced regularly five courses above the beam-holes of the bench: one explanation of this feature may be that they could have received supports for lamps, which would have compensated a little for the lack of a window.

The interpretation of the east end of this church is highly problematical. As has been noted, Eyice's plan includes all the twentieth century alterations. He has, furthermore, shown only one of the secondary walls in hatching which is distinct from that which he uses to denote ancient walls. His plan, therefore, can be used only to correct the distortions in the alignments of Bell's plan. Much more was standing in this part of the church in 1905, and it is surprising that Eyice did not take more account of Bell's observations. The plan published here (figure 37) follows Bell's notes.

It is clear from Bell's photograph and description that that there was a passage behind the apse which communicated with the side-chambers through arches which she denoted 'aa' and 'bb'. Only 'aa' was standing in 1905: it is still present, but has subsequently been filled in with masonry. A modern wall has been built almost exactly on the line of 'bb'. Bell also noted brackets on the apse, marked as 'c' and 'd' on her plan, which had supported arches which she suggested must have rested on the superstructure of the chamber directly east of the apse which is denoted as 'e' on her plan. This chamber is one of a range of three which were set on the east side of the passage. Only two appear on Eyice's plan. Even in 1905 these eastern chambers existed only as the vaulted substructures of some building which had disappeared, the floor of which was probably higher than that of the nave of the church. Bell found them in use as cattle sheds 'much blocked with filth'. They are still in use, and, since whenever I have visited Kanlıdivane they have been locked, I have been unable to examine the relationship between the eastern passage and chamber 'e'. Bell's plan shows dotted lines across the join. Eyice's plan shows an infill. It appears likely therefore that this chamber was originally connected with the eastern passage, as were the chambers on either side of it. Although the alignments are eccentric, and this church does have subsidiary apses, this arrangement is similar to that in the South Church at Yanıkhan, where there is also a square chamber on the east side of the passage directly behind the main apse.

I have thus far avoided referring to the spaces to north and south of the apse as the side-chambers. It may be more correct to suggest that these were part of the passage, and that the chambers on the east side of the passage may have been used as pastophories. This would explain why there were arches across the full width of the east ends of the aisles, and doorways into the eastern chambers which were roughly opposite the ends of the aisles. Although Bell thought that the arches at the east end of the church 'supported the roof of the passage', it is clear from her photograph that there was an upper storey over the passage, and that the arches supported walls which would have risen as partitions at the upper level. A console can be seen in her photograph which would have supported a beam which would have run diagonally across the floor of the awkwardly shaped upper room on the southeast side of the apse, and would thus have given extra support to the joists which were set into the wall above the transverse arch of the passage (this arrangement was also present in the North Church at Yanıkhan). Bell's photograph also shows a section of wall at the north end of the east side of the passage, which shows that there also were two storeys at that point in the building.

A further peculiarity of this church is the extra room at its northeast corner. On Bell's plan this not so much a room as a triangular excrescence with a doorway in its west side. It appears, more convincingly, on Eyice's plan as a chamber at the northern end of the passage, open to the passage for most of its southern side. In 1973 I saw the foundations of a doorway on the north side of the church in line with the west wall of the nave, corresponding exactly to the doorway in the west side of the northeast chamber. By 1975 the stone-robbers who had uncovered this foundation had removed it, and by 1979 scrub-oak was firmly established in the disturbed soil. The presence of this doorway allows the possibility that there was a corridor or walkway along the north side of the church, leading from the narthex to the eastern chambers. The arrangement may be compared either with that of the Necropolis Church at Anemurium, where the northeastern room was used as a baptistery, or with that of the South Church at Yanıkhan, where a colonnaded walkway along the south side of the church leads directly into the eastern passage with its central martyrium.

KANLIDİVANE (Canytela), Church 3[110] (figure 38, plates 87-90)

This church, which stands near the northwestern corner of the cavern was described very briefly by Bell, and has been discussed at greater length by

---

[110] Bell 1906a, 410, figures 19-23; Feld 1965, 134, plates 2a, 3a; Eyice 1977, 426-9, figures 14, 21-2; Hild, Hellenkemper and Hellenkemper-Salies 1984, 208; Hild and Hellenkemper 1990, plate 208.

Eyice. The position of this church is very close to the centre of the ancient settlement, and there is an open space on the east side of the church where a large ancient cistern is still in use. The plan presents few points of dispute, but the walls of the church belong to various periods, and show considerable signs of remodelling. It is possible that the complex east façade of the church contains parts of an earlier domestic structure. In essence Church 3 was a simple basilica with a narthex, side-chambers, and, probably, with galleries. It is likely that the original plan of the church was similar if not identical, since the walls of the eastern part rise directly from the earlier walls, and the west wall of the narthex appears to have been part of a much earlier building.

Church 3 measures approximately 23.5 by 17.5 metres overall. As Bell observed, 'the principal feature of the third church is the exceptionally strong western wall of the narthex.' The outer face of this wall is constructed from well dressed limestone ashlars. The thickness of the wall is reduced by offsets as it rises. As Eyice pointed out, this wall must be earlier than the rest of the church, and I see no reason to doubt his tentative suggestion that it was part of a Roman building. Eyice also points out that the inner face of the wall does not match the outer face. The former is, in fact, exactly similar to the walls of the rest of the church, even to the extent of showing two constructional phases, with coarse small stone facing on the lower half, and more regular, coursed, squared stones in the facing of the upper half. This inner facing, however, is the replacement for the original facing which was presumably in disrepair at the time of the building of the church. Eyice's plan is misleading in two respects. Firstly, he omits the earlier part of the west wall as if it were not part of the church: this is particularly unlikely since it is clear that the rest of the earlier building occupied the space which is now covered by the church. Secondly, he employs different hatching for the west and south walls of the narthex, although the building techniques used in the narthex conform exactly to those in the rest of the church.

The inner face of the west wall runs for an extra 2.4 metres past the south end of the earlier, western, face before turning to meet the south wall of the church. The massive west wall was without windows or doors, but there were arched doorways at the north and south ends of the narthex. The east jamb of the southern doorway is still in position, and Eyice may well be correct in suggesting that the architrave was re-used. On top of the jamb sits the corner of the lintel, and the first springing stone of a relieving arch. A row of beam-holes set in the inner face of the west wall is much more likely, as Feld suggested, to be evidence for an upper floor in the narthex, than, following Eyice, to be evidence for a wooden lean-to roof.

It is possible that in antiquity, as today, the north-south road through Kanlıdivane passed through this narthex. If so, we may compare this with the South Church at Yanıkhan, where the ancient road appears to have passed through the atrium. There may be a further similarity between the two churches, since there is a cistern under the atrium at Yanıkhan, and it is possible that Church 3 at Kanlıdivane controlled the cistern against its eastern side. Thus not only would both churches appear to have been public in the sense that thoroughfares passed through them, but they may also have served as public fountain houses. There is some reason, in both cases, to suppose that these were the parish churches in their settlements. The only other church at Yanıkhan stands in the cemetery: at Kanlıdivane Churches 1 and 2 were probably part of a monastic precinct, and Church 4 was commemorative in character.

Three doorways led from the narthex into the nave and aisles. The moulded architrave of the central door is still standing, but it is not possible to determine whether or not it had a relieving arch. There was a doorway at the centre of the south wall with pairs of arched windows to either side. There was no doorway in the north wall, which does not survive to a sufficient height to show whether it had any fenestration. There is now no trace of any division of the church into nave and aisles since neither fallen columns or piers, nor even the returns of arcading against the east or west walls of the nave, can be seen. It cannot, indeed, be stated with certainty that there were aisles. The placing of the doorways in the west wall would tend to suggest that their presence was likely, but other considerations seem to militate against this. Since no two walls of the church are parallel, it is very difficult even to guess where the stylobates might have been. Given the position of the doors in the west wall, and the alignment of the mouth of the apse, one is presented with the problem that either the north arcade was 1 metre longer than the south arcade, and neither was at a right angle to the east wall of the nave, or else the doors in the west wall of the nave bear no relation to the relative positions of the arcades. The interior plan of Church 4 exhibited similar peculiarities: its north aisle was wider than its south aisle, and it appears that the north colonnade was fractionally longer than the south colonnade, neither being at a right angle to the chord of the apse. It has been suggested that this may have occurred because the builders of Church 4 were obliged to erect it in an inconvenient position too close to the edge of the cavern in order to preserve an association with an existing sacred spot (Forsyth 1961, 132). Since Church 3 is the successor of en earlier building, it is possible that similar considerations may have caused the eccentricities in its plan.

The apse is semi-circular, and is 6 metres in diameter. There is no moulding at the level of the springing of the semi-dome, although the capital which might have supported one is present at the northern corner of the mouth of the apse. The apse is lit by a double arched window, and does not project beyond the line of the east walls of the side-chambers. The highest surviving section of the apse is its northern corner. A row of four sockets has been cut into the masonry joints at the level of the top of the capital at the mouth of the apse, and there is a larger semi-circular socket just above the others slightly to the east of the capital. The latter socket may have supported a wooden screen which shut off the apse (this may be compared the sockets in the apse at Batısandal). The row of smaller sockets may be compared with the puzzling sockets in the apse of Church 2, and again one possible suggestion is that these sockets may have been used for lamp-holders.

The side-chambers reflect the irregular shape of the building, and are themselves odd shapes, especially since the curve of the apse wall is not disguised. The north side-chamber is almost twice as big as the south side-chamber, and their relative importance is reflected in their fenestration, since there is a double arched window in the northern room, and only a small rectangular slit at a high level in the east wall of the southern room. Here, at least, then, it is reasonable to suggest that the northern, well-lit, room was probably used as the prothesis, and the more secure southern room as the diaconicum. Two windows at a high level in the east façade prove that, in the second phase of the church at least, there were rooms above the side-chambers.

The imbalance between the two side-chambers disturbs the symmetry of the east façade of the church, which also displays most clearly the varied phases of building. A section of wall at the base of the northern end of the east wall is constructed from large ashlars which match those of the west wall of the narthex. It is possible, therefore, that the now ruined north wall was also re-used from a much earlier building. Further support for this suggestion may be derived from the observation that the north and west walls would, if projected, meet at a right angle. For the rest, the east wall shows how the lower parts of the walls are constructed much more roughly than the upper parts.

KANLIDİVANE (Canytela), Church 4[111] (figure 39, plates 91-3)

This church has, to date, been more fully discussed than any other basilica in Cilicia. It was the subject of a lengthy discussion by Forsyth, and has subsequently been studied by Eyice. It would, therefore, be inappropriate to provide a detailed account of the building here, and I shall concentrate mainly on points where the accounts of Forsyth and Eyice can be amplified or which are helpful for the general analysis of Cilician church planning. The church has been a subject of controversy since Strzygowski discussed it in 1903. He had never visited the site, but published a sketch plan made by Heberdey and Wilhelm, and drew attention to the square choir in front of the apse, which is the central bay of the transept. Unfortunately, when Bell visited the site in 1905, she felt that Strzygowski's account was adequate, and limited herself to photographing the building, and noting a few omissions from Heberdey's and Wilhelm's plan. Strzygowski's ideas were repeated by Liesenberg, who had also not visited Kanlıdivane, and it was not until Forsyth published the findings from his visit in 1954 that some of Strzygowski's misconceptions could be

---

[111] Bell 1906b, 410-2, figures 24-6; Bent 1891, 209; Eyice 1977, 429-36, figures 23-7; Forsyth 1961, 127-37, figures 1-20; Hild, Hellenkemper and Hellenkemper-Salies 1984, 208-10; Hild and Hellenkemper 1990, plates 205-7; Hill 1981, 33-4; Langlois 1861, 225-6; Liesenberg 1928, 114-5, figure 35; Strzygowski 1903, 52.

rectified. Forsyth's description of the building is exhaustive, and is basically accepted by Eyice, who has finally produced a measured plan of the building, and differs from Forsyth mainly in proposing that the eastern passage is an original feature.

Church 4 is situated close to the north edge of the cavern. Its function has never been defined, but since there is an extensive cemetery to north and east of it, it is likely that it was built as a cemetery or memorial church. Forsyth seems to agree with this since he commented on the fact that the church is so close to the precipice:

> 'A far easier solution would have been to erect the church farther to the west, where a more level site was available. Perhaps, however, the position of the sanctuary of the church was dictated by the presence of some holy spot or immovable object, such as a tomb.' (Forsyth 1961, 132)

The church is one of the most developed examples of the Cilician basilica. Its overall measurement, including atrium and eastern passage, is approximately 45 by 15.5 metres. The main part of the church, from the west wall of the narthex to the outer face of the apse is approximately 28 metres long. The atrium, or forecourt appears not to have had a peristyle since, as Forsyth noted, there is no trace of a return for this on the surviving part of the west wall of the narthex. Nor is there any trace of the former presence of a lean-to roof against the west wall of the narthex. The northern pilaster and springing of the triple-arched western entrance to the narthex is still in position. The narthex has a doorway at its northern end, with a relieving arch over its lintel. The outer side of the door, which is the only opening in the north wall, is protected by an arched canopy which is supported by projecting consoles, and is very similar in appearance to those on the exterior of the Tomb Church at Corycus, and the 'Domed Ambulatory Church' at Dağ Pazarı. Forsyth suggested that the church must somewhere have had a wooden staircase to provide access to the galleries. Slots in the north wall of the narthex, immediately to the west of the north door, were probably intended to support such a structure. The upper floor of the narthex would have allowed communication round the church at gallery level, and a fine view down the nave through the wide window above its doorway. Forsyth thought that this window 'looked like an afterthought. It appears to have been set into a far taller opening, whose surviving jamb runs straight up to the roof.' (Forsyth 1961, 129). This is an unnecessary argument. The window in the narthex gallery could not have admitted much light into the nave since it was under the roof of the narthex, but a window at a high level in the gable end would have been a useful source of light in the late afternoon. I am not wholly convinced by Forsyth that the basilica had no clerestory (Forsyth 1961, 130), but if this were true, then a window in this position would have been essential. The tall window in the west wall may be compared with such windows in the

churches on Erciyes Dağı in southern Cappadocia such as that formerly existing
at Tomarza, where the architrave of the west door sits inside the bottom part of
a very tall opening which rises towards the gable (Hill 1975, plate 2). The
comparison is not perfect since Tomarza is an Anatolian cross-church, but it is
close enough to suggest that there is no need to argue that the window in
Church 4 at Kanlıdivane was a secondary feature. Its presence would also have
provided the necessary support for a few courses of masonry against which the
roof of the narthex could lean. There would only be a point to Forsyth's
argument if it could be shown that the narthex was itself a secondary feature,
but this is impossible, since there is no change in the masonry of the north wall,
and since the gallery of the narthex was essential to allow communication
between the galleries over the aisle. There was a window in the apex of the
west gable of the basilica at Manaz.

Three doors led from the narthex into the nave and aisles. The presence of
galleries over the aisles is proved by the corbels in the north wall which once
supported its floor joists, and by the upper arch to the north of the triumphal
arch. As has been noted, the north aisle (3.67 metres) was wider than the south
aisle (3 metres).

The only surviving traces of the nave arcades are part of the south pilaster
on the west wall of the nave, and the western pilasters of the cruciform piers of
the triumphal arch. Forsyth suggested that there were four columns in the
arcades, but his argument is, again, somewhat suspect.

'Wilhelm's plan shows a very narrow, fragmentary pier which is oblong
in an east-west sense and which corresponds to a broken pilaster against
the west wall of the nave. Between the two is the figure "2.60?". If it is
assumed that the pier was originally square and was 0.50m. wide, like
the three other responds of the nave arcade, four intercolumniations and
three piers will give a total length for the arcade, not including the end
pilasters, of 11.90m. This is somewhat smaller than my measurement of
12.70m., which implies an intercolumniation of 2.80m. rather than
2.60m. Strzygowski assumes that there were five piers and hence six
arches; but such an arrangement would imply an incredibly small
intercolumniation of only 1.70m. He was probably misled by Langlois'
drawing. I have assumed that the arches rested on columns because such
a combination was standard for nave arcades in this coastal region and is
without exception as far as I know.' (Forsyth 1961, 129, note 13)

There are no columns, or even fragments of columns, to be seen in the vicinity
of Church 4, and I can see no sound reason for suggesting that the rectangular
pier drawn by Heberdey and Wilhelm was 'originally square'. Furthermore, in
making this assumption Forsyth creates the problem that each of his
intercolumniations is 20 centimetres too short. If we assume that there were
three piers, each measuring 50 by 70 centimetres, then the conditions imposed

by Forsyth's measurements would be met perfectly, and there would be no need to tamper with the only evidence we have for the appearance of the arcade. Such an arrangement would not be unparalleled, since the arcades of the churches at İmamli, Hasanalıler and Susanoğlu were also supported by rectangular piers.

Eyice follows Forsyth in suggesting columns, but, for no apparent reason, reverts to Strzygowski's figure of five intercolumniations rather than four. Strzygowski, who wrote 'Vor 1861 standen im Mittelschiff noch Bogen auf Pfeilern aufrecht', was presumably drawing this conclusion from Langlois' drawing of the church which was made in 1852 or 1853 (Strzygowski 1903, 52). But Langlois' drawing shows four intact narrow arches, and the springs of two more, in a row which would extend to no less than twelve if projected along the full length of the nave. Forsyth dismisses Strzygowski, and argues that Langlois' drawing shows the windows of the south wall of the church (Forsyth 161, 128, note 6). But an unbroken row of six or more arched windows at ground floor level in the south wall of a Cilician basilica would be much more remarkable than the presence of piers in its nave arcades, and the possibility must be considered that Langlois' drawing actually shows four courses of the south wall of the church still standing in front of the then surviving part of the north arcade. The position of the westernmost pier visible drawn by Langlois would correspond closely, if not exactly, to the position of the pier planned by Heberdey and Wilhelm. The south wall might well have been preserved to the height shown by Langlois because its collapsed windows had stood at that level. Only excavation would reveal whether Langlois had drawn too many piers in the nave. The point is important because Forsyth argues from the weakness of his proposed reconstruction that the church was unlikely to have had a clerestory. Piers would have been much stronger than columns, and an arrangement of columns with the close intercolumniations which appear in Langlois' drawing would have provided excellent support for an elaborate superstructure.

Cruciform piers at the east end of the nave supported the triumphal arch, as well as the ends of the nave arcade, and the arches which sprang across the ends of the aisles and across the north and south sides of the bay in front of the apse. The section of the church between the triumphal arch and the apse forms, as Forsyth observed, a transverse unit, but one which is compartmentalized since the aisles and galleries are continued eastwards through it. Forsyth makes much of the independent character of this part of the church, which, he says, 'is marked by a drop in levels, since the spring of its lateral arches is lower than that of the nave arcades, and since the moulding at the base of its gallery is lower than the corresponding one in the nave.' (Forsyth 1961, 130). Whilst not disagreeing with the proposal that this section of the building is marked out for special treatment, I am not entirely convinced that the differing levels of the arches is anything more than a symptom of the tentative nature of the architectural scheme. The wider arches beside the choir must, of necessity, have sprung from a lower level than the narrower arches of the nave arcades. Forsyth also pointed out that the triumphal arch and the mouth of the apse were effectively buttressed by the pairs of arches which stood on either side of them. But Forsyth dismissed the possibilities that the bay immediately in front of the apse might have been surmounted by a tower like that of the East Church at Alahan, or that there might have a transverse roofing system across the full width of the church at this point (Forsyth 1961, 131). Eyice does not question this argument which is based on the assumption that the substructure of the church was too weak to support such arrangements, and also that the wall above the apse would have been thinner than that over the triumphal arch. I have noted that Forsyth's similar argument for the lack of a clerestory above the nave can be questioned, and doubt whether his case for the roofing above the choir is any more convincing. If we follow his arguments about the buttressing effects of the side-arches which create what he terms 'diaphragm walls', we can perhaps extend it by pointing out that the semi-dome of the apse would also have had some buttressing effect, and that the eastern 'diaphragm wall' could therefore have been slighter than the more independent western one. Neither Forsyth nor Eyice saw the church at Öküzlü, which is only a few kilometres from Kanlıdivane. There the piers which supported the triumphal arch are less massive than those in Church 4 at Kanlıdivane, although they differ in being T-shaped rather than cruciform since no arches bridged the space between the triumphal arch and the apse. This point is important since there can be no doubt that the church at Öküzlü had an unbroken transept and it is clear that it had a transverse roofing system since a row of windows is still in position in the north-south wall which surmounts the mouth of the apse. With so similar a building so close to hand it would seem to be going against logic to suggest that Church 4 at Kanlıdivane was devoid of clerestory or a transverse roofing system over its transept. The argument for a tower over the choir bay of this church is perhaps weaker, since the proven Cilician examples are in churches where the naves are shorter, but the possibility cannot be wholly discounted.

Eyice's plan shows how the outside walls of the church start to converge after the line of the mouth of the apse. This is probably a direct response to the environment, since the northeast corner of the church is cut deeply into the rock, and the southeast corner is so close to the edge of the cavern. Eyice's plan also shows that the outer faces of the apse are straight and parallel to the outer walls of the church. The chambers on either side of the apse are, therefore, rhomboidal in plan. To the east of the apse can be seen the remains of an eastern passage. Forsyth thought that this could not have been part of the original plan of the church because the apse was lit by a double-arched window, with a drip-stone moulding on its outer face, and the lean-to roof of the passage overshadowed this window. There are numerous examples of churches in Cilicia where the eastern passage blocks light from the apse window: a striking example is the South Church at Yanıkhan where the passage is an original feature of the church, and the presence of a domed martyrium directly behind the apse means that there cannot have been a window in the passage opposite the window of the apse. If Forsyth's argument about the eastern passage in Church 4 were pursued to its logical conclusion, we would also be obliged to conclude that all two-storeyed nartheces in Cilicia were also secondary features since they block light from the windows at gallery level in the west wall of the nave. This cannot be the case here, nor does any structural observation support the idea that the passage in this church was not part of the original building. To justify his conclusion Forsyth has to resort to unnecessary special pleading:

> 'The eastern hall was probably added soon after the completion of the main body of the church, if we may judge by the masonry, the arch construction, and the impost mouldings. So close is the resemblance that it suggests a change of plan while the church was under construction rather than a later addition to a completed project. In either case, the revised plan represents a radical change in the functioning of the whole east end. The chambers flanking the choir and the apse must have been intended originally as adjuncts to those sacred areas, and therefore reserved for the priests and for subsidiary liturgical actions, as in the case of the pastophoria adjoining the apse of a typical Syrian church of the Early Byzantine period. After remodelling, however, the side-chambers seem to have become mere corridors leading from the aisles of the nave to the eastern hall, as if to admit crowds to some ceremony therein or to permit pilgrims to circulate around the back of the apse. The general effect is that of a primitive ambulatory.' (Forsyth 1961, 132)

Forsyth's suggestion that the eastern passage was a secondary feature may be unnecessary, but he does make an important point when he stresses the open nature of the side-chambers in this church. It does seem that open access to the east end of the church was of the greatest importance to the architects. A pair of chambers was added at some later date to the northeast corner of the church. It is just possible that they may have been used for some of the offices usually associated with the pastophories, but they are at a much higher level than the rest of the church, and appear to have communicated with the eastern passage at first floor level. Forsyth misses the point that there was probably an upper storey at the east end of the church, but it is conceivable that the rooms at that level might have been used for the traditional purposes of the side-chambers. The opposite would appear to have been the case in the Tomb Church at Corycus, where there were side-chambers at ground level, and an eastern passage at first floor level.

Forsyth proposed to date the construction of the building to the end of the sixth century or the beginning of the seventh, but this requires re-examination. He noted the relationship between Church 4 and the Tomb Church at Corycus, but did not question Guyer's unlikely conclusion that the latter church was built in the second quarter of the sixth century. We cannot question Forsyth's observation that the capitals in Church 4 are particularly formalized, but we do not know enough about Cilician capitals to state precisely that the capitals of Church 4 'may be a few decades later' than those of the Tomb Church at Corycus. Consideration of the capital in the atrium of the latter church (Herzfeld and Guyer 1930, figure 152) might even lead one to the opposite conclusion, but the canopied porches which appear in both churches, and also at Dağ Pazarı, are sufficiently similar and unusual to suggest that the group may be very close in date. Even more suggestive is the extremely close similarity of some of the capitals of Church 4 at Kanlıdivane with the pier capitals of the nucleus of the Tomb Church at Corycus.

Forsyth's second argument for dating Church 4 is even less persuasive. He claims that the masonry technique is very similar to that of the so-called 'Cathedral' at Corycus, which was completed by 629/30. This cannot, of course, be denied, but the same claim could be made for the South Church at Yanıkhan which was built in the late fourth century. Church 4, in common with many Cilician basilicas, is constructed from rubble and mortar faced with small, squared stones, and covered with stucco. By implication Forsyth distinguishes this technique from the use of larger, better-cut, ashlars, but ashlars are used for the important parts of Church 4, and a glance at Church 2 should have been enough to convince Forsyth that ashlar and small stone construction are used simultaneously in this region.

KANLIDİVANE (Canytela), Church 5[112]

Gertrude Bell reported seeing part of the stone pavement and the curve of the apse of a fifth church at Kanlıdivane which stood a short distance to the west of Church 3. 'No. 5 was much too ruined to promise satisfactory results either to the camera or to the measuring tape'. I have been unable to find any trace of this building.

KARABÖCÜLÜ[113]

Karaböcülü is the site of a small ancient village in the Kanlı Dere about 7.5 kilometres north of Silifke. Hild and Hellenkemper report a small church here which is about 23 by 11 metres overall including the narthex and an extra apse at the end of the north aisle. The church has the peculiarity (like the small church at Canbazlı of having only a north aisle: this was probably divided from the nave by a colonnade, but the one column standing at the site is probably not in its original position since it is in line with the northern apse. The main apse was 4.3 metres wide and constructed from large ashlars, but smaller stonework

[112] Bell 1906b, 403, 405.
[113] Hild and Hellenkemper 1986, 54, figure 3, plate 46; Hild and Hellenkemper 1990, 268.

was used in other parts of the church. There is in effect a northern side-chamber since the subsidiary apse is set to the east of the main apse.

KARADEDELİ[114]
Three early Byzantine basilicas are reported at this ancient site 6 kilometres westnorthwest of Susanoğlu.

KARAKABAKLI[115]
The site of Karakabaklı (near İşıkkale, about 10 kilometres northeast of Silifke) has the substantial remains of domestic buildings and traces of two three-aisled basilicas with columns which are situated very close together.

KARAKİLİSE[116] (plate 94)
The remains of an early Byzantine church are incorporated within the Armenian monastic complex of Kastalawn near Baka (Feke). The church was probably a three-aisled basilica, but only its apse survives at the east end of a single-chambered Armenian church which was probably constructed on the stylobate of the early Byzantine colonnades. The apse is 6.39 metres wide and rounded on the exterior with three horizontal projecting bands, and a heavy modillioned cornice. Hild and Hellenkemper saw traces of the foundations of the presumed southern aisle. Other early Byzantine walls in the vicinity of the basilica were probably monastic.

KARLIK, Basilica[117] (figure 40)
The site of Karlık was studied by Gough in 1958 and 1959. The village is 14 kilometres northeast of Adana, 2.5 kilometres west of the road to Kozan. Gough described it as an extensive site with the remains of several large buildings of the Byzantine period. The main building recorded was a basilical church which was discovered by the villagers in the process of building a trellis. The church proved to have been extensively robbed in antiquity, and by the time of Gough's excavation, the west end had been covered by modern houses.

Gough's excavation revealed that a few courses of masonry survived only in the area of the apse, but he was able recover the lines of the foundations of parts of the stylobates and the south wall. Gough (1974, 412) described the church as being 'about the same size as the West Basilica at Alahan, though clearly of less opulence in its appointments.' The area which was not covered by modern houses extended to at least 24.1 metres from east to west by 17.5 metres from

---

[114] Eyice 1988, 19; Hild and Hellenkemper 1990, 289.

[115] Dagron 1973; Eyice 1981b, 207, Eyice 1988, 19; Hild and Hellenkemper 1990, 290.

[116] Hild and Hellenkemper 1990, 295, plates 135-6.

[117] Gough 1959a, 8; Gough 1960a, 7; Gough 1960b, 23; Gough 1972, 211-2; Gough 1974, 411-9, figures 62-3, plates 129-30; Hild, Hellenkemper and Hellenkemper-Salies 1984, 202; Hild and Hellenkemper 1990, 292.

north to south. Gough estimated that the whole building would originally have measured approximately 35 by 17.5 metres. He found no remains of the colonnades other than the foundations of the stylobates. The apse was stilted in plan and measured 5.3 metres at its chord. The greater part of a stone synthronum was still in position. The apse projected slightly from the main line of the east wall of the church, and may, therefore, have appeared similar to the church at Kadirli. It is reasonable to assume that the apse would have been lit by three windows. Side-chambers on either side of the apse were entered by doors which, to judge by the southern example, were set towards the outer walls of the aisles. The apse floor was at a slightly higher level than the nave.

There are some indications in Gough's plan which are not mentioned in his text. The apse is not shown in a central position, but 1 metre nearer to the northern stylobate than the southern stylobate. Three lines which appear 3 metres to the east of the mouth of the apse presumably indicate the position of the bema.

Apart from the nave the church was floored with flagstones which had been patched with tiles in some places. The nave floor was covered with a mosaic in two panels which faced westwards. The eastern, larger, panel consisted of a field of diamond shapes which contained birds, baskets of fruit, and other simple motifs. This section of the floor may be compared with the northern, earlier, section of the mosaic in the narthex of the Basilica at Dağ Pazarı. At the west end of the eastern section of the Karlık mosaic was a perfectly preserved dedicatory inscription recording that the mosaic was laid in the time of Sabbatius the presbyter and hegoumenos, and Cyriacus the archdeacon, in the month of Artemisium in the thirteenth year of the Indiction. Sabbatius' status as a hegoumenos raises the possibility that this church was monastic. The eastern part of the mosaic contained a representation of Isaiah's 'Peaceful Kingdom', the scenes of which were separated by the lines of an inaccurate and semi-illiterate transcription of the text of Isaiah.

Gough argued that this mosaic, along with those in the 'Cathedral' at Corycus, and the Temple-Church at Ayaş, (to which may now be added the mosaic in the Necropolis Church at Anemurium), should be attributed to the reign of Zeno after the publication of reconciliatory *Henotikon* in 482. The first thirteenth year of an Indiction which is available is 490/491. This would suggest that the western part of the mosaic was laid by March/April of 491. The standard of illiteracy in the eastern section of the mosaic is such as to lead Gough to the following amusing hypothesis:

'A suspicion that once Sabbatius and the Archdeacon had seen the work of the eastern mosaic and its commemorative inscription duly completed they went off to spend the summer at a resort in the Taurus is hard to dismiss, for the wierd (sic) orthography and comical appearance of the animals suggest that the work was left to an odd-job man under the

unexcating (sic) supervision of the temporary incumbent at Karlık.'
(Gough 1974, 417)

Hild and Hellenkemper question the attribution to the late fifth century on the grounds that it is inconsistent with the style of the mosaic which they would attribute to the sixth century. The format of the pavement with animals and fruit in compartments in not in principle dissimilar from pavements such as that at the north end of the narthex in the basilica at Dağ Pazarı which have been attributed to the fifth century.

KASTALAWN see KARAKİLİSE

KEŞLİ[118]
Eyice reported the presence of an early Byzantine basilica and the apse of a smaller church in what he considered to be a monastic complex near Hasanalıler.

KEŞLİTÜRKMENLİ[119]
Keşlitürkmenli is a locality on the ancient road from Silifke to Uzuncaburç about 15 kilometres north of Silifke. Hild and Hellenkemper found here the remains of an unusual church which was cut deeply into the rock at its east end. Though rock-cut, the church still had the form of a basilica (cf Anavarza, Rock-Cut Church) with its main apse and two subsidiary apses cut out of the rock. Cramp holes indicated that the surface of the main apse was revetted in marble. The rest of the church is relatively poorly preserved, though the lines of some walls can be made out, and a terrace indicates where the narthex and atrium were. There is an entrance to a vaulted undercroft on the north side of the church.

KIZILALİLER[120]
Kızılaliler is the site of an ancient village some 6 kilometres northnorthwest of Anemurium. The ruins include the remains of a small (17.5 by 13 metres including narthex) basilica constructed from roughly coursed mortared rubble. The church apparently had galleries since the two side-chambers were two-storeyed. The short main section of the church was divided into nave and aisles by two rows of four arches supported on three piers. The most interesting feature of this church is the slight stilt (about 2 metres) in front of the apse which has the effect of extending the chancel westwards and provides room for a door between the chancel and the southern side-chamber.

---

[118] Eyice 1988, 22; Hild and Hellenkemper 1990, 299.

[119] Hild and Hellenkemper 1986, 62, figures 61-2; Hild and Hellenkemper 1990 299-300

[120] Hild and Hellenkemper 1986 119, figure 19, plates 179-82; Hild and Hellenkemper 1990 303.

KÖŞKERLİ[121]

In this locality (about 3 kilometres northwest of Üç Tepe, 8 kilometres from Erdemli) Hild and Hellenkemper found the remains of two early Byzantine churches, one well-preserved, the other with only a small apse surviving and a small single-chambered medieval chapel.

Hild and Hellenkemper published no plan of the larger basilica, but their photographs are particularly interesting. The church was constructed from a combination of ashlars (in the area of the apse) and coursed small stones. Hild and Hellenkemper report that the church had columns and four cross-shaped piers. From the photographs it is clear that the church had galleries, since there are two storeyed side-chambers entered through arches at ground and gallery level. But there is no sign on the west façade of the apse (Hild and Hellenkemper 1990, plate 269) of a nave arcade meeting the east wall of the church, and all the signs are that there was a transept at this point in the building. The arrangement was thus similar to that in the South Church at Öküzlü. In this context the reference to cross-shaped piers is intriguing, and the view of the northeast corner of the nave (Hild and Hellenkemper 1990, plate 270) shows such a pier rising to gallery level and supporting arches across the aisle: the arrangement may be compared with the west end of the East Church at Alahan where similar piers support diaphragm arches across the area of the nave. A decorated column lying at the west end of the church (Hild and Hellenkemper 1990, plate 271) may be compared with one in the narthex of the South Church at Yanıkhan.

MAHRAS DAĞI (Kale Pınar), Monastery[122] (figure 41. Plates 95-6)

The inaccessible rocky promontory of Mahras Dağı is a notable landmark in the upper Göksu valley, about 15 kilometres west of Alahan from where it is clearly visible. The monastery is near the summit at the same altitude as Alahan, about 1200 metres above sea level. Owing to the difficulties of the precipitous ascent, the site has not often been visited by Europeans. The first description is that of Sykes, who ascended in 1913, and published what is still the only general plan of the site. A party led by Michael Gough climbed to the monastery in 1957: his account of the site appeared posthumously in 1974. Gough, who was unaware of Sykes' visit, admitted the possibility that others may have written about Mahras Dağı before him, and invited communications about the site (Gough 1974c, 65, note 3). Harrison, who did not visit the site, responded to Gough's request by producing a short note in which Sykes' plan is reproduced, and Gough's photographs are supplemented by some taken by Michael Ballance

---

[121] Hild and Hellenkemper 1990 320, plates 267-71.

[122] Gough 1974c, 65-72, figures 1-3, plates 1-4; Harrison 1980, 22-4, figures 1-4; Hild, Hellenkemper and Hellenkemper-Salies 1984, 254; Hild and Hellenkemper 1990 336; Sykes 1915, 535-6.

who accompanied him in 1957. The accounts and plans of Sykes and Gough do not agree on some points of detail.

The monastery was constructed on a north-facing slope. This is so bizarre, considering the altitude, that it may be the explanation for the considerable confusion in Gough's article in which north and south are regularly reversed (Gough 1974c, 66-7). It is fortunate that we have Sykes' plan and Gough's photographs, since from them some degree of order can be restored. Gough also considered that Mahras monastery, like the complex at Alahan, was built to be defensible. The case may be stronger for Mahras, which is more inaccessible, but neither complex occupies the summit of a slope, and it may be that remoteness and a spectacular view were stronger attractions to the monastic community than any considerations of security. The buildings on Mahras Dağı are imperfectly defined, but seem to consist, from west to east, of a group of poorly preserved walls which may have been monastic quarters, then the basilical church, and finally a trefoil building which Gough thought was a baptistery. The western buildings were less well constructed than the rest of the complex and are, accordingly, less well preserved. Sykes and Gough both noted a cistern to the west of the church, and Gough reported that the southwest corner of the building still stood to a height of seven metres in 1957. No other details are given, but it appears from Sykes' plan that the western buildings were enclosed within an irregular courtyard which was attached to the west side of the basilica. It is likely, therefore, that the monastery consisted, in effect, as Harrison observed, of a basilical church, with an irregular atrium in front of it (Harrison 1980, 24).

The east end of the church appears to be the only section which is substantially preserved. Here the north side-chamber stood to a height of 7 metres at the time of Gough's visit, and the first course of the semi-dome of the main apse was still in position. The main apse is 5.5 metres wide; its semi-dome sits on a simple cyma reversa moulding, and it is lit by two arched windows. Beneath these windows is a range of niches in the wall of the apse. Gough does not describe these in detail, but they are visible in two of the published photographs (Gough 1974c, plate 3; Harrison 1980, figure 3). Immediately beneath the block which divides the apse windows is a central semi-circular niche with a monolithic conch-shaped head. On either side of the head of the niche can be seen carefully cut rectangular holes. These were perhaps settings for lamp brackets: it is unlikely that they could relate to an amphitheatrical seating arrangement, since any such provision would have blocked the niches. The central niche is without ornament: this is a little surprising since the lower niches on either side are adorned with a simply carved frame. It is just possible, therefore, that the rectangular settings beside the central niche may have held wooden blocks to which some applied decoration for the central niche could be affixed. The decoration of the pair of smaller semi-circular niches is exactly comparable to that of the niches in the east wall of the narthex of the East Church at Alahan. I can find no parallel for these niches other than the single arched niche in the apse of Church C at Tapureli. On either side of the smaller niches were 'rectangular cupboard-like' recesses (Gough 1974c, 66), which Gough likened to the recesses in the south pastophory of the East Church at Alahan. Such niches are common in Cilician basilicas, especially in the southern side-chambers, but their position in this church is remarkable.

The main apse is flanked by a side-chamber which projects about 4.5 metres beyond the outer face of the apse, and 1.5 metres westwards from the mouth of the apse. This has the effect of creating a shallow fore-choir in front of the apse. There is, unfortunately, no indication of how this fore-choir was roofed.

The apse of the northern side-chamber projects slightly from the line of the north wall of the church, and has the same arrangement of niches as the main apse. It was lit by two small windows in its north wall, and had a doorway in its south wall which communicated with the area outside the main apse and a doorway in its west wall which communicated with the north side of the main part of the church. Gough also noted that 'a door in the south wall leads into the main apse, or sanctuary of the church (Pl.2)' (Gough 1974c, 66). This doorway is not shown on either Gough's or Sykes' plan, and could not possibly lead into the main apse since there is not sufficient space between the niches. If there were to have been a doorway between the side-chamber and the fore-choir, this could have been 75 centimetres wide at the most. Unfortunately Gough's plate 2 does not show any such door, and, indeed, it could not since it is a reproduction of a photograph which was taken from a position due west of the main apse, and shows the ruined north wall of the apse in section. Gough assumed that the buried south side-chamber would have matched the north side-chamber, but it appears on Sykes' plan as having no apse, and being in line with the outer face of the main apse.

The assumption that this church was originally a basilica is based on Gough's discovery of 'column bases and of some simple "basket" capitals with a single lower register of leaves and a small Greek cross (on each face)' (Gough 1974c, 67). Gough's plan, however, raises doubts in my mind, since, if we assume that the south aisle was equivalent in size to the proposed north aisle, then the main part of the church between the mouth of the apse and the west wall would have been an almost perfect square measuring 14 metres from north to south, and fractionally less from east to west. I can find no precise parallel for such proportions in any conventional Cilician basilica. The church at Akdam is a more pronounced version of the same thing since the body of the church is strikingly wider that it is long. The outline plan at Mahras is reminiscent of the 'Domed Ambulatory Church' at Dağ Pazarı, even to the detail of the rectangular fore-choir immediately in front of the apse. This particular comparison would be all the more apposite if Gough has stated correctly that there was a doorway between the side-chamber and the sanctuary.

The semi-circular niches in the north and south walls of the 'Domed Ambulatory Church', and the west wall of the East Church at Alahan, could be compared with the niches in the apse at Mahras. If these similarities are not merely accidental, the church on Mahras Dağı may be of greater architectural significance than has hitherto been realized.

Seven metres to the east of the north side-chamber, with which it almost certainly shared a north wall, is the triconch building. This latter consists of a triconch set within a rectangle measuring 11 metres from north to south, and 12 metres from east to west. The entrance on the west side of the building gave access to a rectangular bay with a doorway into the chamber at the northwest corner of the structure, and presumably a similar doorway to the south. There was a passage between the eastern apse and the eastern wall of the building which could be entered through doorways in the north apse, and through the north end of the east wall. Gough suggested that there would have been a similar pair of doors on the south side of the building for reasons of symmetry. According to Gough, the north and south walls of the triconch touched the walls of the enclosing rectangle. His account is quite at variance with that of Sykes, who shows the east apse of the triconch touching the enclosing wall, and the north apse as separate from it. There was evidently a problem in regard to lighting this building; Gough observes: 'As for the rest of the lighting of the trefoil itself, the western side was open, and a window in the southern apse, which is now completely ruined, may be considered as likely' (Gough 1974c, 68). This statement is somewhat oracular: the 'rest' has no context, and it is quite unclear whether one is supposed to draw the conclusion that there was a window in the north apse. The apses were covered with horse-shoed semi-domes, and the central space must have been covered by a dome or domical vault, since Gough found the base of a pendentive block.

Gough's identification of the building as a baptistery is rather vague:

'Without excavation it is hard to determine beyond doubt whether the trefoil building east of the church was a baptistery or a martyrium, though everything suggests that it was the former. In the first place, it is at least 7.00 m. east of the northern pastophory of the church, with which it almost certainly shared an outer (northern) wall, for which the evidence is a long block, in situ, projecting eastwards from the north-east corner of the church. Furthermore, there was a gate in the wall, for the lintol (sic) block, decorated with a Greek cross in the centre, was found a short way down the slope. There seems little doubt, therefore, that church and trefoil building were independent units. At Alahan, for example, there is no more tangible connexion between the western basilica and the baptistery than there is between the buildings of Mahras.' (Gough 1974c, 67)

If Gough is saying that the triconch should be identified as a baptistery because it is separate from the basilica, this would seem to me to be a very weak argument. Alahan is the only site in Cilicia where it can be definitely shown that a detached building was used as a baptistery: in most cases the baptistery was either in, or attached to, a side-chamber or the narthex. The one certain example of a martyrium, in the South Church at Yanıkhan, is also attached to the church.

The masonry of the basilica and the triconch is consistently comprised of large ashlars which are friction-bonded. In this expensive detail the buildings again resemble Alahan, and it seems reasonable to agree with Gough that the monasteries are likely to have been contemporary, built during the second half of the fifth century.

MANASTIR (Mylae)[123]

The ruins at this site in the gulf of Taşucu (12.5 kilometres southwest of Silifke) include two early Byzantine basilicas. Hild and Hellenkemper report that one of them is 33 metres long, including an eastern passage, by 14.45 metres wide. This must be the church for which Hellenkemper has recently published a plan (Hellenkemper 1994, figure 5) with no description. The plan shows a long basilica with two rows of seven columns. It has the unusual feature of small apses projecting from the mid-way points on the north and south end walls. The arrangements at the west end are unclear but there appears to have been no narthex. An eastern passage ran round the back of the apse; it communicated with the church through doorways at the ends of the northern and southern aisles, and had two eccentrically positioned apses, one at the extreme south end of its eastern wall and one midway between that apse and the northeast corner of the building.

MANASTIR[124]

Hild and Hellenkemper report the apse of an early Byzantine basilica at the mahalle known as Manastır in western Cilicia about 4 kilometres west of Bozyazı (Nagidus).

MANDANE see AKYAKA

MANAZ, Basilicas[125]

This yayla (now called Beylice), which is about 15 kilometres north of Tarsus, evidently preserved extensive ruins at the time of Langlois' visit in 1853. These

---

[123] Hellenkemper 1984, figure 5; Hild and Hellenkemper 1986, 41; Hild and Hellenkemper 1990, 362.

[124] Hild and Hellenkemper 1990, 340.

[125] Alishan 1899, 80; Hild, Hellenkemper and Hellenkemper-Salies 1984, 204; Hild and Hellenkemper 1990, 340; Hill 1981, 29; Langlois 1861 358-9, plate 22; Rott 1908, 293.

had already been demolished by 1905 when Rott passed through, and nothing now remains to be seen.

Langlois described two churches, and published a drawing of the Town Church which in his day was standing to roof level. This church was a substantial basilica, which in Langlois' time still preserved its apse, and most of the walls of the church proper. According to Langlois, five columns were still standing in the nave. From Langlois' drawing we can see that the church had a narthex, the triple-arched portal of which was still intact. The masonry at the south end of the narthex is shown preserved to a sufficient height to suggest that the narthex had two storeys. The west wall of the church proper still had its gable. There was an intact triple-arched window of great height overlooking the nave, and above it a single window in the apex of the gable. The surviving window at a high level on the south wall shows the extent of the south aisle, and suggests that the church had galleries over the aisles. However the west wall of the basilica, as it is drawn, appears too narrow for the building. What appear to be the north and south ends of the west wall must have been the jambs of the doors between the galleries and the upper hall of the narthex, even though on the north side the vertical edge apparently drops into the narthex. If this is the case, what appears to be a corbel projecting from the north corner must be the end of the broken lintel of the door into the north gallery. Through the triple-arched window in the west wall of the church can be seen a high, wide arch which is presumably the mouth of the apse.

The other church mentioned by Langlois stood in a cemetery on the south side of the settlement surrounded by rock-cut tombs. This was of equivalent size to the Town Church but only its foundations survived. Alishan adds the information, presumably gained from Langlois, that there was still an altar in the Town Church, and that Manaz had 'plusieures églises'. Thus it appears that there were more than two, a fact that is supported by Rott's account since he refers to a ruined monastery in addition to the churches mentioned by Langlois. All the churches of Manaz, including the Town Church which was so well-preserved when Langlois saw it, had been razed to the ground by 1905, and their stones re-used for building material.

MARAŞ HARABELERİ (Arsinoe)[126]

The site of Arsinoe in western Cilicia contains the foundations of three basilicas (Hild and Hellenkemper 1990, 198). Hellenkemper has recently published the plan of one of them without commentary (Hellenkemper 1994, figure 5). His plan shows a three-aisled basilica (21 by 12 metres overall) with a short nave which is 11 metres long. There was a narthex with a single central door at the west end, entrances to the nave and north aisle from the narthex, but not, apparently to the south aisle. An eastern passage with a central subsidiary apse

---

[126] Hellenkemper 1994, figure 4; Hild and Hellenkemper 1990, 198.

behind the main apse presumably communicated with the aisles. An external wall continued the line of the north wall of the church, and a doorway in the east wall of the church, in line with the north aisle, led into the space to the east of the basilica. Hellenkemper attributes the structure to the fifth or sixth century.

MAZILIK, Basilica[127]

This church was first described by Strzygowski, who wrote a short note on the building for Grothe, who supplied him with a sketch plan and a photograph. From Grothe's description of the rest of the ruin-field, it can be seen that the basilica stood at the south end of a large cemetery at the base of Mazılık Dağı about 1 kilometre southwest of the village of Mazılık Köy. This village is approximately 40 kilometres west of Kozan in the Taurus highlands, in the Cappadocian marches. Grothe believed that the site had been urban, but identified it incorrectly as Augusta. The church has been discussed at greater length by Edwards, who visited the site in 1979. Whilst his description is useful, his general observations on the early Byzantine architecture of Cilicia are marred by misconceptions, including the problem that this was not 'new' in terms of publication.

The basilica at Mazılık measures approximately 32 by 17 metres overall, including the southern side-chamber which projects for 3 metres beyond the east face of the main apse. Most of its walls survive at least at ground level, and some features from the first floor survive at the southwest corner. The central and southern apses are preserved up to the level of the springing of their semi-domes, and the western arches of both apses are still standing. Apart from the apses, where reasonably dressed ashlars were employed, the church is constructed rather roughly. Most walls consists of coarsely squared stones which face rubble and mortar, but the lower courses often include large polygonal boulders, and two bulges of the native face of the cliff against which the church was built project from the base of the north wall into the north aisle. The doors throughout the church do not have moulded jambs, but consist simply of breaks in the wall which are surmounted by simple monolithic lintels.

Edwards found that there is a network of caves underneath the church: he speculates that the caves 'may be associated with the life and death of a local saint' (Edwards 1982, 28-9). It certainly seems reasonable to suppose that the caves were sufficiently important to justify building the basilica inconveniently close to the cliff face on the north side. In this respect Mazılık may be compared with the West Church at Alahan, which is also inconveniently positioned near to a cliff on the north side, perhaps because of the significance

---

[127] Edwards 1982, 23-9, figure 2, plates 1-5; Grothe 1911, 229-32, figure 17; Hild, Hellenkemper and Hellenkemper-Salies 1984, 202; Hild and Hellenkemper 1990, 345; Strzygowski 1911, 218-9; figures 6-7.

attached to whatever was in its undercroft. Edwards' description of the entrance to the caves is somewhat obscure:

'The entrance to this maze is on the exterior of the nave below the south-east corner. On the outside this passage is covered by a vault of five voussoirs which are incised with mouldings identical to those on the exterior of the windows of the central apse. Today the lower half of this door is buried in debris, but it appears that it was once preceded by a small porch. On the interior of the entrance-portal is a narrow passage which descends directly to the north... A few metres south of the entrance to the caves is a wall that runs parallel to the south wall of the nave. This parallel wall is probably the north side of a now vanished auxiliary building. The sill of a small window is located at the west end of this wall.' (Edwards 1982, 28)

Although it emerges from this account that the entrance must have been part of the original plan of the basilica, we have to work out for ourselves that the incised voussoirs of a vault form an arched doorway. Two tiny nubs of masonry which appear on Edwards' plan projecting from the east end of the south wall of the church on either side of an indentation must be the supports for the porch to which he refers. The parallel wall to the south of the church may not simply be the northern wall of another building. Edwards' photograph shows that there is a marked drop on the south side of this wall which would render it a still more inconvenient building site than that which is occupied by the basilica (Edwards 1982, plate 1b). Furthermore, Edwards' plan of this south wall shows that at its west end it returns northwards in line with the west wall of the church. It thus appears possible that there is here one of the passages which so often ran along the outsides of Cilician basilicas. One example which may be compared with especial relevance is the passage along the south side of the great Basilica at Meryemlık, which contained the entrance to Thecla's cave. This suggestion gains support from the beam-holes which are visible in the outer face of the south wall of the basilica at Mazılık. These can be seen in Edwards' plate 1b at the west end of the south wall, one course above the lintel of the western south door. That these are not merely putlog holes which run through the wall can be seen by comparing Edwards' plate 1c (incorrectly captioned 'looking south-east'), which shows the interior of the southwest corner of the nave. Here the beam-holes for the joists of the gallery floor can be seen to be one course higher. The west side of the church was not equipped with a narthex, and there is only one door in the west wall, which is set somewhat south of centre, a fact which is all the more remarkable since the north aisle was narrower than the south aisle, and any displacement of the west door in order to set it opposite the main apse should have involved setting it north of the centre of the west wall. The position of the west doorway is hardly compatible with its having been the main entrance to the church. Since there are also two doors in the south wall, it seems possible that a corridor along the south side may have served instead of a narthex, as was probably the case at Şaha. Cilician basilicas with only one doorway in the west wall of the nave are not common: the Temple-Church at Ayaş, and the chapel east of Corycus were tiny; in the church at Hasanalıler there were no entrances in the west side of the narthex, and there is some reason to suppose that the southern entrances may have been more important.   The absence of a western narthex might be considered characteristic of the upper parts of the Cilician Plain, since two churches at Anavarza were without one, and nartheces appear to have been secondary additions to the churches at Bodrum and Kadirli. This is one aspect of the relationship between this area and Cappadocia, since churches in the latter province were never equipped with nartheces.

The south wall had at least four windows at ground level. The western window still preserves its arch as does a window above the western door in the south wall. The surviving window in the west wall is at gallery level, and is rectangular, but it appears that there was probably a larger window over the west door. The interior of the church is not at all preserved. Edwards found part of a monolithic column and a simple capital from the colonnades. Nine matching columns were to be found in the village (Edwards 1982, 26). Beam-holes in the north and south walls show that there were galleries over the aisles. Edwards states baldly that,

> 'Following the Cilician models the thin columns of Mazılık probably formed two parallel arcades creating a central nave and flanking aisles. It is likely that the inner sides of the upper-level rested on the entablatures of the arcades. These galleries were constructed entirely of wood... Wooden piers probably stood on the entablature to support the roof' (Edwards 1982, 27).

If by this Edwards means that there was an upper row of wooden columns, this would an interesting observation, but no evidence is offered to support the idea. The exact lines of the nave colonnades are not marked by piers or capitals on the east and west walls of the nave, but a large hole in the east wall of the nave beside the south angle of the apse, which is best seen in Grothe's photograph, may mark the termination of the south colonnade (Strzygowski 1911, figure 6). This hole may well have received a large wooden beam, which was supported by the colonnade, and it may therefore be correct to assume that the galleries were wooden, but in this event the colonnades must have been trabeated rather than arcaded. The appearance of the interior of this church would thus have been similar to that of the North Church at Yanıkhan. The conclusion that the north aisle was narrower than the south aisle arises from the fact that the main apse is slightly north of centre.

The main apse was lit by three unusually high arched windows. There was no moulding at the level of the springing of the semi-dome. The arch at the mouth of the apse is still in place: its springing stones, again best seen in Grothe's photograph, are remarkably long. The apse is semi-circular on the inside, and pentagonal on the outside. A continuous string course runs over the arches of the windows, and above them is a modillioned drip-stone moulding. In these details Mazılık exactly resembles Kadirli, and Edwards observes that this is one of the 'typical' Cilician drip-stones (Edwards 1982, 26). Both Kadirli and Mazılık are very much in the upper part of Cilicia Pedias, and the appearance here of these modillioned drip-stone mouldings is an indicator of the strong connection of this area with Cappadocian. The full use of modillioned mouldings is well better illustrated, for example, by the Ak Kilise in Soğanlı Dere (Rott 1908, 132-3; figure 40).

Small doorways in the north and south sides of the central apse led into the side-chambers, which also communicated, through wider doorways, with the aisles. The north wall of the church jogs out where it joins the north side-chamber. This was possible because, as Edwards observes, the cliff retreats at this point. Even taking account of the jog, the northern side-chamber is still slightly narrower than the south side-chamber, and Edwards explains this by arguing that the architects were concerned about the symmetry of the east façade (Edwards 1982, 28): Cilician side-chambers regularly project beyond the aisles. Only the west end of the north wall of the north side-chamber is visible: from this it emerges that there was a window in the north side of the room, and a small rectangular niche in the north wall just west of the window. Edwards assumes that the plan of the north side-chamber would have matched that of the south side-chamber. This is not a safe assumption, since they are not of equivalent width, and Cilician side-chambers are as commonly irregular as regular since they had less liturgical significance than their Syrian equivalents. Edwards' view of the north outer face of the apse reveals no scars which might suggest the former position of the wall of the side-chamber. The south side-chamber projects, as has been noted, eastwards beyond the main apse, and is a roughly pentagonal shape. Edwards finds both of these features remarkable. Since the main apse is polygonal externally, it comes as no surprise to find that the subsidiary apse is also, and I attach little significance to the fact that the architects have simply extended the northern face of the apse to meet the outside of the main apse. This provided extra floor space, as well as allowing room for an extra window. Edwards' comments on the east façade as a whole are problematic:

'What we know of the chevet indicates that its design is quite unique for the Byzantine churches of Cilicia. Normally the rooms flanking the central apse do not extend as far east as the apse. Occasionally when the central apse is moved west into the area of the chancel the *pastophories* are joined by a high wall giving the east end a flat appearance on the exterior. In Mazılık Kilise we have the only example in Cilicia of an independent *prothesis* and *diaconicon* extending east beyond the perimeters of the central apse. Architecturally this is a rather bold experiment for such a cultural backwater.' (Edwards 1982, 29)

Edwards' footnote 14 refers us to the churches of Corycus, and it is clear from his argument that he has failed to understand the significance of the arrangements at the east ends of the Transept Church and the Tomb Church, where, if there was a passage in the primary plan, it appears to have been at gallery level in order to preserve the independence of the side-chambers. Projecting side-chambers, where there are no eastern enclosure walls, can be seen, for instance, in the Necropolis Church at Eski Anamur, and the church on Mahras Dağı. In the latter case the identical systems of elaborate niches show beyond any doubt that the subsidiary apse must be contemporary with the main apse. I do not myself believe that this is a 'bold experiment', or that, in terms of early Byzantine architecture, Cilicia was a 'cultural backwater'.

Edwards' analysis of the purpose of the building is self-contradictory:

'The significance of Mazılık Kilise lay not only in its design, but in its location. The caves below the church may be associated with the life and death of a local saint. These caves also may have been important for earlier pagan worship. The proximity of the caves to the cliff explains the peculiar axis and alignment of the church as well as its asymmetry. The extant remains do not suggest that this church is a martyrium. There are no known martyria in Cilicia; the martyria near Cilicia in eastern Anatolia and Syria (i.e., Seleucia Pieria, Diyarbakır and Apamea) are all the aisled tetraconch type with a central dome.' (Edwards 1982, 28-9)

This is uncontroversial until Edwards makes the claim that there were no martyria in Cilicia, and indicates that, if there were, they should have been aisled tetraconches. There are, of course, martyria in Cilicia, and they are basilicas, not aisled tetraconches. The most famous of all Cilician martyria, that of St Thecla at Meryemlık, consisted of a basilical Cave Church, over which a series of basilical martyria were built above ground, and it is a notable feature of Cilician martyria, that their plans never depart from the basilical tradition. The Basilica at Meryemlık has already been mentioned as providing a useful point of comparison for the apparent corridor along the south face of the church at Mazılık, since in both churches the corridor contains the entrance to subterranean caves. I would suggest, therefore, and this is the conclusion towards which Edwards at first appeared to be moving, that there is a strong case for supposing that the basilica at Mazılık, which is inconveniently sited over a system of caves, and in the midst of an ancient cemetery, was another Cilician martyrium.

Edwards does not consider the dating of this church, but since it appears that a horizontal wooden beam was supported by the colonnades, and there was no narthex, a relatively early date, in the fourth or early fifth century, would seem appropriate, and would also suit the circumstantial evidence that this was a martyrium erected over the cave of a local saint.

MERYEMLIK[128] (figures 42-5):

The remains of the sacred- precinct of St Thecla stand about 2 kilometres south of Silifke. The sanctuary was visited by Egeria in the fourth century, and is also mentioned by Gregory of Nazianzus, and by Basil, who was bishop of Seleucia from 431 to 459. Hild and Hellenkemper (1990) have produced a useful survey of the literary references to Thecla's sanctuary. Egeria's account is particularly useful:

'Holy Thecla's is on a small hill about a mile and a half from the city, so, as I had to stay somewhere, it was best to go straight on and spend the night there.

Round the church there is a tremendous number of cells for men and women. And that was where I found one of my dearest friends, a holy deaconess called Marthana. I had come to know her in Jerusalem when she was up there on pilgrimage. She was the superior of some cells of apotactites or virgins, and I simply cannot tell you how pleased we were to see each other again. But I must get back to the point.

There are a great many cells on that hill, and in the middle a great wall round the martyrium itself, which is very beautiful. The wall was built to protect the church against the Isaurians, who are hostile, and always committing robberies, to prevent them trying to damage the monastery which has been established there. In God's name I arrived at the martyrium, and we had a prayer there, and read the whole Acts of holy Thecla; and I gave heartfelt thanks to God for his mercy in letting me fulfil all my desires so completely, despite all my unworthiness. For two days I stayed there, visiting all the holy monks and apotactites, the men as well as the women; then, after praying and receiving Communion, I went back to Tarsus to rejoin my route.' (*Peregrinatio* 23, 2-6; Wilkinson 1971, 121-2)

Basil's account of the life and miracles of St Thecla has been the subject of study by Dagron: he has provided a useful analysis of the content of the work, but, although critical of the archaeological work of Herzfeld and Guyer, he has not fully reconsidered their findings (Dagron 1978, 63-79). Basil's account is particularly important because it is our main source of information concerning

---

[128] Herzfeld and Guyer 1930, 1-89; Hellenkemper 1986; Hild, Hellenkemper and Hellenkemper-Salies 1984, 228-39; Hild and Hellenkemper 1990, 441-3, plates 383-90.

the site in the fourth and early fifth centuries. We learn that Thecla's sanctuary was a major pilgrimage shrine with a reputation for miraculous medical cures. There were gardens which were remarkable for their collections of birds, some of them very exotic, which were brought as offerings by the pilgrims. There were also baths and a plentiful supply of water, and these play a central part in many of Thecla's cures (Dagron 1978, 67-70: *Miracula* 12, 24-5). The fourth century church was a basilica, which contained the actual martyrium, although it should be noted that the term was also used in a wider sense to denote the whole church, or indeed the whole site at Meryemlık (Dagron 1978, 72). It seems that there was a garden which served as the atrium, and that there was actually a bath in the church itself (Dagron 1978, 68-9). The 'bema-martyrium' of the basilica had marble cladding, and a concentric geometric mosaic on its floor (Dagron 1978, 71-2; *Miracula* 17, 3-6). Behind its screens was a sanctuary lamp, and the altar (Dagron 1978, 72: *Miracula* 7, 24-6; 18, 41-2).

Basil (*Vita* 28, 7-11) states clearly that Thecla did not die but went down into the earth alive at the very site of the altar.

δὲ ζῶσα καὶ ὑπεισῆλθε τὴν γῆν, οὕτω τῷ Θεῷ δόξαν, διαστῆναί τε αὐτῇ καὶ ὑπορραγῆναι τὴν γῆν ἐκείνην, ἐν ᾧπερ τόπῳ ἡ θεία καὶ ἱερὰ καὶ λειτουγικὴ πέπηγε τράπεζα, ἐν περιςτύλῳ καὶ ἀργυροφεγγεῖ καθιδρυμένη κύκλῳ...

It thus appears that the altar was set within a circular silver ciborium. There were requests for burial in the church, but this was a privilege granted only very occasionally to bishops and saintly people who were interred in the south aisle (Dagron 1978, 70: *Miracula* 30).

In his attempt to reconcile the literary record with the remains at Meryemlık Dagron is insistent that the martyrium proper must have been a circular chamber because of its pavement, the circular silver colonnade, and Thecla's reference to 'τῶν περικειμένων τῷ ἐμῷ θαλάμῳ κιγκλίδων' (*Miracula* 18, 41-2). Dagron therefore suggested that a basilical hall may have been combined with a 'martyrium en rotonde' (Dagron 1978, 72-3). It is perhaps possible that Basil's text could be reconciled with the assumption that the ciborium stood over an altar in a semi-circular apse which may have had a semi-circular chancel screen in front of it: such an arrangement could even be compared with the semi-circular colonnade on the west side of the sanctuary of the Tomb Church at Corycus. But it may be more relevant to mention here the one other certain martyrium in Cilicia, the South Church at Yanıkhan. There the martyrium proper was a square chamber on the east side of an ambulatory passage directly behind the main apse. The chamber was almost certainly domed and clad with marble. Egeria's description, 'ecclesiam, in qua est martyrium, quod martyrium satis pulchrum est' (*Peregrinatio* 23, 2), suggests that the martyrium was part of the church, but she does seem to imply that it had some sort of architectural independence.

We must accept the literary evidence that the martyrium proper was circular, or at least centralized, and this would appear to rule out the simple suggestion that the Cave Church, on its own, was regarded as the martyrium. The two main fifth century basilicas at Meryemlık both had eastern ambulatory passages, and it would not, therefore, be entirely improbable to suggest that there might have been one in the fourth century basilica, which was associated with a centralized chamber which was actually Thecla's martyrium. This would certainly seem to be a more attractive suggestion than to propose that some alien building form might have been introduced. If there was such an arrangement at Meryemlık in the fourth century, this would go a long way towards explaining the subsequent obsessions of Cilician church builders whose tenacious loyalty to the basilica precluded all other plans, although their basilicas regularly, and somewhat idiosyncratically, included ambulatory passages. The alternative possibility would be that the smaller basilica at the site of the great basilica, which Herzfeld and Guyer interpreted as Armenian, was in fact the early church. Its plan contains a large pier, supported by a pair of columns in the crypt, in the position of the equivalent piers at the west end of the nucleus of the 'Domed Ambulatory Church' at Dağ Pazarı. This very tentative suggestion would mean that the combination of the basilical and centralized forms of the early Byzantine church could have been found at a very early date in Thecla's sanctuary.

There remains the question of where the fourth century basilica was actually situated. Dagron was seriously troubled by the failure on the part of Herzfeld and Guyer to find any convincing remains of the early church.

'Dans l'état actuel des recherches, l'archéologie nous fait donc connaître trois églisss (sic) sensiblement contemporaines dont la plus important, la basilique au-dessus de la grotte, est sans doute celle de Zenon (construite à partir de 476); elle est probablement la première à occuper le site de la grotte où s'est progressivement étendu le culte de Thècle et que sa présence confirme nouveau centre de culte[1]. En tout cas l'église-martyrium du IVe s., qui est encore celle des *Miracles*, est à chercher ailleurs.'

Footnote 1:

'Je me ne prononcerai pas sur la date du premier amenagement de la grotte. Si les sondages necessaires ne bouleversent pas les conclusions archéologiques de Herzfeld et Guyer, il faudrait supposer un premier amenagement postérieur à 444/448 (date de la composition des *Miracles*) et antérieur a 476, puis une modification importante à cette date ou après cette date, en rapport avec la construction de l'église supérieure.' (Dagron 1978, 63).

The conclusion towards which Dagron is driven in the footnote is barely credible, and indicates the lengths to which his innocent acceptance of the account of Herzfeld and Guyer has driven him. His attempt to find another site for the fourth century martyrium is equally hard to accept:

> 'Son emplacement se trouvait, et ses fondations se trouvent sans doute encore, à quelques dizaines de metres de la Grotte, vers l'Est, là où la carte de Herzfeld et Guyer indique "Feld", et où les paysans d'aujourd'hui ont amenagé une aire à battre[4]. Son type general était celui d'une basilique à trois nefs, precedée d'un atrium.'

Footnote 4:

> 'En 1973, j'ai vu des restes de fondations qui pourraient être celles de l'église, en limite de la depression Nord-Sud qui borne le site à l'Est.'
> (Dagron 1973, 69)

The positive tone of this last extract is somewhat at odds with Dagron's earlier comment that the site of the fourth century church was still to be found. I take his last sentence about the form of the church to be a general observation on the kind of building which is indicated by the literary sources. That Dagron in fact found no positive evidence for this hypothetical building is evident from the footnote, and from his general plan of Meryemlık, in which an area to the east of the great Basilica is designated '?Emplacement du martyrium primitif' (Dagron 1978, 163). His argument is open to two important objections. Firstly, the foundations he saw could be those of any type of building: even in 1973 they were so insubstantial that there was no trace of an apse, or even of what could vaguely be termed a basilical building. Secondly, and much more significantly, the area which Dagron is indicating is outside the temenos, and it is quite clear, both from Egeria and from Basil, that the temenos surrounded the fourth century church. Dagron is in fact seriously troubled by the whole problem: in two successive pages he states that the northeast chamber of the Cave Church was the actual scene of Thecla's disappearance into the earth and proposes that the actual martyrium should be sought in the fields to the east (Dagron 1978, 62-3). But Basil, as has been seen, stated quite explicitly that Thecla went down into the earth at the very site of the altar.

I would like to propose a solution to this problem which does not involve abandoning the cave and going outside the temenos to find yet another church at Meryemlık. There must have been a fourth century church which included a martyrium, and this cannot have been the Cave Church, if only because, as Wilkinson observed, its size is insufficient for the large numbers of people Egeria saw at Meryemlık (Wilkinson 1971, 288). It follows that Thecla's disappearance cannot have taken place in the cave, unless we ignore Basil's statement that she went down into the earth at the site of the altar. Surely Basil's term ὑπεισῆλθε (which Dagron translated as 'pénétra') implies that

Thecla went under the earth, i.e. downwards, presumably from a position above ground. This would suggest that there were at Meryemlık two spots of great significance to Thecla's cult, the cave in which she spent her last days, which was presumably turned into the Cave Church, and a point above ground where she disappeared, and where was established subsequently the altar of her martyrium, which was evidently in a substantial basilica which stood above ground. I would suggest that these sites were very close together, and that the fourth century basilica was not only built above the Cave Church but was actually discovered by Herzfeld and Guyer. This proposal arises from the simple observation that Herzfeld and Guyer have misunderstood the stratigraphy of their trenches in the area of the great Basilica, and having found the fourth century basilica assumed that it was the medieval successor of the larger fifth century basilica. To be more precise, it was Guyer who made this mistake, since on Herzfeld's plan the correct stratigraphical relationship is clearly indicated (Herzfeld and Guyer 1930, figure 7). This argument is set out more fully below, in the section on the great fifth century Basilica. It is not to be wondered that Herzfeld, who was a competent archaeologist, was later to publish a carefully worded statement disclaiming responsibility for the text of his joint publication with Guyer (Herzfeld 1943, 56, note 57). There is no need, therefore, to doubt the straightforward suggestion that Thecla's sanctuary developed around the cave in which she was reputed to have spent her last days, and included the spot where she disappeared alive into the bowels of the earth, but it would seem that the scenes of these two events were distinct, although sufficiently close that they could both be included within one building complex.

Evagrius (III. 8) records that Zeno built a μέγιστον τέμενος in honour of St Thecla to commemorate his victory over a rival. Zeno's involvement with Meryemlık is thus firmly established, and provides one secure date to help towards the creation of a chronological system for the early Byzantine architecture of Cilicia. Gough has suggested that Zeno's influence can be detected from the presence in the province of several paradeisos mosaics, which reflect the conciliatory tone of the *Henotikon*, which he published in 482 (Gough 1972, 210-2). From Basil's references to the birds at Meryemlık it would appear that there was a paradeisos at Meryemlık. Such animal sanctuaries are recorded in other pilgrimage shrines, including the monastery of St Simon Stylites at Kal'at Sim'an in northern Syria (Kötting 1964, 209-14). Zeno's involvement with Thecla and the paradeisos at Meryemlık may have been an incentive for him to encourage the use the use of the motif. The victory mentioned by Evagrius is presumably that over Basiliscus in 476. The reference to the μέγιστον τέμενος has led to considerable discussion of precisely which of the monuments at Meryemlık was donated by Zeno, and archaeology has done little to resolve the controversy, but we must surely accept, with Hellenkemper (1986, passim), that the 'Cupola Church' is the one which was Zeno's specific dedication.

In the late nineteenth century, as today, there was very little actually standing at Meryemlık. Langlois saw the cisterns, and the remains of churches with mosaic tesserae, and the churches are noted also in *Murray's Guide*. With only such vague indications to supplement the literary references, Strzygowski made his sole comment on the site: 'Meriamlik muß ausgegraben werden' (Strzygowski 1903, 51). This was duly effected in 1907 by Herzfeld and Guyer. Their excavations certainly justified Strzygowski's optimism regarding the potential significance of the site, but there is still much more work to be done.

The debate about Meryemlık has centred on two issues, the identification of Zeno's church, and the question of whether the 'Cupola Church' was actually domed. Guyer at first believed that the great Basilica of St Thecla was the church dedicated by Zeno, but he changed his mind and decided that it must have been the 'Cupola Church', which has far richer decorations, including huge quantities of Proconnesian marble, and is much more ambitious architecturally. This latter argument has been developed by Gough in his article on 'The Emperor Zeno and some Cilician Churches', although he never actually states which church at Meryemlık he believed to have been Zeno's (Gough 1972, 202-3). Other authorities, notably Forsyth, Mango, and now Dagron, have reverted to the idea that the Basilica was Zeno's church, because of its impressive size (over 80 metres long), and because it is the only church at Meryemlık which is surrounded by a temenos. Hellenkemper (1986) argues the case of the 'Cupola Church' convincingly. All this does not, of course, remove from the Basilica its status as a martyrium.

The temenos walls round the Basilica must have been in existence at least by the time of Egeria's visit in the late fourth century. Its walls are in fact quite distinct in constructional terms from the other buildings at Meryemlık, since they consist of very large ashlars which are friction bonded. Only foundations remain, but the temenos walls may actually belong to a pre-Christian building, and the Cave-Church contains re-used Doric columns which have come from some Roman building. It is not unlikely, then, that the cult of Thecla succeeded that of some pagan deity who had a temple and precinct at Meryemlık. Such successions are not uncommon in early Byzantine Cilicia: we may compare the precincts at Uzuncaburç, Cennet Cehennem, and Canbazlı. Guyer believed, in any event, that the two churches were very close in date. I see no reason to contradict this view, and it is, therefore, of little consequence in chronological terms whether Zeno was the donor of the Basilica or of the 'Cupola Church'. The south side of the temenos around the basilica at Meryemlık has not been defined, but it seems unlikely to have been any bigger than the temenos around the Temple-Church at Uzuncaburç. The term μέγιστον τέμενος could presumably apply to the entire tract of holy ground at Meryemlık, in the same way that the whole site was referred to as a martyrium. This would indeed be μέγιστον, and it would not be unreasonable to suggest that the emperor supported the building of both the major churches at Meryemlık as well as some of the ancillary buildings such as the bath-house and cisterns. The monastery at Alahan was clearly designed as an architectural unity: it would be illogical to think of Meryemlık as a collection of unrelated buildings.

The other debate about Meryemlık concerns the roofing of the 'Cupola Church'. Guyer regarded it as certain that this church had a masonry dome, but Forsyth and Gough have subsequently argued equally strongly that it had a wooden pyramid, and Hellenkemper (1986, 77), somewhat reluctantly, seems to have accepted their conclusion. Gough made the point that:

> 'At Alahan there was no dome, for excavation has proved it; and had Guyer found positive evidence of such a feature at Meryemlık during his own work, he would assuredly have mentioned it, which he does not.'
> (Gough 1972, 203)

I am convinced that archaeology has proved the Alahan did not have a dome, and by 1907 Meryemlık had already suffered from stone-robbing on a massive scale, particularly at the site of the 'Cupola Church'. Since no part of the church stood above the level of the ground floor arcades even in 1907, the argument is pointless. Even if the 'Cupola Church' did not have a masonry dome, there is no reason to suppose that the Cilicians of the fifth century were not perfectly capable of building one, and the difference in effect upon the visitor of wood or masonry, pyramid or dome, would have been negligible.

More than any other early Byzantine site in Cilicia, Meryemlık has suffered terribly from stone-robbing during this century. Feld has already stressed the urgency of an archaeological rescue operation to save what information can still be extracted (Feld 1963/64, 95). Hellenkemper ended his article on the 'Cupola Church' at Meryemlık by re-quoting Strzygowski (Strzygowski 1903, 51; Hellenkemper 1986, 88): I can only do the same thing - 'Meriamlik muß ausgegraben werden'. Such an excavation would not only help to resolve the architectural problems associated with this important site, but controlled excavation of what is a historically well attested complex would provide very useful archaeological data, such as secure pottery sequences for the early Byzantine period in Cilicia, which could supplement the information from Anemurium, and help to interpret the excavated material from Alahan.

MERYEMLIK, Cave Church[129] (figure 42)
The Cave Church is situated under the eastern half of the south aisle of the fifth century Basilica of St Thecla. The cave itself is of natural origin: the erosion by water which originally created it continues, and there has been considerable expansion of the area of the cave even during this century. Clearance of the

---

[129] Herzfeld and Guyer 1930, 38-46, figures 39-44; Dagron 1978, 61-2; Hild, Hellenkemper and Hellenkemper-Salies 1984, 228-31; Hild and Hellenkemper 1990, 442, plates 385-8; Hill 1981, 30; Wilkinson 1971, 288-92.

floor of the church during this century has revealed material which was covered when Herzfeld and Guyer studied the church, and has enabled Wilkinson to revise their account of the building. Although this may not be the martyrium which was included in the fourth century basilica, it must have existed at that time, and was used as a crypt, which was probably visible through the floor of the upper church, rather in the manner of the cave under the Church of the Nativity at Bethlehem. There were certainly light-wells in the floor of the fifth century upper church. The Cave Church presumably deserved conversion into a subterranean basilica measuring approximately 18 by 12 metres, since it included the spot where Thecla spent her last days, which part of the cave probably became the north side-chamber. Clearly the relationship of the Cave Church with the basilica above it was always very close, and it is impossible to prove whether the Cave Church ever had an independent existence, or was always the crypt of a larger basilica. Guyer does not comment upon this issue, but since he devotes some space to establishing the possibility that the Cave Church might have been established in the third century, we must assume that he thought that the upper basilica was a secondary development.

Our understanding of the Cave Church is confused by the major alterations it underwent at the hands of the builders of the great Basilica above it, but it is clear that in the fourth century there was a small basilica which could be entered through a doorway at the south end of a western chamber which was the equivalent of a narthex. This southern entrance is at the bottom of a flight of steps which was included within a colonnaded walkway along the south side of the upper fifth century basilica. In the original scheme, there were probably three archways between the western chamber and the church proper. Wilkinson has shown that a kink in the west wall of the church reflects the re-alignment caused by the fifth century alterations (Wilkinson 1973, 292). The northwest corner of the church has been extended by erosion since 1907, but there is still an archway across a passage which leads from this part of the cave. The passage is blocked, but it is possible that it once provided access to the north end of the entrance hall from some point to the west of the church, which would have been in the atrium of the first upper church.

The Cave Church was divided into nave and aisles by two rows of three Doric columns, which Wilkinson says were repositioned in the fifth century. Herzfeld and Guyer thought that these had come from a Hellenistic building, but the clearance of the nave has revealed that the lower sections of the flutes of the columns are filled, and it is more likely, as Wilkinson observed, that the columns have originated from a Roman building (Wilkinson 1973, 289). Since the temenos wall which surrounds the Basilica and the Cave Church also seems likely to have belonged to a Classical building, it seems logical to suggest that Thecla's sanctuary is the successor of a pagan shrine, which may also have been built above the cave. When the fifth century basilica was constructed, part of the stylobate of its south arcade ran nearly over the north colonnade of the Cave

Church. To provide support for his new stylobate, the fifth century architect apparently re-aligned the colonnade in the Cave Church to match the stylobate above it, and built against the north side of the columns a solid wall which provided a strong basis for the building above ground. This alteration had the effect of creating a side-chapel on the north side of the Cave Church. At the east end of what had been the north aisle were placed two windows.

The Cave Church was provided with a certain amount of natural light through windows at the west and east ends of the south wall. The eastern window appears on Herzfeld's plan as a doorway. There were also two light wells in the floor of the fifth century basilica, which presumably also served the purpose of allowing a view into the cave for the crowds in the upper church. Wilkinson has shown that the original south wall of the church is embedded with the fifth century alterations (Wilkinson 1973, 289). Herzfeld's plan incorrectly shows native rock at this point in the structure.

The apse and the south side-chamber were cut out of the rock and lined with masonry. As is the case with the west wall, there is a kink in the east wall of the church, which reflects the change of alignment in the fifth century. The south side-chamber preserves the original alignment, but the masonry in front of the apse has been altered to suit the new position of the nave. It seems likely that there was a north side-chamber, but its form must remain conjectural unless excavation is carried out in this part of the church. Doorways pierce the north and south sides of the apse. These are omitted from Wilkinson's plan, but after the north aisle had become a side-chapel, the northern door in the apse would have been the only means of access to whatever lay in the northeast corner of the church. That this latter may not have been a simple replica of the south side-chamber appears from the windows which were inserted at the east end of the north aisle. These suggest that the north side-chamber was wider than the southern one. Guyer and Wilkinson have suggested that the area to the north of the apse may be the actual cave in which Thecla lived (Herzfeld and Guyer 1930, 45: Wilkinson 1973, 292). This is an attractive proposal since it would give some point to the re-arrangement of the north aisle, which would allow pilgrims to view Thecla's section of the cave, whilst restricting access to it to the clergy, who could enter it through the doorway in the side of the apse.

The possibility that the Cave Church had a funerary function has arisen from the discovery of the inhumation of a young man in a rough grave in the south side-chamber (Ciner 1964, 251-71). This discovery has led Dagron to speculate that there may have been more burials on the south side of the church (Dagron 1978, 61, note 5).

There is a further masonry-lined room to the north of the underground basilica. This is on a different alignment, and appears on Herzfeld's plan as 'nachzenonisches mauerwerk'. The same convention is used to distinguish the masonry which fills the intercolumniations of the northern arcade. This masonry must be later than the fifth century alterations since patches of wall mosaic are visible on the surface behind it. The infilling of the intercolumniations was presumably meant to counteract settlement in the upper church, or a weakening of the ceiling of the lower church. The same considerations may have prompted the insertion of a pair of Corinthian columns against the north face of the substructure of the fifth century upper stylobate. Traces of wall mosaic can also be seen in the apse and inside the south side-chamber. Loose mosaic tesserae, including some gold glass ones, can be seen in the debris which still covers parts of the floor of the nave. It seems therefore that although the Cave Church was reduced in size in the fifth century, it was provided with a very lavish decorative scheme. A fragment of mosaic seen by Wilkinson was part of the floor of the original north aisle. The first church may also, therefore, have been lavishly decorated.

There can be little doubt that the Cave Church in its earlier form, if not the actual martyrium seen by Egeria in the late fourth century, was nevertheless firmly associated with her cult, which Hild, Hellenkemper and Hellenkemper-Salies (1984, 235), consider was recognised architecturally by about AD 375. It is interesting to see that the plan chosen for the Cave Church, and for the first church above it was that of a simple basilica.

MERYEMLIK, Basilica of St Thecla[130] (figure 43, plate 98)

This basilica was built over the Cave Church, which was, in effect, its crypt, in the second half of the fifth century. It was the largest of the Cilician basilicas; thus, as Guyer observed, 'so hätte die Basilika von S. Apollinare in Classe bei Ravenna bequem im inneren der Thekla-Basilika platz gefunden' (Herzfeld and Guyer 1930, 17). With its precinct, the Basilica filled the southern part of Thecla's sanctuary. Only part of the south half of the apse survives, but this still dominates the site at Meryemlık. The northern part of the apse fell on 15 May 1942 (Hild, Hellenkemper and Hellenkemper-Salies 1984, 232). The church was excavated by Herzfeld and Guyer in 1907, by when it had already suffered stone-robbing on a massive scale. Guyer's account makes it clear that they were looking for the fifth century basilica, and, having found it, rarely, if ever, dug through to see what was beneath. It is also clear that their excavation consisted of a series of test-holes. Since the Basilica had been extensively robbed out by 1907, any conclusions which Guyer has formed on the basis of his stratigraphical observations must be viewed with caution.

From Egeria's account and references by Gregory of Nazianzus, it is clear that there must have been a basilica on the site during the fourth century. Herzfeld and Guyer found a building block with dowel holes for the pegs for marble cladding under a fifth century threshold, and several capitals which could have come from the fourth century church. 'Der Grösse dieser Kapitäle

---

[130] Herzfeld and Guyer 1930, 4-38, figures 1-38; Hild, Hellenkemper and Hellenkemper-Salies 1984, 231-5; Hild and Hellenkemper 1990, 442, plates 389-90; Hill 1981, 30.

nach zu schliessen muss diese alteste oberirdische Theklakirche ein ganz ansehnliches Bauwerk gewesen sein' (Herzfeld and Guyer 1930, 7). I am particularly doubtful about Guyer's conclusion, which is advanced as a matter of factual record and accepted by Hild and Hellenkemper, that the fifth century basilica was once repaired and afterwards replaced by a smaller basilica which occupied the site of the eastern half of the nave and the south aisle (Herzfeld and Guyer 1930, x, 18, 36-38; figures 7, 16, 38; Hild and Hellenkemper 1990, 443). From Herzfeld's plan it can be seen that this was a substantial building measuring at least 33 by 26 metres. Guyer concluded that this smaller basilica was Armenian, and so it appears on Herzfeld's plan. But Guyer seems to have been inclined to assign any building which he considered to have abnormalities of plan to the Armenians. Although there are occasional medieval conversions of basilicas which utilized the former aisles as side-chapels (e.g. the Basilica at Kadirli, where new solid walls were built along part of the original stylobates, and roofs provided between this new wall and the original outer walls of the church), there is no other instance of a Cilician basilica which can be shown conclusively to have been erected in the medieval period, whether by Armenians or by anyone else, and churches of the medieval period are normally single-naved (e.g. Kastalawn). Nor do any of the known medieval chapels in Cilicia aspire to such impressive proportions. The importance of Meryemlık, which certainly continued as a pilgrimage centre, might have justified such an exception, but a close scrutiny of the evidence presented by Herzfeld and Guyer produces nothing which might support their conclusion, and I would suggest that it is much more likely that the smaller basilica should in fact be assigned to the fourth century.

The smaller basilica had its apse in the southern half of the fifth century apse, directly over the irregular section at the northeast corner of the Cave Church which appears to have been the cave in which Thecla actually lived. The south angle of the smaller apse is clearly shown on Herzfeld's plan as being cut by the fifth century apse. Since this section of the fifth century apse is still standing, there can be no question that Herzfeld's plan shows this detail incorrectly. In 1907 the great apse of the fifth century basilica was much better preserved, and if we were to follow Herzfeld and Guyer in saying that the smaller church was the later structure, this would involve accepting that its apse was built in the shadow of the huge apse, but off centre. It appears from Herzfeld's plan that the smaller apse had a stone bench round its inner face, and that there was a burial at the central point on the chord of the apse. Since Thecla descended into the earth alive, this grave cannot be hers, but it must presumably be that of someone of significance to have justified the occupation of such a prominent position in an important martyrium. It is impossible to say whether or not the smaller church had side-chambers flanking the apse, since Herzfeld and Guyer did not excavate to a sufficient depth in the appropriate places. This is particularly unfortunate since the eastern chambers would be, as

I have indicated previously, the first place to look for the actual site of the martyrium.

The stylobates of the arcades which divided the smaller basilica into nave and aisles are on almost exactly the same alignment as the arcades of the fourth century Cave Church. It can be clearly seen from Herzfeld's trench plan that the north wall of the smaller church was cut by the piers which replaced some of the columns of the fifth century basilica. This fact is also apparent from one of the few photographs of the 1907 excavation (Herzfeld and Guyer 1930, figure 16). This shows part of the northern stylobate of the fifth century church: the pier which replaced the fifth column from the east can be seen standing at least six courses high, and there is also visible the base of a smaller pier in the position of the next column but one towards the east. The presence of these piers would seem to be quite incompatible with the suggestion that a later wall was built through them. No trace of the south stylobate of the smaller basilica appears in Herzfeld's trench plan, and it would appear that the building of the south stylobate of the fifth century basilica has obliterated the stylobate of its predecessor. Herzfeld's confusion about this matter emerges clearly from his reconstructed plan in which the west end of the nave of the smaller basilica is 1 metre narrower than the east end because Herzfeld has shown the two stylobates as coterminous, although no other parts of the two churches are shown as sharing the same alignment. No photographs of the piers against the south wall of the fifth century basilica were published, but the shadows in Herzfeld's trench plan show that they, too, seem to have been preserved to the extent of several courses, and in both of Herzfeld's plans the piers are drawn as though they were secondary to the foundations of the smaller church. If the smaller basilica was built after the larger basilica, then the new south wall was built in such a way that there was a gap of a few centimetres between it and the south wall of the fifth century church, and the secondary piers of the latter were partially included in the new wall. This proposal seems even more unlikely than the idea that a smaller apse was built at one side of a still standing larger apse.

One last piece of evidence in favour of Guyer's conclusion that the smaller basilica was the latest church on the site must be mentioned. He tells us that the smaller basilica included re-used building materials (Herzfeld and Guyer 1930, 36-37). This would be a telling argument if it could be shown that these spolia came from the fifth century basilica, but Guyer made no attempt to do this. Since the Cave Church contains re-used Doric columns, it is quite reasonable to suppose that the re-used materials in the smaller of the churches above ground may have come from the same source. Only further excavation could prove this, but if true, this would mean that the Cave Church and the fourth century basilica were likely to have been constructed simultaneously, perhaps on the site of an earlier pagan sanctuary.

At the west end of the smaller basilica there was a narthex with a tower-like expansion at its south end. Guyer reported traces of a staircase in this chamber (Herzfeld and Guyer 1930, 37). We can assume, therefore, that the smaller church had a two-storey narthex, and is likely to have had galleries over the aisles. The south wall of the smaller basilica was directly above the south wall of the Cave Church. If I am correct in assuming that the smaller basilica should be assigned to the fourth century, then the expansion of the west end of its narthex may have been effected in order that the staircase did not obstruct access through the south wall of the narthex to the entrance to the Cave Church. There may also have been an entrance to the Cave Church from the atrium of the fourth century basilica. Since the latter is known to have contained a bath, the possibility exists that this may also have been incorporated in the stout chamber at the south end of the narthex.

The most remarkable feature of the fifth century basilica was its size: it measured no less than 81 metres by 43 metres. As has been noted, the building was already largely robbed out by 1907. Herzfeld and Guyer were able to recover a general picture of the plan, but since their excavation consisted of a series of small trial trenches, various details remain obscure, especially those relating to the arrangement of the chancel. The overall plan of the basilica, as reconstructed by Herzfeld and Guyer, was very simple indeed.

Since the basilica stood within a precinct, there was no need for an atrium. A flight of steps across the west end led up to the narthex. According to Guyer, this was probably only one storey high with a triple-arched portal in which the central arch was wider than the two outer arches, and with a lean-to roof at the same height as the roof over the aisles (Herzfeld and Guyer 1930, 29-30). No other Cilician narthex has a portal with arches of varying diameter, and this suggestion is incompatible with the idea of a simple lean-to roof, since the greater height of the central arch would seem to necessitate some form of gable. Guyer's reconstruction of the narthex is in any case improbable, since the proposed central arch of his portal would have been 9 metres wide, whilst the intercolumniation of the nave arcades was merely 3 metres. Thus, unless the columns of the narthex portal were extraordinarily short and squat, it is inconceivable that the walls of the narthex could have been the same height as the outer walls of the aisles. Herzfeld and Guyer found two porphyry columns a few paces to the west of the basilica which they assumed came from the narthex: there is no suggestion that these were remarkably dumpy, although they do appear to be about 1 metre in diameter on Herzfeld's reconstructed plan (Herzfeld and Guyer 1930, 29; figures 6-7). A more likely solution is that, as befitted a church of such width, the portal of the narthex had five arches. This would not be unparalleled, since Herzfeld and Guyer themselves discovered that there was a five-arched portal in the narthex of the Tomb Church at Corycus. In the case of the Basilica at Meryemlık, if we assume that the columns were in the region of 75-80 centimetres in diameter, the five arches would then have had the same intercolumniation as the nave arcades, and Guyer's proposed lean-to roof would become a feasible possibility. This not in itself sufficient reason for accepting Guyer's view that the narthex had only one storey. This idea related to his theory that there were no galleries over the aisles, to which point I shall return, and to his failure to find any trace of a staircase in the narthex. The latter evidence could only be admitted if the narthex had been preserved to a considerable height. Evidently it was not, and it is clear from Herzfeld's trench plan that the north end of the narthex was not even explored. Guyer's conclusions concerning the narthex contrast strangely with his opinion that the proportions of the side-chambers suggest that these must have had upper floors (Herzfeld and Guyer 1930, 15-16). These, Guyer suggested, must have been approached by wooden staircases. But Guyer found no trace of such a staircase in the north side-chamber which was completely excavated, and yet, if we are to believe that there was no gallery over the north aisle, then the only possible access to the upper floor would have been from the side-chamber itself. Although the columns of the narthex portal were not in position, Guyer noted that there seemed to have been a jamb against one of them: this would suggest that doors were set in the arches. Herzfeld and Guyer found a well-head inside the narthex against the west wall, immediately south of the southern arch of the portal.

There were three doorways which led from the narthex into the nave and aisles. These together measured 55 by 36.8 metres, thus enclosing a space in excess of 2,000 square metres. As reconstructed by Herzfeld and Guyer, the nave and aisles were separated by two rows of fifteen tall Corinthian columns. The nave was exactly twice the width of the aisles. Only occasional column bases were seen by them, since some of the columns were strengthened or replaced at some date by square piers. Herzfeld's positioning of the original columns is thus to some extent conjectural, and there is an anomaly at the east ends of the colonnades, since the final intercolumniation is wider than all the others. This is clear on all three relevant plans, and is most apparent on the plan of the Cave Church (Herzfeld and Guyer 1930, figure 39). A discrepancy of 40 centimetres is perhaps not enormous, but it would be sufficient to create problems, since the final arches of the arcades would either have been 20 centimetres higher than the others, or else could not have been complete semi-circles.

As has been noted, Guyer believed that there had been no galleries over the aisles. The reason for this conclusion was presumably that he found no remains from an upper order. This would not be a particularly powerful argument since the replacement of the columns of the arcade by piers suggests that the building was re-roofed after a disastrous collapse. In the same reconstruction, the floors of the nave appear to have been re-laid (Herzfeld and Guyer 1930, 20-1). It would be natural to assume that the galleries fell with the roof, and that their debris was cleared away when the floors were replaced. Guyer in fact gives no reason for supposing that there were no galleries, although their absence from a Cilician basilica of such size would be very remarkable. The only slight evidence for the superstructure of the church is the surviving portion of the main apse. A console still projects from the south corner, 9.8 metres above floor level. Guyer assumed that this console received the eastern arch of the south arcade (Herzfeld and Guyer 1930, 17; figure 8). This is certainly the simplest solution, but it involves accepting that the slender columns of the nave, the lowest diameter of which was 58 centimetres, also rose to the impressive height of 9.8 metres. This would give a column height in excess of sixteen lower diameters, when the norm for even the Corinthian order is only ten diameters. Allowing for Guyer's so tall and thin order, there might still have been room for a gallery, but any clerestory lighting would have been above the apex of the arch at the mouth of the apse. Guyer suggested that the arches of the arcade rose a further 2.3 metres above the columns (Herzfeld and Guyer 1930, 17). The calculation was reached by taking a figure of half the largest total distance from centre to centre of two columns. Most columns were not so widely spaced, and Guyer's figure makes no allowance for the thickness of the columns, or the further reduction in the diameters of the arches which would have been caused by the impost blocks which he thought belonged to the arcades (Herzfeld and Guyer 1930, figure 18). The actual extra height created by the arches is thus more likely to have been about 1.5 metres.

There is a possibility that the plan of the great Basilica was not as simple as Herzfeld and Guyer believed. Herzfeld's positions for the two eastern columns of the arcades are hypothetical, and the relevant photograph and plans show that there was a rectangular pier in the position of the penultimate column of the north arcade: a similar pier is marked on the reconstruction plan (Herzfeld and Guyer 1930, figure 7) directly above the window which looked into the northern side-chamber of the Cave Church. The thick wall which the latter window pierces would thus have provided extra support for the southern rectangular pier. The other secondary piers in the upper church were square and larger, but the rectangular piers were the same thickness as the spurs of wall which project to north and south from the mouth of the apse. It is possible, therefore, that these piers were not, after all, secondary insertions, but part of the fifth century scheme, and they may have been all that survived of a triumphal arch set 8 metres to the west of the mouth of the apse. Thus there may well have been a transept, 8 metres wide, in the Basilica of St Thecla. This proposal has the merit of resolving several anomalies. If there was a triumphal arch, then it would be possible to reconstruct a view of the nave in which columns of normal proportions, between 5 and 6 metres high, supported a lower arcade above which ran a similar order at gallery level. The console next to the mouth of the apse could then have received a wide arch which sprang from the rectangular pier, at a higher level than the lower nave arcade. In this event there would be no need to suppose that the eastern arch of the nave arcade was wider than the others. If there was a sanctuary area, which was defined by a triumphal arch, it would have been directly above the most holy sections of the Cave Church. The final eastern column of the north arcade would support the screen which cut off the north side of the chancel, as in the Church of the Apostles at Anavarza.

There is a possibility that the sanctuary and the Cave Church were directly connected. Herzfeld's excavation plan shows that the east part of the south wall of the south aisle was heavily encumbered by rubble, but there is a row of what might be paving slabs which run up to a tiny nub of the south wall, which is no thicker than a door jamb at the east end of the south wall. It seems, therefore, that there was a wide opening in this part of the south wall which would have allowed easy access from the sanctuary to the Cave Church. Not the least of the problems which this tentatively suggested triumphal arch would help to resolve is one which troubled Guyer.

'Es mag wundernehmen, dass der wohl in der zweiten Hälfte des V. Jahrhunderts errichtete grossartige Neubau der Theklakirche die Form einer Basilika aufweist... Denn es ist ja eine weit verbreitete Ansicht, die frühchristlich-byzantinische Baukunst habe für Martyrien gerne zentrale und zentralisiernde Grundrisse bevorzugt.' (Herzfeld and Guyer 1930, 8)

Early Byzantine architecture in Cilicia always remained loyal to the basilical tradition, but it would be remarkable if by the late fifth century an entirely simple design had been chosen for a church which was such an important martyrium. Special treatment of the east end of the nave of the basilica would have emphasized the role of the church as the site of Thecla's miraculous disappearance, at the same time as bringing the entrance to Cave Church into more direct contact with the sanctuary of the upper Basilica.

The entrance to the Cave Church was protected by a passage along the south side of the basilica. Herzfeld and Guyer found the east and west walls of the nave extended beyond the south wall of the south aisle. They accordingly carried out a trial excavation at the west end which uncovered the corner of the west wall, and its return eastwards on a line parallel with the south wall of the basilica, and 5 metres to the south. Guyer was of the opinion that there was an open colonnade along the south side of the passage, which was perhaps a lean-to structure resting against the south wall below the level of the windows (Herzfeld and Guyer 1930, 30-1). If there were galleries over the aisles, then the windows might have been lower than those postulated by Guyer, but it seems reasonable to assume that the southern passage was a single storey structure. If Guyer was correct in suggesting that there was a colonnade rather than a wall, then the feature could be compared with the colonnade along the south side of the South Church at Yanıkhan, which also contained a martyrium. The entrance to the caves under the Basilica at Mazılık also appear to have been protected by a corridor which had a wall along its south side.

Apart from the possible sanctuary at the east end of the nave, Herzfeld and Guyer found fragments of small stylobates running from east to west along the nave at a distance of 5 metres from the main arcades (Herzfeld and Guyer 1930, 21-8). Guyer suggested that these were the remains of a Schola Cantorum which occupied the greater part of the nave, and was defined by rows of columns which were broken by monumental doorways. Herzfeld and Guyer found a quantity of fragments of columns and small capitals from an order which cannot have been more than 3 metres high, and which seems likely to have belonged to this feature, but it is clear that they saw so little of the stylobate that they cannot be considered to have established its total form or extent.

The apse was 13.6 metres wide, and 8.2 metres deep. Its wall were clad in marble up to the sima moulding at the springing of its semi-dome. This moulding is 12.85 metres above floor level, and the crown of the arch at the mouth of the arch must have risen to a height in the region of 20 metres. The apse was lit, unusually, by a pair of double windows (this feature was also present in the Temple-Church at Silifke, so may have been a very local characteristic). Each pair of windows was divided by a column with a white marble capital with very stylized acanthus decoration. Three great buttresses strengthened the semi-circular outer face of the apse. One of these was set against the division between the double windows, the other two were on either side of the windows (Herzfeld and Guyer 1930, 8-12). There were also, in effect, two further buttresses on either side of the mouth of the apse, which were not mentioned by Guyer. Short sections of thick wall ran on a north-south alignment between the corners of the apse and the inner walls of the side-chambers. The south corner of the apse is still standing along with the section of wall up to the first buttress beside the former south window. The buttresses are the highest surviving masonry of the church, and can be seen to continue rising with the semi-dome of the apse. This point is not discussed by Guyer, but it creates a situation where, so far from helping to support the semi-dome, the upper parts of the buttresses actually rest on top of the masonry of the semi-dome. It is difficult to think of any purpose for this arrangement, unless there was an unusual roofing structure which needed support. Two mouldings ran round the outer face of the apse: one was at the same level of the interior sima moulding, the other would appear to be the cornice which would support the ends of the tiled roof were it not for the curious manner in which the buttresses rise above it.

Side-chambers on either side of the apse were entered through doorways in their west walls. Herzfeld and Guyer excavated the north side-chamber and suggested, as seems likely, that the south side-chamber would have been its mirror image (Herzfeld and Guyer 1930, 12-17). The chamber measured 11.4 by 8.8 metres, and proved to have a small horse-shoed apse at its east end. It was originally enriched with marble cladding. A door in the south wall of the side-chamber led into the area behind the main apse which was enclosed by an eastern wall which ran across the end of the building at a tangent to the subsidiary apses. A limestone pine-cone was found in the north side-chamber, which Guyer thought was either part of a fountain, or a knob from the corner of a balustrade (Herzfeld and Guyer 1930, 16-17; figure 15). If the former suggestion is correct, this church might be added to the list of Cilician basilicas in which there is some indication that water was available in one of the side-chambers, possibly for baptismal purposes. There is a discrepancy in Herzfeld's plans: from the two plans of the basilica as a whole it appears that the east wall continued beyond the north and south building lines of the church; but on the detailed plan of the area of the apse (Herzfeld and Guyer 1930, figure 8), there is a definite northeast corner to the building, and there are openings beside the subsidiary apse which lead into tiny side-chambers.

At some stage the basilica had to undergo extensive repairs. Herzfeld and Guyer found that the mosaic floors of the nave and the Schola Cantorum had been replaced. Piers were built around some of the columns, against the outer walls of the church, and against the long walls of the side-chamber, as though parts of the church were re-roofed with barrel-vaults (Herzfeld and Guyer 1930, 33-6).

The major problem with this building is whether or not it was the μέγιστον τέμενος donated by Zeno. Guyer at first believed that the Basilica was Zeno's church, but then changed his mind (Herzfeld and Guyer 1930, 31-2). Forsyth reverted to Guyer's first position:

> 'Such vast size, combined with the excellence of the construction, suggests that Guyer's first opinion, which he discusses and finally rejects, may be correct and that the church was actually built soon after 476 by the Emperor Zeno to commemorate a victory... The surviving fragment still has the magnificence appropriate to imperial patronage.' (Forsyth 1957, 224)

This view was endorsed by Mango:

> '...for Meriamlik we have the explicit statement of Evagrius, III. 8 that Zeno built a μέγιστον τέμενος in honour of St Thekla (hence probably the great basilica rather than the "domed church")' (Mango 1966, 364, note 23)

But the temenos which surrounds this church has been shown to belong either to the fourth century church, or, more likely, to some earlier building, and the case cannot, therefore, be so easily proven. The main point, about which there can be no disagreement, is that the great Basilica and the 'Cupola Church' must be very close in date, and that both may be attributed with confidence to the late fifth century.

MERYEMLIK, 'Cupola Church' ('Kuppelkirche')[131] (figure 44, plate 99)
Although this is one of the most famous and controversial of the Cilician basilicas, it is extremely poorly preserved, and little more was standing in 1907 when it was explored by Herzfeld and Guyer. Guyer's conclusions about the building have been somewhat controversial, but Hellenkemper (1986) has provided a very useful revised description and new plans of the building, which he firmly attributes to Zeno.

The main part of the church is much smaller than the basilica, but the overall dimensions of the 'Cupola Church' (78 by 35 metres including its fore-courts) are still on a grand scale. Although it was a more complicated building, Guyer's description of the remains causes less problems than his description of the great Basilica of St Thecla. This is largely because all the evidence suggests that the 'Cupola Church' was a one period building. Where Guyer's account has caused problems is in regard to his conclusion that the church had a masonry dome.

The 'Cupola Church' was built about 160 metres to the north of the Basilica, on the very edge of the cliff. The east end of the church is, accordingly, built up on massive substructures. There is no obvious reason why the architect should have chosen so inconvenient a position, but it is likely that it was chosen because of functional considerations. Immediately to the west of the 'Cupola Church' was a bath-house, which was presumably served by the mass of cisterns further to the west. Herzfeld and Guyer thought that the 'Cupola Church' and the bath-house were founded jointly, and noted that the opus sectile floor of the bath-house matched that of the church (Herzfeld and Guyer 1930, 84-7). The bath-house was an interesting building in its own right. Its main hall was a circular chamber flanked by eight alternating circular and rectangular niches. The site of the building is littered with masonry voussoirs, and it seems reasonable to conclude that this building had a masonry dome, even if no other building at Meryemlık did. The masonry of the bath-house is identical with that of the 'Cupola Church'.

It is clear from the writings of Basil of Seleucia that Thecla's sanctuary at Meryemlık was famous for miraculous cures. It is likely that this bath-house would have played its part in the healing process, as did the bath in the fourth century church. The therapeutic aspect of Meryemlık also seems to have been associated with the bird gardens. The position of the latter has not been determined, but it would have been logical to erect the bath-house near to it. The 'Cupola Church' may also have been associated with the curative aspect of the sanctuary, in which case its position would have been dictated by already existing structures. If the 'Cupola Church' was associated with the bird

---

[131] Feld 1963/64, 95; Forsyth 1957, 224-5; figures 4, 6; Gough 1972, 202-5, figure 2; Herzfeld and Guyer 1930, 46-74, figures 46-66; Hellenkemper 1986; Hild, Hellenkemper and Hellenkemper-Salies 1984, 235-9; Hild and Hellenkemper 1990, 443; Hill 1981, 32; Kramer 1963, 303-7, figure 5, plates 3-4.

sanctuary, this might explain the presence of birds as protomes in the capitals of the narthex and the nave, and the eagles which decorated the brackets in the nucleus.

Guyer's description, as I have indicated, presents few problems, and need only be summarized here, with the addition of some details which have become apparent at the east end of the church as the result of continued stone-robbing. The church was built throughout of well-cut ashlars, with most of the details being worked in Proconnesian marble. Exposed wall surfaces were either clad in marble or covered in mosaic, and where areas of floor were uncovered, these were regularly covered with opus sectile, even in the atrium.

At the west end of the complex was a semi-circular fore-court. This unusual feature was also present in the 'Domed Ambulatory Church' at Dağ Pazarı, and may be compared with the hexagonal courtyard to the west of the Transept Church at Öküzlü.   Sigma courtyards are a regular feature of palatial architecture, and it has even been argued that they are a particular feature of imperial palaces and churches (Lavin 1962, 9).   The presence of one here may be another symptom of the imperial involvement in the building programme at Meryemlık.   The western courtyard appears to have had a single wide entrance on the main axis, behind which a flight of curved steps led downwards into the courtyard.   There was a bench around the outer wall, and the courtyard was paved with square stone flags. The east side of the courtyard was occupied by a building which Herzfeld and Guyer did not explore very fully. It seems to have had the character of a propylaeum, being open, perhaps through a colonnade on the west side, and closed on the east side by a wall through which three doorways led into the atrium proper. The excavation produced a series of highly elaborate entablatures and cornices from this part of the church (Herzfeld and Guyer 1930, 49-52; figures 47-51). A square room at the north end of the propylaeum, presumably one of a pair, may have supported a tower. Guyer does not discuss the function of this chamber, which he did not excavate, but since he believed that there may have been an upper floor in the atrium, it is possible that the square room could have contained a staircase.   Guyer considered and rejected the possibility that there was a hall on the east side of the propylaeum. (Herzfeld and Guyer 1930, 48-53).

Herzfeld and Guyer uncovered a small area of the northeast corner of the atrium. From this it emerged that there had been a colonnade along the north side, which was paved with opus sectile. The narthex filled the west side of the atrium. The excavators uncovered enough of the north half of this to produce a reconstruction drawing (Herzfeld and Guyer 1930, figure 54). This shows the north half of a triple-arched portal in which moulded jambs and lintels were set between the columns. The capitals which supported the arches were adorned with birds. As well as the central portal, there was an extra doorway between the narthex and the northern colonnade of the atrium. Guyer was certain that the narthex had two storeys although he found no trace of a staircase. Three doorways seem to have led from the narthex into the main part of the church. (Herzfeld and Guyer 1930, 56-57).

In the published reconstruction plan (Herzfeld and Guyer 1930, figure 46), the triple-arched portal of the narthex is shown off-centre in the east side of the atrium, because the south colonnade of the atrium did not correspond to the position of the south aisle of the church. This peculiarity is not discussed by Guyer, but, presumably in order to restore symmetry to the interior of the narthex, Herzfeld's plan shows a doorway into the centre of the atrium opposite the doorway into the south aisle. No evidence for this emerges from the plan of the excavations (Herzfeld and Guyer 1930, figure 45), and I suspect that it is more likely that there were five arches in the portal, as was certainly the case in the Tomb Church at Corycus, and probably also in the great Basilica at Meryemlık. The extra width of the atrium must be assumed from the arc of the hemi-cycle at the west of the building. It may relate to the heavy foundations against the southwest corner of the church proper which were not discussed by Guyer. Smith suggested that these may have been the remains of a tomb (Smith 1971, 126). It is perhaps more likely that there was a bath at this point in the church, as there may have been in the fourth century basilica. Whether bath or tomb, the structure appears to have been sufficiently important to justify extending the atrium and the narthex southwards in order to provide access to it.

The main section of the church retained the basilical principle of having nave and aisles, but the nave was divided into two sections. Immediately in front of the apse was a central bay. The inner sides of this formed an almost perfect square (10.6 by 10.65 metres). The corners were defined on the west side by piers which were 2.2 metres square, and on the east side by the walls at the mouth of the apse which were 2 metres thick. There was certainly a colonnade on the north side of this central nucleus, which was presumably mirrored by one on the south side. Guyer does not say whether there was a colonnade on the west side of the nucleus. By analogy with the 'Domed Ambulatory Church' at Dağ Pazarı, this might have been expected, but Herzfeld's excavation plan shows paving at the north end of the west side of the bay. The western bay of the nave was defined to north and south by two pairs of arches which were separated by square piers. The capitals of the colonnades in the nave were very similar to those of the narthex, and the excavators also found smaller capitals from the galleries (Herzfeld and Guyer 1930, 56-61).

It is Guyer's attempt to reconstruct a picture of the roofing system of the main part of the church which has provoked most controversy. He concluded that the aisles and the west bay of the nave were covered with barrel vaults, and that high arches sprang from the four piers of the central nucleus which was surmounted by a masonry dome:

'Und nun die wichtige Frage: wie war dies Haupt-Joch eingedeckt?? Um die Antwort gleich vorweg zu nehmen: nur eine Kuppel kann in Frage kommen. Diese massiven, über die Fluchtlinien der Scheidebogenreihen vorspringenden Pfeiler, diese mächtigen Blendbögen auf allen vier Seiten, sie haben nur einen Sinn, wenn sie das Auflager einer richtigen Kuppelkonstruktion sind; eine hölzerne Kuppel oder ein Zeltdach wie in Alahan Monastir kommt da nicht in Frage. Steht diese Thatsache völlig ausser Zweifel, so lassen sich alle anderen Fragen nach der Gestaltung dieser Kuppel nur mit z. T. recht fragwürdigen Vermutungen beantworten. So lässt sich - um mit einer der wichtigsten dieser Fragen zu beginnen - nicht mehr genau ermitteln, wie der Übergang vom Viereck zum Kuppelrund beschaffen war.' (Herzfeld and Guyer 1930, 61-2)

Forsyth was not so easily convinced:

'Any reader who is accustomed to regard this church as an important point of reference for the development of Byzantine domical structures may share my own disappointment in the meagre amount of evidence actually available to support such a view. Guyer confidently asserts that the great square bay... was originally covered by a stone dome... To be sure, the ruin has suffered depredations since 1907 and, as a result, some of his evidence may have been destroyed. Thus the large pier... is shown in Guyer's figure 64 as it looked when it still retained its ashlar facing and carried fragments of the nave arcade and of the tunnel vault over the south aisle. Its facing and voussoirs have now disappeared, leaving only the shapeless rubble core of the pier. Yet Guyer's photograph shows that it stood no higher in his day than at present, so that it could hardly have yielded him evidence about the upper parts of the church... Indeed the only evidence he offers for the very existence of a dome is the outline of the plan which his excavations revealed... To him this is conclusive - there must have been a massive masonry dome above such massive supports - and he firmly rejects any comparison to the wooden pyramid which must have covered the corresponding bay of the church at Alahan Kilisse... In my opinion, such reasoning is not at all conclusive and the comparison with Alahan Kilisse seems very appropriate... The latter has, of course, certain features which are not found in the Meriamlik church, namely a choir bay, a small apse terminating each aisle, and nave columns prefixed to the two western piers of the nave arcade; and the Meriamlik church, in turn, possesses more closely spaced nave supports and, above all, is distinguished by the four massive corner piers which define its eastern bay. Such differences can be regarded, however, as mere local variants within one basic concept of a church plan as a large square box containing a smaller box which is more or less square and is placed against the eastern side of the large box so as to be near the main apse. ...we are entitled to believe that our church at Meriamlik being of similar plan and located in the same region was crowned by a wooden pyramid also - not by a dome. The heavier substructure at Meriamlik can be explained by the tunnel vaults over the aisles, without any need to conjecture a masonry dome above them. Curiously enough, Guyer himself came close to associating the two churches when he noted that certain corbels decorated with animal and bird forms which he dug up in the Meriamlik church, were similar in size and style to those still in position at the top of the Alahan Kilisse tower... So obsessed was he by the notion of a dome on the church at Meriamlik, however, that he finally rejected the implications of his corbels on the ground that they were too small to support the great weight of a dome and must, therefore, have come from some other part of the building. Domes seem to have an irresistible attraction for some architectural historians.' (Forsyth 1957, 224-5)

Gough was entirely convinced by Forsyth's rhetoric (Gough 1972, 202-3), and Hellenkemper has felt obliged to agree.

Als Eindeckung über dem Zentraljoch scheint nach heutigem Kentnisstand nur ein flach geneigtes pyramidales Dach mit wohl offenem Dachstuhl wahrscheinlich. Eine einfachere, doch ästhetisch unbefriedigende Lösung wäre ein Pultdach. Gegen eine Kuppel über dem Zentraljoch und eine Tonne über dem Westjoch sprechen nicht nur die fehlende Befunde, sondern insbesondere statische Gründe: Pfeiler und Außenmauern sind trotz genenteiler Ansicht zu gering dimensioniert, um den erheblichen Horizontalschub aufzufangen. (Hellenkemper 1986, 77)

Like Forsyth, Hellenkemper compares the East Church at Alahan and the 'Cupola Church' at Meryemlık, but I feel that the comparison of these churches is not as straightforward as Forsyth would have it. To say that the heavier substructure at Meryemlık is the result of the presence of barrel vaults over the aisles is absurd, since there are similar vaults at Alahan, and in both cases the barrel vaults were presumably constructed for a specific reason. The western supports of the tower at Alahan are cruciform piers, the maximum dimensions of which are 0.7 by 1.6 metres: by contrast the piers at Meryemlık are 2.2 metres square, and the walls at Meryemlık are twice as thick as those at Alahan. The masonry dome of the tetrapylum beside the Transept Church at Corycus was supported on L-shaped piers which were only 51 centimetres thick, and that dome was supported on pendentives which had squinch arches in their bases. This combination of squinch and pendentive removes some of the force from the argument that the corbels could not have supported squinches strong enough to carry the weight of a masonry dome. Such squinches might have been combined with pendentives, as at Corycus, or could have been essentially ornamental, as at Kala'at Sem'an (for a reconstruction drawing of Kala'at Sem'an, see Krencker 1939, figure 6). In the absence of a surviving Cilician example, it is useful to compare Butler's reconstruction of the church at Kasr Ibn Wardan, which has a dome set on pendentives which were pierced by arched windows (Butler 1907, plate 3).

The differences between the churches at Meryemlık and Alahan might simply have arisen from the fact that the 'Cupola Church' is larger, but it is relevant here to note that the piers at Meryemlık are marginally bigger than those in the 'Domed Ambulatory Church' at Dağ Pazarı, which almost certainly supported a masonry dome. In fact the relationship of the 'Domed Basilicas' at Meryemlık and Dağ Pazarı is much closer than any relationship of either with the East Church at Alahan. They may all be regarded as 'mere local variants', but I cannot see why this should preclude the possibility that there should have been variations in the roofing systems. Furthermore Forsyth's arguments concerning Alahan and Dağ Pazarı are less than convincing since his reconstruction of the roofing systems there is inaccurate. It is evident in both churches that there would have had to be either a continuation of the tower, or a tambour, in order to allow any fenestration in the upper walls of the nucleus. The tower evidently did not continue upwards at Dağ Pazarı since there was a cornice immediately above the mouth of the apse. Since there was a low tambour in the church at Kasr Ibn Wardan, which contained the pendentives and the windows, it must be likely that the arrangements at Alahan and Dağ Pazarı were similar. It would be most illogical to suggest that the tower at Meryemlık was not also similar. Herzfeld and Guyer did not clear the central bay of the 'Cupola Church', which is still encumbered by about 5 metres depth of debris, and there is, therefore, little to commend Gough's argument ex silentio:

> 'At Alahan there was no stone dome, for excavation has proved it; and had Guyer found positive evidence of such a feature at Meryemlık during his own work, he would assuredly have mentioned the fact, which he does not.' (Gough 1972, 203)

Gough did find that large holes had had to be repaired in the floor of the East Church at Alahan, which may be taken as evidence for the possibility that something massive had fallen on it. This cannot have originated from the surviving part of the tower, but might well have fallen from a still higher level. There is, accordingly, much to be said for a view expressed by Gough in an earlier article:

> 'Nevertheless, when all is said and done, the use of squinch arches at the angles of the tower strongly suggests that the architect was familiar with the basic principles of domical construction, and this alone would make Koja Kalessi a building of exceptional interest if, as some scholars have believed, it was built a good half century before the most distinguished

of all domed basilicas, the church of St Sophia in Istanbul, begun in 532.' (Gough 1968, 463)

But it is much more likely than the squinch arches marked the transition to the tambour, and they may also have been included in the base of the pendentives (in this respect it is useful to compare the setting of the dome of the Tetrapylum at Corycus). The argument can be applied as readily to the 'Cupola Church' at Meryemlık, and I regard the presence of the elements of squinch arches like those of the tower at Alahan as conclusive evidence that there was a dome at Meryemlık. The massive blocks of masonry which clutter the site of the 'Cupola Church' to a depth of four or five metres must have fallen from the superstructure of the building: excavation might well reveal the voussoirs of the masonry dome at the bottom, since this would have been the first part of the building to fall. In fact fragments of architectural sculpture have been found in the 'Cupola Church' which resemble the brackets which support the squinches in the tower at Alahan (Herzfeld and Guyer 1930, 63, figure 61). Hellenkemper has discussed these pieces (1986, 76-7, figures 13-16), but observes that they probably came from the archivolts of the nave because on one piece, a bracket with an eagle, there is the trace of a bronze fixing which presumably supported a hanging lamp. Hellenkemper does not mention such traces on the other brackets, and whilst one might cite the opposed peacocks in the exedrae of St Polyeuktos in Constantinople (Harrison 1989, 81-4) as a loose parallel for Hellenkemper's positioning of the brackets in the nave archivolts, lamps were suspended from the semi-dome of the apse in the east Church at Alahan, and one only has to look inside Santa Sophia to see that lamps can hang from a very great height indeed in Byzantine churches.

Guyer's comments on the east end of the church were very brief. He observed that the apse was semi-circular on the inside, which had stone benches for the clergy, and presented five faces of an octagon on its outer face. Herzfeld and Guyer did not explore the side-chambers in any detail, but indications of their form can be seen on Herzfeld's plans. Guyer noted that there might have been an eastern enclosure wall as in the great Basilica (Herzfeld and Guyer 1930, 66-7).

The southeast corner of the church was buried in 1907, but has been uncovered by stone-robbers. This area has been described by Kramer, who has amplified Herzfeld's plan of this section of the building (Kramer 1963, figure 5). Kramer's plan shows that the arrangements at this corner of the church were unusually complicated, but he made no detailed attempt to explain them, merely noting that there was a pair of rooms at the southeast corner of the church which were not directly connected either to the apse or to the south aisle. Kramer's most important discovery was made in this room where he saw a quatrefoil basin carved from a single block of marble measuring 1.5 metres across (plate 99). Kramer identified this basin as a font (Kramer 1963, 304). This is the most likely identification, since the shape is so commonly associated with baptismal fonts, and this basin is very similar to the fragmentary marble basin found in the Tomb Church at Corycus, which was believed by Khatchatrian to be a font (Khatchatrian 1962, 100; figure 130). The possibility cannot, however be entirely discounted that this was a bath associated with Thecla's miraculous cures. Since Kramer's visit, more robbing has taken place at this corner of the building, and the font, which is a fine piece of Proconnesian marble, has been further uncovered and partially smashed. It is a little over a metre deep and has, in one conch, two wide, deep steps, the lower of which may have been used as a seat. The walls which appear in Kramer's sketch plan are no longer distinct, but, by combining the plans of Herzfeld and Kramer, we can gain an impression of the plan of the eastern apartments.

The font is placed near the centre of the chamber, with its conches aligned to the points of the compass (Kramer 1963, 304). There seems little reason to suppose that it is not in its original position, although Feld has raised this as a possibility (Feld 1965, 93). Baptisteries in the side-chambers of Cilician basilicas are known, and, often enough, as here, there are ranges of associated rooms (compare, e.g. Anemurium, Necropolis Church; church north of Corycus). Here rectangular spaces are interposed between the baptistery and the apse and south aisle. These spaces are connected by a doorway which is shown on Herzfeld's plan and provided communication with the vaulted substructures which are visible at this point in the church (Hellenkemper 1986, 81). It would appear, therefore, that in this church the integrity of the side-chamber, which had a special function, was preserved by placing it beyond the passage round the apse, the eastern section of which is indicated on Herzfeld's plan as a long rectangular chamber. The northeast corner of the church is still buried: it appears from Herzfeld's plan that the passage turned again to hug the north side of the apse, but that the plan of the northern side-chambers was different from that of those on the south side.

Herzfeld and Guyer uncovered so little of this church that they found few traces of its fittings. The only significant find of this nature was a rectangular marble basis which lay in the central position of the west side of the nucleus, projecting into the west bay of the nave: lying beside this were fragments of a circular plinth (Herzfeld and Guyer 1930, 68-70; figures 65-6). Guyer could not decide whether these belonged to an ambo or to a bishop's throne, but there can be no doubt that the former identification was correct. The ambo in the Funerary Basilica at Dağ Pazarı was very similar, and was found in situ projecting from the sanctuary into the nave. The position of these fragments in the 'Cupola Church' thus gives credence to the obvious conclusion that the central nucleus served as the chancel. Though smaller than the Basilica, the 'Cupola Church' appears to have been more lavishly decorated, and much more ambitious architecturally. Guyer concluded that this was the church which was sponsored by Zeno, and that the Basilica was slightly earlier (Herzfeld and

Guyer 1930, 73-4). I have much sympathy for this view, but I am not entirely convinced that it is necessary to select one of the churches at Meryemlık. I would prefer to suggest that Zeno had a hand in the design and financing of both churches since both (to misapply Forsyth's comment on the Basilica - Forsyth 1957, 224) have the 'magnificence appropriate to imperial patronage'.

MERYEMLIK, North Church[132] (figure 45)

Although this building was largely ignored by Herzfeld and Guyer, it approached the more famous churches in size, measuring roughly 60 by 30 metres, and would have been the first church at Meryemlık to be seen by visitors from Seleucia. Though very ruinous, it is hardly more so than the other basilicas, and as Feld observed, the excavation of this building should prove worthwhile (Feld 1965, 93).

Without excavation, very little can be added to the brief comments of Herzfeld and Guyer, and the outline provided on their general plan. This appears to have been a simple basilica, with an atrium, a narthex, a projecting semi-circular apse, and no side-chambers. Herzfeld and Guyer found an acanthus window capital, two simple foliate capitals, and part of an ambo. The latter was very similar to the ambo of the 'Cupola Church'. Feld noted fallen columns on the north side of the atrium, which thus appears to have had colonnades. The few surviving decorative elements are similar to those of the two larger basilicas, and it would be reasonable to suppose that the North Church was probably of similar date.

MERYEMLIK, Church Northwest of 'Cupola Church'[133]

Herzfeld and Guyer noted a small ruined church some 40 metres to the northwest of the 'Cupola Church', which they thought was certainly a basilica since the apse was visible. On the general plan, the building appears to be about 30 metres long. No trace of this building can be seen today.

MEZAROLUK[134]

Langlois saw 'une petite église en forme de basilique' near the Han at Mezaroluk (Güzeloluk) 12 kilometres south of the Cilician Gates.

---

[132] Feld 1963/64, 93; Herzfeld and Guyer 1930, 74-7, figures 2, 67-73; Hild, Hellenkemper and Hellenkemper-Salies 1984, 239.

[133] Herzfeld and Guyer 1930, 77, figure 2.

[134] Langlois 1861, 367, Hild and Hellenkemper 1990, 349

MİSİS (Mopsuestia), Basilica[135]

The remains of a large basilica which stands in an ancient cemetery to the west of the mound which marks the site of the city of Mopsuestia were uncovered by the excavations of Bossert and Budde in 1955 to 1958. Budde has published various accounts of the mosaics, which are of unusual magnificence, but his publications are unhelpful in terms of the architectural remains of the basilica. Budde's plan merely gives the layout of the mosaics, and does not cover the entire building and we are dependent on a sketchy plan of the building which was included by Bossert in a preliminary note on his work on Misis Höyük. Even this latter was poorly reproduced, and did not include a scale (Bossert 1957, figure 1). By combining the two inadequate plans is it possible to work out that the basilica measured roughly 37 by 25 metres overall, and appears to have had an extra corridor or annex on its north side, and perhaps a narthex at the west. The apse is indicated roughly, and it is clear that the areas around it were not excavated. It is, therefore, impossible to say whether the apse had side-chambers, or was backed by a passage. Brief references to the building reveal that it was destroyed by an earthquake, and subsequently used as an Arab cemetery. Budde believed that the basilica was a martyrium, which was possibly dedicated to Tarachus, Probus and Andronicus, the martyrs of Anazarbus (see Hild and Hellenkemper 1990, 352, 357), but the argument is very thin. Budde was also convinced that the church belonged to the period when Theodore was Bishop of Mopsuestia (392-428), more particularly to the late fourth century (Budde 1969, 34), but Buschhausen and Kitzinger (followed by Hild and Hellenkemper) have shown that the mosaics must be later, and are unlikely to have been laid earlier than the late fifth century.

Kitzinger's review of Budde's publication of his work at Misis is very telling:

'It must be said at once that the book falls sadly short of the full documentation of the Misis mosaics which it was expected to provide. Dazzled by the wealth of illustrations spread before him the reader may not immediately realize that the visual apparatus is actually quite deficient; and its deficiencies are all the more serious since, by Budde's own account, some of the material he uncovered has since been lost irretrievably.

Most grievous of all is the inexplicable absence of an architectural plan. There is not even a reference to what appears to be the only such plan ever published. All that Budde provides is a situation diagram of extant portions of the mosaics, insufficient for relating the floors to their architectural setting, and inadequate as a record of the mosaics

---

[135] Bossert 1960, 15, figure 1; Budde 1969; Buschhausen 1972,, 57-71; Hild, Hellenkemper and Hellenkemper-Salies 1984, 202-4; Hild and Hellenkemper 1990, 357; Kitzinger 1973a, 140-2; Kitzinger 1973b, 136-44.

themselves... Budde interprets the building as a three-aisled martyrium church, but the material evidence he presents, inadequately documented as it is, does not bear this out. It suggests a basilica of either four (sic) or five aisles; and while there is little to support its identification as a martyrium, the plan has certain affinities with some synagogues. The possibility that the building and its mosaics are Jewish rather than Christian should be explored carefully.' (Kitzinger 1973a, 141)

Kitzinger has developed his argument that the building may have been a synagogue in a subsequent paper on the Samson mosaic of the north aisle. The essential element in this argument is the comparison with two synagogues:

'In particular, mention should be made of the synagogue at Hammath-Tiberias, which, in its earlier state, was a building roughly square in overall shape with two aisles to the left of the nave and one to the right; and of another synagogue discovered a few years ago at Gaza which had two aisles on either side of the nave. Both buildings were richly decorated with mosaic floors. In the light of these analogies, the possibility that the Misis basilica was a synagogue rather than a church should be examined closely.' (Kitzinger 1973b, 136-7)

Although there is much to be said for this, especially since the representational mosaics of the building are concerned exclusively with Old Testament subjects, it must be noted that it would not be surprising to discover that a Christian basilica in Cilicia had had four aisles, or three aisles and a passage, since there are numerous examples of churches with a corridor along one side, and in cases where it has been possible to recover more than the ground plan, some of these corridors have been shown to have been open to the body of the church through colonnades, and thus had the character of extra aisles (compare e.g. the Necropolis Church at Eski Anamur). Kitzinger is correct to note the square plan of the church: the nave and aisles together appear to have measured 25 by 25 metres. This would not in itself be surprising in a province which has so many basilicas with centralized elements, but the nave and the two immediately adjoining aisles formed a rectangle measuring roughly 25 by 20 metres, proportions which can be passed over without comment.

The presence of the fourth 'aisle' would suggest that if this was indeed a church, there would have been either a baptistery in the north side-chamber, or an eastern passage. The presence of either of these features would secure the identification of the building. In the light of these observations, it is all the more to be regretted that Budde did not fully explore the east end of the church. In the present state of knowledge it is safest to assume that this building was indeed a church.

MOPSUESTIA see MISIS

MYLAE see MANASTIR

NESULION see BOĞŞAK ADASI

OLBA see URA

OVACİK (Aphrodisias), Church of Pantaleimon[136]
This basilica was excavated by Budde, whose prime concern was with its mosaic floors, but its plan is of considerable interest in its own right. The basilica with narthex and side-chambers measured about 28.4 by 13.5 metres overall, with walls about 55 centimetres wide. Two rows of five columns separated nave and aisles. The south wall is better preserved but the north wall, on the sea side, has fallen. The small apse (diameter 2.4 metres) which is visible was the inner part of the eastern ambulatory which filled the space between the side-chambers, and probably extended for the full width of the nave (4.6 metres). The bema was marked out and stretched into the first, eastern, intercolumniation of the nave. Fine Proconnesian marble architectural members and capitals attest to the richness of the building, and there were also limestone capitals in the galleries The floor mosaics include benefactors' names as well as that of the dedicatee of the church, St Pantaleimon. There were rectangular graves with multiple burials at the south end of the narthex, and a Christian limestone sarcophagus stands nearby. Budde puts the mosaics in early fifth century; and Hild and Hellenkemper suggest a fifth century date for the sculpture. The basilica was later converted into a single-naved church by the insertion of inner blocking walls.

ÖKÜZLÜ ('UKUSLÜKÜ'), North Church[137] (figure 46, plates 100-4)
The ruined village site at Öküzlü stands about 5 kilometres southwest of Yanıkhan on an ancient road which leaves the road from Limonlu to Canbazlı just south of Yanıkhan. The site has no permanent residents, but is used by the Yürüks as a halting place when on the move between winter and summer pastures. The Yürüks keep an ancient cistern, which is sited immediately to the west of the basilica, in repair. This must be the 'Ukuslükü' where Bent saw 'a fine early Christian church, and a few remains of earlier date' (Bent 1891, 219). The ruins are visible from Yanıkhan, and I first saw them from a distance in 1975, and resolved to visit the site on a future occasion. I returned to do so in 1979, but my visit was made in less than ideal circumstances. Petrol was not available anywhere south of Karaman, and on the drive up from Limonlu the rear differential on the Land Rover started to fail. The culminating indignity

---

[136] Budde 1973; Budde 1987; Hild and Hellenkemper 1986, 27-30; Hild and Hellenkemper 1990, 195-6.
[137] Bent 1891, 219; Eyice 1982, figure d, plates 1-2; Hild, Hellenkemper and Hellenkemper-Salies 1984, 205-6; Hild and Hellenkemper 1990, 369, plate 322; Hill 1981, 34.

was that I was bitten by a Karabaş and had to withdraw from Öküzlü with a wounded foot. I give this preamble to explain why I had to rush past the South Church at Öküzlü and was unable to conduct more than a very cursory survey of the North Church, even though I was aware at the time that it was a monument of unusual interest. As well as the basilica, the site preserves a number of ruined ancient houses and olive presses.

The North Church at Öküzlü (32 by 17.5 metres) is the larger of its two churches. The east end of the church is much better preserved than the west end, where there is evidence of secondary building, but the basic outlines of the original plan are clear. The church had a polygonal forecourt or atrium at the west end which could be entered through doorways in its three western faces. It is not large enough to have had internal colonnades. Its unusual shape is somewhat reminiscent of the semi-circular courtyards on the west sides of the 'Cupola Church' at Meryemlık and the 'Domed Ambulatory Church' at Dağ Pazarı. On the east side of the fore-court there are vestiges of a narthex which may have had an arched portal. Three doorways led into the nave and aisles: the central doorway is larger, and has a simple moulding on its jambs and lintels. The nave and aisles were separated by two rows of columns. Three of the columns of the north arcade are still standing, and there were evidently five columns in each row.

A T-shaped pier at the east end of the north arcade still stands up to the level of the springing of the gallery arcade. This pier is a precious survival, for it proves that this church had a fully developed transept. The springings of five arches are preserved on this pier. On its west face can be seen the eastern arches of the north colonnade at ground and gallery levels. The north face of the pier shows the beginnings of arches which sprang across the aisle and its gallery from north to south. On the south face of the pier, a single arch sprang from a capital which is just above the base moulding of the aisle gallery: we have here part of the triumphal arch which sprang across the width of the nave, and marked the west side of the transept. Most significantly, the east face of the pier is entirely plain, proving that no arches linked the triumphal arch with the wall at the mouth of the apse. It is clear, therefore, that the transept in this basilica formed a unified lateral space 4.5 metres wide. If any further proof were needed that this church had a fully developed transept, this is provided by the wall at the mouth of the apse. Not only is the main apse perfectly preserved, but there are courses of masonry above the arch at its mouth, and even the evidence for fenestration at this high level in the church. Four arched windows survive from a row of six above the mouth of the apse. There can be no question that here walls continued upwards above the mouth of the apse. There can only be one explanation for this: the transept at Öküzlü must have had a transverse roofing system, which was also supported by a wall which rose above the triumphal arch. The row of windows above the mouth of the apse is the only clerestory lighting which is still fully in position in a Cilician basilica: it is doubly remarkable since it is the clerestory lighting of a transept.

The main apse itself is very plain. A simple sima moulding marks the springing of its slightly horse-shoed semi-dome, but there are no capitals at its angles since no colonnades or arches crossed the transept. Because the masonry is here preserved to such a height, the characteristic Cilician mixture of small stones and ashlar work is especially apparent. The apse is constructed from well-cut large blocks, but the walls above and beside its mouth are in small stones. The array of putlog holes in the small stonework, and traces of plaster in the semi-dome show that all wall surfaces were stuccoed. The apse was lit by a double arched window, and is inscribed within a flat east wall. On either side of the mouth of the apse are the doorways of the side-chambers. These doorways are entirely plain, and have relieving arches which would presumably have been hidden by plaster. The side-chambers were wider than the aisles, and therefore project beyond the outer walls of the aisles. They also project eastwards, beyond the central apse, thus defining a square space, which could be entered through doorways in the side walls of the side-chambers. There are traces of an enclosure wall on the east side of this space, running between the east walls of the side-chambers. This wall may have been a later insertion, but the equivalent unbonded wall in the Transept Church at Corycus is probably a primary feature. Both side-chambers have small projecting apses which are lit by single windows. The better-preserved north side-chamber has a cupboard-like recess in its south wall which is let into the outer face of the central apse, and a small rectangular window on either side of the semi-dome of its absidiole. Beam-holes in the outer face of the main apse show that the side-chambers had upper floors. With only trivial differences, such as the projection of the absidioles, and details of fenestration, the east end of this basilica, is very similar to that of the Transept Church at Corycus.

A scrap of the outer wall of the south aisle is the only other section of the church which survives to gallery level. From this section it can be seen that there was a doorway at the centre of the south aisle. Arched windows with drip-stones ran along the wall above the level of the top of the lintel of the south door. A console which projects from the north side of the south wall is the only surviving support for the gallery floor. At the top of this short section of wall can be seen parts of two arched windows at gallery level.

The T-shaped pier on the north side of the triumphal arch preserves three matching engaged capitals which all consist of two rows of highly stylized acanthus leaves. These capitals are strikingly reminiscent of the engaged capitals of the nave arcade and the triumphal arch of Church 4 at Kanlıdivane (plate), and closely resemble the pier capitals in the central bays of the 'Domed Basilicas' at Corycus and Dağ Pazarı (plates 43 and 69). The basilica at Öküzlü is therefore a member of the important Cilician group of Transept Basilicas and

'Domed Basilicas', and presumably belongs with the others to the late fifth century.

ÖKÜZLÜ ('UKUSLÜKÜ')[138], South Church

The South Church stands prominently on a small hill outside the centre of settlement. Only the apse is well preserved. The basilica was equipped with a narthex and an eastern passage. The main part of the church was divided into nave and aisles by two rows of six columns. Eyice was unable to tell whether or not there were galleries, but the height of the apse and the presence of an upper storey over the eastern passage would together suggest the likelihood that galleries were present. The round apse was lit by a double window and surrounded by the irregular passage with a larger, eastwards projecting, south side-chamber. Eyice noted that the apse had to be strengthened at some date after its original construction

SELEUCIA see SİLİFKE

SELINUS see GAZİPAŞA

SİLİFKE (Seleucia), Temple-Church[139] (plate 108)

Although Seleucia was the metropolis of Isauria, and important as the seat of the Council of 359, and the home of Bishop Basil, no traces of its churches have survived to the present day. Egeria saw a very beautiful church in the city, but went straight on to Meryemlık rather than spending a night in Seleucia (*Peregrinatio*, 23, 1-2). Langlois saw the remains of two churches at Silifke. Of one he merely noted that some of its column bases survived. This may have been the building which Keil and Wilhelm found a short distance to the west of the Temple-church which had columns, and capitals with crosses (Keil and Wilhelm 1931, 7).

Langlois also briefly described the temple which was converted into a Christian temple, and published a useful line-drawing of the building (plate 108). Its existence had previously been noted by Laborde, who reported that the church had twelve columns. Langlois noted that the Basilica had been created by re-using the blocks from the cella of the temple and that its apse was pierced by two double windows, the arches of which were separated by red marble columns which had impost capitals. By 1907, when Keil and Wilhelm planned the temple, the apse had presumably fallen since they do not mark it, but they note that in 1925 a trench at the west end revealed that the intercolumniations

---

[138] Eyice 1982, 365-6, figure e, plate 3; Hild, Hellenkemper and Hellenkemper-Salies 1984, 369; Hild and Hellenkemper 1990, 369.

[139] Feld 1963/64, 89-93; Hild, Hellenkemper and Hellenkemper-Salies 1984, 227-8; Hild and Hellenkemper 1990, 404, plate 342; Keil and Wilhelm 1931, 7-8, figure 13, plate 12; de Laborde 1838, 130; Langlois 1861, 182-93.

had been filled to create the church. The temple was Corinthian with a peristyle of fourteen columns by eight. Its platform measured 40 by 22 metres. Laborde's statement that the church had twelve columns has been contested by Feld who argued that he was confused by the number of columns in the long sides of the temple (Feld 1963/64, 89-93). But Langlois' drawing shows the outside of the apse, with a column still standing a short distance to the east. This column is one of only two which stood to the height of their capitals, and the only one with a fragment of masonry above the capital. It must therefore be the column which Keil and Wilhelm photographed (Keil and Wilhelm 1931, plate 12). This fact established, it is clear that the apse of the basilica was set to the west of the east colonnade of the temple. But it can be seen from Langlois' drawing, and from the published photograph, that the intercolumniations of this east colonnade were also filled with secondary masonry. It therefore emerges that there must have been a passage behind the apse, and Laborde may well have been correct in his statement that twelve columns were taken up by the length of the main part of the church. Since we know that the western intercolumniations were filled with masonry we may conclude that the church covered the whole temple platform. This would leave 32.5 metres available for the length of the nave. There would have been ample room for a narthex at the west end of the platform. By blocking only the outer pair of intercolumniations at the north and south ends of the west facade, it would have been possible to leave a triple entrance similar to that of the Temple-Church of Uzuncaburç. The Christian conversion of temples seems to have been in progress in the fourth century in Cilicia. This building would have been transformed into a large and impressive basilica, and may well have been in existence as such by the time of the Council of Seleucia in 382, or Egeria's visit in 384, although there are literary references to the use of temples in Seleucia as churches in the fifth century (Hild and Hellenkemper 1990, 404).

SÖMEK[140]
Keil and Wilhelm report a church at a ruin-site 1.2 kilometres westsouthwest of Sömek ('Sümek') on the road from Limonlu to Canbazlı (15 kilometres northwest of Limonlu).

SUSANOĞLU (Çok Ören) (Corasium), Town Church[141] (figure 48)
The village of Susanoğlu stands on the coast at the extreme east end of the Göksu delta, 12 kilometres east of Silifke. It is surrounded by ruin-fields, but the modern development has involved extensive robbing, and few monuments stand for more than a course or two above foundation level.

---

[140] Keil and Wilhelm 1931, 101; Hild and Hellenkemper 1990, 419.

[141] Feld 1963/64, 94; Hild, Hellenkemper and Hellenkemper-Salies 1984   239-40; Hild and Hellenkemper 1990, 313; Keil and Wilhelm 1931, 105-6, figure 140.

The Town Church, which is now flattened, stood on the west side of the site on the steep slope up to the city walls. The basilica measured roughly 32 by 16 metres overall, and was already so ruinous and deeply covered by scrub in 1907 that Keil and Wilhelm were able to discover little about its internal arrangements. The west end was cut deeply in the rock, and the church was therefore entered through doorways towards the west ends of the north and south walls. There was a fore-hall on the south side, which may have contained the main entrance. The apse was semi-circular on both faces, and had consoles attached to its outer face from which arches sprang across to the east wall of the passage behind the apse. There were thus no firmly delineated side-chambers. The presence of the arches may indicate that the side-chambers had an upper storey, since such arches normally seem to have supported the joists of upper floors rather than roofing systems over the passages (compare, e.g. Church 2 at Kanlıdivane). The plan published by Keil and Wilhelm shows pilasters on either side of the apse which presumably mark the terminal points of the nave arcades (Keil and Wilhelm 1931, figure 140).

The arrangements at the west end of the basilica are puzzling. Keil and Wilhelm recorded a pier which supported a partly preserved arch against the south wall just west of the south door. A fragment of a wall which was in line with the arch was also opposite the eastern pier of the north arcade. This scrap of wall contained a semi-circular niche which Keil and Wilhelm thought might have contained an offertory box (Keil and Wilhelm 1931, 106). It seems more likely that the niche contained a stoup, as was the case in the Cemetery Church. From the evidence of the arch and the section of wall, it appears likely that Keil and Wilhelm were correct to suggest there was a narthex-like hall at the west end of the basilica, which could not be entered directly from outside. They did not consider the consequences of this, but it is possible that the enclosed nature of the 'narthex' would not have affected its function as a place of withdrawal for the catechumens. Since there appears to have been an upper floor above the passage, it is likely that the basilica had galleries. In this event the main function of the western hall may have been to support the gallery across the west end of the church. This would have been an essential element in communication at first floor level, and it is not inconceivable, given the topography, that access to the galleries could have been through a portal at first floor level in the west wall.

Feld found a capital in the church which matched one in the garden of the village school. From these he concluded that the basilica should be assigned to the late fifth century, but this type of capital had a long currency in Cilicia, and could easily be found in a fourth century building.

SUSANOĞLU (Çok Ören) (Corasium), Cemetery Church[142] (figure 49)

This church was sited close to the harbour at the eastern end of the west necropolis. The building has suffered so badly since 1907 that the account given by Keil and Wilhelm cannot be supplemented (Keil and Wilhelm 1931, 106; figure 141; plate 142). It was smaller than the Town Church (25 by 17 metres overall), but very similar in plan. As was the case in the Town Church, there was no entrance on the west side of the church. This basilica was provided with a narthex of broad proportions which could be entered through a doorway in the north wall, and from a corridor which ran along the south side of the building. This corridor also communicated with the main part of the church through a doorway in the south wall of the south aisle, and with the passage behind the apse. Three doors led into the nave and aisles from the narthex. In the east wall of the narthex, just to the north of the moulded doorway into the nave, was set a stone block with a basin under a lion's head spout. It is unfortunate that Keil and Wilhelm did not illustrate this stoup, which was evidently a particularly fine example. Keil and Wilhelm were able to plot the lines of the nave colonnades. The semi-circular apse was pierced by a single arched window, and had a simple moulding at the springing of its semi-dome. Doorways at the east ends of the aisles led into the eastern passage, which again had two lateral arches springing from consoles on the outer curved face of the apse. This again allows the assumption that the eastern passage had two storeys, and that the basilica may have had galleries. An unusual feature of this church was that a small apse, 2 metres wide at its mouth was positioned halfway along the length of the north aisle, and projected from the north wall of the basilica. Keil and Wilhelm thought that this may have been the position of a saint's or martyr's tomb. That the apse had a funerary function is perfectly possible, given the position of the church, but it could as well have been a memorial to a priest.

Feld considered that this church was likely to have been contemporary with, or slightly earlier than, the Town Church (Feld 1963/64, 94). Since the churches are so similar in design, and it is clear that Corasium was a planned city founded in the fourth century (Hild and Hellenkemper 1990, 311), it is tempting to suggest that both churches were erected following the σχῆμα of Vranius in the third quarter of the fourth century. The suggestion is particularly attractive since Bent (1891, 207) noted that Vranius' inscription, in which he, as 'λαμπρότατος ἄρχων τῆς 'Ισαύρων ἐπαρχίας' recorded his personal interest in the project, was positioned on one of the churches.

---

[142] Bent 1891, 207; Feld 1963/64, 94; Hild, Hellenkemper and Hellenkemper-Salies 1984, 240; Hild and Hellenkemper 1990, 313; Keil and Wilhelm 1931, 106, figure 141, plate 142.

ŞAHA ("Sheher"), Basilica[143] (figure 50, plates 106-7)

The ruin-field known as Şaha stands on the crest of a hill a few kilometres northwest of Erdemli. It was first reported by Keil and Wilhelm, who reported the presence of the church, houses with polygonal masonry, and some impressive sarcophagi (Heberdey and Wilhelm 1896, 46). Gertrude Bell visited the site in 1905, and published a description of the church (Bell 1906, 388-90). The site can only be approached on foot, and remains substantially as it must have been in 1905. As well as ancient houses, there are still impressive remains of a public building, perhaps an andron at the centre of the settlement. The land to the west and south was terraced in antiquity, presumably for the cultivation of olives. The basilica stands on the southeast edge of the settlement.

In 1905, Gertrude Bell was hampered by scrub and rubble in her attempts to plan the church. The rubble is now considerably deeper, and only a programme of clearance and excavation could clarify the plan further. This was a large basilica, measuring 39 by 17 metres. Parts of the west wall, the north wall, and the main apse are still reasonably well preserved, but all have deteriorated since 1905, and, in particular, the 'tower-like edifice' seen by Bell outside the west door has disappeared. The church was entered through a single door in the west wall. Outside this was the chamber which has disappeared. This structure was not really a narthex, since it did not extend for the full width of the building. It was entered through archways on its south and west sides (the north was already missing in 1905). In Bell's photograph the arch appears to have been inserted into the west wall of the church (Bell 1906, figure 3). What had in fact happened was that the pressure of the arch had weakened the west wall of the church, and, as a result, the arch and its support slipped into the west wall. A hole in this wall, just south of the doorway shows that the arch eventually collapsed through the wall. There is no need, therefore, to assume that the fore-hall was a secondary addition. The scar in the wall above the position of the arch shows that this western construction was properly keyed in. The west archway of the fore-hall rested on a simple capital: it is thus possible that this fore-hall may have had an arcaded portal in the normal manner of Cilician church fronts. Beam-holes above the west door show that the fore-hall had two storeys, and there is still visible above the west door, but offset slightly to the north, the south side of a doorway between the outer chamber and the church at gallery level. The doorway into the church has a huge lintel and is entirely undecorated. It is hard to believe that this was the main entrance to the church.

Nothing remains of the interior of the church, but a stack of column fragments in the northwest corner of the building must have come from the nave colonnades, and it is clear from the surviving section of the north wall that there was a gallery over the north aisle. The north wall is entirely devoid of doors

---

[143] Bell 1906b, 388-90, figures 1-3; Heberdey and Wilhelm 1896, 46; Hild, Hellenkemper and Hellenkemper-Salies 1984, 204; Hild and Hellenkemper 1990, 394.

and windows: its single point of interest is the step in its inner face on which must have rested the joists of the gallery floor. The main apse is very simple, having no moulding at the base of the semi-dome, and being pierced by no windows. There is a row of regular fixing holes in its inner face. A doorway on the north side by the mouth of the apse allowed entry to the eastern passage. In 1905 part of the semi-dome of the subsidiary apse at the north end of the passage was still in position, but very little of this apse is left. The north angle of the south subsidiary apse is just visible although Gertrude Bell in 1905 could see no vestige of it (Bell 1906, 389). It may therefore be assumed that there was also a door into the passage at the end of the south aisle. Beam-holes in the outer face of the apse and in the eastern wall show that the passage was two storeys high.

Gertrude Bell noted that 'The disproportionate length of the nave and aisles tempts me to believe that the foundations marked on the plan (a pier and a returning wall) may have been part of the division between the body of the church and the narthex...' (Bell 1906, 389). Had she considered the galleries, which she does not mention, she would have seen that there can be no question that there was a hall across the west end of the nave, since beam-holes in the west wall show that there was a gallery across this end of the building. This could be entered from the upper floor of the hall in front of the west door. It may be that the main purpose of the fore-hall was to contain the staircase.

The west wall of the church has another peculiarity which Bell overlooked. There is a very noticeable scar where the south wall of the south aisle has fallen away, but the western wall continues southwards beyond this line, as does the row of beam-holes which contained the gallery supports. The continuation is shown on Bell's plan extending for 6 metres before turning to a diagonal alignment. There seems to have been a courtyard on the south side of the church, and it is clear that there was once a two-storeyed hall on this side of the building. It seems most likely, therefore, that excavation would reveal that the main entrance to this building was on this side of the building. Taking as points of comparison the South Church at Yanıkhan, and the Cemetery Church at Susanoğlu, we may assume that the southern passage would have provided direct access not only to the narthex, but also to the south aisle and to the eastern passage. Such passages are a regular feature of basilicas with the eastern passage, and emphasize the significance which must have been attached to them. The southern passage at Şaha is the only example which can certainly be shown to have had an upper storey. A row of beam-holes at a low level in the west wall of the south passage may have been for wooden benches. Seating provision, albeit in stone was made in the forecourts of the 'Cupola Church' at Meryemlık, and the 'Domed Ambulatory Church' at Dağ Pazarı. Columns lying on the south side of the building suggest that the southern hall may have had an arcaded portal.

Bell's plan shows a square chamber against the north side of the west end of the north aisle, but she was unable to tell whether it communicated with the church (Bell 1906, 390). Recent clearance in this chamber, which is used as a stable, has uncovered an opening which was probably once a doorway between this chamber and the north aisle. Smashed fragments of a stone font are included in the rough wall of the stable. It is likely, therefore, that this chamber may have been used as a baptistery.

Squared stones were used throughout the building. These vary in size, the larger blocks being used in the lower courses of the apse all are well laid, and bound by excellent mortar. Putlog holes can be seen throughout the building, and it seems that all surfaces must have been stuccoed. The only recorded decorative element is the now lost, very simple, capital of the western fore-hall. Without excavation it is probably pointless to attempt to suggest a date for the building, though Hild, Hellenkemper and Hellenkemper-Salies (1984, 204) suggest a date in the sixth century on the grounds that the plan of the east end at Şaha resembles that of the 'Große Armenische Kirche' at Corycus..

TAKKADIN[144]

Takkadın is the site of a small ancient village about 4 kilometres east of İmamli. The site was first reported by Keil and Wilhelm who mentioned two chapels and basilica but did not describe them. Further details have been published by Eyice, Feld and Hild and Hellenkemper. Only the side of the apse survives to any height: it was constructed from well-cut ashlars. The church was a basilica, probably with no narthex. The apse was three-sided with a single window. There were side-chambers beside the apse which projected slightly westwards to form a chancel area, and communicated with extra chambers and an eastern passage behind the apse. Doorways were provided between the chancel and the side-chambers. Feld reported a foundation running across the nave about a metre in front of the apse, with a doorway 1.25 metres wide at its centre. This was presumably part of a chancel screen. On the basis of its column capitals Hild and Hellenkemper assigned the church to the fifth or sixth century.

TAPURELİ, Church A[145] (figure 51)

The extensive remains of a Roman village survive at Tapureli, which is situated on a high ridge on the east side of the Lamas gorge 10 kilometres north of Canbazlı. The site was first noted by Bent. The main account of the churches was published by Keil and Wilhelm. Feld, Hild and Hellenkemper have also visited the site, but have added little to the account.

---

[144] Eyice 1981b, 206, plate 83; Feld 1963/4, 96; Hild, Hellenkemper and Hellenkemper-Salies 1984 241, figure 52; Hild and Hellenkemper 1990, 424-5; Keil and Wilhelm 1931, 32.

[145] Feld 1963/64, 96; Hild, Hellenkemper and Hellenkemper-Salies 1984, 241-2; Hild and Hellenkemper 1990, 426, plate 375; Keil and Wilhelm 1931, 95, figure 121, plate 122.

Church A, which Keil and Wilhelm planned in great haste, stands on the east summit of the settlement (Keil and Wilhelm 1931, 95). At the west end of the complex is a forecourt which measured 14 by 16 metres. This has an entrance in its west wall, and a second, wider entrance at its southeast corner. The narthex was entered through two doors in its west wall, the northern of which has a finely moulded architrave (Keil and Wilhelm 1931, plate 122), and this part of the church was constructed from well-cut ashlars. There was also a doorway in the south wall of the narthex. Two, or probably three, doorways led into the nave and aisles. The north side was too ruined for Keil and Wilhelm to be certain about the doorway into the north aisle, or the plan of the northeast corner of the basilica. The main part of the church measured 22 by 13 metres, including the narthex. Fallen columns in the nave showed that there had been colonnades between the nave and aisles. The apse, which was 4.8 metres wide, has the remains of a synthronum against its inner face. The apse was contained within a thick wall, which projected slightly beyond the east walls of the side-chambers. The south side-chamber, at least, extended westwards from the mouth of the apse, and had a doorway in its north wall. It is likely that both side-chambers were extended in this way in order to define a rectangular chancel in front of the apse. The plan made by Keil and Wilhelm shows a solid wall between the side-chamber and the south aisle. It would be unusual for there to be no communication at this point. Feld found a capital in the church which he suggested belonged to the early sixth century.

TAPURELİ, Church B[146] (figure 52)

Church B lies on the south face of the east summit of Tapureli. The complex consists of a very simple church (14.5 by 12 metres overall) with an irregular courtyard (maximum dimensions 24 by 17 metres) to the west. The main entrance to the courtyard was presumably that on its west side, the frame of which is decorated. There is a further doorway at the centre of the south side. Both doorways are surmounted by lintels which carry inscriptions which give the name of Tribemis the archdeacon, patron of the church (Keil and Wilhelm 1931, 97; inscriptions 109 and 110). A range of ill-defined rooms on the north side of the courtyard was cut deeply into the rock, as was the north wall of the church. At the centre of the courtyard can be seen a square stone base with at least two steps. A doorway at the southeast corner of the court leads by way of a short flight of steps to a colonnaded terrace along the south side of the church, which overlooks the steep drop on this side of the building.

The church is entered through a single west door, the frame of which is decorated with a delicately carved scroll (Keil and Wilhelm 1931, plate 124).

---

[146] Gough 1972, 200; Hild, Hellenkemper and Hellenkemper-Salies 1984, 242; Hild and Hellenkemper 1990, 426, plate 374; Keil and Wilhelm 1931, 95-8, figure 123, plate 124.

There is a single apse, rounded on both inner and outer faces. The arcades were supported by two rows of three columns.

Keil and Wilhelm considered that the letter forms of the dedicatory inscriptions were appropriate to the fourth or fifth centuries (Keil and Wilhelm 1931, 98). Gough noted that parts of the monastery were constructed in polygonal masonry, and considered that it could hardly be earlier than the fifth century (Gough 1972, 200).

TAPURELİ, Church C[147] (figure 53, plate 109)

Church C is on the north foot of the saddle, and therefore has its south face partially cut into the rock. This is the most regularly planned of the basilicas at Tapureli, and measures 33 by 12 metres overall. It is entered by a door in the west wall of the courtyard, which is 12 metres square. On the east side of the narthex is a wide arched opening, which is the entrance to an exo-narthex. This is an unusual feature in a Cilician Basilica, the only comparable example being in the Monastic Church at Corycus. Here, given the north-facing situation of the building, the provision of the exo-narthex was presumably intended to protect its occupants during the winter. There were probably three doorways in the west wall of the narthex: Keil and Wilhelm were able to make out the positions of doorways which corresponded with the nave and north aisle. It can be seen from the plan made by Keil and Wilhelm that the east side of the narthex was defined by three arches. Nave and aisles were divided by arcades which were supported by two pairs of columns, and the church was provided with galleries. The apse was equipped with a priests' bench with a central raised seat, and has an arched niche, 1.3 metres high, about 2 metres above ground level (we may compare this with the much more elaborate system of niches in the apses of the church on Mahras Dağı). The side-chambers project slightly to define a chancel immediately in front of the apse. There are doorways between the side-chambers and the chancel, but the east ends of the aisles are defined by archways. The east façade of the church was straight.

The fenestration of the church, at least at ground level, consisted merely of three arrow slits in the outer wall of the north aisle, and one window in the south side-chamber. Although it is clear that this would have helped to counteract the exposed position of the building, the interior of the basilica must have been remarkably gloomy. Keil and Wilhelm do not consider the question of whether this church had galleries, but it is tempting to suggest that they may have been provided, since this would have allowed for extra fenestration. If there was a gallery at the west end of the narthex, it may be that the arches across the west end of the nave and aisles were simply the supports for a

---

[147] Hild, Hellenkemper and Hellenkemper-Salies 1984, 242; Hild and Hellenkemper 1990, 426, plates 372-3; Keil and Wilhelm 1931, 96-7, figure 125.

wooden gallery, and that what has been termed the exo-narthex was in reality a one-storeyed narthex with a triple-arched portal.

TAPURELİ, Church D[148]

Keil and Wilhelm reported a basilica about 80 metres west of the forecourt of Church C. Its apse was 5.7 metres wide. The building was considered too ruinous to be planned without excavation. The site is now marked by a group of broken columns (Hild and Hellenkemper 1990, plate 376). The measurement given by Keil and Wilhelm for the apse makes this larger than those of Churches A, B, and C, the largest of which is the apse of Church B which measures 4.5 metres.

TAPURELİ, Church E[149]

Hild and Hellenkemper report a fifth, probably early Byzantine, church at Tapureli. This stood beside a group of houses (or villa rustica) and was a single-chambered church measuring 8.67 by 3.72 metres.

"TSCHURKILISSE" see ÇUKURKEŞLİ

ÜÇ TEPE, South Church[150] (plate 110)

The ruined village at Üç Tepe, which has remains of churches, houses, olive presses and mills, stands on a small hill about 5 kilometres north of Limonlu. The South Church measures approximately 20 by 12 metres overall, and is deeply buried in its own rubble. The apse is reasonably well preserved, but little else stands above ground level apart from some of the piers of the nave arcades and the jambs of the doorways of the narthex. These features appear to be in situ, and it is likely that the building is covered by over a metre of its own rubble.

Exterior walls can be seen only at the east end. The apse is semi-circular on both inner and outer faces, and projected from the east wall of the church: it was provided with a window. The lowest courses of the apse wall consist of massive blocks which are particularly coarsely dressed. Just above present ground level can be seen a row of beam-holes which presumably took the supports for a wooden bench round the inner face of the apse. The nave arcades were supported on monolithic rectangular piers. The apse was not flanked by side-chambers, but there was an extra chamber on the south side of the church. The jambs which project through the rubble of the narthex show that there were three doorways between the narthex and the nave and aisles, and a wider

---

[148] Hild, Hellenkemper and Hellenkemper-Salies 1984, 242; Hild and Hellenkemper 1990, 426, plate 376; Keil and Wilhelm 1931, 97.

[149] Hild and Hellenkemper 1990, 426.

[150] Heberdey and Wilhelm 1896, 46-7; Hild and Hellenkemper 1986, 92, plate 133; Hild and Hellenkemper 1990, 452-3.

opening in the west wall which was presumably a triple arched portal. There was also a doorway at the north end of the narthex.

ÜÇ TEPE, North Church[151] (plate 111)

This basilica stands at the northeast corner of the settlement. Only the southwest corner of the church survives to any height. At the east end there is a curved line of rubble, deep in scrub oak, which presumably marks the former position of the apse. The two western pillars from the southern arcade are still in situ, and show that the internal appearance of both churches at Üç Tepe must have been very similar. There was a doorway into the south aisle in the centre of the south wall of the church. At the south end of the narthex can still be seen the doorway into the south aisle. It is clear that the narthex had an upper floor, and that the south aisle had a gallery. The doorway into the south gallery was not directly above the entrance to the south aisle. The west wall of the narthex has fallen, but a heap of column drums immediately to the west of the church suggests that it may have had the usual arcaded portal in its west façade.

URA (Uğura) (Olba), Town Church[152] (figure 54, plate 112)

Ura is a small village 26 kilometres northeast of Silifke. It is the site of the ancient city of Olba, which was the capital of the priestly kingdom of Olba in the Hellenistic period. The Town Church stands in the central area of the ancient settlement. Only the apse stands to any height, and it is so battered as to be in danger of collapse. The building was planned by Gertrude Bell in 1905 in what she later described as a 'flying visit' (Ramsay and Bell 1909, 470). Keil and Wilhelm surveyed Ura, but did not study this building since without excavation they did not feel able to add to Bell's plan (Keil and Wilhelm 1931, 87).

Gertrude Bell recorded that she could see the apse, which is described as being lit by a 'charming' double window, and parts of the south and west walls. She was able to find traces of the columns from the nave arcades, and of the narthex. There was a doorway in the south wall of the church. She was also able to plan the south side-chamber, which not only communicated with the south aisle, but also had a doorway into the apse, and a further doorway in its northeast corner leading behind the apse. Gertrude Bell was firmly of the opinion that there had been no north side-chamber, although she noted that the building was 'completely enveloped in brushwood'. Her plan shows that the church measures 36 by 19 metres overall. (Bell 1907 29-30; figure 29) Since 1905, most of the brushwood has been removed, along with a great deal of

---

[151] Hild and Hellenkemper 1986, 92.

[152] Bell 1906, 29-30, figure 29, plate 115; Bent 1891, 221-2; Hild, Hellenkemper and Hellenkemper-Salies 1984, 250; Hild and Hellenkemper 1990, 370, plate 328; Keil and Wilhelm 1931, 87; Voysal 1963.

masonry debris. The foundations of the south and west walls are no longer discernible, but the clearance of the site has elucidated various points of interest.

The surviving parts of the church are built entirely from spolia; many of the blocks of the apse have been cut down from larger blocks, and some have battered traces of inscriptions and mouldings which have been dressed flat. Furthermore, it appears that the church was constructed on the podium of an earlier building, which was probably a temple. A fluted column drum was built into the south side of the apse, and two Corinthian capitals of a simple Classical type can be seen lying beside more fluted column drums in the nave of the church, where they were presumably re-used in the nave colonnades. Visible sections of the podium, at the northeast and southeast corners, are constructed from larger ashlars, which were friction bonded, and dressed much more smoothly than those of the surviving walls of the apse.

It is now also clear that there was, after all, a north side-chamber, which, like the south side-chamber had a doorway which led behind the apse. The eastern walls of the side-chambers sit on the east side of the earlier podium, whilst the apse is set slightly to the west. The apse has the peculiarity that its outer curve projects slightly from the east wall: this would be normal in the Plain (compare e.g. Kadirli), but is matched only by the 'Domed Ambulatory Church' at Dağ Pazarı in western Cilicia. Given this slight projection, there is not sufficient space for a wall enclosing a passage at the east end of the podium, but it was evidently possible to walk between the side-chambers along that part of the podium which was not occupied by the apse. It is likely that there was an eastern chamber in this church, since there is a foundation running parallel to the east face of the podium, about 5 metres to the east. A row of beam-holes in the south face of the apse could have received either the supports of the ceiling of the side-chamber, or the joists for its upper floor. If the fluted columns were re-used to their full height in the nave, then it is likely that the aisles would have had galleries, and thus that there may have two storeys in the side-chambers.

The windows of the apse have drilled holes and slots which must have received grills, and there is an array of drilled holes in the inner face of the apse, up to the level of the tops of the windows. These may have been to receive supports for cladding. The holes are not visible in the upper courses of the apse, but loose glass tesserae in this part of the church may have come from a mosaic in the semi-dome.

URA (Uğura) (Olba), Cemetery Church[153]

Keil and Wilhelm mention the existence of a Cemetery Church to the south of the ancient city. It was too ruined for them to plan, and does not appear on their general plan. No trace of this building is now visible.

---

[153] Hild, Hellenkemper and Hellenkemper-Salies 1984, 250; Hild and Hellenkemper 1990, 370; Keil and Wilhelm 1931, 87.

URA (Uğura) (Olba), Monastery[154] (figure 55, plate 113)

The battered traces of this complex stand on a sloping terraced site at the east end of the Ura valley. It was evidently much better preserved in 1890:

> '...there is a monastery high up on the eastern precipice. We saw it when returning from a three days excursion to Corycus; but were so tired, and so utterly devoid of energy, that we did not climb up the steep side of the ravine to examine. It occupied the same kind of situation as Koja Kalessi, being perched on a long narrow ledge in the face of a mountain. The buildings appeared to be in an excellent state of preservation.' (Headlam 1892, 22)

The monastery was visited by Keil and Wilhelm, who made a plan, but give no other account of its appearance, merely noting that it may have owed its foundation to the spring which is contained in its south courtyard (Keil and Wilhelm 1931, 97; figure 116). The complex has been re-investigated by Hild and Hellenkemper (1986, 62-4, figure 6, plates 65-6). The main church on the north side of the complex was a three-aisled basilica, with re-used columns, measuring 20.5 by 13.5 metres, including the narthex. There is a chamber under the narthex (7.3 by 2.3 metres) which Hild and Hellenkemper interpret as a tomb rather than a cistern. The free-standing apse leant against a rock-face, thus creating two side-chambers which could be entered from the aisles. To the south of the main church there was a smaller second church which had a nave and a north aisle. The apse, which contains an altar base with a slot for a reliquary, is free-standing, but cut from the rock and protected by an eastern wall. To east and south of the second church are a range of rooms approached by way of short flights of steps. The southern room of this complex contained a well-head.

UZUNCABURÇ (Diocaesarea), Temple-Church[155] (figure56, plates 114-7)

The Temple of Olbian Zeus was founded by Seleucus I Nicator, probably early in the third century BC. It is the best preserved of the Cilician temples, and, although little bigger than the temple at Ayaş, it makes a much a greater impression because so much more of it is standing. The temple owes its preservation to the fact that it was converted into a church. Diocaesarea was a flourishing city which grew in extent during the Roman period. Thus when the temple was converted for Christian use, the intercolumniations were filled in to create the outer walls of a basilica, and the addition of an apse and side-

---

[154] Eyice 1988, 22; Headlam 1892, 22; Hild, Hellenkemper and Hellenkemper-Salies 1984, 250; Hild and Hellenkemper 1986, 62-4, figure 6, plates 65-6; Hild and Hellenkemper 1990, 370; Keil and Wilhelm 1931, 87, figure 116.

[155] Feld 1963/64, 97-8; Hild, Hellenkemper and Hellenkemper-Salies 1984, 242-4, figure 25; Hild and Hellenkemper 1990, 240; Hill 1981, 28; Keil and Wilhelm 1931, 47, 62, figures 67-8, 99, plates 69-70.

chambers actually increased the size of the building, whereas in Elaeussa, which was declining in the late Roman period, the church was much smaller than the temple from which it was created. Keil and Wilhelm published Herzfeld's plan of what was visible early in this century: this gives no impression of the arrangements at the east and west ends of the building which were then buried. Voysal's account describes what is visible today; but the building seems to have been cleared in 1958 with no attempt being made to make a record of what was found. The date of this activity, which puzzled Feld, is given by MacKay (Feld 1963/64, 97-8: MacKay 1972, 275). Hild, Hellenkemper and Hellenkemper-Salies (1994, figure 25) have published a re-drawing of the building which shows how the arrangements at the east end worked.

The temple was converted into a standard basilica measuring 39 by 21 metres. As at Canbazlı, and probably at Meryemlık, the temple precinct was retained as the courtyard of the church, which did not have an atrium attached to its west end. All the columns of the peristyle were left in position apart from the two central columns of the east façade which were removed to make way for the mouth of the apse. The walls of the cella were removed, and their materials used to block the intercolumniations of the peristyle. The foundations of the long walls of the cella were included in the stylobates of the interior colonnades of the church. At the west end a narthex was created by building a wall across the church between the infills of the second intercolumniations. This wall was broken by three doorways which led into the nave and aisles. The west façade of the church was given a central triple portal by the device of leaving the three central intercolumniations unfilled. The north end of the narthex is still partially preserved, and contained the staircase which led to the upper floor of the narthex, and the galleries over the aisles. A foundation which runs across the narthex, in line with the north arcade of the nave, is probably to be associated with this staircase. The plan of the narthex, which had small rooms at its north and south ends is more reminiscent of Lycaonia than Cilicia.

All trace of the interior colonnades has been swept away with the clearance of the interior of the building, but the division into nave and aisles is clearly attested by the longitudinal stylobates. The nave was paved with flagstones, while there were geometric mosaic pavements in the aisles. Beam-holes which can be seen cut into the peristyle columns once supported the wooden floors of the galleries over the aisles. There were doorways with relieving arches set in the fifth intercolumniations (from the west) of the north and south outer walls.

The apse was semi-circular in internal plan, and contained within a flat eastern wall, which was pierced by a window. There is no trace of this window today, but it appears on Herzfeld's plan with a dotted dividing column. On either side of the apse were apsidal side-chambers which communicated with the aisles, and directly with the apse, through doorways. The floor of the apse is raised slightly above that of the nave. There is a foundation on a north-south alignment running across the nave in line with the second columns of the peristyle. The plan published by Hild and Hellenkemper shows this foundation extending across the aisles where doorways are shown communicating between the aisles and what were presumably advanced parts of the side-chambers which projected beyond the mouth of the apse to enclose a chancel area. It seems certain, then, that there was a chancel screen in this church, and Herzfeld found fragments of a decorated arch, which look like the parts of the arched entrance to the sanctuary, near the southeast corner of the building.

Keil and Wilhelm considered that:

> '...der alte Tempel später und zwar doch wohl bald nach dem Siege des Christentums..... in eine Kirche umgewandelt worden ist.' (Keil and Wilhelm 1931, 47)

Hild, Hellenkemper and Hellenkemper-Salies (1984, 244) attribute the church to the fifth century on the basis of its plan, but there is really no positive evidence with which to date the church.

UZUNCABURÇ (Diocaesarea), Church near the Theatre[156]

Keil and Wilhelm noted the existence of a second church within the city walls. This was smaller than the Temple-Church and was overgrown with scrub. The church is not located on their plans, but there are still traces of the foundations of a small apse just northeast of the theatre. Hild, Hellenkemper and Hellenkemper-Salies (1984, figure 26) have published a plan based on a drawing in Keil's sketch-book. This shows a three-aisled basilica with no narthex and a nave 23.2 metres long and 16.4 metres wide. The rounded apse is shown projecting slightly from the east wall in a manner similar to the apses of the churches at Bodrum. A chamber on the south side of the apse projected beyond the south wall of the church. It could be entered from the south aisle and directly from the apse.

UZUNCABURÇ (Diocaesarea), Church of Stephanos[157] (figure 58)

This stood outside the ancient city about 200 metres north of the great tower after which Uzuncaburç is named. Keil and Wilhelm saw the apse well preserved, and traces of foundations all around. There is now very little to see. The church was of massive dimensions (52 by 22 metres overall), and must presumably, therefore, have been a basilica. This conclusion gains some slight support from a console found near the apse (Keil and Wilhelm 1931, plate 96). If the tentative plan made by Keil and Wilhelm is correct, The apse was not flanked by side-chambers, and projected from the east end of the church inside a rectangular enclosing wall. I can find no precise parallel for such a

---

[156] Hild, Hellenkemper and Hellenkemper-Salies 1984, 244, figure 26; Hild and Hellenkemper 1990, 240; Keil and Wilhelm 1931, 62.

[157] Hild, Hellenkemper and Hellenkemper-Salies 1984, 244-9; Hild and Hellenkemper 1990, 240; Keil and Wilhelm 1931, 62, figure 95, plate 96.

disposition, and the building is aligned southwest-northeast. It would be interesting to know whether the apse was an original feature of the building, or was inserted into an earlier tribunal. An inscription on the straight outer face of the apse would seem to confirm that it was an original feature (Keil and Wilhelm 1931, 62).

There was an irregular courtyard on the north side of the church, and a cistern near the west of the northwest wall. Without excavation it would be impossible to make any further sense of the building, or, indeed, of the other walls shown on the plan. Keil and Wilhelm expressed the opinion that the letter forms of the inscription were appropriate to the second half of the fourth century.

UZUNCABURÇ (Diocaesarea), Cemetery Church[158] (figure 57, plates 116-7)

This unusual structure is situated in the cemetery which flanks the northern road out of Uzuncaburç. Widening of this road has buried the east end of the complex, and the apse which was planned by Keil and Wilhelm cannot be seen. This apse was 6 metres wide: the large central opening in it, which appears on the plan, could presumably be explained as the position of a double window similar to that of the apse of the Temple-Church. 26 metres to the west is an arched rock-cut tomb which Keil and Wilhelm rightly regarded as the most important feature of the church, and probably also the earliest. The cliff face around it has been cut vertically, and was faced with well-dressed ashlars which have fallen away since 1907 (plate 116). The west end of the church is cut deeply into the hillside, and the west ends of the north and south sides of the church are also rock-cut. The plan shows an irregular line of piers continuing the line on the south side of the building, and two rows of piers on the north side. These are no longer visible, but surely cannot have marked the lines of arcades, since the roof which covered the nave would have had a span of 14 metres, which is exceeded in Cilicia only by the Basilica of St Thecla at Meryemlık, and would have been out of proportion for this building. One possible explanation may be that the centre of the complex was not roofed at all, and that the piers belonged to porticoes which flanked a central open space. This would have given the complex something of the appearance of the martyrium precinct attached to the Anastasius Basilica at Salona-Marusinac, which has been termed a 'basilica discoperta' (see Krautheimer 1986, 180-1, figure 143). There is no Cilician parallel for such a structure, but we could compare this with Church 7 at Maden Şehir (Binbirkilise) in southern Lycaonia, where there is an enclosure on the east side of the church, which has a large apse built into its eastern wall (Ramsay and Bell 1909, 85-99; figures 46-54).

---

[158] Hild, Hellenkemper and Hellenkemper-Salies 1984 , 249; Hild and Hellenkemper 1990, 240; Hill 1981, 28; Keil and Wilhelm 1931, 61-2, figure 92, plates 93-4.

This explanation would make sense of a double row of beam-holes in the rock face at the west end of the building. At the north and south ends of these rows are particularly massive sockets. The rows of beam-holes continue along the returns in the cliff face. These settings may have received the joists of a roof which projected as a sort of canopy over the tomb. It seems hardly likely that there would have been some sort of gallery at this point, and if the whole building had been roofed we would presumably see traces of a gable at the west end rather than horizontal rows of joist-holes.

The church seems to have been richly appointed. Keil and Wilhelm published a photograph of what they believed was a fragment of an ambo (Keil and Wilhelm 1931, 94). The block is more likely to have originated from a chancel screen since it forms part of an arch decorated with scrollwork, and with a conch in the centre. It might have been the tympanum of a relieving arch over a sanctuary door. Part of a round marble drum with spiral fluting, which is lying in the southern part of the building, may have been used as an altar. There is a socket cut into the underside of the keystone of the arch in front of the tomb. It seems likely that this was intended to receive the support for a hanging lamp.

Keil and Wilhelm noted that Diocaesarea was the πόλις τοῦ ἁγίου Λουκίου, and suggested that here may have been the tomb of this local saint which was elaborated into a church as soon as conditions permitted in the fourth century (Keil and Wilhelm 1931, 61-2; 72, inscription 75).

VIRANKÖY[159]
This ruin-site lies about 8.5 kilometres northnortheast of Ura. Sterrett (1888, 4) reported 'a large Christian church or monastery, which, having served as a quarry for the modern huts, has almost entirely disappeared'. No trace of this building can now be identified. Hild and Hellenkemper (1990, 456) saw a small church which is said to be the place of origin of a piece of chancel screen with a cross.

YALNIZCABAĞ see BALABOLU

YANIKHAN South Church[160] (figure 59, plates 118-23)
The remains of an extensive late Roman village lie at a site which the Yürüks call Yanıkhan. It lies on the southern slopes of Sandal Dağı, eight kilometres inland from Limonlu, on the east side of the ancient road from Lamas to Olba by way of Canbazlı. As well as two basilicas, the site preserves extensive remains of domestic houses, and there was apparently a central market place with a three-storeyed public building on its north side. There are numerous

---

[159] Hild and Hellenkemper 1990, 456; Sterrett 1888, 4.
[160] Hild and Hellenkemper 1986, 80-4, figure 13, plate 133; Hill 1981, 27; Hill 1985.

olive presses, and wild olives grow on artificial terraces on the slopes all around. The first definite reference to the site was a brief notice by Gough who mentions that a church at 'Yanıkhan, north of Erdemli' had an example of an eastern ambulatory (Gough 1965, 409). Michael and Mary Gough visited Yanıkhan on 2 September 1959, and copied the inscription which I saw on the fallen lintel of the main doorway of the South Church (Hill 1981).

The South Church stands in the northern part of the settlement directly above the open space at the centre of the village. Only the apse stands to the height of the bottom courses of its window; most walls of the church stand little more than a metre above ground. This was a basilica, which measured 30 by 15 metres, with its narthex and eastern passage. There was also an atrium measuring 20 by 10 metres which was longer on the north-south axis, and extended beyond the building lines of the church. A walkway 4 metres wide ran along the south side of the church. The great interest of this basilica derives from the inscription on the lintel of the main doorway between the narthex and the nave:

ΜΑΡΤΥΡΙΟΝΓΕΩΡΓΙΟΥ   +   ΚΟΝΩΝΟΣΧΡΙΣΤΟΦΟΡΟΥ
ΚΗΡΥΚΩΝΛΙΤΤΑΣΤΟΥΚΥΡΙΥΚΟΜᶜΜΑΤΡΩΝΙΑΝΟΥΚΕΒΟΗΘΗΣΟΝ

Gough's transcription of this inscription is invaluable because I was unable to read the first part of the second line as the left half of the lintel is now lying upside-down. This is the only epigraphical evidence for an early Byzantine martyrium in Cilicia. The Matronianus mentioned in the second line is intriguing. I had assumed (Hill 1981) that he must be the Matronianus who was sent to Isauria in the 380s, and who erected the sea wall at Anemurium (Alföldi-Rosenbaum 1972, 183-6). If this were true, the South Church at Yanıkhan could have been attributed to the fourth century. Hild and Hellenkemper (1986, 82-4) point out that Yanıkhan was not in Isauria, with the implication that the Comes from Anemurium should not have been operating there, and also suggest that, rather than being a contraction of Κόμ(ιτο)ς, ΚΟΜ could be read as the contraction of the patronymic Κομ(ιτᾶ), which name is attested at Corycus (Hild and Hellenkemper 1986, 82). The significance from an architectural point of view is that Hild and Hellenkemper would attribute the building to the late fifth or sixth century, but they apparently did not see the column and capital in the narthex (plate 119) for which a late fourth century date would be much more credible, and the likelihood that the nave colonnades were trabeated rather than arcaded (see below) would also be compatible with an early date for this building.

There was no entrance in the west wall of the atrium, and the only direct access to the complex was through a doorway at the west end of the north wall of the atrium. The basilica was constructed on a slope, with its north side cut into the rock, and the southern walls of the church supported on substructures 2 metres high. There was a flight of steps, therefore, leading from the north entrance down into the atrium. The other approach to the complex was from the south through a monumental doorway, which may have been the main entrance to the church since it stands at the north end of a street which led directly from the centre of the village. This doorway has the only lintel which is still in position in the church. There are narrow voussoirs lying in front of it, and, by analogy with the North Church at Yanıkhan, we may assume that there was a relieving arch above the lintel. The simply decorated corbels of the south doorway would probably have supported an arched canopy similar to those on the Tomb Church at Corycus. The doorway is 7 metres south of the walkway along the south side of the church, and is connected to this by a flight of steps, which are necessary because of the slope. The steps meet the walkway directly opposite the south end of the narthex, but I was unable to find any trace of a doorway into the church at this point, although there was certainly a doorway between the walkway and the atrium. Since the street from the centre of the village leads nowhere else, it seems possible that there may have been a regular thoroughfare through the west end of the church, and that the lack of direct access to the narthex here may have been deliberate. The south side of the building is littered with voussoirs which must have fallen from the windows of the south wall. There also numerous columns and simple capitals, and it seems likely that the walkway had a colonnade along its south side, as was the case in the Basilica of St Thecla at Meryemlık.

It appears that the atrium had a peristyle, since the northwest and southwest corners of its stylobate can seen, in line with the north and south walls of the church. The west stylobate was 1.6 metres from the west wall of the atrium. The east side of the atrium was occupied by the triple arched portal of the narthex. Two fragments of limestone capitals, and a column with a narrow band of decoration at its top, which were lying by the well-head in the atrium had evidently fallen from the narthex. The partner to the column is lying beside the road on the west side of the settlement, presumably having been removed for re-use. The well-head is at the centre of the atrium, and just south of it is the entrance to flight of steps which lead into the cistern below the narthex and atrium. This is still functional, and consists of two barrel-vaulted chambers aligned north-south, and separated by a row of arches directly beneath the entrance to the narthex.

Three doorways led from the narthex into the nave and aisles. The central doorway had a massive lintel with a raised cross in a wreath at the centre, flanked by the dedicatory inscription. The lintels of the smaller doorways into the aisles had a much simpler cross in a circle. The interior of the church is used as a tomato patch, and no trace of its internal divisions can be seen in situ. There are, however, fragments of columns, and capitals of two very simple types, which suggest that there two orders of colonnades separating the nave from the aisles and their galleries. A piece of architrave lying against the north wall may have fallen from the colonnades, and it is likely, therefore, that these were trabeated rather than arcaded. There were no doors, or windows at ground level, in the north wall.

The apse was 6 metres wide, and pierced by a single arched window. Doorways on either side led into the eastern passage, which had subsidiary apses, 4 metres wide, at its north and south ends. Part of the semi-dome of the north apse survives, and it clear that there was no horizontal moulding at the level of its springing. There were no side-chambers as such, but the two arches which sprang from the outer face of the apse across the passage would have had the effect of defining roughly rectangular spaces at the north and south ends of the passage. The tops of these transverse arches would have been at the same level as a row of beam-holes in the outer face of the apse, and these together appear to have been the supports for the floor of the upper level of the passage. The beam holes are set between the base of the window and the springing of its arch. This awkward arrangement must be original, since there is no sign that the springs of the transverse arches were a secondary insertion into the outer face of the apse. If the nave colonnades were trabeated, it is possible that the aisle galleries were relatively low, and this may have affected the relationship between the upper floor of the passage and the window of the main apse.

There was an opening directly behind the main apse which gave access to a square chamber set between the two subsidiary apses. In this chamber there was an arched recess on the north side, inside which, heavily encumbered with fallen voussoirs, is a rectangular stone slab, which appears to be the top of a sarcophagus. Two blocks which are still in situ on the south side of the room suggest that it was once covered with a simple domical structure. Long curved blocks appear to have straddled the corners of the room, thus constituting a crude, but effective substitute for squinches or pendentives. Orange, unweathered, faces in the walls were visible in 1976 and the fallen masonry showed that there had been a fresh collapse in this part of the church: the differential staining of the face of the south wall may therefore reflect the protection which was still afforded by these corner blocks until fairly recently. The rubble which fills this chamber contains large quantities of small slabs of white marble: these are probably fragments of cladding, and it seems that this room was much more lavishly decorated than the rest of the church, a fact which may be taken as an indicator of its importance within the building. Surviving foundations of the east side of this chamber show that it was a straight wall running between the outer faces of the two subsidiary apses, but there is no evidence to indicate whether the room had a window. A doorway in the south wall of the passage communicated with a small chamber at the southeast corner of the church. This had a solid south wall, and was provided with doorways in its east and west sides. The latter led into the walkway along the south side of the church. Thus it appears that the southeast chamber was a vestibule which would be used by persons who proceeded directly to the eastern chambers along the open colonnade on the south side of the church.

The church is consistently constructed from smallish square stones which face a rubble and mortar core. Larger square stones were used for the walls of the central apse. I found no evidence of alterations to the plan: almost the full length of the north wall survives above ground level, and there is no vertical joint at the point where the eastern passage begins. I believe that the church, including the eastern chambers, is of one build. The eastern chamber was thus an original feature of the basilica. Its function is debatable. Hild and Hellenkemper argue that Matronianus was probably the donor of the church, and that the eastern chamber would have contained the donor's tomb, whilst remains of George, Conon and Christopher would have been kept in a reliquary, presumably under the altar. The alternative explanation would be that this was the actual martyrium chamber, kept separate from the parish church proper, with a passage which would have enabled processions of visitors to see the chamber. In any event it is clear that the eastern chamber was a primary feature of this church which definitiely had a martyrial function.

YANIKHAN, North Church[161] (figure 60, plates 124-6)

This basilica stands about 150 metres to the northeast of the South Church in an ancient cemetery. It is the better preserved of the churches, and was extremely similar in plan to the South Church, although lacking an atrium. The basilica measured 27 by 14 metres overall.

The west face of the narthex originally had a triple arched portal. The north end of the narthex still stands to the height of the base of its upper floor, the presence of which is indicated by a rabbet in the inner face of the north wall. At the west end of the north wall is a feature which at first sight appears to be the base of a window. This would be an unusual feature since there is no window in this position in any Cilician basilica which had a narthex with the triple-arched portal, and where there is sufficient evidence to allow consideration of this point (Kanlıdivane, Churches 1 and 4; Manaz). This would, however, be the only window in the church with a monolithic base and jambs. It is more likely that this was a doorway, and that access to the upper floors of this church was by way of an external wooden staircase which was attached to the north end of the narthex, at which point the church is most deeply cut into the rock. The presence of such a staircase would explain the otherwise puzzling corbel which projects from the northwest corner of the narthex. There are three doorways between the narthex and the nave and aisles: all had relieving arches. The central doorway is larger than the other two, and has a simple incised cross in a circle on its lintel. Beside the south jamb of this doorway are the remains of a stoup which consisted of a stone basin set under an arched semi-circular recess. The projecting part of the basin has been smashed off.

---

[161] Hild and Hellenkemper 1986, 84-5, figure 14, plates 107-12; Hill 1981, 27; Hill 1985.

Fragments of columns and their simple bases lie inside the church. It is clear that there were longitudinal colonnades, since there are engaged piers at the east end of the nave, and scars beside the jambs of the doorways at the west end of the aisles where similar piers have fallen away. Neither the scars at the west end, nor the piers at the east end rise to more than the height of a single column, but it is clear from rabbets in the north, west, and south walls of the church, from the doorways above the entrances to the eastern passage, and from the height of the north wall, that this church had galleries. The pier at the east end of the south colonnade is preserved to exactly the height of the rabbet of the south wall, at which level it was capped by a simple block which looks like a console, since the block immediately below it has fallen away. This block was not the springing of an arch; indeed any arch which sprang from it would have been higher than the indicated level of the gallery floor. The simplest way to resolve these anomalies is to assume that the galleries were entirely constructed of wood, and that the piers which stood at both ends of the lower colonnades were intended to support a heavy beam which ran for the length of the nave along the top of the colonnade. It seems, likely, therefore, that both churches at Yanıkhan had trabeated colonnades.

There were no openings in the north wall at ground level, and the eastern part of the north wall survives to a sufficient height to suggest that there were probably no openings at gallery level either. A doorway in the south wall is flanked by one arched window to the west, and two to the east. The foundations of the church are almost entirely rock-cut, a fact which is most apparent in the north aisle where a great mass of bedrock has not been cut back (the same feature is present at Mazılık - Edwards 1982, 25). In other parts of the building the native rock has been cut back to the thickness of the walls, or else turned to advantage. Thus bench seating was provided at the north end of the narthex and the west end of the south aisle by the simple expedient of cutting the bedrock to shape.

The main apse, which is 5 metres wide at its mouth, is almost completely preserved. It has a double arched window, and a simple moulding at the springing of its semi-dome. There were doorways on either side leading into the eastern chambers from both the ground floor and the galleries. The two lower doorways have straight lintels. The passage at the east end of the building has the foundations of subsidiary apses (2.7 metres wide) at the north and south ends of its east wall. No arches sprang across this passage, but there are two massive beam-holes in the outer face of the apse which would have supported joists which ran diagonally to the northeast and southeast corners of the church (similar diagonal joists ran across the passage of Church 2 at Kanlıdivane). That these beams were at the correct level to support the upper floor of the passage is confirmed by a beam-hole beside the doorway from the south gallery. Close to the large beam-holes, but at the same level as the base of the apse window, there are larger square recesses in the wall of the apse. These have socket holes beside them which presumably took wooden plugs against which were fitted cupboard doors. Among the rubble which fills the south apse are fragments of a sarcophagus lid, and a funerary stele. There was an opening in the east wall of the passage opposite the window of the main apse, but there is too much tumbled masonry to establish whether there was a room at this point. This is perhaps unlikely, since the full outer curves of the subsidiary apses can be seen, whereas in the South Church the subsidiary apses and the central chamber were built as one unit. In any event, there is another sarcophagus lid in the space between the subsidiary apses, and the funerary character of this basilica would seem to be assured.

Most of the walls consist of small square stones facing rubble and mortar, and have frequent putlog holes which suggest that they were stuccoed, but the main apse is constructed from very well-cut ashlars. These ashlars were also used for the east wall of the nave up to the level of the gallery floor. This has resulted in vertical joins in the north and south walls of the church, and it seems, therefore, that the apse, and the east wall of the nave, must have been erected before the walls of the aisles or the eastern passage. This may have been normal practice, but it is not usually possible to document it. It is very tempting to assume that the apse was constructed by a gang of master masons, whilst the rest of the building was subsequently completed by journeymen.

The North Church at Yanıkhan did not have an atrium, or a colonnade along its south side, but it is essentially a copy of the South Church. The two churches seem both to have had the primitive feature of trabeated colonnades, and had very similar simple sculptural decoration. They are likely, therefore, to have been contemporary buildings, and I would propose that the North Church should also be assigned to the late fourth century.

YEMIŞKUM, Church 1[162]

A tiny settlement known as Yemişkum stands on a small promontory to the east of Ayaş and is surrounded by one of the ancient cemeteries of Elaeussa-Sebaste. There are the poorly preserved remains of two churches here. The first, according to Hild and Hellenkemper (1986, 71-3, plates 79-81) was an extremely large basilica with an apse 8.8 metres wide and an original length of at least 30 metres. This must be the church which was seen by Irby and Mangles on October 22 1818:

'...close to the sea shore is a large Christian church. The canopy of the altar place has the remains of three saints painted on it; the centre one, by the difference of dress and shape, appears to have been intended for a female; perhaps they represented the trinity. The side walls are mostly fallen, but over the door in front, a cross is sculpted in relief..., and some

---

[162] Irby and Mangles 1823, 514; Hild and Hellenkemper 1986, 71-3, plates 79-81, Hild and Hellenkemper 1990, 401.

visitor has scratched near it, a flag on a staff, probably a banner imprinted by some crusader.' (Irby and Mangles 1823, 514)

Only part of the apse and some subsidiary chambers to the east now survive, but the apse is remarkable since it shares with the Basilica of St Thecla at Meryemlık the feature of having large external buttresses between which are set the windows. A further peculiarity of the apse is that internally the lower courses are constructed from mortared small stones, whilst the upper parts of the semi-dome were constructed in brick: meanwhile the external buttresses were made from large blocks of re-used stone. It seems likely that all surfaces, both inside and out, were plastered, and the inner face of the apse was decorated with mosaic. From the description of Hild and Hellenkemper it emerges that there may have been a passage along the north side of the church.

YEMIŞKUM, Church 2[163] (figure 61, plate 127)

The second much smaller church lies to the west of Church 1. Irby and Mangles noted that 'Farther to the west are the ruins of another church, with part of a mosaic ceiling' (Irby and Mangles 1823, 514). Gertrude Bell visited Yemişkum on her way back from an expedition to Kanlıdivane:

> 'We came down to the sea at the extreme northern end of the Bay of Ayash - Yemishkum, my companions called it, but I think it was a fancy name invented to please me. It will serve, however, to designate a small church which I found on the spur of the hills near the northern end of the bay. It was much ruined and quite irregular in shape. I measured it as well as I could and give the resulting plan, with apologies for its insufficiency. To the south there was a sharp drop in the ground which had forced the builders to set the south wall close up against the curve of the apse. There was a passage between the apse and the east wall of the church and a small apse protruded from the wall, almost, but not quite, in the centre of the church.' (Bell 1906, 412-3)

The church planned by Bell is indeed irregular. It measured 22 metres by 12 metres overall, slightly larger than the church east of Corycus, but still rather small for a late Roman basilica. It may be simplest to regard this as a single chambered chapel which has acquired the additional Cilician features of a passage along the north side of the building, and a passage with a small subsidiary apse behind the main apse. Gertrude Bell's photographs show traces of painted plaster in the semi-dome of the main apse. The larger apse has fallen, but the subsidiary apse has survived.

---

[163] Bell 1906b, 412-3, figures 27-8; Hild and Hellenkemper 1986, 73; Hild and Hellenkemper 1990, 401

YENİYURT KALE (Eski Kale)[164]

Keil and Wilhelm saw three churches in the ruins at Eski Kale on the north side of the Lamus gorge (6 kilometres east of Veyselli). Although Keil and Wilhelm could not make out the plans of these churches, it seems likely that at least one of them was a basilica since Keil and Wilhelm publish a drawing of an impost capital which, as is suggested by Hild and Hellenkemper, must be of sixth century date. Recently Hellenkemper (1994, figure 13) has published the plan of a strangely proportioned small basilica at Yeniyurt Kale. The church is 18 by 12.5 metres overall, with narthex and a stilted apse flanked by side-chambers which could be entered from the aisles and from the chancel area in front of the apse. The area of nave and aisles measures 5.5 metres from east to west and 10 metres from north to south. Compared with a conventional basilica, the main part of the church is thus broader than it is long. Such proportions are unparalleled in southern Turkey though occasional parallels such as the 'Church of the Panagia' at Göreme on Erciyes Dağı in Cappadocia, (Rott 1908, 167, figure 54) are known on the Anatolian plateau.

---

[164] Keil and Wilhelm 1931, 99, figure 128; Hellenkemper 1994, figure 13; Hild and Hellenkemper 1990, 462.

BIBLIOGRAPHY

ALFÖLDI-ROSENBAUM, Elisabeth, HUBER, Gerhard, and ONURKAN, Somay. 1967. *A Survey of Coastal Cities in Western Cilicia* (Ankara).

ALFÖLDI-ROSENBAUM, Elisabeth. 1972. Matronianus, Comes Isauriae: an Inscription from the Sea Wall of Anemurium. *Phoenix*, 26, 183-6.

ALFÖLDI-ROSENBAUM, Elisabeth. 1980. *The Necropolis of Adrassus (Balabolu) in Rough Cilicia (Isauria)*. Ergänzungsbände zu den Tituli Asiae Minoris, 10. Österreichische Akademie der Wissenschaften, Philosophisch-Historische Klasse Denkschriften, 146 (Vienna).

ALISHAN, Ghevont. 1899. *Sissouan ou l'Arméno-Cilicie. Description géographique et historique, traduit du texte arménien* (Venice).

BAKKER, Gerard. 1985. The Buildings at Alahan. In Mary Gough 1985, 75-194.

BALLANCE, Michael H. 1955. Cumanin Cami'i at Antalya: a Byzantine Church. *Papers of the British School at Rome*, 23 (new series, 10), 99-114, plates 22-7.

BARKER, William Burckhardt. 1853. *Lares and Penates* (London).

BAYLISS, Richard. 1996. *The Ala Cami in Kadirli: Transformations of a Sacred Monument*. MA Dissertation (University of Newcastle upon Tyne).

BAYNES, Norman H. 1947. The Pratum Spirituale. *Orientalia Christiana Periodica* 13, 404-14.

BEAN, George Ewart. 1976a. Güney Kalesi. In Stilwell 1976, 368.

BEAN, George Ewart. 1976b. Iotape. In Stilwell 1976, 414.

BEAN, George Ewart. 1976c. Syedra. In Stilwell 1976, 871.

BEAN, George Ewart and MITFORD, Terence Bruce. 1962. Sites Old and New in Rough Cilicia. *Anatolian Studies*, 12, 185-217.

BEAN, George Ewart and MITFORD, Terence Bruce. 1965. *Journeys in Rough Cilicia in 1962 and 1963*. Österreichische Akademie der Wissenschaften, Philosophisch-Historische Klasse Denkschriften, 85 (Vienna).

BEAN, George Ewart and MITFORD, Terence Bruce. 1970. *Journeys in Rough Cilicia. 1964-1968*. Ergänzungsbände zu den Tituli Asiae Minoris Antiqua, 3. Österreichische Akademie der Wissenschaften, Philosophisch-Historische Klasse Denkschriften, 102 (Vienna).

BEAUFORT, Francis. 1817. *Karamania - A Brief Description of the South Coast of Asia Minor and of the Remains of Antiquity* (London).

BELL, Gertrude Lowthian. 1906a. Notes on a Journey through Cilicia and Lycaonia. *Revue Archéologique*[4], 7, 1-29.

BELL, Gertrude Lowthian. 1906b. Notes on a Journey through Cilicia and Lycaonia. *Revue Archéologique*[4], 7, 385-414.

BELL, Gertrude Lowthian. 1906c. Notes on a Journey through Cilicia and Lycaonia. *Revue Archéologique*[4], 8, 1-30.

BELL, Gertrude Lowthian. 1906d. Notes on a Journey through Cilicia and Lycaonia. *Revue Archéologique*[4], 8, 225-52.

BELL, Gertrude Lowthian. 1906e. Notes on a Journey through Cilicia and Lycaonia. *Revue Archéologique*[4], 8, 390-401.

BELL, Gertrude Lowthian. 1907. Notes on a Journey through Cilicia and Lycaonia. *Revue Archéologique*[4], 9, 18-30.

BENT, J. Theodore. 1890a. Explorations in Cilicia Tracheia. *Proceedings of the Royal Geographical Society*, 8, 445-63.

BENT, J. Theodore. 1890b. Recent Discoveries in Eastern Cilicia. *Journal of Hellenic Studies*, 11, 231-5.

BENT, J. Theodore. 1891. A Journey in Cilicia Tracheia. *Journal of Hellenic Studies*, 12, 206-24.

BITTEL, Klaus. 1939. Grabung im Hof des Topkapi Sarayi. *Jahrbuch des Deutschen Archäologischen Instituts*, 54, 179-81.

BLUMENTHAL, Ekkhart. 1963. *Die altgriechische Siedlungskolonization im Mittelmeerraum unter besonderer Berücksichtigung der Südküste Kleinasiens*. Tübinger Geographische Studien, 10.

BOSSERT, Helmuth Theodor and ALKIM, U. Bahadir. 1947. *Karatepe, Kadirli ve Dolayları. İkinci Ön-rapor (Second Preliminary Report)* İstanbul Üniversitesi Edebiyat Fakültesi: Eski Önasya Kültürlerini Araştırma Enstitüsü Yayınları 3 (İstanbul).

BOSSERT, Helmuth Theodor. 1960. 1959 Misis Çalişmaları. *Türk Arkeoloji Dergisi* 10.1, 15.

BRANDES, Wolfram. 1989. *Die Städte Kleinasiens im 7. Und 8. Jahrhundert* (Amsterdam).

BROOKS, E. W. 1893. The Emperor Zenon and the Isaurians. *English Historical Review*, 8, 209-38.

BUDDE, Ludwig. 1969. *Antike Mosaiken in Kilikien*, Volume 1. *Frühchristliche Mosaiken in Misis-Mopsuestia*. Beiträge zur Kunst des christlichen Ostens, 5 (Recklinghausen).

BUDDE, Ludwig. 1973. Die Pantaleons-Kirche von Aphrodisias in Kilikien. *Deutsch-Türkische Gesellschaft E.V. Bonn Mitteilungen*, 60, 1-4.

BUDDE, Ludwig. 1987. *St. Pantaleon von Aphrodisias in Kilikien* (Beitrage zur Kunst des christlichen Ostens, 9 (Recklinghausen).

BUSCHHAUSEN, H. 1972. Die Deutung des Archemosaiks in der justinianische Kirche von Mopsuestia. *Jahrbuch der Österreichischen Byzantinistiks*, 21, 57-71.

BUTLER, Howard Crosby. 1906. The Tychaion at Is-Sanamen and the Plan of the Early Christian Churches in Syria. *Revue Archéologique*[4], 8, 413-23.

BUTLER, Howard Crosby. 1907. *The 'Alā and Kasr Ibn Wardân*. Publications of the Princeton University Archaeological Expedition to Syria, in 1904-1905. Division II, Ancient Architecture in Syria. Section B, Northern Syria, Part 1 (Leyden).

BUTLER, Howard Crosby (edited and compiled by BALDWIN-SMITH, E.). 1929. *Early Churches in Syria* (Princeton).

CALDER, William M. and BEAN, George Ewart. 1958. *A Classical Map of Asia Minor* (London).

CİNER, Refakat. 1964. Ayatekla Kilisesinden Çıkaların İskeletin Tetkiki. *Dil ve Tarih-Cografya Fakultesi Dergisi (Ankara)*, 22, 251-71.

COLLIGNON, Maxime. 1880. Notes d'un voyage en Asie-Mineure, II Adalia, la Cilicia-Trachée, le Taurus. *Revue des Deux Mondes*, 38, 891-917.

CORMACK, Robin. 1969. The Mosaic Decoration of S. Demetrios, Thessaloniki. *The Annual of the British School at Athens*, 64, 17-52.

DAGRON, Gilbert. 1973. Les études byzantines. *L'information de l'histoire de l'art*, 18, 163-7.

DAGRON, Gilbert. 1978. *Vie et Miracles de Sainte Thècle, Text grec, traduction, et commentaire*. Subsidia Hagiographica, 62 (Brussels).

DAGRON, Gilbert and FEISSEL, D. 1987. *Inscriptions de Cilicie*. Travaux et Mémoires du centre du recherche d'histoire et civilisation de Byzance, 4 (Paris).

DAVIS, Edwin John. 1879. *Life in Asiatic Turkey. A Journey of Travel in Cilicia Pedias and Trachaea, Isauria and parts of Lycaonia* (London).

DUCHESNE, L. and COLLIGNON, M. 1877. Rapport sur un Voyage Archéologique en Asie Mineure. *Bulletin de Correspondence Hellenique*, 1, 361-76.

DUPONT-SOMMER, André and ROBERT, Louis. 1964. *La déesse de Hierapolis Castabala (Cilicie)* (Paris).

EDWARDS, Robert W. 1982. Two New Byzantine Churches in Cilicia. *Anatolian Studies*, 32, 23-32.

EDWARDS, Robert W. 1989 The Domed Mausoleum at Akkale in Cilicia. The Byzantine Revival of a Pagan Plan. *Byzantinoslavica* 50, 46-56.

EYICE, Semavi. 1971. Monuments byzantins anatoliens inédits ou mal-connus. *Corsi di cultura sull'arte ravennate e bizantina*, 18, 309-32.

EYICE, Semavi. 1976/77. Silifke Çevresinde İncelemer: Kanlıdivan (=Kanytelleis - Kanytelideis) Basilikaları. Bir Önçalışma. *Anadolu Araştırmaları* (4-5), 411-41.

EYICE, Semavi. 1977. Die Basiliken von Kanlıdivan (=Kanytelideis - Kanytelleis). XX Deutscher Orientalistentag 1977 in Erlangen. *Zeitschrift der Deutschen Morgenländischen Gesellschaft*, Supplement 4, 488-91.

EYICE, Semavi. 1979. La basilique de Canbazlı en Cilicie. *Zograf*, 10, 22-9.

EYICE, Semavi. 1981a. Silifke Çevresinde İncelemer: Elaiussa-Sebaste (=Ayaş) Yakınında Akkale. *VIII Türk Tarih Kongresi (Ankara)*, 865-86.

EYICE, Semavi. 1981b. Einige byzantinische Kleinstädte im Rauhen Kilikien. In *150 Jahre deutsches Archäologisches Institut (Festschrift)* (Mainz), 204-9.

EYICE, Semavi. 1982. Un site byzantine de la Cilicie: Öküzlü et ses basiliques. In Hadermann-Misguich and Raepsaet 1982, 355-67.

EYICE, Semavi. 1986. Akkale in der Nähe von Elaiussa-Sebaste (=Ayaş). In Feld and Peschlow 1986, 63-77.

EYICE, Semavi. 1988. Richerche e scoperte nella regione di Silifke nella Turchia meridionale. *Milion* I (Rome), 15-33.

FELD, Otto. 1963/64. Bericht über eine Reise durch Kilikien. *Istanbuler Mitteilungen*, 13/14, 88-107.

FELD, Otto. 1965. Beobachtungen an spätantiken und frühchristlichen Bauten in Kilikien. *Römisches Quartalschrift*, 60, 131-43.

FELD, Otto. 1986. Die beiden Kirchen in Hierapolis-Kastabala. In Feld and Peschlow 1986, 77-86, plates 19-23.

FELD, Otto. 1989. Kilikische Ambone. *Istanbuler Mitteilungen*, 39, 123-8, plate 15.

FELD, Otto and PESCHLOW, Urs (editors). 1986. *Studien zur spätantiken und byzantinischen Kunst Friedrich Wilhelm Deichmann gewidmet.* Monographien des Römisches-Germanisches Zentralmuseums 10.1, (Bonn).

FELD, Otto and WEBER, Hans. 1967. Tempel und Kirche über der Korykische Grotte (Cennet Cehennem) in Kilikien. *Istanbuler Mitteilungen*, 17, 254-78.

FORSYTH, George H. 1957. Architectural Notes on a Journey through Cilicia. *Dumbarton Oaks Papers*, 11, 223-36.

FORSYTH, George H. 1961. An Early Byzantine Church at Kanlıdivane in Cilicia. *De Artibus Opuscula XL - Essays in Honour of Erwin Panofsky*, 127-37 (New York).

FORSYTH, George H. 1968. The Monastery of St. Catherine at Mount Sinai: the Church and Fortress of Justinian. *Dumbarton Oaks Papers*, 22, 3-19.

FOSS, Clive. 1975. The Persians in Asia Minor and the End of Antiquity. *English Historical Review*, 90, 721-47.

GOTTWALD, J. 1936. Die Kirche und das Schloss Paperon in Kilikisch-Armenien. *Byzantinische Zeitschrift*, 36, 86-100.

GOUGH, Mary. 1954. *The Plain and the Rough Places* (London).

GOUGH, Mary (editor). 1985. *Alahan: an Early Christian Monastery in Southern Turkey Based on the Work of Michael Gough* (Toronto).

GOUGH, Michael R. E. 1952. Anazarbus. *Anatolian Studies*, 2, 85-150.

GOUGH, Michael R. E. 1954. A Temple and Church at Ayaş (Cilicia). *Anatolian Studies*, 4, 49-64.

GOUGH, Michael R. E. 1955a. Early Churches in Cilicia. *Byzantinoslavica*, 16.2, 201-11.

GOUGH, Michael R. E. 1955b. Some Recent Finds at Alahan. *Anatolian Studies*, 5, 115-23.

GOUGH, Michael R. E. 1957. A Church of the Iconoclast period in Byzantine Isauria. *Anatolian Studies*, 7, 153-61.

GOUGH, Michael R. E. 1958a. A Fifth-Century Silver Reliquary from Isauria. *Byzantinoslavica*, 19.2, 244-50.

GOUGH, Michael R. E. 1958b. Report on Archaeological Work Carried out at Alahan in 1957. *Türk Arkeoloji Dergisi*, 8.2, 6-7.

GOUGH, Michael R. E. 1958c. The "Paradise of Dağ Pazarı": A Newly Discovered Early Christian Mosaic in Southern Asia Minor. *Illustrated London News*, 233, 644-6.

GOUGH, Michael R. E. 1959a. Report on Work Carried out during Summer 1958. *Anatolian Studies*, 9, 7-8.

GOUGH, Michael R. E. 1959b. Karlik and Dağ Pazarı. *Türk Arkeoloji Dergisi*, 9, 5-6.

GOUGH, Michael R. E. 1960a. Isauria and Cilicia 1959. *Anatolian Studies*, 10, 6-7.

GOUGH, Michael R. E. 1960b. Dağ Pazarı 1959. *Türk Arkeoloji Dergisi*, 10.2, 23-4.

GOUGH, Michael R. E. 1961. *The Early Christians* (London).

GOUGH, Michael R. E. 1962. The Church of the Evangelists at Alahan. *Anatolian Studies*, 12, 173-84.

GOUGH, Michael R. E. 1963. Excavations at Alahan Monastery Second Preliminary Report. *Anatolian Studies*, 13, 105-16.

GOUGH, Michael R. E. 1964. Excavations at Alahan Monastery Third Preliminary Report. *Anatolian Studies*, 14, 185-90.

GOUGH, Michael R. E. 1965a. Christian Archaeology in Turkey. *Atti del VI Congresso di Archeologia cristiana (Ravenna)* (Rome), 405-12.

GOUGH, Michael R. E. 1965b. A Thurible from Dağ Pazarı. *Anadolu Araştırmaları*, 2, 231-5.

GOUGH, Michael R. E. 1967a. Excavations at Alahan Monastery Fourth Preliminary Report. *Anatolian Studies*, 17, 37-48.

GOUGH, Michael R. E. 1967b. Excavations at Alahan 1967. *Türk Arkeoloji Dergisi*, 14.1, 95-100.

GOUGH, Michael R. E. 1967/68. Alahan Monastery - A Masterpiece of Early Christian Architecture. *The Metropolitan Museum of Art Bulletin*, 26, 455-64

GOUGH, Michael R. E. 1968. Excavations at Alahan Monastery Fifth Preliminary Report. *Anatolian Studies*, 18, 159-68.

GOUGH, Michael R. E. 1970. Alahan Monastery 1970. *Türk Arkeoloji Dergisi*, 19.1, 95-8.

GOUGH, Michael R. E. 1971. The Secular Appointment of Alahan Monastery. *American Journal of Archaeology*, 75, 202-3.

GOUGH, Michael R. E. 1972. The Emperor Zeno and some Cilician Churches. *Anatolian Studies*, 22, 199-212.

GOUGH, Michael R. E. 1973. *The Origins of Christian Art* (London).

GOUGH, Michael R. E. 1974a. Three Forgotten Martyrs of Anazarbus in Cilicia. *Essays in Honour of Anton Charles Pegis* (Toronto), 262-7.

GOUGH, Michael R. E. 1974b. The Peaceful Kingdom, an Early Christian Mosaic Pavement in Cilicia Campestris. *Mansel'e Armağan - Mélanges Mansel* (Ankara), 411-9.

GOUGH, Michael R. E. 1974c. Notes on a Visit to Mahras Monastery in Isauria. *Byzantine Studies*, 1, 65-72.

GOUGH, Michael R. E. 1975. Dağ Pazarı, the Basilical Church 'extra muros'. In Robertson and Henderson 1975, 147-63.

GOUGH, Michael R. E. 1976a. Epiphaneia. In Stilwell 1976, 315.

GOUGH, Michael R. E. 1976b. Flaviopolis. In Stilwell 1976, 330.

GOUGH, Michael R. E. 1976c. Hieropolis Castabala. In Stilwell 1976, 392.

GOUGH, Michael R. E. 1985. Alahan Monastery and its Setting in the Isaurian Country Side. In Mary Gough 1985, 3-17.

GRABAR, Andre. 1946. *Martyrium, Recherches sur le Culte des Reliques et l'Art chrétien antique* (Paris).

GRABAR, Andre. 1962. Un reliquaire provenant d'Isaurie. *Cahiers archéologiques,* 13, 49-59

GRABAR, Andre. 1970. Deux Portails sculptés paleochrétiens d'Égypte et d'Asie Mineure et les Portails Romans. *Cahiers archéologiques,* 20, 15-28.

GROTHE, Hugo. 1911/12. *Meine Vorderasienexpedition 1906 und 1907* (Leipzig)

GUYER, Samuel. 1909/10. Ala Kilise - ein Kleinasiatischer Bau des V Jahrhunderts. Zeitschrift für Geschichte der Architektur, 3, 192-9.

GUYER, Samuel. 1950. *Grundlagen der mittelalterlicherabendländischer Baukunst* (Zurich-Köln).

HADERMANN-MISGIUCH, L. and RAEPSAET, G. (editors). 1982. *Rayonnement grec (Hommages à Charles Delvoye)* (Brussels).

HAMILTON, William John. 1842. *Researches in Asia Minor, Pontus, and Armenia* (London).

HARRISON, R. Martin. 1963. Churches and Chapels of Central Lycia. *Anatolian Studies*, 13, 117-51.

HARRISON, R. Martin. 1980. The Monastery on Mahras Dağ in Isauria. *Yayla*, 3, 22-4.

HARRISON, R. Martin. 1985. The Inscriptions and Chronology of Alahan. In Mary Gough 1985, 21-34.

HARRISON, R. Martin. 1981. The Emperor Zeno's Real Name. *Byzantinische Zeitschrift*, 74, 27-8.

HARRISON, R. Martin. 1986. *Excavations at Saraçhane in Istanbul.* Volume 1 The Excavations, Structures, Architectural Decoration, Small Finds, Coins, Bones and Molluscs (Princeton and Washington DC).

HARRISON, R. Martin. 1989. *A Temple for Byzantium* (Austin).

HEADLAM, Arthur C. 1892. *Ecclesiastical Sites in Isauria.* Occasional Papers of the Society for the Promotion of Hellenic Studies, 2 (London).

HEBERDEY, Rudolf and WILHELM, Heinrich. 1896. *Reisen in Kilikien ausgeführt - 1891 und 1892 im Auftrage der kaiserlichen Akademie der Wissenschaften.* Denkschriften der Kaiserlich Akademie der Wissenschaften, Philosophisch-Historische Klasse, 44 (Vienna).

HELLENKEMPER, Hansgerd. 1980. Zur Entwicklung des Stadtbildes in Kilikien. *Aufstieg und Niedergang der Römischen Welt*, Principat 7.2 (Berlin), 1262-83.

HELLENKEMPER, Hansgerd. 1986. Die Kirchenstiftung des Kaisers Zenon im Wallfahrtsheiligtum der heilige Thekla bei Seleukeia. *Wallraf-Richartz-Jahrbuch*, 47, 63-90.

HELLENKEMPER, Hansgerd. 1994. Early Church Architecture in Southern Asia Minor. In Painter 1994, 213-238.

HELLENKEMPER, Hansgerd and HILD, Freidrich. 1986. *Neue Forschungen in Kilikien.* Veröffentlichungen der Kommission für die Tabula Imperii Byantini, 4. Österreichische Akademie der Wissenschaften, Philosophisch-Historische Klasse Denkschriften, 186 (Vienna).

HERZFELD, Ernst. 1909. Eine Reise durch das westliche Kilikien im Frühjahr 1907. *Petermann's Geographisches Mitteilungen*, 55, 25-34.

HERZFELD, Ernst. 1943. Damascus - Studies in Architecture II. *Ars Islamica*, 10, 13-70.

HERZFELD, Ernst and GUYER, Samuel. 1930. *Meriamlik und Korykos. Zwei christliche Ruinenstätten des Rauhen Kilikiens.* Monumenta Asiae Minoris Antiqua, 2 (Manchester).

HICKS, E. L. 1890. Inscriptions from Eastern Cilicia. *Journal of Hellenic Studies*, 11, 236-54.

HICKS, E. L. 1891. Inscriptions from Western Cilicia. *Journal of Hellenic Studies*, 12, 225-73.

HILD, Friedrich, HELLENKEMPER, Hansgerd and HELLENKEMPER SALIES, G. 1984. Kommagene - Kilikien - Isaurien. *Reallexikon zur Byzantinischen Kunst*, 4, 182-356.

HILD, Friedrich, and HELLENKEMPER, Hansgerd. 1990. *Kilikien und Isaurien.* Tabula Imperii Byzantini, 5. Österreichische Akademie der Wissenschaften, Philosophisch-Historische Klasse Denkschriften, 138 (Vienna).

HILL, Stephen. 1975. The Early Christian Church at Tomarza, Cappadocia - A Study Based on Photographs Taken in 1909 by Gertrude Bell. *Dumbarton Oaks Papers*, 29, 151-64.

HILL, Stephen. 1977. Sarı Kilise. *Yayla*, 1, 16-20.

HILL, Stephen. 1979. Dağ Pazarı and its Monuments - A Preliminary Report. *Yayla* 2, 8-12.

HILL, Stephen. 1981. Early Church Planning in Rough Cilicia. In Hornus (1981), 27-37.

HILL, Stephen. 1984. *The Early Christian Churches of Cilicia*. PhD Thesis (University of Newcastle upon Tyne)

HILL, Stephen. 1985. Matronianus, Comes Isauriae, an Inscription from an Early Byzantine Basilica at Yanıkhan, Rough Cilicia. *Anatolian Studies*, 35, 93-7.

HILL, Stephen. 1994. When is a Monastery not a Monastery? In Mullett and Kirby 1994, 137-45.

HILL, Stephen, RITCHIE, Lynn and HATHAWAY, Barbara. 1982. *Catalogue of the Gertrude Bell Photographic Archive* (Newcastle upon Tyne).

HOPWOOD, Keith. 1983. Policing the Hinterland: Rough Cilicia and Isauria. In Mitchell 1983, 173-87.

HORNUS Jean-Michel (editor). 1981. *Architecture of the Eastern Churches* (Birmingham).

IRBY, Charles Leonard and MANGLES, James. 1823. *Travels in Egypt and Nubia, Syria and Asia Minor during the years 1817 and 1818* (London).

De JERPHANION, P. Guillaume and JALABERT, P. L. 1911. Taurus et Cappadoce. *Mélanges de la Faculté Orientale*, 5, 282-328.

JONES, C. P. 1972. The Inscription from the Sea-Wall at Anemurium. *Phoenix*, 26, 396-9.

JONES, Arnold Hugh Martin. 1937. *The Cities of the Eastern Roman Empire* (Oxford).

JONES, Arnold Hugh Martin. 1964. *The Later Roman Empire* (Oxford).

KAUTZSCH, Rudolf. 1936. *Kapitellstudien. Beiträge zu einer Geschichte des spätantiken Kapitells im Osten vom vierten bis ins siebente Jahrhundert*. Studien zur spätantiken Kunstgeschichte, 9 (Leipzig).

KEIL, Josef and WILHELM, Adolf. 1931. *Denkmäler aus dem Rauhen Kilikien*. Monumenta Asiae Minoris Antiqua, 3 (Manchester).

KHATCHATRIAN, Aram. 1962. *Les Baptistères Paleochrétiens* (Paris).

KING, E. H. 1937. A Journey through Armenian Cilicia. *Journal of the Royal Central Asian Society*, 24, 234-46.

KIRSTEN, Ernst. 1974. Eleiaussa-Sebaste in Kilikien - Ein Ausgrabungswunsch an den Ausgräber von Side und Perge. *Mansel'e Armağ an - Mélanges Mansel* (Ankara), 777-802.

KITZINGER, Ernst. 1973a. Review of Budde 1972. *The Art Bulletin*, 55, 140-2.

KITZINGER, Ernst. 1973b. Observations on the Samson Floor at Mopsuestia. *Dumbarton Oaks Papers*, 27, 135-44.

KÖTTING, Bernhard. 1964. Tier und Heiligtum. *Mullus - Festschrift Theodor Klauser*. Jahrbuch für Antike und Christentum, Ergänzungsband 1 (Münster).

KRAMER, Joachim. 1963. Ein Fund an der Kuppelbasilika von Meriamlik. *Byzantinische Zeitschrift*, 56, 304-7.

KRAUTHEIMER, Richard. 1941. S. Pietro in Vincoli and the Tripartite Transept in the Early Christian Basilica. *Proceedings of the American Philosophical Society*, 84, 417-29.

KRAUTHEIMER, Richard. 1986. *Early Christian and Byzantine Architecture*, fourth edition revised by Richard Krautheimer and Slobodan Ćurčić (Harmondsworth).

KRENCKER, Daniel. 1939. *Die Wallfahrtskirchen des Simeon Stylites im Kal'at Sim'an* (Berlin).

De LABORDE, Leon Emmanuel Simon Joseph. 1838. *Voyage de l'Asie Mineure* (Paris).

De LABORDE, Leon Emmanuel Simon Joseph. 1847. Église d'Aladja dans le Taurus - Inscription grecque inédite. *Revue Archéologique*, 1, 172-6.

LANGLOIS, Victor. 1861. *Voyage dans la Cilicie et dans les montagnes du Taurus executé pendant les années 1852-1853* (Paris).

LAVIN, Irving. 1962. The House of the Lord. *The Art Bulletin*, 44, 1-27.

LESTRANGE, Guy. 1930. *Lands of the Eastern Caliphate* (Cambridge).

LIESENBURG, Kurt. 1928. *Der Einfluss der Liturgie auf die frühchristliche Basilika* (Hamburg).

LIPSIUS, R. A. 1907. Die apokyphen Apostoelgeschichten und Apostellegenden, volume 3 (Leipzig).

LLOYD, John A. 1977. Excavations at Sidi Khrebish, Benghazi. *Libya Antiqua*, Supplement 5.1.

LLOYD, Seton and RICE, D. Storm. 1958. *Alanya (Ala'iyya)* (London).

MacKAY, Pierre A. 1971. The First Modern Visitor to Alahan. *Anatolian Studies*, 21, 173-4.

MacKAY, Theodora Stilwell. 1968. *Olba in Rough Cilicia*. PhD. Thesis, (Bryn Mawr).

MacKAY, Theodora Stilwell. 1976. Diocaesarea. In Stilwell 1976, 275-6.

MADER, E. 1957. *Mambre* (Freiburg).

MAGIE, David. 1950. *Roman Rule in Asia Minor to the End of the Third Century after Christ* (Princeton).

MANGO, Cyril. 1966. Isaurian Builders. *Polychronion (Festschrift Franz Dölger zum 75 Geburtstag)*, 358-65.

MANGO, Cyril. 1976. *Byzantine Architecture* (New York).

MANGO, Cyril. 1986. The Pilgrimage Centre of St. Michael at Germia. *Jahrbuch der Österreichischen Byzantinistik*, 36, 117-32.

MANGO, Cyril. 1991. Germia, a Postscript. *Jahrbuch der Österreichischen Byzantinistik*, 41, 297-300.

MATHEWS, Thomas F. 1971. *The Early Churches of Constantinople Architecture and Liturgy* (Pennsylvania State University).

MIETKE, Gabrielle. Forthcoming. Survey der römisch-frühbyzantinischen Siedlung bei Akören in Kilikien, 1994. *Araştırma Sonuçları Toplantısı*, 13.

MITCHELL, Stephen (Editor). 1983. *Armies and Frontiers in Roman and Byzantine Anatolia.* British Archaeological Reports International Series, 156, (Oxford).

MITFORD, Terence Bruce. 1980. Roman Rough Cilicia. *Aufstieg und Niedergang der Römischen Welt, Principat 7.2* (Berlin), 1230-61.

MULLETT Margaret and KIRBY, Anthony (editors). 1994. *The Theotokos Evergetis and Eleventh-century Monasticism.* Belfast Byzantine Texts and Translations 6.1 (Belfast)

ÖZCAN, Birsel. 1991. Sulusaray-Sebastopolis Antik Kenti. *Müze Kurtarma Kazıları Semineri*, 1, 261-309.

PAINTER, Kenneth. 1994. *Churches Built in Ancient Times. Recent Studies in Early Christian Archaeology* (London).

RAMSAY, William Mitchell. 1890. *The Historical Geography of Asia Minor* (London).

RAMSAY, William Mitchell and BELL Gertrude Lowthian. 1909. *The Thousand and One Churches* (London).

RESTLE, Marcell. 1979. *Studien zur frühbyzantinischen Architektur Kappadokiens.* Österreichische Akademie der Wissenschaften, Philosophisch-Historische Klasse Denkschriften, 138 (Vienna).

RIEFSTAHL, Rudolf. 1931. Turkish Architecture in Southwestern Anatolia, part 2. *Art Studies* (Cambridge, USA), 173-212.

ROBERTSON, Giles and HENDERSON, George (editors). 1975. *Studies in Memory of David Talbot Rice* (Edinburgh).

RODLEY, Lyn. 1985. *Cave Monasteries of Byzantine Cappadocia* (Cambridge).

RODLEY, Lyn. 1994. *Byzantine Art and Architecture, an Introduction* (Cambridge).

ROTT, Hans. 1908. *Kleinasiatische Denkmäler aus Pisidien, Pamphylien, Kappadokien und Lykien.* Studien über Christliche Denkmäler, 5-6 (Leipzig).

RUSSELL, James. 1973a. New Inscriptions from Anemurium. *Phoenix*, 27, 319-27.

RUSSELL, James. 1973b. Excavations at Anemurium (Eski Anamur), 1971. *Türk Arkeoloji Dergisi*, 20.1, 201-19.

RUSSELL, James. 1975a. Excavations at Anemurium (Eski Anamur), 1972. *Türk Arkeoloji Dergisi*, 21.2, 154-63.

RUSSELL, James. 1975b. Excavations at Anemurium (Eski Anamur), 1973. *Türk Arkeoloji Dergisi*, 22.2, 121-38.

RUSSELL, James. 1976a. Excavations at Anemurium (Eski Anamur), 1974. *Türk Arkeoloji Dergisi*, 23.1, 93-6.

RUSSELL, James. 1976b. Anemurium - Eine römische Kleinstadt in Kleinasien. *Antike Welt*, 7, 3-20.

RUSSELL, James. 1976c. Anemurium. In Stilwell 1976, 58.

RUSSELL, James. 1977. Excavations at Anemurium (1976). *Échos du Monde Classique - Classical News and Views*, 21, 5-10.

RUSSELL, James. 1980a. Anemurium: The Changing Face of a Roman City. *Archaeology*, 33, 31-40.

RUSSELL, James. 1980b. Excavations at Anemurium (1979). *Échos du Monde Classique - Classical News and Views*, 24, 1-10.

RUSSELL, James. 1983. Excavations at Anemurium (Eski Anamur) 1982. *Échos du Monde Classique - Classical News and Views*, 27, new series 2, 171-82.

RUSSELL, James. 1986. Excavations at Anemurium (Eski Anamur) 1987. *Échos du Monde Classique - Classical News and Views*, new series 5, 131-4.

RUSSELL, James. 1987. Excavation and Restoration at Roman Anemurium (Turkey). *Transactions of the Royal Society of Canada*, series 5, volume 2, 145-62.

RUSSELL, James. 1988. Conservation and Excavations at Anemurium (Eski Anamur), 1985. *Échos du Monde Classique - Classical News and Views*, new series 7, 173-83.

RUSSELL, James. 1989. Christianity at Anemurium (Cilicia), Recent Discoveries. *Actes du XIe congrés internationale d'archéologie chrétienne (Lyon, Vienne, Grenoble, Genève et Aoste (21-28 Septembre 1986).* Collection de l'école française de Rome, 123; Studi di antichita cristiana 41, 1621-37.

SMITH, E. Baldwin. 1971. *The Dome - A Study in the History of Ideas.* Princeton Monographs in Art and Archaeology, 25 (Princeton).

SOTERIOU, G. A. and SOTERIOU, M. G. 1952. *He basilike tou Hagiou Demetriou Thessalonike* (Athens).

STANZL, Günther. 1979. *Längsbau und Zentralbau als Grundthermen der frühchristliche Architektur - Überlegungen zur Entstehung der Kuppelbasilika.* Österreichische Akademie der Wissenschaften, Philosophisch-Historische Klasse Denkschriften, 139 (Vienna).

STERRETT, J. R. Sitlington. 1888. *The Wolfe Expedition to Asia Minor.* Papers of the American School of Classical Studies at Athens, 3 (Boston).

STILWELL, Richard (Editor). 1976. *The Princeton Encyclopedia of Classical Sites* (Princeton).

STRZYGOWSKI, Josef. 1903. *Kleinasien - ein Neuland der Kunstgeschichte* (Leipzig).

STRZYGOWSKI, Josef. 1911. Kunsthistorisches (Comana Cappadociae. Die Kirche von Masylyk. Die Islamischen Denkmäler von Kaissari). In Grothe 1911, 212-28.

SWOBODA, Heinrich, KEIL, Josef and KNOLL, Fritz. 1935. *Denkmäler aus Lykaonien, Pamphylien und Isaurien.* Deutsche Gesellschaft der Wissenschaften und Künster für die Tschechoslowakische Republik in Prag (Brünn, Prag, Leipzig).

SYKES, Mark. 1915. *The Caliphs' Last Heritage* (London).

TALBOT RICE, David (Editor). 1958. *The Great Palace of the Byzantine Emperors,* Volume 2 (Edinburgh).

TAŞKIRAN, Celâl. 1994. *Silifke (Seleucia on Calycadnus) and Environs* (Silifke)

De TCHIHATCHEFF, P. 1854. Lettre sur les Antiquités de l'Asie Mineure addressée à M. Mohl. *Journal Asiatique,* 49-143.

THIERRY, N. and THIERRY, J-M. Le monastère de Koca Kalesi en Isaurie. *Cahiers archéologiques,* 13, 43-7.

TSUJI, Shigebumi. 1995. *The Survey of Early Byzantine Sites in Ölüdeniz Area (Lycia, Turkey). The First Preliminary Report.* Memoirs of the Faculty of Letters Osaka University, 35.

VAN DEN VEN, Paul. 1962. *La Vie ancienne de S. Syméon Stylite le Jeune.* Volume 1, Introduction et texte grec (Brussels).

VAN DEN VEN, Paul. 1970. *La Vie ancienne de S. Syméon le Jeune.* Volume 2, Traduction et Commentaire; Vie grecque de Sainte Marthe mère de Syméon (Brussels).

VERZONE, Paolo. 1956. Alahan Monastir - *Un monumento dell'arte tardo-romano in Isauria* (Turin).

VERZONE, Paolo. 1985. Ricordi di un breve Soggiorno di Studi ad Alahan. In Mary Gough 1985, 221-4.

VOYSAL, Y. 1963. *Uzuncaburç ve Ura* (Ankara).

WARD-PERKINS, John Bryan. 1958. Notes on the Structure and Building Methods of Early Byzantine Architecture. In Talbot Rice 1958, 52-104.

WILKINSON, John. 1971. *Egeria's Travels* (London).

SETON-WILLIAMS, M. V. 1954. Cilician Survey. *Anatolian Studies,* 4, 121-74.

WILLIAMS, Caroline. 1985. The Pottery and Glass at Alahan. In Mary Gough 1985, 35-61.

WILSON, Charles. 1895. *Handbook for Travellers in Asia Minor, Transcaucasia, Persia, etc.* (London).

ZOROĞLU. K. Levent. 1987. Kelenderis, 1986 Yılı Çalışmaları. *Araştırma Sonuçları Toplantısı,* 5.1, 409-22.

ZOROĞLU. K. Levent. 1988. Kelenderis, 1987 Yılı Kazısı. *Kazı Sonuçları Toplantısı,* 10, 135-55.

INDEX

FIGURES

KEY TO FIGURES

All plans are reproduced at 1:400 unless a different scale is shown.

Construction phases have been indicated where known, according to the following key:

░░░░░	pre-church phases
▇▇▇▇	original church

subsequent modifications:

▨▨▨	1st
▩▩▩	2nd
▨▨▨	3rd
▁▁▁	rock face

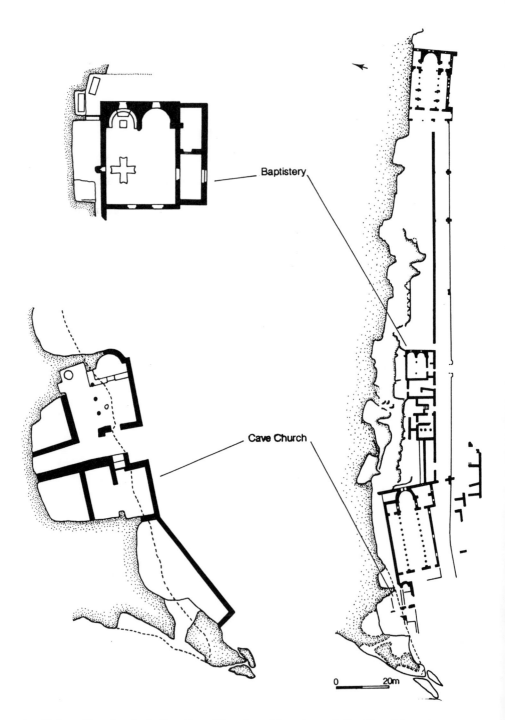

1. Alahan, Site plan including Cave Church and Baptistery (after Gough).

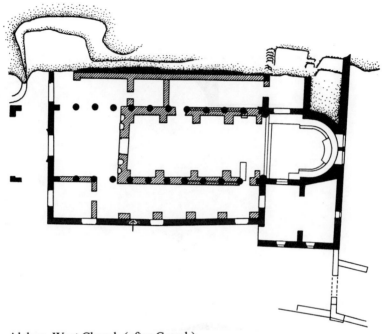

2. Alahan, West Church (after Gough).

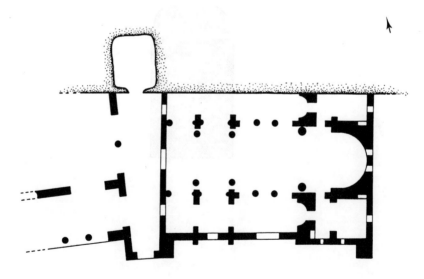

3. Alahan, East Church (after Gough).

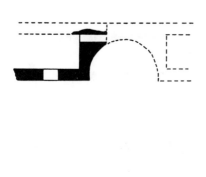

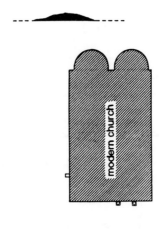

modern church

4. Alakilise (after Guyer).

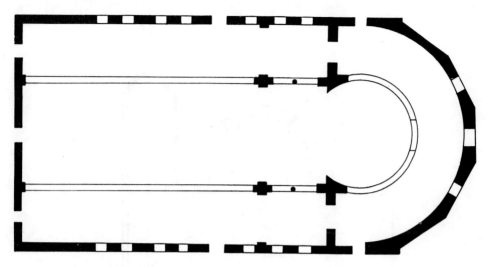

5. Anavarza, Church of the Apostles (after Gough).

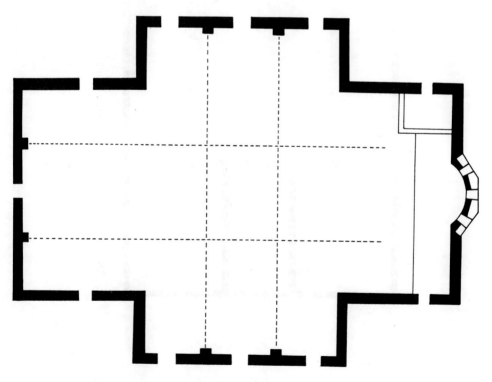

6. Anavarza, Southwest Church (after Gough).

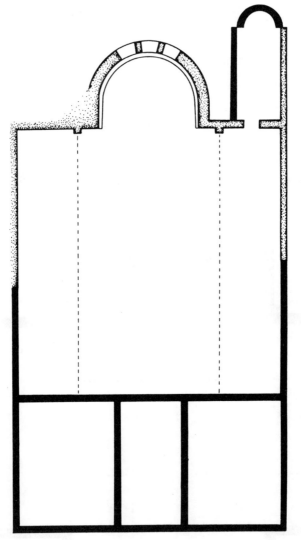

7. Anavarza, Rock-Cut Church (after Gough).

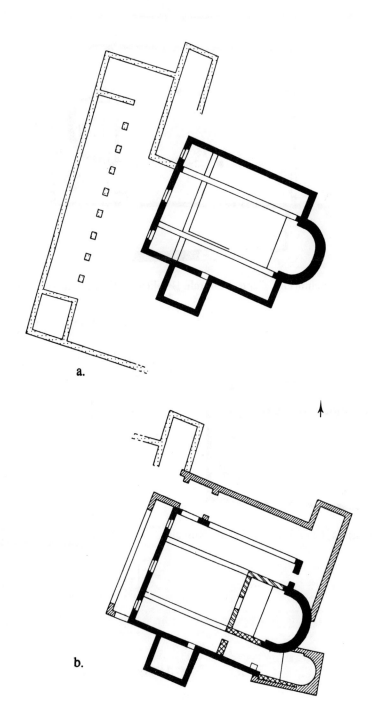

8. Anemurium, Church A II 1, Necropolis Church (after Russell).

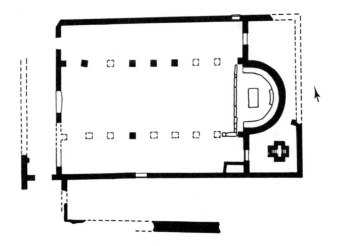

9. Anemurium, Central Church, Basilica III 13 C (after Russell).

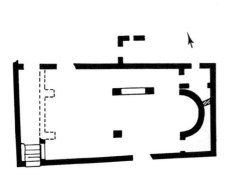

10. Anemurium, Church III 10 C (after Russell).

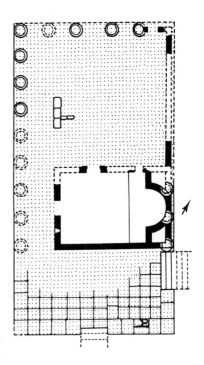

11. Ayaş, Temple-Church (after Gough).

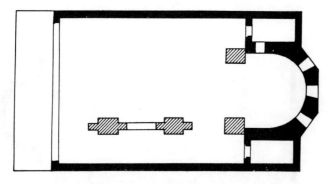

12. Bodrum, North Church, Town Church.

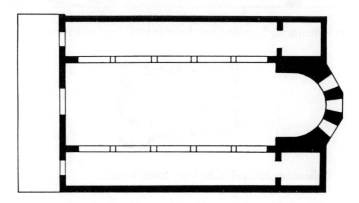

13. Bodrum, South Church (after Bell).

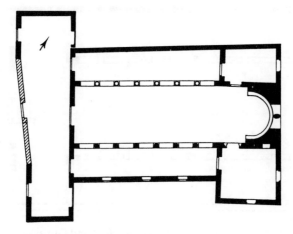

14. Canbazlı, Basilica (after Eyice).

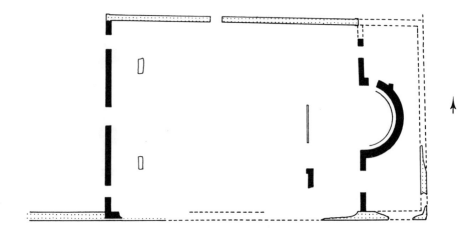

15. Cennet Cehennem, Temple-Church (after Bell, Feld and Weber).

16. Cennet Cehennem, Chapel of St Mary (after Bell).

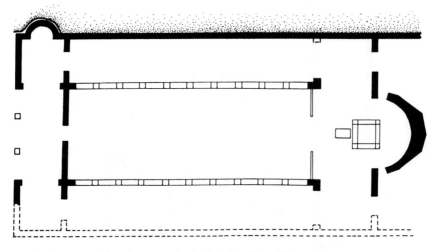

17. Corycus, Church A, 'Cathedral' (after Herzfeld and Guyer).

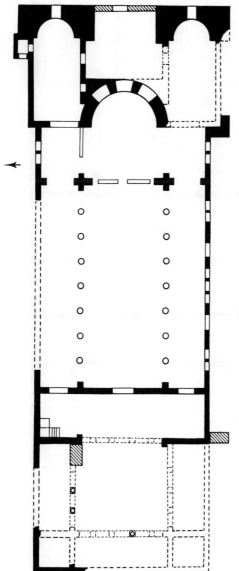

18. Corycus, Church G, Transept Church extra muros (after Herzfeld and Guyer).

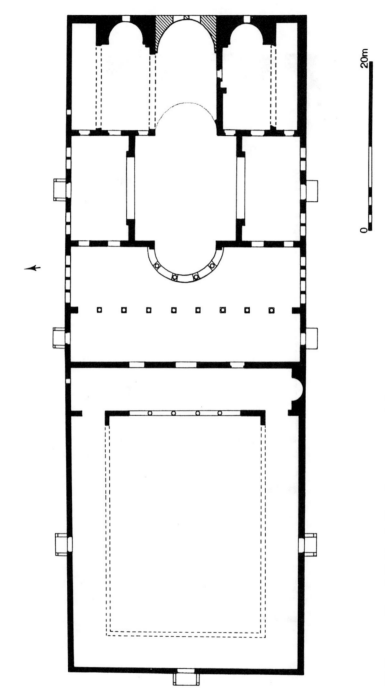

20m

0

19. Corycus, Church H, Tomb Church extra muros (after Herzfeld and Guyer).

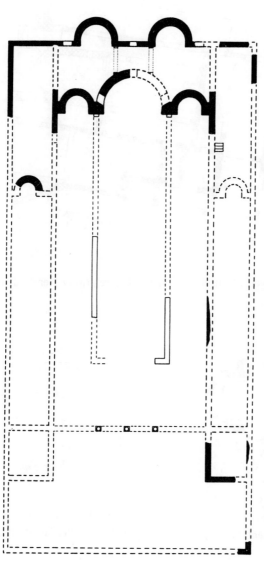

20. Corycus, Church I, 'Große Armenische Kirche extra muros' (after Bell, Herzfeld and Guyer, Hellenkemper).

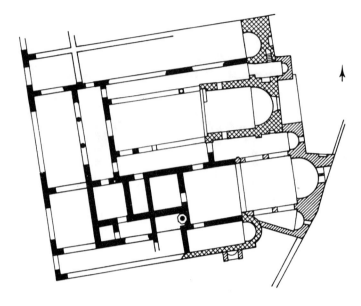

21. Corycus, Church J, Monastic Church (after Herzfeld and Guyer).

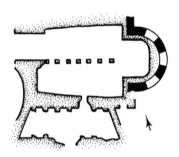

22. Corycus, Church D
(after Herzfeld and Guyer).

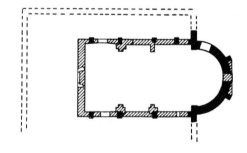

23. Corycus, Church K, Northwest Church inside
Land Castle (after Herzfeld and Guyer).

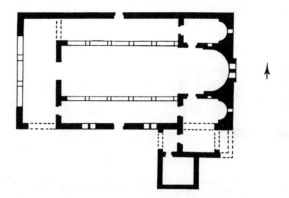

24. North of Corycus (Demirciören) (after Herzfeld and Guyer).

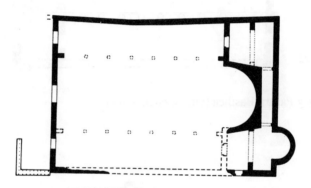

25. Çatıkören (after Gough, Feld).

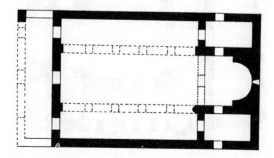

26. Çukurkeşlik (after Liesenburg).

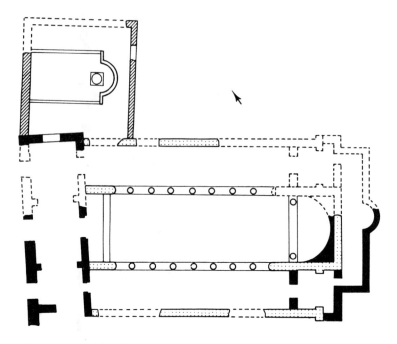

27. Dağ Pazarı, Basilica (after Gough notes).

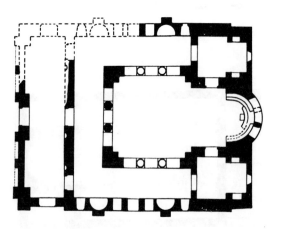

28. Dağ Pazarı, 'Domed Ambulatory Church' (after Gough).

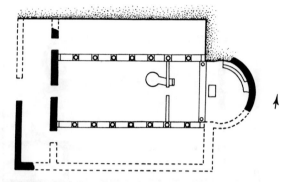

29. Dağ Pazarı, Funerary Basilica extra muros (after Gough).

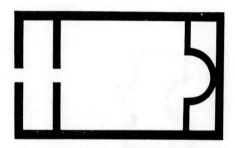

30. Deleli (after De Jerphanion and Jalabert).

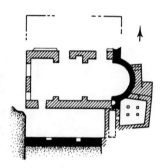

31. Gazipaşa, Church 10 C
(after Alföldi-Rosenbaum).

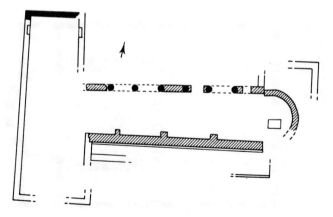

32. Güney Kalesi, Church I 15 (after Alföldi-Rosenbaum).

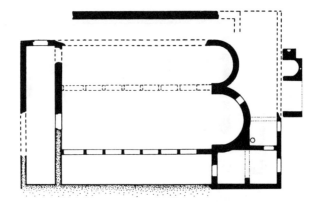

33. Hasanalıler (after Gough notes, Hild and Hellenkemper).

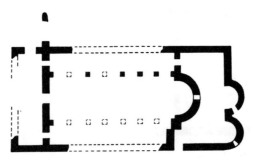

34. İmamli (after Bell).

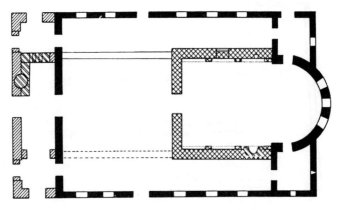

35. Kadirli, Ala Cami (after Gough notes, Bayliss).

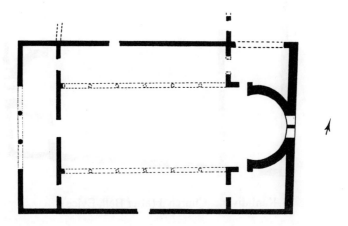

36. Kanlıdivane, Church 1 (after Bell, Eyice).

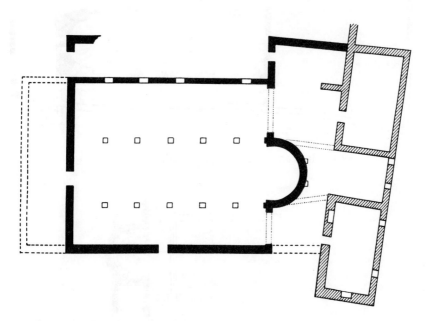

37. Kanlıdivane, Church 2 (after Bell notes, Eyice).

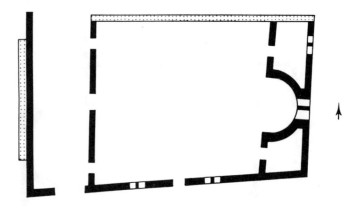

38. Kanlıdivane, Church 3 (after Bell, Eyice).

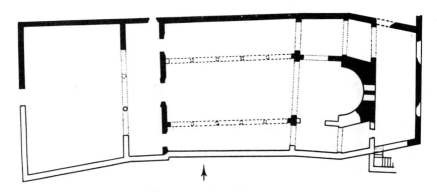

39. Kanlıdivane, Church 4 (after Bell, Eyice).

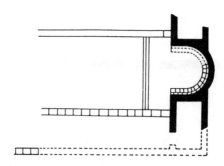

40. Karlık, Basilica (after Gough).

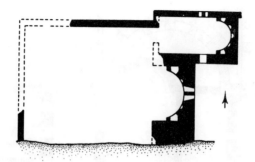

41. Mahras Dağı (after Gough).

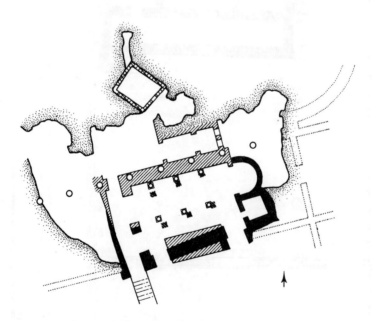

42. Meryemlık, Cave Church (after Herzfeld and Guyer, Wilkinson).

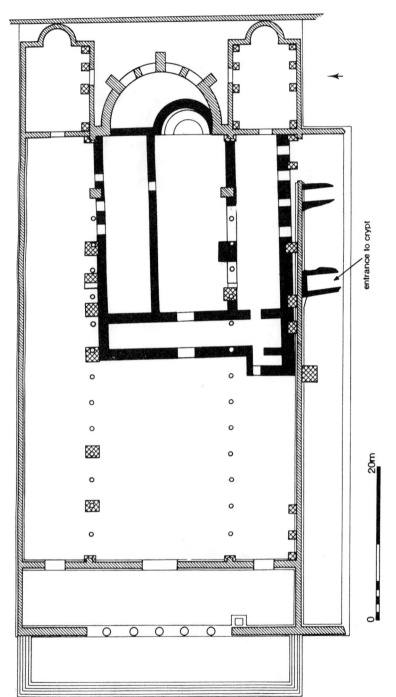

entrance to crypt

20m

0

43. Meryemlık, Basilica of St Thecla (after Herzfeld and Guyer).

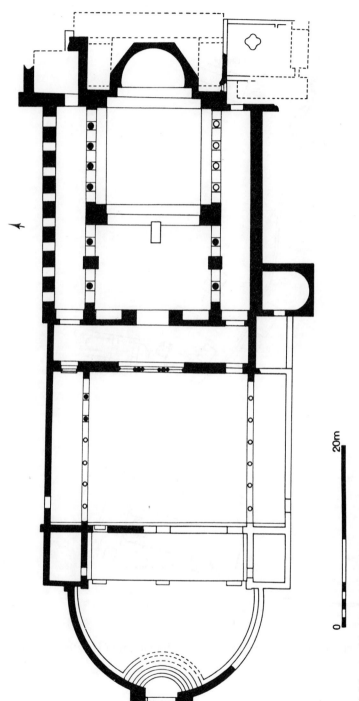

44. Meryemlık, 'Cupola Church' (after Herzfeld and Guyer).

0   20m

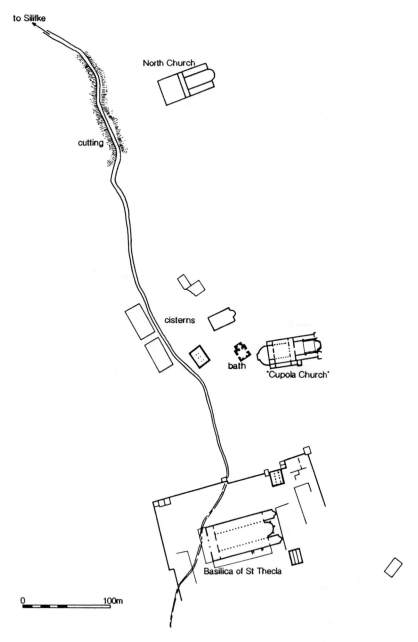

to Silifke

North Church

cutting

cisterns

bath

"Cupola Church"

Basilica of St Thecla

0   100m

45. Meryemlık, site plan (including North Church) (after Herzfeld and Guyer).

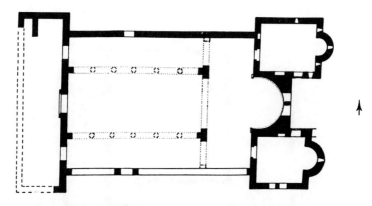

46. Öküzlü, North Church (after Eyice, Gough notes).

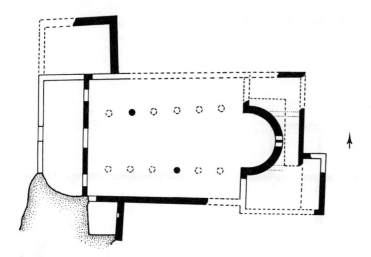

47. Öküzlü, South Church (after Eyice, Gough notes).

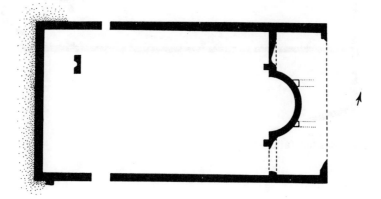

48. Susanoğlu, Town Church (after Keil and Wilhelm).

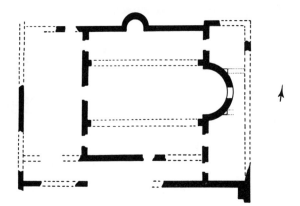

49. Susanoğlu, Cemetery church (after Keil and Wilhelm).

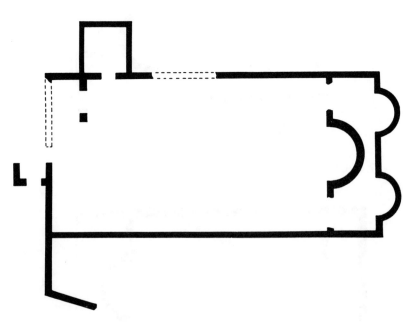

50. Şaha, Basilica (after Bell).

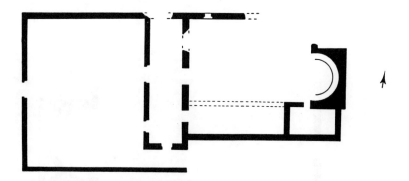

51. Tapureli, Church A (after Keil and Wilhelm).

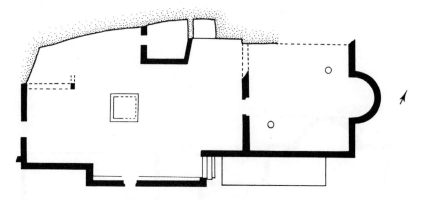

52. Tapureli, Church B (after Keil and Wilhelm).

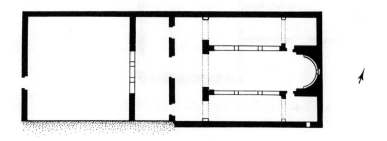

53. Tapureli, Church C (after Keil and Wilhelm).

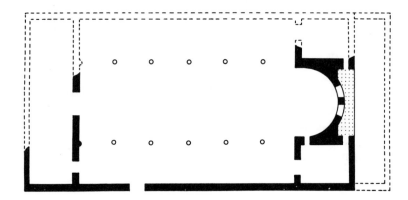

54. Ura, Town Church (after Bell).

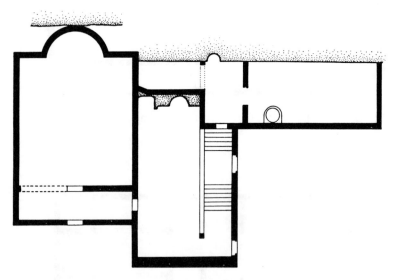

55. Ura, Monastery (after Keil and Wilhelm).

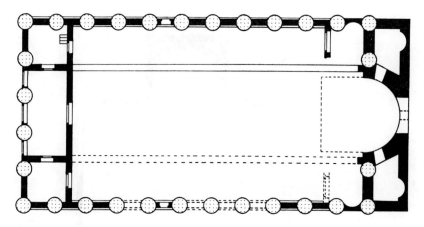

56. Uzuncaburç, Temple-Church (after Keil and Wilhelm).

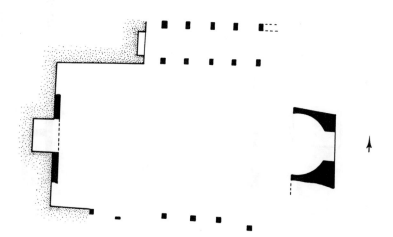

57. Uzuncaburç, Cemetery Church (after Keil and Wilhelm).

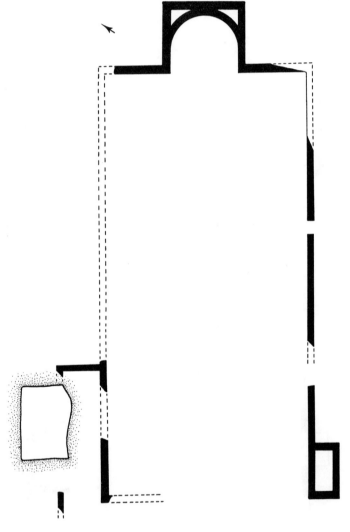

58. Uzuncaburç, Church of Stephanos (after Keil and Wilhelm).

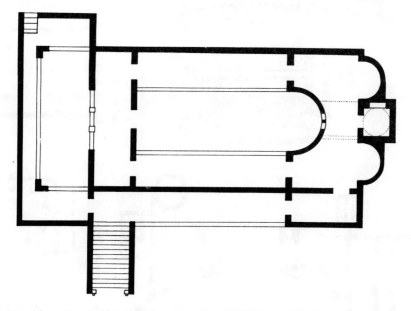

59. Yanıkhan, South Church (after Gough and Hill notes, Hild and Hellenkemper).

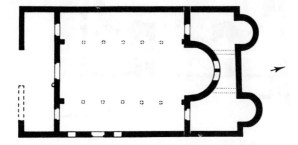

60. Yanıkhan, North Church (after Gough and Hill notes, Hild and Hellenkemper).

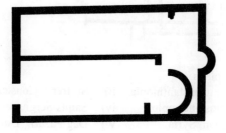

61. Yemişküm (after Bell).

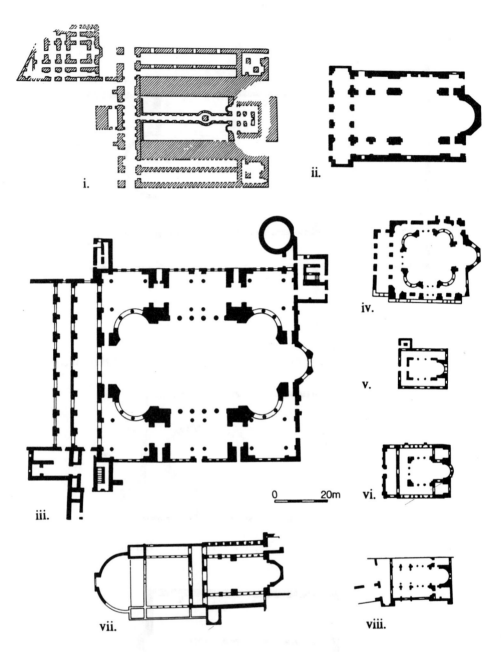

62.   Comparative plans.
  i)   St. Polyeuktos, Constantinople.   ii)   St. Irene, Constantinople.
  iii)   St. Sophia, Constantinople.   iv)   Saints Sergius and Bacchus, Constantinople.
  v)   Kasr ibn Wardan, Syria.   vi)   Dağ Pazarı, 'Domed ambulatory Church'.
  vii)   Meryemlık, 'Cupola Church'.   viii)   Alahan, East Church.

PLATES

1. Alahan, general view from west (Gough).

2. Alahan, Cave Church,
   view from west (Gough).

3. Alahan, West Church, view from
   east before excavation (Gough).

4. Alahan, West Church, view from east showing primary church (Gough).

5. Alahan, West Church, view from east showing secondary church (Gough).

6. Alahan, East Church from north (Gough).

7. Alahan, East Church from southeast (Gough).

8. Alahan, East Church from west (Gough).

10. Alahan, East Church, interior looking east (Hill).

9. Alahan, East Church, interior looking west (Hill).

11. Alahan, East Church, interior of tower looking east (Gough).

12. Alahan, East Church, east side of tower (Gough).

13. Alahan, Baptistery, interior from northeast (Hill).

14. Alahan, Baptistery, exterior
from southwest (Gough).

16. Alahan, East Church,
capital with eagles (Gough).

15. Alahan, East Church, north
end of narthex (Gough).

17. Ayaş, Temple-Church,
    apse (Gough).

18. Anavarza, Rock-Cut Church from
    southwest (1905, Bell C193).

19. Batısandal from west (Hill).

20. Batısandal, sockets at mouth
    of apse (Hill).

21. Batısandal, east façade (Hill).

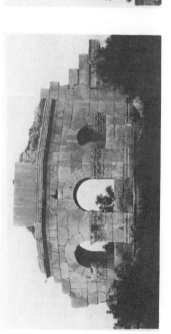

22. Bodrum, North Church, exterior of apse (ca 1925).

23. Bodrum, South Church, exterior of apse (ca 1925).

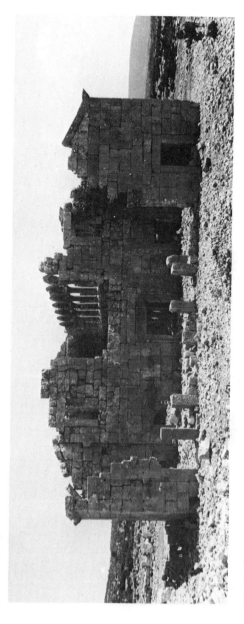

24. Canbazlı, Basilica from west (Hill).

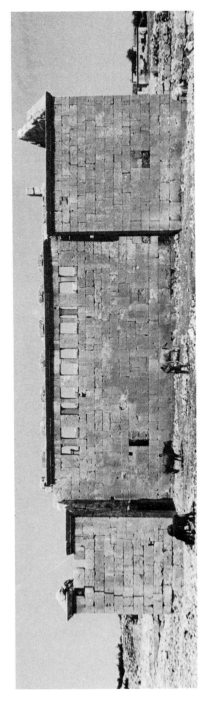

25. Canbazlı, Basilica from south (Hill).

27. Canbazlı, Basilica, gallery (ca 1925).

26. Canbazlı, Basilica, south colonnade (ca 1925).

28. Cennet Cehennem, Temple-Church, apse from south (Hill).

29. Cennet Cehennem, Temple-Church, apse from west (Hill).

30. Cennet Cehennem, Temple-Church, inner face of north wall (Hill).

33. Corycus, Church A, 'Cathedral', apse from west (Hill).

31. Cennet Cehennem, Chapel of St Mary from south (Hill).

32. Cennet Cehennem, Chapel of St Mary, domical vault in southern side-chamber (Hill).

34. Corycus, Church G, Transept Church extra muros, south façade (1905, Bell D4a-b).

35. Corycus, Church G, Transept Church extra muros, east façade (Hill).

36. Corycus, Church G, Transept Church extra muros, interior looking east (Hill).

37. Corycus, Church G, Transept Church extra muros, base of south pier of triumphal arch (Hill).

38. Corycus, Church H, Tomb Church extra muros, south façade from southeast (ca 1925).

39. Corycus, Church H, Tomb Church extra muros, inner face of south wall (ca 1925).

40. Corycus, Church H, Tomb Church extra muros, interior looking east (ca 1925).

41. Corycus, Church H, Tomb Church extra muros, interior looking northwest (Hill).

42. Corycus, Church H, Tomb Church extra muros, atrium and narthex from southeast (Hill).

43. Corycus, Church H, Tomb Church extra muros, pier capital at northeast corner of nucleus (Hill).

44. Corycus, Church H, Tomb Church extra muros from northeast (1905, Bell D16).

46. Corycus, Church I, 'Große Armenische Kirche extra muros' from west (Hill).

48. Corycus, Church I, 'Große Armenische Kirche extra muros' from east (Hill).

45. Corycus, Church B, apse from west (Hill).

47. Corycus, Church I, 'Große Armenische Kirche extra muros' from south (Hill).

49. Corycus, Church J, Monastic Church, general view from southwest (Hill).

50. Corycus, Church J, Monastic Church, west façade of court (1905, Bell D28).

51. Corycus, Church J, Monastic Church from southeast (Hill).

52. Corycus, Church K, Northwest Church inside Land Castle from southeast (Hill).

53. East of Corycus, Funerary Chapel from west (Hill).

54. East of Corycus, Funerary Chapel, apse and hypogaeum from south (Hill).

55. North of Corycus (Demirciören),
interior looking northwest (Hill).

56. North of Corycus (Demirciören),
east end from southwest (Hill).

59. North of Corycus
(Demirciören), capital (Hill).

58. North of Corycus (Demirciören),
southeastern chambers from west (Hill).

57. North of Corycus (Demirciören),
east façade (Hill).

60. Çatıkören from south (Gough).

61. Çatıkören, interior looking west (Gough).

63. Dağ Pazarı, Basilica, eastern passage from southwest (Ballance).

62. Dağ Pazarı, Basilica, narthex from south (Ballance).

64. Dağ Pazarı, 'Domed Ambulatory Church' from southeast (1890, Headlam).

65. Dağ Pazarı, 'Domed Ambulatory Church', east façade (Hill).

66. Dağ Pazarı, 'Domed Ambulatory Church', east end from south (Ballance).

67. Dağ Pazarı, 'Domed Ambulatory Church', interior from west (Gough).

68. Dağ Pazarı, 'Domed Ambulatory Church', east end of south aisle (Ballance).

69. Dağ Pazarı, 'Domed Ambulatory Church', pier capital on north side of apse (Hill).

70. Dağ Pazarı, 'Domed Ambulatory Church', northwest corner of nucleus (Ballance)

71. Dağ Pazarı, Funerary Basilica extra muros from south (Gough).

72. Dağ Pazarı, Funerary Basilica extra muros, apse from northwest (Gough).

73. Dağ Pazarı, Funerary Basilica extra muros, apse and chancel from northwest (Gough).

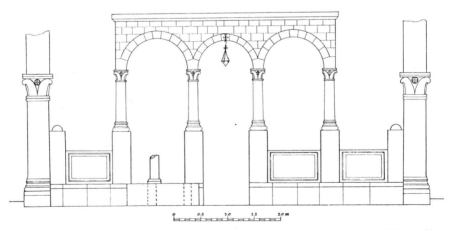

74. Dağ Pazarı, Funerary Basilica extra muros, reconstruction of chancel (Gough). reconstruction of chancel (Gough).

75. Hasanahler, interior from west (Gough).

76. Hasanahler, south arcade (Gough).

77. İmamli from west (Bell D58).

78. İmamli from south (1905, Bell D57).

81. Kadirli, Ala Cami from southeast (1905, Bell C145).

79. Kadirli, Ala Cami from south (1905, Bell C144).

80. Kadirli, Ala Cami from southwest (ca 1925).

82. Kanlıdivane, Church 1, west facade (1905, Bell C236).

83. Kanlıdivane. Church 1, chancel and apse from west (Hill).

84. Kanlıdivane. Church 1, east façade and doorway
   in wall linking Churches 1 and 2 (Hill).

85. Kanlıdivane. Church 2, apse from west (Hill).

86. Kanlıdivane. Church 2 from south (1905, Bell C248).

87. Kanlıdivane, Church 3, south end of narthex (Hill).

88. Kanlıdivane, Church 3 from southwest (1905, Bell C245).

89. Kanlıdivane, Church 3, apse from southwest (Hill).

90. Kanlıdivane, Church 3, east façade (Hill).

91. Kanlıdivane, Church 4 from west (Hill).

92. Kanlıdivane, Church 4 from northeast.

93. Kanlıdivane, Church 4, chancel and apse from west (Hill).

94. Karakilise from southeast showing early Byzantine apse
and Armenian church (Gough).

95. Mahras Dağı, church from
west (Gough).

96. Mahras Dağı, apse from
southwest (Gough).

97. Manaz from west (Langlois 1861, plate 22).

98. Meryemlık, Basilica of St Thecla, apse from west (ca 1925).

99. Meryemlık, 'Cupola Church', font (Hill).

100. Öküzlü, North Church from west (Hill).

101. Öküzlü, North Church from south (Hill).

104. Öküzlü, North Church,
northern side-chamber (Hill).

105. Öküzlü, South Church,
apse from west (Hill).

103. Öküzlü, North Church, chancel
and apse from northwest (Hill).

102. Öküzlü, North Church, northern
pier of triumphal arch (Hill).

106. Şaha, Basilica from west (1905, Bell C215).

107. Şaha, Basilica, west end from north (1905, Bell C215).

108. Silifke, Temple-Church from east (Langlois 1861).

109. Tapureli, Church C from west (Gough).

110. Üç Tepe, South Church from west (Hill).

111. Üç Tepe, North Church, north aisle looking west (Hill).

112. Ura, Town Church from west (Hill).

113. Ura, Monastery from west (Gough).

114. Uzuncaburç, Temple-Church from north (1905, Bell D66).

115. Uzuncaburç, Temple-Church, interior looking east (Hill).

116. Uzuncaburç, Cemetery Church, general view from west (Hill).

117. Uzuncaburç, Cemetery Church, arcosolium from east (ca 1925).

118. Yanıkhan, South Church, general view from west (Hill).

119. Yanıkhan, South Church, column and capital in narthex (Hill).

120. Yanıkhan, South Church, apse from northwest (Hill).

121. Yanıkhan, South Church, northern subsidiary apse (Hill).

122. Yanıkhan, South Church, eastern chamber showing fragment of dome (Hill).

123. Yanıkhan, South Church, arcosolium in eastern chamber (Hill).

124. Yanıkhan, North Church, interior from west (Hill).

125. Yanıkhan, North Church, exterior from southeast (Hill).

126. Yanıkhan, North Church, interior looking northeast (Hill).

127. Yemişküm from west (1905, Bell C257).